SET THEORY AND ITS LOGIC

SET THEORY AND ITS LOGIC

Revised Edition

WILLARD VAN ORMAN QUINE

EDGAR PIERCE PROFESSOR OF PHILOSOPHY
HARVARD UNIVERSITY

THE BELKNAP PRESS
OF HARVARD UNIVERSITY PRESS
CAMBRIDGE, MASSACHUSETTS
LONDON, ENGLAND

Library of Congress Catalog Card Number 68-14271
ISBN 0-674-80207-1
Printed in the United States of America

10 9 8 7

To BERTRAND RUSSELL

whose ideas have long loomed large
in this subject and whose writings
inspired my interest in it

"How quaint the ways of paradox."

W. S. GILBERT

PREFACE TO THE REVISED EDITION

The revisions have been extensive. Most of them made their way meanwhile into the Japanese edition, thanks to the patience of the Japanese translators and publishers. I am much relieved that these improvements are now to go out to readers of English.

The latest major change is the adoption in §23 of an axiom schema which provides in general that a class will exist if its members can be mapped on the ordinals less than some ordinal. In general my policy in the book has been to minimize existence assumptions and to postpone them; but this much compromise proved rewarding. While continuing to defer the assumption of infinite classes, it served to sweep away most of the existence premisses that had formerly cluttered the theorems of §§23–27 and also to simplify a number of proofs. One notable effect of the axiom schema is a proof that there is no last ordinal (new 24.9).

§§25–27 on transfinite recursion were already subject to another major change, prompted by Charles Parsons; see bibliography. He observed that some of my theorem schemata on this subject carried existence premisses that would rule out some of the clearly desirable interpretations of the schematic letters. He showed how to remedy the situation, and I have adopted his central idea.

Parsons also pointed out a second and lesser limitation in my treatment of transfinite recursion, and showed how to overcome it. But it was a limitation that operates only if there is a last ordinal; and this contingency is now excluded, as noted above. So I am not following Parsons on this point.

Another notable revision was instigated by Burton Dreben: the reorganization of §30 on infinite cardinals. Extensions and corrections relating to the axiom of *Fundierung* and the axiom schema of replacement also have been prompted by Dreben and by Kenneth Brown. Findings by Brown and by Hao Wang have led me also to insert some further points on axioms in §13 and elsewhere. §37 on variants of the theory of types has been improved in the light mainly of findings by David Kaplan; a case of this is the elimination of '$(\exists x)\mathrm{T}_0 x$' as axiom at one stage.

Minor improvements have been made throughout the book. Here and there a proof is shortened, a theorem strengthened, a theoretical or clerical error corrected, a space-saving lemma inserted, an obscurity clarified, a historical error corrected or omission supplied, a new event noted. In these connections I am indebted variously to Burton Dreben, John Denton, Jean van Heijenoort, Henry Hiż, Saul Kripke, David K. Lewis, Donald Martin, Akira Ohe, Charles Parsons, Dale R. Samson, Thomas Scanlon, Leslie Tharp, Joseph S. Ullian, and Natuhiko Yosida.

For supporting my work on this revision, as well as the proofreading and indexing of the first edition in 1963, I acknowledge with thanks a grant GP-228 from the National Science Foundation.

W.V.Q.

April 1967

PREFACE TO THE FIRST EDITION

A preface is not, in my book, an introduction. Somewhere, readers already acquainted with the subject need to be told succinctly what a book covers and how. The book itself gives this information the long way, explaining concepts and justifying assertions. The preface gives it the short way, presupposing some command of the technical terms and concepts.

As explained in the Introduction, the book assumes no prior knowledge of set theory but some of logic. Chapter I, entitled "Logic," builds upon this prerequisite. Mainly what it builds is what I have elsewhere called the virtual theory of classes and relations: a partial counterfeit of set theory fashioned purely of logic. This serves later chapters in two ways. For one thing, the virtual theory affords a useful contrast with the later, real theory. The contrast helps to bring out what the genuine assuming of classes amounts to; what power real classes confer that the counterfeits do not. For another thing, the virtual theory eventually gets merged with the real theory in such a way as to produce a combination which, though not strictly more powerful than the real theory alone would be, is smoother in its running.

This departure last mentioned is one of several that are meant for the theoretician's eye. But at the same time the book is meant to provide a general introduction to staple topics of abstract set theory, and, in the end, a somewhat organized view of the best-known axiomatizations of the subject. Paradoxically, the very novelties of the approach are in part devices for neutralizing idiosyncrasy.

Because the axiomatic systems of set theory in the literature are largely incompatible with one another and no one of them clearly deserves to be singled out as standard, it seems prudent to teach a panorama of alternatives. This can encourage research that may some day issue in a set theory that is clearly best. But the writer who would pursue this liberal policy has his problems. He cannot very well begin by offering the panoramic view, for the beginning reader will appreciate neither the material that the various systems are meant to organize nor the considerations that could favor one system in any respect over another. Better to begin by orienting the reader with a preliminary informal survey of the subject matter. But here again there is trouble. If such a survey is to get beyond trivialities, it must resort to serious and sophisticated reasoning such as could quickly veer into the antinomies and so discredit itself if not shunted off them in one of two ways: by abandoning the informal approach in favor of the axiomatic after all, or just by slyly diverting the reader's attention from dangerous questions until the informal orientation is accomplished. The latter course calls for artistry of a kind that is distasteful to a science teacher, and anyway it is powerless with readers who hear about the antinomies from some-one else. Once they have heard about them, they can no longer submit to the discipline of complex informal arguments in abstract set theory; for they can no longer tell which intuitive arguments count. It is not for nothing, after all, that set theorists resort to the axiomatic method. Intuition here *is* bankrupt, and to keep the reader innocent of this fact through half a book is a sorry business even when it can be done.

In this book I handle the problem by hewing a formal line from the outset, but keeping my axioms weak and reasonable and thus nearly neutral. I postpone as best I can the topics that depend on stronger axioms; and, when these topics have to be faced, I still postpone the stronger axioms by incorporating necessary assumptions rather as explicit hypotheses into the theo-rems that require them. In this way I manage to introduce the reader at some length to the substance of set theory without any grave breach of neutrality, and yet also without resorting to studied informality or artificial protraction of innocence. After ten such chapters I find myself in a position to present and compare, in the four concluding chapters, a multiplicity of mutually incompatible axiomatizations of the material with which the reader has been familiarized.

More specifically, the weak axioms that thus govern the main body of the work are such as to imply the existence of none but finite classes. Moreover, they do not even postulate any infinite classes hypothetically. To see what I mean by this, consider, in contrast to my axioms, a pair of axioms providing for the existence of the null class Λ and of $x \cup \{y\}$ for all x and y. These axioms, like mine, imply the existence only of finite classes. But, unlike mine, these provide also that *if* an infinite class x exists then so does the further infinite class $x \cup \{y\}$ for any y.

My axioms do provide for the existence of all finite classes of whatever things there are. They are consequently not altogether neutral toward the systems in the literature. They conflict with those systems, such as von Neumann's, in which some classes—"ultimate" classes, I call them—are counted incapable of being members of classes at all. Though one such system was that of my own *Mathematical Logic*, in the present book I defend the finite classes against the ultimate classes.

My axioms of finite classes are enough, it turns out, for the arithmetic of the natural numbers. A familiar definition of natural number involves infinite classes. Natural numbers are the common members of all classes that contain 0 (somehow defined) and are closed with respect to the successor operation (somehow defined); and any such class is infinite. The law of mathematical induction, based on this definition, can be proved only by assuming infinite classes. But I get by with finite classes by inverting the definition of natural number, thus: x is a natural number if 0 is a common member of all classes that contain x and are closed with respect to predecessor.

Classically the definition of natural number is a special case of that of Frege's ancestral (Dedekind's chain); a natural number is what bears the ancestral of the successor relation to 0. Mathematical induction is a special case of ancestral induction. Now to avoid the need of infinite classes in the special case of natural number, by inversion as above, is all very well; but what of the general case? I answer this question by deriving the general from the special: defining the *n*th iterate of a relation *r*, for variable '*n*', with the help of number theory and then defining the ancestral of *r* in effect as the union of its iterates. Through this channel the general law of ancestral deduction is derived from what is usually looked upon as its special case, mathematical induction, and there is still no need of infinite classes. Incidentally, the notion of the iterate expedites the definition and treatment of arithmetical sum, product, and power. These developments are largely a revival of Dedekind's ideas.

Through these and subsequent developments an illusion is maintained of opulence unaccounted for by the axioms. The trick is the merging of the virtual theory with the real. The notation '$\{x: Fx\}$' of class abstraction is introduced by contextual definition in such a way that much use can be made of it even if the class does not exist; just its substitution for variables requires existence, and even this sanction is lightened somewhat by a use of schematic letters that does not require existence. We find we can enjoy a good deal of the benefit of a class without its existing either as a set or as an ultimate class.

After the natural numbers come the ratios and other real numbers. The reals are construed by essentially the Dedekind cut as usual, but the details of the development are so adjusted that the ratios turn out identical with the rational reals, not just isomorphic to them, and the reals become classes of natural numbers, not relations or classes of relations of them. The classical laws of real numbers, in particular that of the least bound, are found of course to depend on hypotheses of existence of infinite classes.

Then come the ordinal numbers, which I take in von Neumann's sense. My treatment of the natural numbers, earlier, is at variance with this course, for I take them rather in Zermelo's way. My reason is that I seem thus to be able to get by for a while with simpler existence axioms. In the general theory of ordinals we are bound to face serious existence assumptions, but we *can* preserve economy of assumption at the level of natural-number theory; and so I let the natural numbers and the ordinals go their separate ways.

I take comfort in the thought that it is just as well that students familiarize themselves with both Zermelo's and von Neumann's versions of the natural numbers. Still I would have been pleased to find that I could reap all advantages of the Zermelo version by adhering to von Neumann's from the start; and I appreciate the help of my student Kenneth Brown in exploring this alternative. To have rested with his best results, and so adhered first and last to von Neumann numbers, would have been nearly as good as the choice I made.

Transfinite recursion for me, as for von Neumann and Bernays, consists in specifying a transfinite sequence by specifying each thing in the sequence as a function of the preceding segment of the sequence. This matter is formalized in Chapter VIII, and put to use in defining the arithmetical operations on ordinals. It is put to use also in defining the *enumeration* of an arbitrary well-ordering. From the existence of enumerations, in turn, the comparability of well-orderings is deduced. These developments depend on existence assumptions which are written into the theorems as hypotheses. The same is true of the developments in the next two chapters, which are devoted to the Schröder-Bernstein theorem, the infinite cardinals, and the main equivalents of the axiom of choice.

The four concluding chapters are given over to the description and comparison of various systems of axiomatic set theory: Russell's theory of types, Zermelo's system, von Neumann's, two of mine, and, in a sketchy way, some recent developments. Logical connections are traced among them; for example, the theory of types is transformed essentially into Zermelo's system by translating it into general variables and taking the types as cumulative. The systems generally are given an unfamiliar cast by continuing to exploit the vestiges of the virtual theory of classes.

These four concluding chapters embody the origin of the book. One of my short lecture courses at Oxford, when I was there as George Eastman Visiting Professor in 1953–54, was a comparison of axiomatic set theories; and though I had dealt with the topic repeatedly at Harvard, it was the formulation at Oxford that got me to envisaging a little book. Then, for five years after Oxford, the project remained in abeyance while I finished a book on other matters. In 1959 I returned to this one, and that summer I gave a resumé of the material in some lectures at Tokyo. The book bade fair to be finished in a year, as a short book comprising the comparison of set theories along with some minimum preliminary chapters for orientation in the subject matter. But in the writing I got ideas that caused the preliminary chapters to run to five-sevenths of the book, and the book to take two additional years.

Since October the manuscript has had the inestimable benefit of critical readings by Professors Hao Wang, Burton S. Dreben, and Jean van Heijenoort. Their wise suggestions have led me to extend my coverage in some places, to deepen my analysis in others, to clear up some obscurities of exposition, to correct and supplement various of the historical notes, and, thanks to Wang particularly, to give a sounder interpretation of some papers. And all three readers have helped me in the asymptotic labor of spotting clerical errors.

I have been indebted also to Professors Dreben and John R. Myhill for helpful earlier remarks, and to current pupils for sundry details that will be attributed in footnotes. For defraying the costs of typing and other assistance I am grateful to the Harvard Foundation and the National Science Foundation (Grant GP-228).

W. V. Q.

Boston, January 1963

CONTENTS

INTRODUCTION 1

Part One. The Elements

I. LOGIC

1. Quantification and identity 9
2. Virtual classes 15
3. Virtual relations 21

II. REAL CLASSES

4. Reality, extensionality, and the individual 28
5. The virtual amid the real 34
6. Identity and substitution 40

III. CLASSES OF CLASSES

7. Unit classes 47
8. Unions, intersections, descriptions 53
9. Relations as classes of pairs 58
10. Functions 65

IV. NATURAL NUMBERS

11. Numbers unconstrued 74
12. Numbers construed 81
13. Induction 86

V. ITERATION AND ARITHMETIC

14. Sequences and iterates 96
15. The ancestral 101
16. Sum, product, power 107

Part Two. Higher Forms of Number

VI. REAL NUMBERS

17. Program. Numerical pairs 119
18. Ratios and reals construed 124
19. Existential needs. Operations and extensions 130

VII. ORDER AND ORDINALS

20. Transfinite induction 139
21. Order 145
22. Ordinal numbers 150
23. Laws of ordinals 160
24. The order of the ordinals 170

VIII. TRANSFINITE RECURSION

25. Transfinite recursion 174
26. Laws of transfinite recursion 180
27. Enumeration 184

IX. CARDINAL NUMBERS

28. Comparative size of classes 193
29. The Schröder-Bernstein theorem 203
30. Infinite cardinal numbers 208

X. THE AXIOM OF CHOICE
31. Selections and selectors 217
32. Further equivalents of the axiom 224
33. The place of the axiom 231

Part Three. Axiom Systems

XI. RUSSELL'S THEORY OF TYPES
34. The constructive part 241
35. Classes and the axiom of reducibility 249
36. The modern theory of types 259

XII. GENERAL VARIABLES AND ZERMELO
37. The theory of types with general variables 266
38. Cumulative types and Zermelo 272
39. Axioms of infinity and others 279

XIII. STRATIFICATION AND ULTIMATE CLASSES
40. "New foundations" 287
41. Non-Cantorian classes. Induction again 292
42. Ultimate classes added 299

XIV. VON NEUMANN'S SYSTEM AND OTHERS
43. The von Neumann–Bernays system 310
44. Departures and comparisons 315
45. Strength of systems 323

SYNOPSIS OF FIVE AXIOM SYSTEMS 331

LIST OF NUMBERED FORMULAS 333

BIBLIOGRAPHICAL REFERENCES 343

INDEX 353

INTRODUCTION

Set theory is the mathematics of classes. Sets are classes. The notion of class is so fundamental to thought that we cannot hope to define it in more fundamental terms. We can say that a class is any aggregate, any collection, any combination of objects of any sort; if this helps, well and good. But even this will be less help than hindrance unless we keep clearly in mind that the aggregating or collecting or combining here is to connote no actual displacement of the objects, and further that the aggregation or collection or combination of say seven given pairs of shoes is not to be identified with the aggregation or collection or combination of those fourteen shoes, nor with that of the twenty-eight soles and uppers. In short, a class may be thought of as an aggregate or collection or combination of objects just so long as 'aggregate' or 'collection' or 'combination' is understood strictly in the sense of 'class'.

We can be more articulate on the function of the notion of class. Imagine a sentence about something. Put a blank or variable where the thing is referred to. You have no longer a sentence about that particular thing, but an open sentence, so called, that may hold true of each of various things and be false of others. Now the notion of class is such that there is supposed to be, in addition to the various things of which that sentence is true, also a further thing which is the *class* having each of those things and no others as member. It is the class *determined* by the open sentence.

Much the same characterization would serve to characterize the notion of attribute; for the notion of attribute is such that there is supposed to be, in addition to the various things of which a given open sentence is true, a further thing which is an *attribute* of each of those things and of no others. It, with apologies to McGuffey, is the *at*tribute that the open sentence at*trib*utes. But the difference, the only intelligible difference, between class and attribute emerges when to the above characterization of the notion of class we adjoin this needed supplement: classes are identical when their members are identical. This, the *law of extensionality*, is not considered to extend to attributes. If someone views attributes as identical always when they are attributes of the same things, he should be viewed as talking rather of classes. I deplore the notion of attribute, partly because of vagueness of the circumstances under which the attributes attributed by two open sentences may be identified.[1]

My characterization of the notion of class is not definitive. I was describing the function of the notion of class, not defining class. The description is incomplete in that a class is not meant to require, for its existence, that there be an open sentence to determine it. Of course, if we can specify the class at all, we can write an open sentence that determines it; the open sentence '$x \in \alpha$' will do, where '$\in$' means 'is a member of' and α is the class. But the catch is that there is in the notion of class no presumption that each class is specifiable. In fact there is an implicit presumption to the contrary, if we accept the classical body of theory that comes down from Cantor. For it is there proved that there can be no systematic way of assigning a different positive integer to every class of positive integers, whereas there is a systematic way (see §30) of assigning a different positive integer to every open sentence or other expression of any given language.

What my characterization of classes as determined by open sentences brings out is just the immediate utility and motivation of the notion of class, then, not its full range of reference. In fact the situation is yet worse: not only do classes outrun open

---

[1] In what I call referential opacity there is further cause for deploring the notion of attribute. On both complaints see *Word and Object*, pp. 209f.

sentences, but also conversely. An open sentence can be true of some things and false of others and yet fail, after all, to determine any class at all. Thus take the open sentence '$x \notin x$', which is true of an object x if and only if x is not a class that is a member of itself. If this open sentence determined a class y at all, we should have, for all x, $x \in y$ if and only if $x \notin x$; but then in particular $y \in y$ if and only if $y \notin y$, which is a contradiction. Such is Russell's paradox.[2] So, on the heels of finding that not all classes are determined by open sentences, we are now forced to recognize that not all open sentences determine classes. (These ills, by the way, would descend no less upon attributes.) A major concern in set theory is to decide, then, what open sentences to view as determining classes; or, if I may venture the realistic idiom, what classes there are. This is a question from which, in the course of this book, we shall never stray far.

The word 'set' recurred two sentences ago, for the first time since we took leave of it in the second sentence of this Introduction. It will be as well now to reckon a bit further with it. After all, it is on the cover.

Basically 'set' is simply a synonym of 'class' that happens to have more currency than 'class' in mathematical contexts. But this excess terminology is often used also to mark a technical distinction. As will emerge, there are advantages (and disadvantages) in holding with von Neumann and perhaps Cantor that not all classes are capable of being members of classes. In theories that hold this, the excess vocabulary has come in handy for marking the distinction; classes capable of being members are called sets. The others have lamely been called 'proper classes', on the analogy of 'Boston proper' or 'proper part'; I prefer to call them *ultimate* classes, in allusion to their not being members in turn of further classes.

We can know this technical sense of 'set' and still use the terms 'set' and 'class' almost interchangeably. For the distinction emerges only in systems that admit ultimate classes, and even in

---

[2] Russell discovered it in 1901. He did not publish it until 1903, but meanwhile he discussed it in correspondence with Frege. The letters appear in van Heijenoort, pages 124–128.

such systems the classes we have to do with tend to be sets rather than ultimate classes until we get pretty far out. And, as a name for the whole discipline, 'set theory' remains as defensible as 'class theory' even granted ultimate classes; for any properly general treatment of the sets would be bound anyway to relate them incidentally to the ultimate classes if such there be, thus covering the whole ground still. My own tendency will be to favor the word 'class' where 'class' or 'set' would do, except for calling the subject set theory. This is the usual phrase for the subject, and I should not like to seem to think that I was treating of something else.

In Chapter I we shall see how set theory can in part be simulated by purely notational convention, so that the appearance of talking of sets (or classes), and the utility of talking of them, are to some degree enjoyed without really talking of anything of the kind. This technique I call the "virtual theory of classes." When we move beyond it in later chapters to the real thing, we shall still retain this simulation technique as an auxiliary; for in a superficial way it will continue to offer some of the convenience of stronger existence assumptions than we actually make. But a difference between class and set is not to be sought in this, for the simulation is not a case of using things of some other sort to simulate sets; it is a case of seeming to talk of sets (or classes) when really talking neither of them nor of anything in their stead.

I defined set theory as the mathematical theory of classes, and went on to describe the notion of class. Yet I thereby gave no inkling of what prompts set theory. This is best done rather by quoting the opening sentence of Zermelo's paper of 1908: "Set theory is that branch of mathematics whose task is to investigate mathematically the fundamental notions of 'number', 'order', and 'function' taking them in their pristine, simple form, and to develop thereby the logical foundations of all of arithmetic and analysis."[3]

Because of Russell's paradox and other antinomies, much of set theory has to be pursued more self-consciously than many

[3] The English is Bauer-Mengelberg's, from van Heijenoort's *Source Book.*

other parts of mathematics. The natural attitude on the question what classes exist is that any open sentence determines a class. Since this is discredited, we have to be deliberate about our axioms of class existence and explicit about our reasoning from them; intuition is not in general to be trusted here. Moreover, since the known axiom systems for the purpose present a variety of interesting alternatives, none of them conclusive, it would be imprudent at the present day to immerse ourselves in just one system to the point of retraining our intuition to it. The result is that the logical machinery is more in evidence in this part of mathematics than in most.

But in this respect the literature on set theory divides conspicuously into two parts. The part that concerns itself mainly with foundations of analysis gets on with much the same measure of informality as other parts of mathematics. Here the sets concerned are primarily sets of real numbers, or of points, and sets of such sets and so on. Here the antinomies do not threaten, for questions like '$x \in x$' do not come up.

It is rather in what Fraenkel has called abstract set theory, as against point-set theory, that we have so particularly to call our shots. A book in this branch typically takes up, in order, the following topics. First there are the general assumptions of the existence of classes, and other general laws concerning them. Then there is the derivation of a theory of relations from this basis, and more particularly a theory of functions. Then the integers are defined, and the ratios, and the real numbers, and the arithmetical laws are derived that govern them. Finally one gets on to infinite numbers: the theory of the relative sizes of infinite classes and the relative lengths of infinite orderings. These latter matters are the business of set theory at its most characteristic. They are the discovery or creation of Cantor, and thus virtually coeval with set theory itself.

This is a book on abstract set theory, and it falls generally into the above outline. It thus belongs to the branch of set-theoretic literature that has to be rather explicit about its logic. And this requirement is somewhat heightened, in this book, by two special circumstances. One is that in the last four chapters I shall compare and connect alternative systems more than is commonly done. The other is that I keep exploiting the "virtual theory."

In books that depend thus heavily on concepts and notations of modern logic, it has been usual to strive for self-sufficiency by devoting an opening chapter to a short course in logic. But knowledge of modern logic is now so widespread that those dreary and ever more perfunctory preparatory chapters can at last be dispensed with, I think, even in as introductory a presentation of set theory as this one is going to be. Still today, admittedly, many who take up set theory are unread in logic; but today a reader who goes at set theory by means of a book that leans heavily on logic is likely to have studied logic elsewhere. And if he has not, there are plenty of convenient texts with which to fill the lack.[4] Of mathematics apart from logic, on the other hand, I mean to presuppose nothing that a freshman is unlikely to know.

Oddly enough, Chapter I is called "Logic." But it assumes a grounding in logic, and builds out upon it in ways especially relevant to foundations of set theory. Specifically its main burden is the virtual theory of classes and a virtual theory of relations.

Readers already acquainted with set theory can quickly get further word on the aims of this book by turning to the Preface. Meanwhile I have been keeping this Introduction intelligible, I believe, to readers in every likely walk of life. Even the reader who has only the modest knowledge of logical theory needed for pushing on in the book will already have known most of what I have thus far been saying about classes; but I wrote below his level for the sake of those who are not prepared to read the book. For they may as well know what it is that they are not pressing on with. Some of them might decide to read a little logic and come back.

---

[4] The material covered by my *Methods of Logic* is more than enough. Any of various other texts at that level would likewise suffice, for my demands will be of a generalized character.

PART ONE
THE ELEMENTS

I | LOGIC

1. Quantification and identity

We shall need the usual notational apparatus of elementary logic: the quantifiers '(x)', '$(\exists x)$', '(y)', '$(\exists y)$', etc., their associated variables 'x', 'y', etc., and the truth-function signs '$\sim$', '$.$', '$\vee$', '$\supset$', and '$\equiv$'. This elementary logical vocabulary is a general apparatus for building complex sentences from atomic sentences, within particular theories about objects of any particular sorts. The particular theory concerned, whatever it may be, provides its special predicates for use in forming the atomic sentences, each of which consists of such a predicate and one or more variables in the role of subjects of the predicate.

Note that when I speak thus of predicates I speak merely of expressions of a certain sort: any verblike expressions, such as produce sentences when completed with one or more variables or other singular terms. In construing predicates thus as mere notation, rather than as properties or attributes, I am espousing no nominalistic sort of philosophy, but merely keeping the terminology straight. Properties or attributes, when discussed, will be called attributes.

The schematic predicate letters 'F', 'G', . . . attach to variables to make dummy clauses 'Fxy', 'Gx', 'Gy', etc., as expository aids when we want to talk about the outward form of a complex sentence without specifying the component clauses. Any actual compound sentence intended would contain, in place of the dummy clauses 'Fxy', 'Gx', etc., some genuine component sentences formed with the help of the special vocabulary of the particular theory under consideration—such component sentences as '$x < y$', '$x < 5$', '$y < 5$' if the theory is arithmetic. As long as we adhere to the dummy clauses instead of introducing express subject matter, we are working not with sentences but with sentence *schemata.* The sentence schemata used in elementary logic, called *quantificational* schemata, comprise the atomic sentence schemata 'p', 'q', 'Fx', 'Gx', 'Gy', 'Fxy', '$Gxyz$', and the like, and all compounds constructible of these by truth functions and quantification.

So the letters 'F', 'G', ... are never to be thought of as variables, taking say attributes or classes as values. Abstract objects, these or others, may of course still belong to our universe of discourse, over which our genuine variables 'x', 'y', ... of quantification are allowed to range. But the letters 'F', 'G', ... are withheld from quantifiers, indeed withheld from sentences altogether, and used only as dummies in depicting the forms of unspecified sentences.

The atomic schemata 'Fxy', 'Gx', 'Gy', etc. may represent sentences of any degree of complexity; they do not stand merely for atomic sentences with simple explicit predicates in place of 'F' and 'G'.

Particular theories, while they are like one another in using quantifiers and truth functions, will ordinarily differ from one another in point of universe of discourse and in point of their special predicate vocabularies. But, whatever these particulars, we can count on sentences of certain forms to come out true every time. Schemata depicting such forms are called *valid.* Typical ones are:

$$(y)((x)Fx \supset Fy), \qquad (y)(Fy \supset (\exists x)Fx), \qquad (x)Fx \supset (\exists x)Fx,$$
$$(x)(Fx \supset Gx) \supset. \ (x)Fx \supset (x)Gx.$$

Whatever nonempty universe of discourse a given special theory may impose as the range of the variables 'x' and 'y', and whatever special sentences involving 'x' and 'y' may be concocted of the special vocabulary of the theory as interpretations of 'Fx',

'Fy', and 'Gx', we may count on sentences of the above forms to turn out regularly true (for all values of whatever further free variables they may contain).

The theorems of any special theory will include, as a start, all the sentences that are thus instances of valid schemata. In addition there will be special theorems suited to the intended interpretations of the vocabulary of the special theory in question. Some of these theorems may be postulated as axioms. Others will *follow* logically, in this sense: they stand as 'q' in sentences of the conditional form '$p \supset q$', where the position of 'p' is occupied by axioms and the conditional sentence as a whole is an instance of a valid schema.

The literature of modern logic is rich in efficient and complete techniques for proving validity of schemata. I shall assume the reader's familiarity with one or more of these techniques, and present none in particular. When occasion arises to appeal to the validity of some unobvious schema, or to show that some particular sentence follows logically from another, I shall merely present so much intuitive argument as bids fair to enable the reader to fill in the formal argument according to the logical techniques of his choice.

I shall assume familiarity also with the conventions governing substitution of sentences for 'p', 'Fx', 'Fy', etc.[1] For instance, if a sentence substituted for 'Fx' has free variables beyond 'x', they must not be ones that can be captured by outlying quantifiers of the schema in which the substitution is made. Thus in the valid schema:[2]

$$(x)(y)(Fx \equiv Gy) \supset (x)(y)(Gx \equiv Gy)$$

it would be wrong to substitute '$y = x - x$' for 'Fx' so as to infer the falsehood:

$$(x)(y)(y = x - x \mathrel{.{\equiv}.} y = 0) \supset (x)(y)(x = 0 \mathrel{.{\equiv}.} y = 0).$$

---

[1] See for example my *Methods of Logic*, §§23, 25.

[2] A mechanical test of validity is known for schemata which, like this one, contain only one-place predicate letters. See for example *Methods of Logic*, pp. 107–117, 192–195.

Students of logic are familiar also with certain second-order generalizations regarding the validity of quantificational schemata. Conspicuous among these is the *substitutivity of the biconditional*, which may be represented thus:

$$(x_1) \ldots (x_n)(A \equiv B) \,.\, C_A \;.\!\supset C_B.$$

Here 'A', 'B', 'C_A', and 'C_B' represent any quantificational schemata such that the last two are alike except for containing as corresponding parts the respective schemata represented by 'A' and 'B'; and 'x_1', . . . , 'x_n' represent all variables, free in the schemata represented by 'A' and 'B', that are captured by quantifiers in the schemata represented by 'C_A' and 'C_B'.[3]

So much for quantification theory: the logic of the outward forms of sentences, which abstracts from all actual predicates of specific theories. Next let us turn our attention to one particular predicate which, for its persistent recurrence in all sorts of theories and its relevance to all sorts of universes of discourse, is also customarily considered under the head of logic. It is the two-place predicate '=' of *identity*. Adequate axioms of identity are '$x = x$' and all instances of the schema '$x = y \,.\, Fx \;.\!\supset Fy$' of *substitutivity of identity*. From these, by quantification theory, all laws of identity follow.[4] For example, as an instance of the schema we have that

$$x = y : x = x \;.\!\supset\!.\; x = x :\supset: x = y \;.\!\supset\!.\; y = x,$$

which reduces by truth-functional logic to '$x = y \;.\!\supset\!.\; y = x$'.[5] Another example: from '$y = y$' we have that $Fy \supset\!.\; y = y \,.\, Fy$ and so

$$Fy \supset (\exists x)(x = y \,.\, Fx),$$

and from '$x = y \,.\, Fx \;.\!\supset Fy$' we have conversely that

$$(\exists x)(x = y \,.\, Fx) \supset Fy,$$

---

[3] See for example my *Mathematical Logic*, §18.

[4] Gödel, 1930, Satz VIII.

[5] This proof, which does not use the axiom '$x = x$', is due to Hilbert and Bernays, vol. 1, p. 376 n.

so, combining,

$$Fy \equiv (\exists x)(x = y \,.\, Fx).$$

Incidentally this last schema suffices by itself conversely to deliver both '$x = y \,.\, Fx \,.\!\supset Fy$' and '$y = y$' and hence all laws of identity.[6] For it obviously delivers '$x = y \,.\, Fx \,.\!\supset Fy$', and further it has the substitution instance:

$$y \neq y \,.\!\equiv (\exists x)(x = y \,.\, x \neq y),$$

which, by virtue of the contradiction in its right side, reduces to '$y = y$'.

Each specific theory has its basic vocabulary of predicates. These are called *primitive*, to distinguish them from further predicates that may be introduced by definition merely to afford abbreviations of complex sentences. Usually the primitive predicates will be finite in number. When they are, we never need count '=' among them; we can always define this in terms of the rest. Thus suppose the only primitive predicate of some theory is a two-place predicate, 'ϕ'. Then '=' may be defined adequately for that theory by explaining '$x = y$' as:

$$\text{(i)} \qquad (z)(\phi xz \equiv \phi yz \,.\, \phi zx \equiv \phi zy).$$

For obviously '$x = x$' becomes a mere instance of a valid quantificational schema when construed according to this definition. Furthermore, the same happens to all instances of '$x = y \,.\, Fx \,.\!\supset Fy$', insofar as they are sentences involving no predicates beyond 'ϕ'. This is seen as follows. Consider first any instance where the sentences represented by 'Fx' and 'Fy' differ at only one place. The immediate contexts of these single distinctive occurrences of 'x' and 'y' will have to be respectively either 'ϕxv' and 'ϕyv', or else 'ϕvx' and 'ϕvy', where 'v' represents some one variable (possibly 'x' or 'y' in turn). By the substitutivity of the biconditional we have:

$$(z)(\phi xz \equiv \phi yz) \,.\, Fx \,.\!\supset Fy$$

---

[6] This was pointed out to me by Wang.

if the immediate contexts were 'ϕxv' and 'ϕyv', and in the other event we have:

$$(z)(\phi zx \equiv \phi zy) \, . \, Fx \, .\supset Fy;$$

so in either event we have '$x = y \, . \, Fx \, .\supset Fy$', with '$x = y$' defined as (i). So our schema is proved for the case where the sentences represented by 'Fx' and 'Fy' differ at only one place. Finally the extension to the case of n places is as follows. Let '$G_i y$', for each $i \leqq n$, represent what the sentence represented by 'Fx' becomes when we put 'y' for just the first i of the n occurrences of 'x' in question. Then our theorem for the case of one place gives '$x = y \, . \, G_i y \, .\supset G_{i+1} y$' for each i from 0 to $n - 1$, and these together imply '$x = y \, . \, G_0 y \, .\supset G_n y$', or '$x = y \, . \, Fx \, .\supset Fy$'.

We see therefore that all laws of identity are forthcoming without special assumptions, so long as the sole primitive predicate is 'ϕ'; for all laws of identity issue from '$x = x$' and '$x = y \, . \, Fx \, .\supset Fy$', and we have just seen that the definition (i) suffices for these.

If the primitive predicates of a theory comprise not just the two-place predicate ϕ but also, say, a one-place predicate ψ and a three-place predicate χ, then we would define '$x = y$' for purposes of that theory not as (i) but as:

$$\text{(ii)} \qquad \psi x \equiv \psi y \, . \, (z)(\phi xz \equiv \phi yz \, . \, \phi zx \equiv \phi zy \, . \\ (w)(\chi xzw \equiv \chi yzw \, . \, \chi zxw \equiv \chi zyw \, . \, \chi zwx \equiv \chi zwy)).$$

Similarly for other theories: we define '$x = y$' by exhaustion of atomic contexts as in (i) and (ii) and then establish '$x = x$' and '$x = y \, . \, Fx \, .\supset Fy$' by reasoning essentially similar to what we have seen.

The sense of '$x = y$' given by the plan of definition illustrated in (i) and (ii) may or may not really be identity; this will depend on the interpretations adopted for the primitive predicates and the universe of quantification. If the universe is taken as that of the real numbers, and 'ϕ' is construed as '<', then (i) will imply '$(z)(z < x \, .\equiv. \, z < y)$' and thus certainly will endow '$x = y$' with the sense of genuine identity. There not being a distinctive expressible condition for singling out every individual real number is immaterial to this favorable result. But if the universe is taken as that of persons, and the predicates are interpreted in ways depending on nothing but people's incomes, then the proposed manner of defining '$x = y$' will equate any persons who have equal incomes; so here indeed is an unfavorable case, where '$x = y$' does not come out with the sense of genuine identity. In cases of this kind we could protest that the interpretation of the universe and predicates is ill chosen, and that it might better be so rectified as to construe the members of the universe as whole income groups. But even at worst, even if we do not thus rectify the interpretation in order to sustain our method of defining '$x = y$', still no discrepancies between it and genuine identity can be registered in terms of the vocabulary of the theory itself. Even in the perverse case, thus, the method defines something as good as identity for purposes of the theory concerned.[7]

Clearly the plan illustrated in (i) and (ii) is available whenever the number of primitive predicates is, as usual, finite. Even when their number is infinite, commonly their interpretation is such that '$x = y$' can be adequately defined in terms of some few of them. But the contrary case can arise. Thus consider a theory whose primitive predicates are 'ϕ_1', 'ϕ_2', 'ϕ_3', . . . , each of them one-place and such that for each i

$$(\exists x)(\phi_1 x \mathbin{.} \phi_2 x \mathbin{.} \ldots \mathbin{.} \phi_{i-1} x \mathbin{.} \sim\phi_i x).$$

Here '$=$' must be added as a primitive predicate if it is to be available.

2. Virtual classes

In subsequent chapters we shall be concerned not with theories in general but with theories specifically of classes; and these will regularly be conceived in such form as to involve a single primi-

---

[7] This way of eliminating identity was recognized by Hilbert and Bernays, vol. 1, pp. 381f. On its relation to the identity of indiscernibles see my *Word and Object*, p. 230.

tive predicate, the two-place predicate 'ϵ' of class membership. Much, however, of what is commonly said of classes with the help of 'ϵ' can be accounted for as a mere manner of speaking, involving no real reference to classes nor any irreducible use of 'ϵ'. To this part of class theory, which I call the *virtual* theory of classes, and to an analogous virtual theory of relations I shall devote the rest of this chapter. So for the rest of this chapter the point of view of preceding pages continues: we continue to think generally of theories on whatever subject, each with its special primitive predicates, and not just of theories with primitive 'ϵ'.

Let us see how, into any such theory, a plausible and serviceable auxiliary 'ϵ' of ostensible class membership can be introduced by definition as a purely notational adjunct. The basic trick consists in defining 'ϵ' jointly with the form of notation '$\{x: Fx\}$' of class abstraction, which purports to designate the class of all objects x such that Fx.

In the eliminable combination here envisaged, 'ϵ' occurs only before class abstracts and class abstracts occur only after 'ϵ'. The whole combination '$y \epsilon \{x: Fx\}$' reduces, by what I call the *law of concretion*,[1] to 'Fy', so that there remains no hint of there being such a thing as the class $\{x: Fx\}$. Turning the tables and speaking not of elimination but of introduction, we may view 'ϵ' and class abstraction simply as fragments of a combination defined *in toto* thus:

2.1 '$y \epsilon \{x: Fx\}$' for 'Fy'.

If we were unwisely to agree to write, say, '$*(Fx)$' for '$x = 1 . (\exists y)Fy$', we should err in inferring '$*(F0) \equiv *(F1)$' from '$F0 \equiv F1$'. Now in view of this sort of fallacy we must mistrust a definition which, like 2.1, shows 'Fx' in the definiendum and not in the definiens. However, we can rectify 2.1 thus:

2.1′ '$y \epsilon \{x: Fx\}$' for '$(\exists x)(x = y . Fx)$'.

The definientia in 2.1 and 2.1′ were equated on p. 13.

---

[1] 1934, p. 48. It was stated by Whitehead and Russell (*20.3) and by Frege (1893, p. 52).

Incidentally 2.1′ clarifies the status of the variable of abstraction—the 'x' of '$\{x: Fx\}$'—as that simply of a bound variable of quantification, whereas 2.1 introduced that variable rather in an unprecedented role, without counterpart in the definiens 'Fy'.

When I state a definition in terms of 'x', 'y', 'Fx', etc., I mean it for all choices of variables in the positions of 'x', 'y', etc., and for all choices of sentences (of whatever theory we may be working in) in the position of 'Fx'. For 2.1 the intended relation of the sentences represented by 'Fx' and 'Fy' was, of course, that they be alike except that the latter have free 'y' where the former has free 'x'. If the sentence represented by 'Fx' happens to contain a quantifier capable of binding the 'y' of 'Fy', then an evasive relettering of the quantification is to be understood; e.g., we are to understand 2.1 as explaining:

$$y \in \{x: (\exists y)(x = y^2)\}$$

not as '$(\exists y)(y = y^2)$' but as '$(\exists z)(y = z^2)$'. Now a third virtue of 2.1′ is that this need of evasive relettering lapses; the definiens in 2.1′ is indifferent to there being quantification of 'y' in the sentence represented by 'Fx'.

However, 2.1′ raises a new difficulty instead: we can no longer put 'x' for 'y'. In 2.1 we could; '$x \in \{x: Fx\}$' came quite properly to 'Fx'. But under 2.1′ '$x \in \{x: Fx\}$' would come very improperly to '$(\exists x)(x = x \,.\, Fx)$', or '$(\exists x)Fx$'. Now one more dose of the same medicine cures this too. We can write:

2.1″ '$y \in \{x: Fx\}$' for '$(\exists z)(z = y \,.\, (\exists x)(x = z \,.\, Fx))$'.

Granted, 'z' must now not be free in the sentence represented by 'Fx'. But that much is standard convention; always, when using a definition whose definiens has a bound variable foreign to the definiendum, we are prepared to represent the variable by a letter new to the context.

Having noted these refinements, I shall for brevity keep to 2.1.[2]

Our ostensible talk of classes can be furthered by introducing the familiar notations of the Boolean class algebra through the

---

[2] For a further remark on 2.1″ see §4.

following conventions, where the Greek letters other than 'ϵ' are schematic letters standing for any class abstracts.[3]

2.2	'$\alpha \subseteq \beta$' for '$(x)(x \in \alpha .\supset. x \in \beta)$',	(inclusion)
2.3	'$\alpha \subset \beta$' for '$\alpha \subseteq \beta \nsubseteq \alpha$',	(proper inclusion)[4]
2.4	'$\alpha \cup \beta$' for '$\{x: x \in \alpha .\mathbf{v}. x \in \beta\}$',	(union)
2.5	'$\alpha \cap \beta$' for '$\{x: x \in \alpha . x \in \beta\}$',	(intersection)
2.6	'$\bar{\alpha}$' or '$^{-}\alpha$' for '$\{x: x \notin \alpha\}$'.	(complement)[4]

All such class notation is reducible, as observed, to prior terms. It can be seen as a notational elaboration upon the schematism of the logic of quantification, or as a notational elaboration upon the notation of any specific theory having any specific vocabulary of primitive predicates.

Definition of the notation '$x = y$' on the basis of such a vocabulary (cf. (i), (ii) of §1) does not extend to '$\alpha = \beta$'; for the class abstracts represented by the schematic letters 'α' and 'β' arise only through 2.1 and are not eligible to the positions of the genuine variables 'x' and 'y'. But an independent definition of '$\alpha = \beta$' is arrived at by similar reasoning:

2.7 '$\alpha = \beta$' for '$(x)(x \in \alpha .\equiv. x \in \beta)$', or '$\alpha \subseteq \beta \subseteq \alpha$'.

The prior '$x = y$' can itself be exploited in forming some useful class expressions, as follows. For the unit class of x, and further finite classes given by enumeration, we can define the

---

[3] When you are referred back to these definitions from beyond §4, the Greek letters stand rather for both abstracts and variables; cf. §4.

[4] Certain obvious contractions may well be taken for granted, without the ceremony of numbered definitions. In this spirit let us recognize the cancellation in '$\nsubseteq$', '$\notin$', and '$\neq$' as a displaced '$\sim$', and let us recognize '$x = y = z$', '$\alpha \subseteq \beta \nsubseteq \alpha$', '$x, y \in \alpha$', and the like as contracted conjunctions. —Regrettably, '$\subset$' is the old sign for '$\subseteq$', and is used in that sense in publications from Whitehead and Russell to the present day, including many of my own. But it is used nowadays in the narrower sense, as of 2.3, by those who use '$\subseteq$' for the broader sense. I have decided to go along with this trend, since '$\subseteq$', at any rate, will invite no confusion.

notations:

$$\text{`}\{x\}\text{' for `}\{z\colon z = x\}\text{',} \qquad \text{`}\{x, y\}\text{' for `}\{x\} \cup \{y\}\text{',}$$

etc.,[5] and, for the null class,

2.8 $\text{`}\Lambda\text{' or `}\{\ \}\text{' for `}\{z\colon z \neq z\}\text{'.}$

We may define also, as a companion to Λ, the universal class:[6]

2.9 $\text{`}\mathcal{V}\text{' for `}\{z\colon z = z\}\text{', or `}^{-}\Lambda\text{'.}$

The virtual theory of classes and relations was so called in my Brazil lectures of 1942.[7] Confusion of this idea with some others in the literature could impede the understanding of things to come in later chapters. So let me sort out these ideas.[8]

The definition 2.1 is reminiscent of Russell's introduction of classes by contextual definition.[9] But there is an essential difference. Russell's apparent counterpart of the schematic '*F*' of 2.1 is for Russell not a schematic letter, but a quantifiable variable taking attributes as values. This point was obscured to Russell and some of his readers by an inexact terminology: he used 'propositional function' to refer both to attributes and to open sentences or predicates. In reality he only reduced the theory of classes to an unreduced theory of attributes. He might better have assumed classes outright, for attributes are no clearer or more economical; on the contrary. (Cf. Introduction.)

The various operations on classes and relations are introduced by Behmann (1927) as mere variant notation for sentence connectives; '$\alpha \cap \beta$' and '$\alpha \cup \beta$', for instance, are introduced by explaining '$x \in \alpha \cap \beta$' and '$x \in \alpha \cup \beta$' as short for '$x \in \alpha \,.\, x \in \beta$' and '$x \in \alpha \;.\mathrm{v}.\; x \in \beta$'. Insofar, in effect, I follow Behmann in my

---

[5] The reason for not numbering these definitions appears in §7

[6] My use of script is accounted for at the end of §6.

[7] *O Sentido da nova lógica*, §51. See also Martin, who urged the idea concurrently; also my "Theory of classes presupposing no canons of type," p. 325.

[8] Readers new to the subject may reasonably settle for an imperfect grasp of the rest of this section, pending an acquaintance with later chapters.

[9] 1908. Also in Whitehead and Russell. See below, §35.

virtual theory of classes and, below, of relations. But again the difference is crucial: Behmann assumes classes and relations as values of quantifiable variables.

The distinction between set and ultimate class (cf. Introduction) is not to be confused with that between real and virtual class. Ultimate classes, for theories that admit them, are real: they belong to the universe of discourse, they are values of quantifiable variables. The virtual theory of classes, on the other hand, does not invoke classes as values of variables; it talks much as if there were classes, but explains this talk without assuming them.

The axiom system partly projected in Cantor's historic letter of 1899 (pp. 443f) could be developed in either vein. He described a set (*Menge*) as a class or multitude (*Klasse, Vielheit*) that can be "thought of as being together" as "*one* thing," "a finished thing." He went on to postulate that a class or multitude is a set if it is of the same size as a set; likewise if it is a subclass of a set; likewise if it is the class of all members of members of a set. Now such axioms could be formalized in either vein: by allowing the classes other than sets the status of ultimate classes, or by dismissing them as virtual. It is a choice upon which there hinges a difference as to what else can or cannot be said, for it is a question whether quantification is to be freely available over the wider domain. But either course would accommodate the Cantor passage.

What Bernays in his 1958 system calls classes as opposed to sets are precisely virtual classes in my sense; they are not real classes, ultimate or otherwise. In that system (unlike his earlier one) there are no ultimate classes; the only values of his variables are sets. In this respect the set theory that I shall develop in succeeding chapters, II–X, will resemble his. But I shall join the virtual theory more intimately to the real one than he does: unlike him I shall identify the virtual class with the corresponding set when such there is.

When in Chapters XIII and XIV and in a few intermediate parentheses we come to contemplate ultimate classes after all, we shall have the three headings side by side: sets, ultimate classes, and virtual classes. This pattern is much the same as in Gödel's

1940 monograph; for my virtual classes are precisely Gödel's "notions," apart from two points of style. One point is that unlike Gödel I talk of them as if of classes, subjecting them to class operations and the like. The other point is, again, that I shall eventually identify the virtual class with the corresponding real class, whether set or ultimate, when such there is.

Between the assumption of ultimate classes and the pretense of virtual ones there is, I emphasized, a difference in respect of available machinery for saying further things. If the extra machinery is not used, the significance of the difference dwindles. Thus it is that in the case of Cantor's letter we cannot choose between the two points of view. In the case of Bernays's earlier system (1937–54) the situation is somewhat similar; there indeed his assumption of ultimate classes was explicit, but still, as he has since remarked (1958, p. 43), he put little burden upon them. In the system of my *Mathematical Logic* they have figured more centrally.[10]

3. Virtual relations

Analogous to this virtual theory of classes, and connecting with it, there is a virtual theory of *relations*. Parallel to the notation of class abstraction there is the notation '$\{xy: Fxy\}$' of relation abstraction, purporting to designate the relation of anything x to anything y such that Fxy. Parallel to the use of 'α', 'β', . . . as schematic letters for class abstracts, I shall use 'P', 'Q', 'R', . . . as schematic letters for relation abstracts. Parallel to the notation '$x \in \alpha$' of class membership, finally, there is a notation for *relational attribution:* 'xRy' means that x bears the relation R to y. Just as the law of concretion for classes was used in 2.1 to provide a joint definition of membership and class abstraction, so the law of concretion for relations provides a joint definition of the attribution and abstraction of relations:

$$'z\{xy: Fxy\}w' \text{ for } 'Fzw'.$$

[10] See below, §§42–44, for more on these matters.

Parallel to 2.2–2.7 we may define:

$$
\begin{aligned}
`Q \subseteq R\text{' for }`(x)(y)(xQy \supset xRy)\text{'},\\
`Q \subset R\text{' for }`Q \subseteq R \not\supseteq Q\text{'},\\
`Q \cup R\text{' for }`\{xy\colon xQy \vee xRy\}\text{'},\\
`Q \cap R\text{' for }`\{xy\colon xQy \,.\, xRy\}\text{'},\\
`{}^{-}R\text{' for }`\{xy\colon {\sim} xRy\}\text{'},\\
`Q = R\text{' for }`(x)(y)(xQy \equiv xRy)\text{'}.
\end{aligned}
$$

Parallel to 'Λ' and '$\mho$' we have '$\Lambda \times \Lambda$' and '$\mho \times \mho$', both of which are forthcoming as cases of this general definition of the *Cartesian product* of two classes:

$$`\alpha \times \beta\text{' for }`\{xy\colon x \in \alpha \,.\, y \in \beta\}\text{'}.$$

This latter notion is typical of a cluster of useful notions that emerge only with relations, having no analogues within the class algebra. Others of them are as follows:

'$\breve{R}$' or '$\smile R$' for '$\{xy\colon yRx\}$',	(converse)
'$Q \mid R$' for '$\{xz\colon (\exists y)(xQy \,.\, yRz)\}$',	(resultant)
'$R``\alpha$' for '$\{x\colon (\exists y)(xRy \,.\, y \in \alpha)\}$',	(image)
'I' for '$\{xy\colon x = y\}$'.	(identity as relation)

They could be multiplied. Some of the further useful notions, however, are compactly expressible in the symbols already introduced. Thus $\{x\colon (\exists y)\, xRy\}$, which may be called the *left field* of R, is $R``\mho$; the *right field* is $\breve{R}``\mho$; the *field* is $(R \cup \breve{R})``\mho$. Again $\{x\colon xRy\}$, a useful notion by whatever name, is $R``\{y\}$.

Formulas come ready to hand corresponding to the familiar and useful terminology for special sorts of relations:

R is connected: $(x)(y)(x, y \in (R \cup \breve{R})``\mho \,.\!\supset x(R \cup \breve{R} \cup I)y)$,

reflexive: $(x)(x \in (R \cup \breve{R})``\mho \,.\!\supset xRx)$,

irreflexive: $R \subseteq {}^{-}I$,

symmetric: $R = \breve{R}$,

asymmetric: $R \subseteq {}^{-}\breve{R}$,
antisymmetric: $R \cap \breve{R} \subseteq I$,
transitive: $R \mid R \subseteq R$,
intransitive: $R \mid R \subseteq {}^{-}R$.

Relations as thus far treated are dyadic relations. Analogously one can provide also for triadic relations, $\{xyz\colon Fxyz\}$, and higher.

An important use of relations is as functions; for a function may be explained as a relation. The function "square of," e.g., may be explained as the relation $\{xy\colon x = y^2\}$ of square to root. Not that every relation rates as a function; the distinguishing trait of functions is that when R is a function we can speak uniquely of *the* R of x, if any: *the* square of n. A dyadic relation is a function if no two things bear it to the same thing. Thus we may define

'Func R' for '$R \mid \breve{R} \subseteq I$', or '$(x)(y)(z)(xRz \,.\, yRz \,.\supset.\, x = y)$'.

This means that 'function' is to be used in the sense of 'single-valued function'. What are sometimes spoken of as many-valued functions may best be referred to merely as relations. In analytical geometry and the differential calculus there is indeed point in distinguishing between so-called many-valued functions and other relations, out of considerations of continuity; but not here.

A typical function in the intended sense is

$$\{xy\colon (\exists z)(\exists w)(w \neq 0 \,.\, x = z/w \,.\, y = 2^z \cdot 3^w)\}.$$

Note that this function assigns the same ratio $\frac{2}{3}$ both to 108 $(=2^2 \cdot 3^3)$ and to 11,664 $(=2^4 \cdot 3^6)$; also that there are numbers, e.g. 5, or for that matter 0, to which it assigns nothing. Neither of these infirmities counts against its being a function. What makes it a function is that it never assigns more than one thing to the same thing.

Besides being able to write 'Func R', which means that no two things bear R to the same thing, it is convenient to be able to say even of a nonfunction R and a thing x that just one thing bears

R to x. Such things x will be called *arguments* of R, and the class of them is definable thus:

$$\text{`arg } R\text{' for `}\{x\colon (\exists y)(R``\{x\} = \{y\})\}\text{'}.$$

For example, where R is the son relation, arg R is the class of those persons who have one and only one son. Clearly

$$\text{(i)} \qquad \text{Func } R \equiv. \text{ arg } R = \breve{R}``\mathrm{V}.$$

In taking functions as dyadic relations we have provided only for functions like father, square, half, double, which are functions of single arguments. A parallel account provides, more generally, for functions of n arguments, as $(n + 1)$-adic relations; thus the power and sum functions, as functions of two arguments, may be explained as the triadic relations

$$\{xyz\colon x = y^z\}, \quad \{xyz\colon x = y + z\}.$$

In construing functions as I do, I follow Peano (1911) and agree with Gödel (1940). But in recent decades there has developed a divergence of style in this matter, logically inconsequential and practically exasperating. Instead of reckoning the values to left field and the arguments to right, the opposite plan is no less frequently adopted. The square function, e.g., is then taken as the relation not of square to root, but of root to square.

My way (Peano's, Gödel's) is natural in that if we are going to identify functions with relations at all, it is natural to identify the square (or father) function with the square (or father) relation; and certainly the square relation is the relation of square to root, as the father relation is the relation of father to child. This way is natural also in that, when Q and R are functions so construed, Q of R of x turns out to be $Q \mid R$ of x; on the other version it becomes $R \mid Q$ of x.

The reverse way might be said to be more natural on one count: a function transforms the argument into the value, thus leads from the argument *to* the value, and thus is naturally identified with the relation of the argument *to* the value. But the reasoning seems lame to me.

This reverse way is sustained incidentally by a concomitant accident of terminology, as follows. $R``\mathrm{V}$ has been called, at least since 1903 (Russell), the *domain* of the relation; $\breve{R}``\mathrm{V}$ the converse domain. On the other hand the arguments of a function are commonly said to constitute the domain, and the values the range. Taking functions oppositely to my way (and Peano's) makes the domain of the function the domain of the relation.

It might seem that on so arbitrary a point the majority usage should be decisive; and I fear that a majority now favors the switch. But awkwardness accumulates. Thus what are we to do with $R``\alpha$ when $R$ is a function? If we keep the above definition of the image $R``\alpha$ but switch the version of function, then $R``\alpha$ becomes the class *not* of values of $R$ for arguments in $\alpha$, but of arguments of $R$ for values in $\alpha$. So we find writers switching the definition of $R``\alpha$ to match; $R``\alpha$ becomes

$$\{y: (\exists x)(xRy \,.\, x \in \alpha)\}.$$

Thereupon $R``\alpha$ is again, as desired, the image of $\alpha$ by the function $R$, in the switched sense of function. But then $R``\alpha$ has ceased, for relations R in general, to be the class of things bearing R to members of α; and so usage is mixed up anew.

This latter sorry business, and the glaring perversity of the $R \mid Q$ phenomenon, are what have made me decide to hold, with Gödel, to the old Peano convention against the tide. My first point in defense of its naturalness has force too, but I should have been glad to waive that one. As for the contrary trouble about 'domain', I have cut the knot by abandoning the word in connection with relations. 'Left field' and 'right field' leave nothing to the imagination; and one then becomes free to speak of the arguments of a function steadfastly as comprising its domain, whether this be the right field (as it is for me) or the left.

I have given much space to a logically trivial point of convention because in practice it is so vexatious. The trouble of thinking through proofs and theorems, considerable at best, is aggravated time and again by the need to think which way functions are to be taken and what then to make of '$R``\alpha$' and '$Q \mid R$'. The mathematician who switched a seemingly minor point of usage out of willfulness or carelessness cannot have suspected what a burden he created.

A wealth of notation is now before us, having to do with classes and relations; and we have seen how to define it in such a way as to recognize no such things as classes and relations at all except as a defined manner of speaking. A motive for talking thus ostensibly and eliminably of classes and relations is compactness of expression. Thus take again our recent observation (i). It amounts, like any valid schema of the virtual theory of classes and relations, to a valid schema of the logic of quantification and identity. But what schema? Taking 'R' in (i) as '$\{xy: Fxy\}$' and expanding the whole by our definitions, we come out with the exorbitant schema:

$$(x)(y)(z)(Fxz \,.\, Fyz \,.\!\supset\!.\, x = y) \equiv$$
$$(x)((\exists y)(z)((\exists w)(Fzw \,.\, w = x) \equiv.\, z = y) \equiv (\exists y)(Fyx \,.\, y = y)).$$

(i) is one among countless laws that gain much in brevity and intuitiveness by translation from the schematism of pure quantification and identity into the schematism of virtual classes and relations. Other examples are the familiar laws of Boolean algebra, e.g.:

$$\overline{\ }(\alpha \cap \beta) = \bar{\alpha} \cup \bar{\beta}, \qquad \alpha \cap \beta \subseteq \alpha \subseteq \alpha \cup \gamma, \qquad \Lambda \subseteq \alpha \subseteq \mathcal{V},$$

and these laws of the algebra of relations:

$$R``(\alpha \cup \beta) = R``\alpha \cup R``\beta, \qquad \breve{\ }\breve{R} = R,$$
$$R``\alpha \subseteq \alpha \,.\!\equiv\!.\, \breve{R}``\bar{\alpha} \subseteq \bar{\alpha}, \qquad R \subseteq R``\mathcal{V} \times \breve{R}``\mathcal{V},$$
$$Q \mid (R \mid S) = (Q \mid R) \mid S, \qquad R \mid I = I \mid R = R,$$
$$\breve{\ }(Q \mid R) = \breve{R} \mid \breve{Q}, \qquad (Q \mid R)``\alpha = Q``(R``\alpha),$$

R is transitive and symmetric $\supset$ R is reflexive,

R is asymmetric $\supset$ R is irreflexive.

Down the centuries a major motive, certainly, for assuming such objects as relations and classes or attributes has been this kind of convenience, and we now see that this kind of convenience can be served as well by a virtual theory that ultimately assumes no such objects after all.

But there are also further purposes for assuming such objects, purposes not served by the virtual theory. To these we now turn.

II | REAL CLASSES

4. Reality, extensionality, and the individual

The virtual theory of classes and relations does not assume classes and relations as values of variables of quantification. The expressions that were accounted for in positions to the right of 'ϵ' or in the middle of relational attribution were invariably class abstracts and relation abstracts (or abbreviations and schematic representations thereof); they never were variables. Once we admit classes and relations irreducibly as values of variables of quantification, and only then, we are committed to recognizing them as real objects. The range of values of the variables of quantification of a theory is the theory's universe.

By admitting classes genuinely into the universe of a theory, as values of variables, we can often add significantly to what can be said in the theory about the rest of the objects in that universe. A good illustration of this effect is provided by the definition of ancestor in terms of parent. To simplify the illustration let us stretch the term 'ancestor' to the slight extent of counting everyone among his own ancestors. Then the ancestors of y fulfill, as a class, these two conditions: the *initial condition* that y is a member of the class, and the *closure condition* that all parents of members are members. Moreover, the ancestors of y compose the smallest such class, and are the common members of all such classes. So we can explain 'x is an ancestor of y' as saying that x belongs to all classes fulfilling that initial condition and closure condition; hence as saying that

$$(z)(y \in z \,.\, (u)(w)(w \in z \,.\, u \text{ is a parent of } w \;.\supset.\; u \in z) \;.\supset.\; x \in z).$$ [1]

Given the predicate 'is a parent of' and the apparatus of truth functions and quantification, but not given the predicate 'ϵ' of class membership and the right to quantify over classes z, we should be deprived of this means of expressing 'x is an ancestor of y'.

Further motives for quantifying over classes will appear in connection with number in Chapter IV. There are motives equally for quantifying over relations; but let us forget relations for a while.

When we take this step of admitting classes as real, we can no longer rest content with defining 'ϵ' as a mere fragment of a compound '$y \in \{x: Fx\}$'; for we need '$y \in z$' also, with quantifiable 'z'. We have to accept 'ϵ' rather as a primitive two-place predicate.

Once we accept 'ϵ' thus as primitive, we gain yet more than the right to use quantifiable variables after 'ϵ'; we gain also the right to mention classes to the left of 'ϵ', affirming their own membership in further classes. For, if classes are to count as values of variables, then the 'y' of '$y \in z$' may in particular refer to a class just as 'z' does. We could, indeed, forego this further profit by adopting one style of quantifiable variables for classes and another for individuals and allowing only the one style after 'ϵ' and only the other style before. But, as will be abundantly illustrated in later chapters, the acceptance of classes as members of further classes adds very significantly to what can be said about numbers and other mathematical objects; it is scarcely less urgent than the initial acceptance of quantification over classes of individuals. Let us therefore proceed with our single style of variables 'x', 'y', 'z', . . . and our primitive predicate 'ϵ', accepting '$y \in z$' as significant equally for individuals and classes as values of 'y' and 'z'.

---

[1] This construction, which is due to Frege, will occupy us further in §§11, 15.

Thereupon the question arises how to interpret '$y \in z$' where z is an individual. The convention that first suggests itself and has commonly been adopted in the literature is that in such a case '$y \in z$' is simply false for all y; individuals do not have members. But there is a different convention that proves much more convenient, as we shall see two pages hence.

Now that '$\in$' is to figure as a primitive predicate, we must consider what axioms to adopt to govern it. One axiom that we shall certainly want in some form or other is that of *extensionality*, also known as that of *Bestimmtheit* or definiteness: classes are the same whose members are the same. A natural rendering is:

$$(x)(x \in y .\equiv. x \in z) \supset. y = z.$$

The '$y = z$' here may be thought of as defined according to the plan of (i) of §1, with '$\in$' as sole primitive predicate; hence as short for:

$$\text{(i)} \qquad (x)(x \in y .\equiv. x \in z : y \in x .\equiv. z \in x).$$

We shall reopen the question of definition three pages later. Meanwhile let us ponder this awkward point: if y and z are memberless, then, according to the law of extensionality as we have it, $y = z$. This means that there is but one memberless entity. If it is the empty class, then individuals are not memberless; if individuals are memberless, and there are any, then there is but one individual and no empty class.

We could avert this consequence by inserting into the law of extensionality the further condition '$(\exists x)(x \in y)$', but then we would lose a case of that law that needs preserving; for we do still want to say that there is but one empty *class*. Evidently what is wanted as a further condition governing the law of extensionality is not that there are members of y (and z), but just that y and z are classes rather than individuals. But how is this to be written?

This would not be a problem if we quantified over individuals and classes with distinctive styles of variables. We could choose to do so for the sake of this problem, even while permitting both styles of variable before 'ϵ' (contrary to the passing impulse of a page back). Or we could keep to a single style of variables but adopt as a primitive predicate, additional to 'ϵ', the one-place predicate 'is an individual' (or 'is a class'). Adoption of the additional predicate is in theory perhaps preferable to admitting two styles of variables of quantification, in that it leaves the underlying logic undisturbed. This is always a live option: instead of adopting n distinctive styles of variables we can always add $n - 1$ one-place predicates, one for each of the domains but one to which the distinctive styles of variables would have been reserved. The one is saved by being definable by negation of the rest. (See further §§33, 37.)

However, even the adding of a single primitive predicate of individuality, or one of classitude, is an unwelcome sacrifice of elegance, and happily it can be avoided. For there is no need to reckon individuals as memberless. We are interested in '$x \epsilon y$' to begin with only for classes y; such are the only cases of '$x \epsilon y$' that are subject to preconceptions worth respecting. If for the sake of smooth systematization we see fit to assign meaning to further cases, let us assign a meaning that maximizes the smoothness. The first plan, of so assigning meaning as to count all the further cases false, has proved rough. Instead let us rule '$x \epsilon y$' true or false according as $x = y$ or $x \neq y$, when y is an individual. The problem of applying the law of extensionality to individuals y and z then vanishes; where y and z are individuals and 'ϵ' before individuals is given the force of '$=$', the law comes out true.

But what if y is an individual and z is the unit class of y? On our new interpretation of 'ϵ' before individuals, '$x \epsilon y$' then becomes true if and only if x is the individual y; but also '$x \epsilon z$' is true if and only if x is the individual y; so $(x)(x \epsilon y .\equiv. x \epsilon z)$ and therefore $y = z$. This result is *prima facie* unacceptable, since y is an individual and z a class. But actually it is a harmless result; none of the utility of class theory is impaired by counting an individual, its unit class, the unit class of that unit class, and so on, as one and the same thing. True, we are well advised now to adjust our terminology to the extent of ceasing to explain 'individual' as 'nonclass'; let us take to saying that what constitutes them individuals is not inclassitude, but identity with their unit classes (or, what comes to the same thing, identity with their own sole members). Individuals are what rated as nonclasses until we decided to give 'ϵ' the force of '$=$' before them; now they are best counted as classes. Everything comes to count as a class; still, individuals remain marked off from other classes in being their own sole members.

For I am by no means blurring the distinction between y and its unit class where y is not an individual. If y is a class of several members or of none, certainly y must be distinguished from its unit class, which has one member. If y is the unit class of a class of several members or of none, still y must be distinguished from its unit class, since the one member of y is, by the preceding sentence, different from the one member of the unit class of y. In general thus the distinction between classes and their unit classes is vital, and I continue to respect it. But the distinction between individuals and their unit classes serves no discoverable purpose, and the awkwardnesses that attended the law of extensionality can be resolved by abolishing just that distinction.

There is no need to assert that there are individuals, in the sense '$x = \{x\}$' or another. It suffices for our purposes, now and in the higher reaches of set theory as well, to rule merely that '$x = \{x\}$' is what characterizes individuals if such there be. As Fraenkel observed with reference to Zermelo's set theory, all formal demands can be met in a universe in which there are only *pure* classes, as he calls them: just Λ, $\{\Lambda\}$, $\{\Lambda, \{\Lambda\}\}$, and further classes composed of such materials, and no individuals in any sense.[2] Still, if one wants to apply set theory outside pure mathematics, he may want any manner of odd things as members of his classes. My version of individuals is intended to reconcile any such wishes with the formal benefits of making everything in some sense a class.

---

[2] Fraenkel, *Einleitung*, pp. 355f. Of my system NF (§40 below), Scott has proved that if it is consistent it remains so when an axiom, '$(\exists x)(x = \{x\})$' or '$(x)(x \neq \{x\})$', is added affirming or denying the existence of individuals in my sense.

These formal benefits are, up to now, elimination of a primitive predicate of individuality and simplification of the axiom of extensionality. Further benefits will be noted at scattered points in §§5, 7, 8, 38. And one further one to note now is that we are enabled to simplify our definition of identity: instead of explaining '$y = z$' as (i), we may define

$$`y = z\text{' for }`(x)(x \in y .\equiv. x \in z)\text{'}.$$

For clearly this pattern of definition, already envisaged for '$\alpha = \beta$' in 2.7, comes out right for individuals as well now that we have identified individuals with their unit classes.

Instead of numbering this definition, I shall adopt a convention that causes this definition to be covered by 2.7. The convention is that all the definitions 2.1–2.9 be retained still and that 'α' and 'β', therein and in future, be understood as schematic letters standing for occurrences not just of class abstracts but of class abstracts and ordinary free variables indiscriminately. When 'α' is taken as representing a class abstract, the '$x \in \alpha$' in any of the definitions 2.2–2.7 counts still as what was defined in 2.1; when 'α' is taken rather as representing 'y', the '$x \in \alpha$' in those same definitions 2.2–2.7 involves rather the primitive predicate '$\in$'. Thus I shall use the sign '$\in$', undifferentiated, in two very different statuses. This practice will make for some smooth techniques, as we shall see; and any ambiguity is resolved contextually by what comes after '$\in$'—variable or abstract.

The '$=$' in 2.8 and 2.9 was meant at the time as prior equipment of unspecified origin. Under our new attitude, that '$=$' is to be understood as issuing from 2.7.

Similarly, indeed, for the '$=$' in 2.1″, if as purists we favor 2.1″ over 2.1; but here steps are needed to avoid apparent circularity, since 2.7 comes necessarily after 2.1″. A solution, of course, is simply to begin with 2.1″ in expanded form:

'$y \in \{x\colon Fx\}$' for

$$`(\exists z)((w)(w \in z .\equiv. w \in y) \,.\, (\exists x)((w)(w \in x .\equiv. w \in z) \,.\, Fx))\text{'}.$$

But if we think in terms rather of 2.1, as we shall, this detail lapses.

Now that '$y = z$' is defined as '$(x)(x \in y .\equiv. x \in z)$' instead of as (i), the axiom of extensionality as hitherto formulated loses its content and must be rewritten. What it really said, abbreviations aside, was that

$$(x)(x \in y .\equiv. x \in z) \supset (x)(x \in y .\equiv. x \in z : y \in x .\equiv. z \in x),$$

or, what is logically equivalent,

$$(x)(x \in y .\equiv. x \in z) \supset (w)(y \in w .\equiv. z \in w).$$

As an axiom for this purpose the simpler formula:

$$(x)(x \in y .\equiv. x \in z) . y \in w .\supset. z \in w$$

obviously suffices, since '$(x)(x \in y .\equiv. x \in z)$' is symmetrical in '$y$' and '$z$'. Here, then, abbreviations aside, is the desired *axiom of extensionality*. 2.7 abbreviates it to:

4.1 *Axiom.* $y = z . y \in w .\supset. z \in w.$

In this axiom we see an instance of the substitutivity of identity (§1). The axiom is needed because '$(x)(x \in y .\equiv. x \in z)$', unlike (i), is of itself inadequate to assure the substitutivity law by logic alone.

5. The virtual amid the real

Originally 2.7 defined '$=$' only between class abstracts. In letting 'α' and 'β' stand now for free variables as well as class abstracts we have caused 2.7 to define '$=$' also between variables, as remarked. And indeed we have done more: we have caused 2.7 to define '$=$' also between a variable and an abstract. By 2.7 and 2.1,

5.1 $\alpha = \{x: Fx\} .\equiv (x)(x \in \alpha .\equiv Fx)$

whether 'α' represents variable or abstract.

Taking 'Fx' in particular as '$x \in \alpha$', we have from 5.1 that

5.2 $$\alpha = \{x: x \in \alpha\}.$$

Note that this embraces as theorems all sentences of the form:

$$\{z: Fz\} = \{x: x \in \{z: Fz\}\}$$

and, in addition, '$y = \{x: x \in y\}$'. The y in this last can be anything, even an individual; here is a further illustration of the simplicity gained in §4 by taking individuals as members of themselves.

In 5.1 the link is forged between, on the one hand, the primitive '$\in$' with its ensuing variable 'y', and, on the other hand, the defined '$\in$' with its ensuing abstract '$\{x: Fx\}$' of virtual class theory; we now equate the 'y' and the '$\{x: Fx\}$' to say, when we want to, that $(x)(x \in y .\equiv Fx)$. It is perhaps misleading to continue to speak of our abstraction notation '$\{x: Fx\}$' as virtual, now that the virtual theory and the real are thus fused.

This fusion is a departure from *O Sentido* and from Bernays's 1958 procedure as well. For Bernays, $\{x: Fx\}$ is steadfastly virtual and unreal even when a set exists with the same members. (Cf. §2.) For me, on the other hand, $\{x: Fx\}$ *is* that set if such there be. We might therefore do well hereafter to speak of the abstraction notation '$\{x: Fx\}$' not as virtual, for us, but as *noncommittal:* its use merely carries no general presumption of existence of the class (nor, if it exists, of its sethood).

Whether to say in particular that there is such a class as $\{x: Fx\}$ will depend on what sentence we interpret 'Fx' to represent and what axioms of existence we may eventually decide to adopt. It may seem that this latter theme could be satisfactorily managed by a single axiom schema:

(i) $$(\exists y)(x)(x \in y .\equiv Fx),$$

guaranteeing for every formulable condition (schematized 'Fx') a class y whose members are just the things fulfilling that condition. Such is the *law of abstraction*, or *comprehension*, in its naïve form. More compactly, thanks to 5.1, it may be put:

$$(\exists y)(y = \{x\colon Fx\}), \quad \text{i.e.,}\ (\exists y)(y = \alpha).$$

In any event it is untenable; there are no end of instances to the contrary, all of them valid simply by the logic of quantification. The simplest of these, noted in the Introduction as *Russell's paradox*, runs thus:

5.3 $$\sim(x)(x \in y \;.\!\equiv\!.\; x \notin x).$$

Proof. If $(x)(x \in y \;.\!\equiv\!.\; x \notin x)$ then $y \in y \;.\!\equiv\!.\; y \notin y$.

Another is as follows, where '$x \in^2 x$' is short for '$(\exists z)(x \in z \in x)$'.

5.4 $$\sim(x)(x \in y \;.\!\equiv \sim(x \in^2 x)).$$

Proof. Suppose on the contrary that

$$(x)(x \in y \;.\!\equiv \sim(x \in^2 x)). \qquad [\text{i}]$$

Since $y \in y \in y \;.\!\supset\!.\; y \in^2 y$, and also, by [i], $y \notin y \;.\!\supset\!.\; y \in^2 y$, it follows that $y \in^2 y$. So there is something x such that $y \in x \in y$. But then $x \in^2 x \in y$, contrary to [i].

What 5.3 and 5.4 tell us is that $\{x\colon x \notin x\}$ and $\{x\colon \sim(x \in^2 x)\}$ do not exist. We can likewise disprove the existence of $\{x\colon \sim(x \in^3 x)\}$, $\{x\colon \sim(x \in^4 x)\}$, and so on.[1]

From these examples one might suppose that the cyclic pattern '$x \in z_1 \in z_2 \in \ldots \in x$', perhaps with negation, is essential to the exceptions to (i). It is not. An example to the contrary is:

$$(\exists z)((w)(w \in z \;.\!\equiv\!.\; w \in x)\,.\, z \notin x).$$

For its atomic components '$w \in z$', '$w \in x$', '$z \in x$' cannot be joined to spell out any cycle; yet the whole reduces by 2.7 to '$(\exists z)(z = x\,.\, z \notin x)$', which amounts after all to the '$x \notin x$' of 5.3.

---

[1] *Mathematical Logic*, §24. The contractions '$\in^2$', '$\in^3$', etc., like those mentioned in note 4 of §2, seem not to warrant the ceremony of a numbered definition.

A further paradox in the same vein is Mirimanoff's, which comes of taking the y of (i) as the class of all *grounded* classes: all classes x for which there is no infinite progression $z_1, z_2, \ldots$ such that $\ldots \in z_2 \in z_1 \in x$. For, if y itself is grounded, then $y \in y$ and so $\ldots \in y \in y \in y$, contrary to groundedness of y. If on the other hand y is not grounded, then there are $z_1, z_2, \ldots$ such that $\ldots \in z_2 \in z_1 \in y$; but then z_1 in turn is not grounded, contrary to '$z_1 \in y$'.

Can we perhaps limit (i) satisfactorily by ruling simply that each instance of (i) whose negation is not logically valid be counted as an axiom? It could be objected to this course that there is no general technique for disproving logical validity, as there is for proving logical validity. This objection is minor. But there is also an objection that is devastating: the axioms thus specified, individually consistent, would be collectively inconsistent.

Thus consider the principle of *Aussonderung:*[2]

(ii) $$(\exists y)(x)(x \in y \;.\!\equiv.\; x \in z \,.\, Gx),$$

or more compactly:

$$(\exists y)(y = z \cap \{x\colon Gx\}), \quad \text{i.e.,}\ (\exists y)(y = z \cap \alpha).$$

This is a specialization of (i), embracing just those cases of (i) where 'Fx' is interpreted as implying '$x \in z$'. Now all such cases can be simultaneously assumed true, for all z, without engendering any logical contradiction. (Proof: reinterpret '$x \in y$' trivially as false for *all* x and y, and (ii) will become trivially true regardless of 'G'.) Furthermore, the separate case:

(iii) $$(\exists y)(x)(x \in y \;.\!\equiv.\; x = x)$$

of (i) can individually be assumed true; indeed it reduces to '$(\exists y)(x)(x \in y)$', or '$(\exists y)(y = \mathcal{V})$'. But the combination of (ii) and (iii) leads to contradiction. For, if we take z in (ii) as the y

---

[2] From Cantor (1899) and Zermelo (1908). See below, §37.

of (iii), hence as $\mathcal{V}$, then '$x \in z$' can be dropped from (ii), and what remains has the full force of (i) itself.

Zermelo's theory accepts (ii) in full, and hence rejects (iii). The theory in my "New foundations" accepts (iii) and hence has to make exceptions to (ii). (See below, §§38, 40.) Still other theories reject (iii) and make exceptions to (ii) besides. Because of this incompatibility among separately tenable cases of (i), many radically unequivalent set theories have been put forward; there is no evident optimum.

My policy on comprehension axioms—cases of (i)—will be to adopt such axioms piecemeal and with reluctance as need presses. In §7 I shall assume all classes of fewer than three members. In §13 I shall assume finite classes generally, but no more. In later chapters the consequences of assuming further classes in various ways will be weighed. But in the present chapter I shall assume no cases of (i), no comprehension axioms at all.

Let us compare this ontological attitude with that of Chapter I. In Chapter I the question of there really being classes did not arise. Class talk, as far as it went in Chapter I, was explained away as a mere manner of speaking, superimposed definitionally on one or another special theory having its own primitive predicates for its own special subject matter, whatever that might be. Now in the present chapter we are still refraining from assumptions of class existence, but with the difference that now the question very decidedly arises: we now have 'ϵ' as primitive predicate, and it will be a trivial and pointless one unless there are classes and lots of them. Even the many theorems which, because they are governed by universal rather than existential quantifiers, we can prove without axioms or premisses of existence, would lose all potential content and interest if classes were excluded. We now certainly intend there to be classes, but we are not yet prepared to say just which.

It can be argued that in any event we are committed to there being at least one class. For we are assuming the classical logic of quantification, which, as is well known, assumes there to be at least one thing (since '$(\exists x)(Fx \supset Fx)$' and the like are counted valid); and on our version of individuals anything is a class, individuals being classes of themselves.

The need of existence assumptions beyond that technical minimum is somewhat less continually pressing than might be expected, thanks to our noncommittal version of class abstraction, which I shall continue to exploit. For our contextual definition 2.1 of class abstraction allows us to speak freely of membership in $\{x: Fx\}$, and even truly on occasion, without having to assume the existence of any such class as $\{x: Fx\}$. In proceeding thus there is no risk of involving ourselves in logical contradiction, since the procedure rests only on the definition 2.1, and on no assumption; any contradiction encountered would have to be present independently of the defined notation. We can even speak of the class $\{x: x \notin x\}$ underlying Russell's paradox, to the extent of affirming or denying membership in it; indeed, by 2.1,

$$y \in \{x: x \notin x\} \ .\equiv.\ y \notin y.$$

If we were allowed to substitute '$\{x: x \notin x\}$' for 'y' here, we would be in contradiction; but there is no license thus far for substituting class abstracts for variables, nor has any definition even been adopted thus far to explain a class abstract to the left of '$\in$'.

The latter gap will now, however, be filled. How to fill it is evident from 5.1.

5.5 '$\{x: Fx\} \in \beta$' for '$(\exists y)(y = \{x: Fx\} \,.\, y \in \beta)$'.

To affirm membership in $\{x: Fx\}$ is not to suggest that $\{x: Fx\}$ exists. But to affirm membership on the part of $\{x: Fx\}$ is, by 5.5, definitely to imply that $\{x: Fx\}$ exists: that $(\exists y)(y = \{x: Fx\})$.

2.1 and 5.5 together account for occurrences of class abstracts in all places where free variables can occur. For they account for abstracts on either side of '$\in$', and '$\in$' is our sole primitive predicate. Hereafter our schemata can therefore admit '$F\alpha$' and '$F\{x: Gx\}$' as freely as 'Fy'. 'Fy' stands for any sentence built of '$\in$', variables, quantifiers, and truth functions (definitions aside); and '$F\alpha$' or '$F\{x: Gx\}$' stands for the same with 'α' or '$\{x: Gx\}$' in place of 'y'.

But let us not jump to the conclusion that we may freely substitute abstracts for variables as a rule of inference. Such substitution changes the status of '$\in$', from the status of a primitive predicate as in '$y \in z$' to the status of a contextually defined particle as in '$y \in \{x: Fx\}$' or '$\{x: Fx\} \in \beta$'; and the two sorts of '$\in$' are *prima facie* the merest accidental homonyms. Our tendentious choice of notation looks certainly to eventual inference by substitution of abstracts for variables, at least within limits; but any rule to this effect demands justification in the light of the definitions and antecedent assumptions. Such is the subject matter of the next section.

6. Identity and substitution

The law '$x = y \,.\, Fx \,.\!\supset Fy$' of substitutivity of identity is recoverable in the present system as follows. By 4.1, $x = y \,.\, x \in z \,.\!\supset\!.\, y \in z$ and $y = x \,.\, y \in z \,.\!\supset\!.\, x \in z$. But, by 2.7, $x = y \,.\!\equiv\!.\, y = x$. So

$$x = y \,.\!\supset:\, x \in z \,.\!\equiv\!.\, y \in z.$$

Hence, by 2.7,

$$x = y \,.\!\equiv (z)(z \in x \,.\!\equiv\!.\, z \in y :\, x \in z \,.\!\equiv\!.\, y \in z).$$

From this, by the argument seen in connection with (i) of §1, we conclude that $x = y \,.\, Fx \,.\!\supset Fy$.

Further, by 2.7, $y = y$. From these two results all laws of identity follow, as was mentioned in §1. In particular we may now set down:

6.1 $$Fy \equiv (\exists x)(x = y \,.\, Fx),$$

for its derivation from '$x = y \,.\, Fx \,.\!\supset Fy$' and '$y = y$' was seen explicitly in §1. As a corollary of it we have further the dual:

6.2 $$Fy \equiv (x)(x = y \,.\!\supset Fx).$$

For, substituting in 6.1,

$$\begin{aligned} \sim Fy &\equiv (\exists x)(x = y \,.\, \sim Fx) \\ &\equiv \sim(x)(x = y \,.\!\supset Fx). \end{aligned}$$

But when I say that all laws of identity are forthcoming I am supposing them couched, like 6.1 and 6.2, in genuine variables, not Greek letters or abstracts. With the latter we immediately encounter failures. For example, '$(\exists y)(y = z)$' is a valid law of identity, following from '$z = z$'; yet '$(\exists y)(y = \alpha)$' fails, since, by 5.3, $y \neq \alpha$ for all y when α is $\{x: x \notin x\}$. For that matter, even 6.1 and 6.2 can fail with 'α' for 'y'; for if $\sim(\exists x)(x = \alpha)$, then definitely $\sim(\exists x)(x = \alpha \,.\, Fx)$ and $(x)(x = \alpha \,.\!\supset Fx)$, while certainly not both $\sim F\alpha$ and $F\alpha$.

We do get this special case of 6.1 with 'α' for 'y'.

6.3 $$\alpha \in \beta \,.\!\equiv (\exists x)(x = \alpha \,.\, x \in \beta).$$

Proof by 5.5 or 6.1 according as 'α' represents an abstract or a variable.

In the failure of '$(\exists y)(y = \alpha)$', and of 6.1 and 6.2 with 'α' for 'y', we have ample illustration that the substitution of abstracts (or Greek letters) for variables is not a generally justifiable mode of inference. Many laws of identity do, unlike 6.1 and 6.2, happen to hold under such substitution; but it takes more than the substitution to show that they do. For instance, we are not entitled to conclude outright from '$x = x$' and '$x = y \,.\!\equiv\!.\, y = x$' that

6.4 $$\alpha = \alpha,$$

6.5 $$\alpha = \beta \,.\!\equiv\!.\, \beta = \alpha.$$

But we *can* quickly prove these latter by observing that they are mere abbreviations, under 2.7, of:

$$(x)(x \in \alpha \,.\!\equiv\!.\, x \in \alpha),$$
$$(x)(x \in \alpha \,.\!\equiv\!.\, x \in \beta) \equiv (x)(x \in \beta \,.\!\equiv\!.\, x \in \alpha),$$

which are true by the pure logic of quantifiers and truth functions. We could prove '$\alpha = \beta \,.\, \beta = \gamma \,.\!\supset\!.\, \alpha = \gamma$' similarly; however, it is covered also by 6.7 below.

Again the law of substitutivity of identity holds also for abstracts in place of either or both variables, thus:

$$\textbf{6.6} \qquad \alpha = \beta \,.\, F\alpha \,.\!\supset F\beta,$$

but we have to prove this anew, as follows. First we consider the case where '$F\alpha$' and '$F\beta$' represent sentences differing only at one place. The immediate context of that one occurrence of 'α' will be either '$\gamma \in \alpha$' (Subcase 1) or '$\alpha \in \gamma$' (Subcase 2); for we may suppose any overlying definitions expanded.

Subcase 1: Let '$G\alpha$' represent the sentence formed by putting '$(\exists x)(x = \gamma \,.\, x \in \alpha)$' for the occurrence of '$\gamma \in \alpha$' in the sentence represented by '$F\alpha$'. So, by 6.3 and the substitutivity of the biconditional, $F\alpha \equiv G\alpha$.

Subcase 2: Let '$G\alpha$' represent the sentence formed by putting:

$$(\exists z)((x)(x \in z \,.\!\equiv\!.\, x \in \alpha) \,.\, z \in \gamma)$$

for the occurrence of '$\alpha \in \gamma$' in the sentence represented by '$F\alpha$'. So, by 2.7 and 6.3 and the substitutivity of the biconditional, $F\alpha \equiv G\alpha$.

Both subcases: $F\alpha \equiv G\alpha$. Similarly $F\beta \equiv G\beta$. But the sentences represented by '$G\alpha$' and '$G\beta$' are alike except that the one has '$x \in \alpha$' where the other has '$x \in \beta$'; so, by the substitutivity of the biconditional,

$$(x)(x \in \alpha \,.\!\equiv\!.\, x \in \beta) \,.\, G\alpha \,.\!\supset G\beta.$$

That is, by 2.7, $\alpha = \beta \,.\, G\alpha \,.\!\supset G\beta$. That is, $\alpha = \beta \,.\, F\alpha \,.\!\supset F\beta$.

So 6.6 is proved for the case where the sentences represented by '$F\alpha$' and '$F\beta$' differ at only one place. The extension to *n* places then proceeds as in the argument from (i) in §1.

A more useful variant of 6.6 is:

$$\textbf{6.7} \qquad \alpha = \beta \,.\!\supset\!.\, F\alpha \equiv F\beta,$$

which comes of it in view of 6.5.

We saw in 6.4 and 6.6 that '$x = x$' and '$x = y \,.\, Fx \,.\!\supset Fy$' still hold when Greek letters are put for the free variables. But all laws of identity theory follow by quantification theory from '$x = x$' and '$x = y \,.\, Fx \,.\supset Fy$' (cf. §1). Yet some laws of identity theory were seen to fail when Greek letters are put for the free variables. How is this possible? The answer is that the deductive steps of quantification theory themselves do not carry over to Greek letters. That Greek letters are not regularly justifiable as instances of quantified variables is, after all, substantially what we have been talking about. The proof of 6.1, e.g., used quantification theory thus:

$$y = y \,.\, Fy \,.\supset (\exists x)(x = y \,.\, Fx).$$

With 'α' for 'y' this step would not be justifiable.

In general it is the schema '$(x)Fx \supset F\alpha$' for substitution of class abstracts for variables that fails, along with its dual '$F\alpha \supset (\exists x)Fx$'. These are in general justifiable only subject to a supporting comprehension premiss to the effect that α exists, $(\exists x)(x = \alpha)$. Clearly therefore we shall have much use for such premisses.

A more convenient notation than '$(\exists x)(x = \alpha)$' for such premisses is '$\alpha \in \mathcal{V}$'. For, we have by 6.4 that $x = x$ and so by the definitions 2.1 and 2.9 that

6.8 $$x \in \mathcal{V},$$

whence, since

$$\alpha \in \mathcal{V} \,.\!\equiv (\exists x)(x = \alpha \,.\, x \in \mathcal{V})$$

according to 6.3, we can conclude that

6.9 $$\alpha \in \mathcal{V} \,.\!\equiv (\exists x)(x = \alpha).$$

This and 5.1 give us three ways of saying that $\{x\colon Fx\}$ exists:

$$\{x\colon Fx\} \in \mathcal{V}, \quad (\exists y)(y = \{x\colon Fx\}), \quad (\exists y)(x)(x \in y \,.\!\equiv Fx).$$

So in particular we can now transcribe 5.3 and 5.4 thus:

6.10 $$\{x\colon x \notin x\}, \quad \{x\colon \sim(x \in^2 x)\} \notin \mathcal{V}.$$[1]

[1] On '$\alpha, \beta \in \gamma$' see note 4 of §2.

The appropriately restricted schema for substitution of class abstracts for variables is now easily proved, along with its dual.

6.11 $\alpha \in \mathcal{V} \,.\, (x)Fx \,.\!\supset Fa$, $\alpha \in \mathcal{V} \,.\, F\alpha \,.\!\supset (\exists x)Fx$.

Proof. By hypothesis and 6.9, there is something y such that $y = \alpha$. By 6.7, then, $Fy \equiv F\alpha$. So $(x)Fx \supset F\alpha$ and $F\alpha \supset (\exists x)Fx$.

That '$\alpha \in \beta$' implies existence of α was already remarked, and will be used much.

6.12 $\alpha \in \beta \,.\!\supset\!.\, \alpha \in \mathcal{V}$. *Proof* by 6.3, 6.9.

More fully, we have that

6.13 $\alpha \in \{x\colon Fx\} \,.\!\equiv\!.\, \alpha \in \mathcal{V} \,.\, F\alpha$.

Proof. By 2.1, $(y)(y \in \{x\colon Fx\} \,.\!\equiv Fy)$; so, by 6.11,

$$\alpha \in \mathcal{V} \,.\!\supset\colon \alpha \in \{x\colon Fx\} \,.\!\equiv F\alpha.$$

But also, by 6.12,

$$\alpha \in \{x\colon Fx\} \,.\!\supset\!.\, \alpha \in \mathcal{V}.$$

6.13 then follows by truth-functional logic.

When we put 'y' for 'α' in 6.13, of course the existence clause drops by 6.8. What remains is just 2.1.

We may add here the dual of 6.8. But it admits of a schematic letter.

6.14 $\alpha \notin \Lambda$.

Proof. By 6.13 and 2.8, $\alpha \in \Lambda \,.\!\equiv\!.\, \alpha \in \mathcal{V} \,.\, \alpha \neq \alpha$. So, by 6.4, $\alpha \notin \Lambda$.

Both 6.8 and 6.14 can be strengthened, thus:

6.15 $(x)(x \in \alpha) \equiv\!.\, \alpha = \mathcal{V}$, $(x)(x \notin \alpha) \equiv\!.\, \alpha = \Lambda$.

Proof. By 6.8 and 6.14 respectively,

$$(x)(x \in \alpha) \equiv (x)(x \in \alpha \,.\!\equiv\!.\, x \in \mathcal{V}),$$

$$(x)(x \notin \alpha) \equiv (x)(x \in \alpha \,.\!\equiv\!.\, x \in \Lambda),$$

q.e.d. (cf. 2.7).

Or, taking α in 6.15 as $\{x: Fx\}$ or $\{x: \sim Fx\}$ and looking to 2.1,

6.16 $(x)Fx \equiv. \{x: Fx\} = \mathcal{V} .\equiv. \{x: \sim Fx\} = \Lambda.$

The warning in §2 against confusing existence with sethood, and virtual classes with ultimate classes, must be renewed and intensified now that '$\alpha \in \mathcal{V}$' has emerged as our means of saying that α exists. Existence of α is membership in $\mathcal{V}$, and sethood of α is membership in something; the catch is just that $\mathcal{V}$ is not known to be something. If we do postulate existence of $\mathcal{V}$, i.e., that $\mathcal{V} \in \mathcal{V}$, then indeed all things become sets; existence reduces to sethood. If there are ultimate classes at all, $\mathcal{V}$ is unreal; $\mathcal{V} \notin \mathcal{V}$.

If there are ultimate classes, i.e., if not all classes are sets, then it is useful to distinguish in general between the class $\{u: Fu\}$ of all classes u such that Fu (hence all objects whatever u such that Fu) and the class $\hat{u}Fu$ merely of all sets u such that Fu.[2] The latter is definable in terms of the former thus:

'$\hat{u}Fu$' for '$\{u: (\exists z)(u \in z) . Fu\}$'.

When $\hat{u}Fu$ and $\{u: Fu\}$ differ, it is because there is an ultimate class x such that Fx. In this event we have $x \notin \hat{u}Fu$ but still $x \in \{u: Fu\}$ and so $\{u: Fu\} \notin \mathcal{V}$ (since $(y)(x \notin y)$), though quite possibly $\hat{u}Fu \in \mathcal{V}$. (Indeed '$\hat{u}Fu \in \mathcal{V}$' recommends itself as axiom

[2] The difference of notations '$\hat{u}Fu$' and '$\{u: Fu\}$' was never before meant to reflect this distinction. The one notation goes back to Whitehead and Russell; the other is more recent, and increasingly in vogue. By chance I used the old '$\hat{u}Fu$' in *Mathematical Logic;* and I gave it the sense 'the class of all sets such that Fu' only because committal abstraction is bound to have that sense and noncommittal abstraction did not cross my mind. By chance Bernays (1958) favored rather the notation '$\{u: Fu\}$' (nearly enough), and, for no related reason, limited his use of abstraction to virtual classes. Now it proves convenient to exploit this chance divergence of notation to register the chance divergence of connotation. Since this new distinction remains empty (like that between set and class) for systems without ultimate classes, it may quite possibly conflict with no literature in which either of the forms '$\hat{u}Fu$' and '$\{u: Fu\}$' has turned up.

schema categorically, for theories admitting ultimate classes.[3]) Now once this distinction between $\{u: Fu\}$ and $\hat{u}Fu$ emerges, care must be taken not to confuse $\{x\}$, $\mathcal{V}$, etc., in our own sense of $\{u: u = x\}$, $\{u: u = u\}$, etc., with say ιx, V, etc. in the sense of $\hat{u}(u = x)$, $\hat{u}(u = u)$, etc. If x is an ultimate class then

$$x \in \{u: u = x\} \notin \mathcal{V}, \qquad x \notin \hat{u}(u = x) = \Lambda.$$

Furthermore everything belongs to $\mathcal{V}$ in our sense $\{u: u = u\}$; while just sets belong to V in the sense $\hat{u}(u = u)$;

$$(x)(x \in \{u: u = u\}), \qquad (x)(x \in \hat{u}(u = u) .\equiv (\exists z)(x \in z)).$$

In my *Mathematical Logic* there was no thought of noncommittal abstraction, so the V of that book is $\hat{u}(u = u)$, not $\{u: u = u\}$, and consequently '$x \in \mathrm{V}$' in that book is the regular way of expressing sethood of x; whereas for us here '$x \in \mathcal{V}$' holds for all x, and '$\alpha \in \mathcal{V}$' is our regular way of expressing existence of α while leaving sethood unsettled. Readers familiar with *Mathematical Logic* should particularly note this contrast. I have been working it into the typography by using the roman 'V' as in that book for the firmer class, and the script '$\mathcal{V}$' for the less probably existent class of absolutely everything.

In the many systems without ultimate classes, the distinction of course lapses; there all classes are sets, $\hat{u}Fu$ is $\{u: Fu\}$, and in particular V is $\mathcal{V}$, which may or may not exist. Among such systems are those of Russell, Zermelo, Bernays (1958), my "New foundations," Rosser. And in the present book the distinction between sets and classes will not concern us, except in cautionary passages such as this, until the last two chapters. When it does come to concern us, we shall not need to lean upon the typographical distinction between 'V' and '$\mathcal{V}$'; for '$\mathrm{U}\mathcal{V}$' will conveniently emerge in §8 to do the work of 'V'.

---

[3] Von Neumann did not assume it categorically, but I did in *Mathematical Logic*. My saying so will seem odd to readers who know that book, but only because of the discrepant use of 'V' explained in the next sentences.

III | CLASSES OF CLASSES

7. Unit classes

Everything is for us a class, since anything that threatens to be otherwise is brought into line by the ruling of §4 that made individuals their own members. It follows that every class is a class of classes, and hence that everything is a class of classes.

A good thing about everything's being a class is that wherever a free variable would make sense a class abstract makes sense too. Intuitive sense, that is; formally the sense is provided by 2.1 and 5.5, and by our continuing to write all further definitions with Greek letters rather than variables in the free positions.

Greek letters in places available to variables were an impossibility for §2, for these two reasons: Greek letters there stood only for abstracts and not also for variables, pending the retroactive convention to the contrary in §4; and abstracts had access only to positions barred to variables, viz., post-epsilon position (and abbreviations of such). Substantively stated, the original situation in §2 was that classes were virtual only, only their members were real, and so classes of classes came in for not even so much as virtual status.

Thus in particular we were able in §2 to define '$\{x\}$' and '$\{x, y\}$' but not '$\{\alpha\}$' or '$\{\alpha, \beta\}$'. This was why I withheld reference numbers from the definitions of '$\{x\}$' and '$\{x, y\}$' in §2. At that stage '$z = x$' and '$\gamma = \alpha$' were available but '$z = \alpha$' was not; so we could not define '$\{\alpha\}$' as '$\{z: z = \alpha\}$', and had to rest content with defining '$\{x\}$' as '$\{z: z = x\}$'. Correspondingly for '$\{x, y\}$' as against '$\{\alpha, \beta\}$'. In §4, the revised convention of Greek letters caused 2.7 to make sense of '$z = \alpha$' after all, as in 5.1. So let us now define '$\{\alpha\}$' and '$\{\alpha, \beta\}$'.

7.1 '$\{\alpha\}$' for '$\{z: z = \alpha\}$', '$\{\alpha, \beta\}$' for '$\{\alpha\} \cup \{\beta\}$'.

Getting the Greek letter into '$\{\alpha\}$' is not, indeed, quite what makes it meaningful to talk of unit classes of classes. Since adopting 'ϵ' as a primitive predicate, in §4, and so viewing classes as real, we view 'x' itself as admitting classes as values—all classes whatever (that exist, of course); and so $\{x\}$ may already be the unit class of any class. What '$\{\alpha\}$' accomplishes is little more than the formal office of letting the class x be referred to in that position also by abstract instead of variable. The little more is that in defining '$\{\alpha\}$' we make sense also of the case '$\{\{x: Fx\}\}$' where there is no such class as $\{x: Fx\}$; but the profit here is slight, $\{\{x: Fx\}\}$ being in this case Λ. Indeed,

7.2 $$\alpha \notin \mathcal{V} .\equiv. \{\alpha\} = \Lambda.$$

Proof. By 6.9

$$\alpha \notin \mathcal{V} .\equiv (x)(x \neq \alpha)$$

(by 2.1, 7.1) $$\equiv (x)(x \notin \{\alpha\})$$

(by 6.15) $$\equiv. \{\alpha\} = \Lambda.$$

In future theorem schemata, as opposed to definitions, it is therefore usually pointless to use 'α' in '$\{\alpha\}$'; 'x' adequately covers the ground. For, 'α' always remains freely substitutable for 'x' anyway in view of 6.11 so long as $\alpha \in \mathcal{V}$, and otherwise interest in $\{\alpha\}$ lapses in view of 7.2.

Likewise it is usually pointless in future theorem schemata, as opposed to definitions, to use 'α' before 'ϵ'; again we can do with 'x'. For, 'α' remains substitutable for 'x' so long as $\alpha \in \mathcal{V}$, and otherwise the clauses having 'α' before 'ϵ' simply go false by 6.12. In short, by 6.12 and 6.11,

7.3 $$\alpha \in \beta \,.\, (x)Fx .\supset F\alpha.$$

But to get back to unit classes, here are some theorems and theorem schemata formulated with ordinary variables in the braces as proposed.

7.4 $$\{x\} \subseteq \alpha .\equiv. x \in \alpha.$$

Proof. By definitions,

$$\{x\} \subseteq \alpha .\equiv (y)(y = x .\supset. y \in \alpha)$$

(by 6.2) $$\equiv. x \in \alpha.$$

7.5 $$\{x, y\} \subseteq \alpha .\equiv. x, y \in \alpha.$$

Proof. $\{x\} \cup \{y\} \subseteq \alpha .\equiv. \{x\} \subseteq \alpha . \{y\} \subseteq \alpha$

(by 7.4) $$\equiv. x, y \in \alpha.$$

7.6 $x \in \{x\}, \quad x, y \in \{x, y\}.$ *Proof* by 7.4, 7.5.

7.7 $$\{x\} = \{y\} .\equiv. x = y.$$

Proof. By 7.4 and definition, $\{x\} \subseteq \{y\} .\equiv. x = y$. So, by definition,

$$\{x\} = \{y\} .\equiv. \{x\} \subseteq \{y\} \subseteq \{x\}$$
$$\equiv. x = y = x.$$

7.8 $$\{x, y\} = \{z\} .\equiv. x = y = z.$$

Proof. By definition, $\{x, x\} = \{x\}$. So, by 6.7,

$$x = y = z .\supset. \{x, y\} = \{z\}.$$

Conversely, by definition,

$$\{x, y\} = \{z\} .\supset. \{x, y\} \subseteq \{z\}$$

(by 7.5) $$\supset. x, y \in \{z\}$$

(by definition) $$\supset. x = y = z.$$

7.9 $$\{x, y\} = \{x, w\} .\equiv. y = w.$$

Proof. If $\{x, y\} = \{x, w\}$, then, by definition, $\{x, y\} \subseteq \{x, w\}$ and so, by 7.5, $y \in \{x, w\}$, which is to say, by definitions, $y = x$ .v. $y = w$. Similarly $\{x, w\} \subseteq \{x, y\}$ and so $w = x$ .v. $w = y$. Combining, $y = x = w$ .v. $y = w$; hence $y = w$. Conversely, if $y = w$ then $\{x, y\} = \{x, w\}$ by 6.7 and 6.4.

I shall not record all the elementary theorems and theorem schemata that will figure in subsequent reasoning. Such ones as '$x \in \bar{\alpha}$.≡. $x \notin \alpha$' or '$x \in \{\alpha\}$.≡. $x = \alpha$', which are cases simply of '$p \equiv p$' in view of 2.1 and other definitions, will be left unlisted and simply used when need arises. Similarly for laws of Boolean algebra—'$\alpha \subseteq \alpha$', '$\alpha \cap \beta = \beta \cap \alpha$', and the like; these again reduce to essentially truth-functional considerations when definitions are consulted. One such Boolean law, viz.:

$$\beta \cup \gamma \subseteq \alpha \;.\!\equiv\!.\; \beta \subseteq \alpha \,.\, \gamma \subseteq \alpha,$$

was taken for granted just now in the proof of 7.5; another, '$\alpha \cup \alpha = \alpha$', in the first step of the proof of 7.8.

We have come thus far without assuming any particular classes, indeed without assuming there to be any at all, beyond some one (cf. §5). I shall now mar a good record by postulating some modest classes on account, viz., all classes of fewer than three members.

7.10 *Axiom.* $\Lambda, \{x, y\} \in \mathcal{V}$.

Such is the joint axiom of *pairing* and of the *null class*. It assumes that Λ exists, also that $\{x, y\}$ exists for all objects x and y in our universe, and also that $\{x\}$ exists (for $\{x, x\}$ is $\{x\}$).

This axiom, for all its modesty, commits us against ultimate classes. For an ultimate class is a class x such that $(y)(x \notin y)$; and we have rather by 7.6 and 7.10 that $x \in \{x\} \in \mathcal{V}$ and so by 6.11 that

7.11 $(\exists y)(x \in y)$.

That is, there are only sets.

Let me sketch the policy that lies behind this decision. Only because of Russell's paradox and the like do we not adhere to the naïve and unrestricted comprehension schema, briefly '$\alpha \in \mathcal{V}$'. Having to cut back because of the paradoxes, we are well advised to mutilate no more than what may fairly be seen as responsible for the paradoxes. Thus I do not mutilate truth-function logic (e.g. by denying the law of the excluded middle) nor the logic of quantification, but only set theory, the laws of '$\in$'. But within set theory there is in turn the conspicuous distinction between finite and infinite classes; the obscure classes are infinite ones, and only the infinite ones give rise to paradox. Our maxim of minimum mutilation then favors admitting all finite classes of whatever things we admit; and so I shall do, in the axiom schema 13.1. Meanwhile 7.10 is a short step in that direction.

The above argument is vague at a crucial point, and is not meant to prove anything. But it may help to lend a certain air of reason to the course I am taking.

Ultimate classes are admittedly a boon, as we shall see in the concluding chapters. I shall there air the alternative of accepting ultimate classes and revoking 7.10 and 13.1. Also I shall there speculate on compromise that would preserve 7.10 and 13.1, hence all finite classes, and provide still for something rather like ultimate classes: classes capable of membership only in classes smaller than themselves.

For the present, at any rate, and right through to the last two chapters of the book, everything is a set. The distinction between $\hat{u}Fu$ and $\{u\colon Fu\}$, noted late in §6, accordingly vanishes for the duration; hence also the distinction there noted between V and $\mathcal{V}$, ιx and $\{x\}$.

Let us return now to our axiom and derive two modest comprehension schemata that will prove convenient.

7.12 $\{\alpha\} \in \mathcal{V}$.

Proof. $\{x\} = \{x\} \cup \{x\} = \{x, x\}$ by definition. So, by 7.10, $(x)(\{x\} \in \mathcal{V})$. So, by 6.11, $\alpha \in \mathcal{V} .\supset. \{\alpha\} \in \mathcal{V}$. But also, by 7.2,

$$\alpha \notin \mathcal{V} .\supset. \{\alpha\} = \Lambda$$

(by 7.10, 6.7) $\supset. \{\alpha\} \in \mathcal{V}$.

7.13 $\{\alpha, \beta\} \in \mathcal{V}$.

Proof. Case 1: $\alpha, \beta \in \mathcal{V}$. But, by 7.10,

$$(x)(y)(\{x, y\} \in \mathcal{V}).$$

So, by 6.11, $(y)(\{\alpha, y\} \in \mathcal{V})$. So, by 6.11 again, $\{\alpha, \beta\} \in \mathcal{V}$.

Case 2: $\beta \notin \mathcal{V}$. Then, by 7.2, $\{\beta\} = \Lambda$. Then, by definition,

$$\{\alpha, \beta\} = \{\alpha\} \cup \Lambda = \{\alpha\}$$

and so $\{\alpha, \beta\} \in \mathcal{V}$ by 7.12 and 6.7.

Case 3: $\alpha \notin \mathcal{V}$. Similar.

In view of 7.10, 7.12, and 7.13, this welcome convention can be adopted: We shall hereafter substitute 'Λ' and all expressions of the forms '$\{\alpha\}$' and '$\{\alpha, \beta\}$', and their abbreviations, freely for variables without benefit of special references. This is a matter of tacit use of 7.10 or 7.12 or 7.13, along with 6.11. Even when the variable is free, 6.11 is of course in point; for we imagine a universal quantifier.

The convention is used in the first step of the following proof.

7.14 $\quad \alpha = z \,.\!\equiv (x)(z \in x \,.\!\supset\!.\, \alpha \in x).$

Proof. $(x)(z \in x \,.\!\supset\!.\, \alpha \in x) \supset: z \in \{z\} \,.\!\supset\!.\, \alpha \in \{z\}$

(by 7.6) $\quad \supset\!.\, \alpha \in \{z\}$

(by 6.13 and 7.1) $\quad \supset\!.\, \alpha = z.$

The converse holds by 6.6, since $(x)(\alpha \in x \,.\!\supset\!.\, \alpha \in x)$.

Our definition 2.7 of identity explains '$y = z$' as '$(x)(x \in y \,.\!\equiv\!.\, x \in z)$'. A prior and more cumbersome version of '$y = z$' was (i) of §4. And now we have from 7.14 the further version '$(x)(z \in x \,.\!\supset\!.\, y \in x)$'. From this we easily see that '$(x)(y \in x \,.\!\supset\!.\, z \in x)$' and '$(x)(y \in x \,.\!\equiv\!.\, z \in x)$' would also serve. But it is interesting that these last three versions depend on the existence axiom 7.10, or its corollary 7.12. The role of 7.12 in the proof of 7.14 is inconspicuous because of the convention that just preceded.

8. Unions, intersections, descriptions

Until we were in a position to talk of classes of classes, the useful notion now to be defined was not available.

8.1 $\quad$ '$\mathsf{U}\alpha$' for '$\{x\colon x \in^2 \alpha\}$'.

The clause '$x \in^2 \alpha$' is short for '$(\exists y)(x \in y \in \alpha)$', and so has a variable after '$\in$', putting it as effectively out of reach of the virtual theory of Chapter I as was the ancestor construction that launched Chapter II.

$\mathsf{U}\alpha$ is the class of all members of members of α, hence the *union of the members of* α. Often it is called the *sum* of α. If α has finitely many members $x_1, x_2, \ldots, x_n$, then $\mathsf{U}\alpha$ is the union $x_1 \cup x_2 \cup \ldots \cup x_n$ in the familiar Boolean sense; cf. 8.4, below. But $\mathsf{U}\alpha$ generalizes the Boolean notion of union in making sense equally when α has infinitely many members. Further it has this degenerate case:

8.2 $\quad$ $\mathsf{U}\{x\} = x.$

Proof. By 6.1,

$$y \in x \mathrel{.\equiv} (\exists z)(y \in z = x)$$

(by 2.1, 7.1) $$\mathrel{\equiv.} y \in^2 \{x\}$$

for all y, i.e., by 5.1 and 8.1, $x = \mathsf{U}\{x\}$.

That we are able to affirm 8.2 categorically, rather than having to provide somehow that x be a class of classes, illustrates again the convenience of everything's being a class and hence a class of classes.

8.3 $\quad$ $\mathsf{U}(\alpha \cup \beta) = \mathsf{U}\alpha \cup \mathsf{U}\beta.$

Proof. By 2.1 and 2.4,

$$\begin{aligned} x \in^2 \alpha \cup \beta \mathrel{.\equiv} &\ (\exists y)(x \in y : y \in \alpha \mathrel{.\mathsf{v}.} y \in \beta) \\ \mathrel{\equiv.} &\ (\exists y)(x \in y \in \alpha) \mathrel{\mathsf{v}} (\exists y)(x \in y \in \beta) \\ \mathrel{\equiv:} &\ x \in^2 \alpha \mathrel{.\mathsf{v}.} x \in^2 \beta. \end{aligned}$$

That is, by 2.1 and 8.1,

$$x \in \mathsf{U}(\alpha \cup \beta) \,.\!\equiv\!:\, x \in \mathsf{U}\alpha \,.\mathbf{v}.\, x \in \mathsf{U}\beta$$

for all x, i.e., by 5.1 and 2.4, $\mathsf{U}(\alpha \cup \beta) = \mathsf{U}\alpha \cup \mathsf{U}\beta$.

It has as a corollary the title theorem itself:

8.4 $$\mathsf{U}\{x, y\} = x \cup y.$$

Proof. By 7.1,

$$\mathsf{U}\{x, y\} = \mathsf{U}(\{x\} \cup \{y\})$$

(by 8.3) $$= \mathsf{U}\{x\} \cup \mathsf{U}\{y\}$$

(by 8.2) $$= x \cup y.$$

A main law of unions is this:

8.5 $$\mathsf{U}\alpha \subseteq \beta \,.\!\equiv (x)(x \in \alpha \,.\!\supset\!.\, x \subseteq \beta).$$

Proof. $(y)(y \in^2 \alpha \,.\!\supset\!.\, y \in \beta) \equiv (y)(x)(y \in x \in \alpha \,.\!\supset\!.\, y \in \beta)$

$$\equiv (x)(x \in \alpha \,.\!\supset (y)(y \in x \,.\!\supset\!.\, y \in \beta)).$$

By 2.1 and other definitions, this is 8.5.

We may call β an *upper bound* of α, with respect to class inclusion, when each member of α is a subclass of β. Then the point of 8.5 is that $\mathsf{U}\alpha$ is the least upper bound of α.

As a corollary, taking β as $\mathsf{U}\alpha$, we have that

8.6 $$x \in \alpha \,.\!\supset\!.\, x \subseteq \mathsf{U}\alpha.$$

The union of all members of Λ is as we might expect.

8.7 $$\mathsf{U}\Lambda = \Lambda.$$

Proof. By 6.14, $(x){\sim}(x \in^2 \Lambda)$; i.e., by 6.16 and 8.1, $\mathsf{U}\Lambda = \Lambda$.

Also, symmetrically,

8.8 $$\mathsf{U}\mathcal{V} = \mathcal{V}.$$

Proof. By 7.11 and 6.8, $(x)(x \in^2 \mathcal{V})$. That is, by 6.16 and 8.1, $\bigcup \mathcal{V} = \mathcal{V}$.

But 8.8 is less platitudinous than it looks. Through 7.11 it depends on our existence axiom 7.10 ('$\{x\} \in \mathcal{V}$'). If at 7.10 we had taken the other turning and allowed ultimate classes, 8.8 would have been false. Absolutely, $\bigcup \mathcal{V}$ is $\{x: (\exists y)(x \in y)\}$ by 8.1 and 6.8, hence the class of all sets, what was called $\hat{u}(u = u)$ late in §6. 8.8 holds for us only because everything is, according to 7.11, a set.[1] 8.8 simply repeats the sentiment, identifying the class $\bigcup \mathcal{V}$ of all sets with the class $\mathcal{V}$ of everything.

The idea of the union of the members of α has as its dual that of the *intersection*, $\bigcap \alpha$, of the members of α.

8.9 '$\bigcap \alpha$' for '$\{x: (y)(y \in \alpha \,.\supset.\, x \in y)\}$'.

It comprises the common members of all members of α. So, if the members of α are again $x_1, x_2, \ldots, x_n$, then $\bigcap \alpha$ is $x_1 \cap x_2 \cap \ldots \cap x_n$. Just as $\bigcup \alpha$ was the least upper bound of α with respect to inclusion, so $\bigcap \alpha$ is the greatest lower. Parallel to 8.2–8.7 we have:

8.10 $\bigcap \{x\} = x$,

8.11 $\bigcap (\alpha \cup \beta) = \bigcap \alpha \cap \bigcap \beta$,

8.12 $\bigcap \{x, y\} = x \cap y$,

8.13 $\beta \subseteq \bigcap \alpha \,.\equiv\, (x)(x \in \alpha \,.\supset.\, \beta \subseteq x)$,

8.14 $x \in \alpha \,.\supset.\, \bigcap \alpha \subseteq x$,

8.15 $\bigcap \Lambda = \mathcal{V}$,

the proofs of which I leave to the reader. And finally, parallel to 8.8, we have:

8.16 $\bigcap \mathcal{V} = \Lambda$.

---

[1] So 8.8 fails in *Mathematical Logic*. The reader of that book who is surprised by this remark must remind himself of the distinction noted at the end of §6 above. What is called 'V' in *Mathematical Logic*, viz. $\hat{u}(u = u)$, is precisely our $\bigcup \mathcal{V}$.

Proof. By 7.10, $\Lambda \in \mathcal{V}$. So, by 8.14, $\bigcap\mathcal{V} \subseteq \Lambda$.

It is interesting that whereas the proof of '$\bigcup\mathcal{V} = \mathcal{V}$' depended on the aspect 7.11 of 7.10, this proof of '$\bigcap\mathcal{V} = \Lambda$' depends only on the part '$\Lambda \in \mathcal{V}$' of 7.10. Indeed '$\bigcap\mathcal{V} = \Lambda$' needs less than '$\Lambda \in \mathcal{V}$'; even if $\Lambda \notin \mathcal{V}$, we still get '$\bigcap\mathcal{V} = \Lambda$' so long as there are two mutually exclusive classes. We cannot get '$\bigcap\mathcal{V} = \Lambda$' without some comprehension axiom or other, but no reasonable set theory would fail to include an adequate one. So '$\bigcap\mathcal{V} = \Lambda$' is common coin in set theories, unlike its dual '$\bigcup\mathcal{V} = \mathcal{V}$', which holds only for set theories without ultimate classes.

This circumstance bears upon the dilemma of §7 between 7.11 ('$(\exists y)(x \in y)$') and ultimate classes, by favoring 7.11 as the more symmetrical choice. We are bound to have '$\bigcap\mathcal{V} = \Lambda$', and its dual '$\bigcup\mathcal{V} = \mathcal{V}$' amounts to 7.11.

A consequence of the theorems '$\bigcup\{x\} = x$' and '$\bigcap\{x\} = x$' is that the form of notation '$\bigcup\{x\colon Fx\}$', or equally '$\bigcap\{x\colon Fx\}$', comes to serve the purposes of the idiom of singular description '$(\imath x)Fx$', 'the object x such that Fx', whenever there is indeed one and only one object x such that Fx. That is,

8.17 $(x)(Fx \equiv. x = y) \supset. \bigcup\{x\colon Fx\} = \bigcap\{x\colon Fx\} = y.$

Proof. By hypothesis and definitions, $\{x\colon Fx\} = \{y\}$. So y is $\bigcup\{x\colon Fx\}$ by 8.2, and $\bigcap\{x\colon Fx\}$ by 8.10.

The fundamental law and desideratum of singular description is that

$$(x)(Fx \equiv. x = y) \supset. (\imath x)Fx = y,$$

and this, 8.17 tells us, would be fulfilled by defining '$(\imath x)Fx$' as '$\bigcup\{x\colon Fx\}$' or as '$\bigcap\{x\colon Fx\}$'. But there is another course that proves more convenient in relation to comprehension premisses. If we define '$(\imath x)Fx$' in such a way rather as to make it come out arbitrarily and invariably Λ when $\sim(\exists y)(x)(Fx \equiv. x = y)$, then we can get '$(\imath x)Fx \in \mathcal{V}$' for all cases. This is the reason for the more complex definition:

8.18 '$(\imath x)Fx$' for '$\bigcup\{y\colon (x)(Fx \equiv. x = y)\}$'.

Now we get the fundamental law thus:

8.19 $(x)(Fx \equiv . \; x = y) \supset . \; (\imath x)Fx = y.$

Proof. By hypothesis,

$$(x)(Fx \equiv . \; x = z) \supset (x)(x = y \; . \equiv . \; x = z)$$
$$\supset : z = y \; . \equiv . \; z = z$$
$$\supset . \; z = y.$$

Conversely, by hypothesis and 6.7,

$$z = y \; . \supset (x)(Fx \equiv . \; x = z).$$

Combining,

$$(z)((x)(Fx \equiv . \; x = z) \equiv . \; z = y).$$

So, by 8.17,

$$\bigcup\{z\colon (x)(Fx \equiv . \; x = z)\} = y.$$

So, by 8.18, $(\imath x)Fx = y$.

It follows further that

8.20 $(x)(Fx \equiv . \; x = y) \supset : Fz \equiv . \; z = (\imath x)Fx.$

Proof. By hypothesis, $Fz \equiv . \; z = y$. But $y = (\imath x)Fx$ by hypothesis and 8.19.

Incidentally,

8.21 $y = (\imath x)(x = y).$

Proof by 8.19, since $(x)(x = y \; . \equiv . \; x = y)$.

Finally the vacuous case:

8.22 $\sim(\exists y)(x)(Fx \equiv . \; x = y) \supset . \; (\imath x)Fx = \Lambda.$

Proof. By hypothesis and 6.16,

$$\{y\colon (x)(Fx \equiv . \; x = y)\} = \Lambda.$$

So, by 8.18, $(\imath x)Fx = \bigcup\Lambda$. That is, by 8.7, $(\imath x)Fx = \Lambda$.

Description is wanted for any sort of object, yet $(\imath x)Fx$ as of 8.18 is a class. That this definition nevertheless suffices—and even '$\bigcup\{x: Fx\}$' or '$\bigcap\{x: Fx\}$' would have served—is a benefit of our having assimilated individuals to classes.

Finally let us reap the benefit of having adopted 8.18 instead of the simpler '$\bigcup\{x: Fx\}$' or '$\bigcap\{x: Fx\}$'.

8.23 $$(\imath x)Fx \in \mathcal{V}.$$

Proof. By 8.22 and 8.19,

$$(\imath x)Fx = \Lambda \,.\mathsf{v}\, (\exists y)((\imath x)Fx = y).$$

So, by 7.10 or 6.9 as the case may be, $(\imath x)Fx \in \mathcal{V}$.

The time-saving convention adopted near the end of §7 can accordingly be extended now to descriptions. That is, we shall hereafter freely substitute 'Λ' and all expressions of the forms '$\{\alpha\}$', '$\{\alpha, \beta\}$', and '$(\imath x)Fx$', and their abbreviations, for variables.

In illustration we may substitute '$(\imath x)Fx$' for 'z' in 8.20, and so conclude that

8.24 $$(x)(Fx \equiv. x = y) \supset F(\imath x)Fx.$$

9. Relations as classes of pairs

Something further that is made available by allowing talk of classes of classes is a simple and serviceable notion of *ordered pair* $\langle x, y\rangle$. What is wanted of a notion of ordered pair is that the pair determine its two paired objects uniquely and in an order. The class $\{x, y\}$, though determining x and y, fails to determine which is which; that is, $\{x, y\} = \{y, x\}$. The fundamental law demanded of ordered pairs is that $\langle x, y\rangle = \langle z, w\rangle$ not whenever $\{x, y\} = \{z, w\}$, but only when $x = z$ and $y = w$. Any definition of '$\langle x, y\rangle$', however arbitrary and artificial, is to the purpose if it fulfills this fundamental law. Wiener solved this problem by explaining $\langle x, y\rangle$ as a certain class of classes. A variant of his definition, due to Kuratowski, is:

9.1 '$\langle \alpha, \beta\rangle$' for '$\{\{\alpha\}, \{\alpha, \beta\}\}$'.

Thus $\langle x, y\rangle$ is the class whose members are the classes $\{x\}$ and $\{x, y\}$. Happily any ordered-pair expression may be freely substituted forthwith for variables, thanks to the convention that was summed up at the end of the preceding section. For '$\langle\alpha, \beta\rangle$' is defined as an abbreviation of an expression of the form '$\{\gamma, \delta\}$'.

We proceed to establish the fundamental law of ordered pairs.

9.2 $$\langle x, y\rangle = \langle z, w\rangle \;.\supset.\; x = z \,.\, y = w.$$

Proof.[1] By 7.6 and 9.1, $\{x\} \in \langle x, y\rangle$. So, by hypothesis, $\{x\} \in \langle z, w\rangle$. That is, by 2.1 and other definitions,

$$\{x\} = \{z\} \;.\mathrm{v}.\; \{x\} = \{z, w\}.$$

That is, by 7.7 and 7.8, $x = z \;.\mathrm{v}.\; x = z = w$. So $x = z$. So, by hypothesis, $\langle x, y\rangle = \langle x, w\rangle$. That is, by 7.9 and 9.1, $\{x, y\} = \{x, w\}$. That is, by 7.9, $y = w$.

A useful variant of 9.2 is:

9.3 $$\langle x, y\rangle = \langle z, w\rangle \;.\equiv.\; x = z \,.\, y = w.$$

Proof. $\langle x, y\rangle = \langle x, y\rangle$; so, by 6.6 twice,

$$x = z \,.\, y = w \;.\supset.\; \langle x, y\rangle = \langle z, w\rangle.$$

Converse by 9.2.

The principal virtue of ordered pairs is that they make it possible to simulate relations within the theory of classes. What simulates the relation $\{xy\colon Fxy\}$ is the class of all pairs $\langle x, y\rangle$ such that Fxy.

Thus far we have seen relations only as virtual (§3). 'R' and kindred letters for relations have stood only as schematic letters for relation abstracts of the form '$\{xy\colon Fxy\}$', defined only in the position 'zRw' of relational attribution. But we shall see in succeeding chapters that the admission of something like relations as real members of the universe of discourse, as values of the genuine quantifiable variables 'x', 'y', etc., enables us to formulate

[1] Shortened by John C. Torrey.

some important matters for which the virtual theory of relations is of itself inadequate. Just as in moving to the real theory of classes we went beyond the contextually defined 'ϵ' of 2.1 to adopt a primitive predicate 'ϵ' for use between genuine variables, so we might now go beyond the contextually defined 'xRy' of §3 and adopt a primitive notation of relational attribution allowing a genuine variable 'z' in the position of the 'R' of 'xRy'. Thanks to the ordered pair, however, no such further primitive notation will be needed; '$\langle x, y\rangle \epsilon z$' will serve.

We saw in §5 that it is impossible, on pain of contradiction, to suppose a real class $z = \{x: Fx\}$ for every open sentence in the role of 'Fx'; Russell's paradox, e.g., obtruded when 'Fx' was taken as '$x \notin x$'. Now the corresponding situation obtains, as Russell also observed, with relations: it is impossible, on pain of contradiction, to admit, for every open sentence in the role of 'Fxy', a pair-class z such that

$$\text{(i)} \qquad (x)(y)(\langle x, y\rangle \epsilon z .\equiv Fxy).$$

For, take 'Fxy' as '$\langle x, y\rangle \notin x$'; then (i) becomes:

$$(x)(y)(\langle x, y\rangle \epsilon z .\equiv. \langle x, y\rangle \notin x),$$

which implies the contradiction:

$$(y)(\langle z, y\rangle \epsilon z .\equiv. \langle z, y\rangle \notin z).$$

So the question which cases of (i) to accept is one to be settled by eventual existence axioms of a selective kind, like the corresponding problem of classes. Indeed the one problem is subsumed by the other, as a question of existence of classes of ordered pairs. Thanks to the notion of ordered pair and the supporting existence axiom 7.10, the virtual theory of relations as of §3 can now be set aside altogether in favor of classes, virtual and real, of ordered pairs.

As a preparatory step let me introduce a general notational device that will be useful in both this connection and later ones. Think of '$\ldots x_1 \ldots x_2 \ldots x_n \ldots$' for the moment as some class abstract whose free variables are as shown. I define

$$\textbf{9.4}\quad `\{\ldots x_1 \ldots x_2 \ldots x_n \ldots : Fx_1x_2 \ldots x_n\}\text{' for}$$
$$`\{z\colon (\exists x_1)(\exists x_2) \ldots (\exists x_n)(Fx_1x_2 \ldots x_n \,.\, z = \ldots x_1 \ldots x_2 \ldots x_n \ldots)\}\text{'.}$$

For example, taking '$\ldots x_1 \ldots x_2 \ldots x_n \ldots$' as '$\langle x, y\rangle$' (which is an abbreviation of a class abstract), we have:

$$`\{\langle x, y\rangle\colon Fxy\}\text{' for }`\{z\colon (\exists x)(\exists y)(Fxy \,.\, z = \langle x, y\rangle)\}.$$

Thus $\{\langle x, y\rangle\colon Fxy\}$ is the class of all ordered pairs $\langle x, y\rangle$ such that Fxy. Similarly $\{\{x\}\colon Fx\}$ is the class of all unit classes of things x such that Fx; correspondingly for $\{\bar{x}\colon Fx\}$, or again $\{\langle x, \Lambda\rangle\colon Fx\}$. This last is the class of all pairs $\langle x, \Lambda\rangle$ such that Fx. Note this limitation: whereas

$$\{\langle x, \Lambda\rangle\colon Fx\} = \{z\colon (\exists x)(Fx \,.\, z = \langle x, \Lambda\rangle)\},$$

we must not construe $\{\langle x, y\rangle\colon Fx\}$ with variable 'y' as

$$\{z\colon (\exists x)(Fx \,.\, z = \langle x, y\rangle)\};$$

rather

$$\{\langle x, y\rangle\colon Fx\} = \{z\colon (\exists x)(\exists y)(Fx \,.\, z = \langle x, y\rangle)\}.$$

The other expression, when meant, must be spelled out. The point is that all variables to the left of the colon count as bound variables of the whole.[2]

Our present interest in 9.4 is its yield of the notation '$\{\langle x, y\rangle\colon Fxy\}$', which will hereafter serve all purposes, and more, of '$\{xy\colon Fxy\}$'. We get the law of concretion:

$$\textbf{9.5}\qquad \langle z, w\rangle \in \{\langle x, y\rangle\colon Fxy\} \;.{\equiv}\; Fzw.$$

[2] Rosser's convention in *Logic for Mathematicians*, pp. 221f, is a little different.

Proof. By 9.4 and 2.1,

$$\langle z, w\rangle \in \{\langle x, y\rangle: Fxy\} \;.\!\equiv (\exists x)(\exists y)(Fxy \,.\, \langle z, w\rangle = \langle x, y\rangle)$$
(by 9.3) $$\equiv (\exists x)(\exists y)(Fxy \,.\, z = x \,.\, w = y)$$
(by 6.1) $$\equiv Fzw.$$

This law takes the place, for future purposes, of the contextual definition in §3 that introduced the forms of notation '$\{xy: Fxy\}$' and 'zRw' into the virtual theory of relations. Those forms of notation will be dropped hereafter in favor of '$\{\langle x, y\rangle: Fxy\}$' and '$\langle z, w\rangle \in \alpha$', the schematic relation letters 'Q', 'R', etc. being superseded by our general 'α', 'β', etc. Of course $\{\langle x, y\rangle: Fxy\}$ still may or may not be real, in the sense of membership in $\mathcal{V}$.

The definitions of the Boolean notions of inclusion, union, and intersection for relations can now be dropped without benefit of substitutes; for the parallel definitions 2.2–2.5 for classes now cover the whole ground. On the other hand the definition in §3 of relation complement is not covered by its class analogue 2.6, since, where α is a class of pairs, $\bar{\alpha}$ has all nonpairs among its members. However, this matter is easily adjusted along with others by defining the *relational part* $\cdot\alpha$ of a class α as the class of all ordered pairs in α, thus:

9.6 '$\cdot\alpha$' for '$\{\langle x, y\rangle: \langle x, y\rangle \in \alpha\}$'.

Thereupon the relation complementary to α becomes $\cdot\bar{\alpha}$ in contrast to the class complement $\bar{\alpha}$.

The class of all ordered pairs comes out as $\cdot\mathcal{V}$. So

9.7 $$\cdot\alpha = \alpha \cap \cdot\mathcal{V}.$$

Proof. By 6.7,

$$\{z: (\exists x)(\exists y)(z = \langle x, y\rangle \in \alpha)\} = \{z: z \in \alpha \,.\, (\exists x)(\exists y)(z = \langle x, y\rangle)\}.$$

That is, by 2.1 and other definitions, $\cdot\alpha = \alpha \cap \cdot\mathcal{V}$ (since $\langle x, y\rangle \in \mathcal{V}$).

An analogue of the definition in §3 of inclusion for relations is worth noting still as a theorem schema.

9.8 $\cdot\alpha \subseteq \beta \mathrel{.\equiv} (x)(y)(\langle x, y\rangle \in \alpha \mathrel{.\supset.} \langle x, y\rangle \in \beta)$.

Proof. By definitions,

$$\cdot\alpha \subseteq \beta \mathrel{.\equiv} (z)((\exists x)(\exists y)(\langle x, y\rangle \in \alpha \,.\, z = \langle x, y\rangle) \supset.\ z \in \beta)$$

$$\equiv (x)(y)(z)(z = \langle x, y\rangle \mathrel{.\supset:} \langle x, y\rangle \in \alpha \mathrel{.\supset.} z \in \beta)$$

(by 6.2) $$\equiv (x)(y)(\langle x, y\rangle \in \alpha \mathrel{.\supset.} \langle x, y\rangle \in \beta).$$

The definition in §3 of identity between relations fares like that of inclusion. It gives way to the general 2.7 so far as definition goes, and to this in the way of a theorem schema:

9.9 $\cdot\alpha = \cdot\beta \mathrel{.\equiv} (x)(y)(\langle x, y\rangle \in \alpha \mathrel{.\equiv.} \langle x, y\rangle \in \beta)$.

Proof. By Boolean algebra,

$$\alpha \cap \cdot\mathcal{V} \subseteq \beta \cap \cdot\mathcal{V} \mathrel{.\equiv.} \alpha \cap \cdot\mathcal{V} \subseteq \beta.$$

That is, by 9.7, $\cdot\alpha \subseteq \cdot\beta \mathrel{.\equiv.} \cdot\alpha \subseteq \beta$. Similarly for $\cdot\beta \subseteq \cdot\alpha$. So, by 2.7,

$$\cdot\alpha = \cdot\beta \mathrel{.\equiv.} \cdot\alpha \subseteq \beta \,.\, \cdot\beta \subseteq \alpha$$

(by 9.8) $$\equiv (x)(y)(\langle x, y\rangle \in \alpha \mathrel{.\equiv.} \langle x, y\rangle \in \beta).$$

By 9.5 and 9.6,

9.10 $\cdot\{\langle x, y\rangle : Fxy\} = \{\langle x, y\rangle : Fxy\}, \qquad \langle x, y\rangle \in \cdot\alpha \mathrel{.\equiv.} \langle x, y\rangle \in \alpha.$

So we can ignore the dot when it occurs on a pair-class abstract (or any abbreviation thereof) or after an epsilon that is preceded by an ordered-pair expression. This right will be exercised hereafter without comment.

Further definitions in §3 call for outright readoption, *mutatis mutandis*. Signs for *confinement* of right and left field are added.

9.11 '$\alpha \times \beta$' for '$\{\langle x, y\rangle : x \in \alpha \,.\, y \in \beta\}$',

9.12 '$\breve{\alpha}$' or '$\smile\alpha$' for '$\{\langle x, y\rangle : \langle y, x\rangle \in \alpha\}$',

9.13 '$\alpha \mid \beta$' for '$\{\langle x, z\rangle : (\exists y)(\langle x, y\rangle \in \alpha \,.\, \langle y, z\rangle \in \beta)\}$',

9.14 '$\alpha``\beta$' for '$\{x : (\exists y)(\langle x, y\rangle \in \alpha \,.\, y \in \beta)\}$',

9.15 'I' for '$\{\langle x, y\rangle : x = y\}$',

9.16 '$\alpha\restriction\beta$' for '$\alpha \cap (\mathcal{V} \times \beta)$',

9.17 '$\beta\upharpoonleft\alpha$' for '$\alpha \cap (\beta \times \mathcal{V})$'.

Similarly for the terms 'connected', 'reflexive', etc. Also the various sample laws from the algebra of relations that were stated late in §3 continue to hold in translation, except that the dot of relational part is now wanted in a few of them, thus:

$$\cdot\alpha \subseteq \alpha``\mathcal{V} \times \breve{\alpha}``\mathcal{V}, \qquad \breve{\breve{\alpha}} = \cdot\alpha, \qquad \alpha \mid I = I \mid \alpha = \cdot\alpha.$$

It seems unnecessary to develop an explicit background of theorem schemata at this level, for the proofs run to type. It is a matter of lifting definitions and applying the concretion law 9.5 and perhaps 9.10 and then observing that the theorem schema concerned is a familiar or obvious one of the logic of quantification and truth functions or perhaps identity (often 6.1 or 6.2). So I shall use the typical laws of the algebra of relations, in proofs, as informally as I have been using the laws of the Boolean algebra of classes. I shall suppose the reader to be familiar with the equivalences and implications displayed in §3 and others at that level, and with the definitions 9.11–9.17. It should be clear without reflection that anything x is a member of $\alpha``\{y\}$ or $\breve{\alpha}``\{y\}$ or $\alpha``\mathcal{V}$ or $\breve{\alpha}``\mathcal{V}$ according as $\langle x, y\rangle \in \alpha$ or $\langle y, x\rangle \in \alpha$ or $(\exists y)(\langle x, y\rangle \in \alpha)$ or $(\exists y)(\langle y, x\rangle \in \alpha)$; also that $\alpha \cap (\beta \times \beta)$ is α with its field confined to β; also that $\alpha``\beta$ is the left field of $\alpha\restriction\beta$ and that $\alpha``(\breve{\alpha}``\mathcal{V})$ is $\alpha``\mathcal{V}$.

10. Functions

Part of what needed to be said about functions was said in §3. More, which would have been less readily manageable in the virtual theory, has been reserved for here, along with some details that would have fitted either place.

The notation for being a function, and that for the domain or class of arguments, are now to be defined by adapting their definitions in §3. For convenience of reference I give the definitions their succinct forms and their more discursive forms as well. In the case of function it proves best in the long run to add the clause '$\alpha = {}^{\cdot}\alpha$', thus trimming off the waste members, the nonpairs, and requiring functions to be pure relations. This was an option that could not arise at the level of §3.

10.1 'Func α' for '$\alpha \mid \breve{\alpha} \subseteq I \,.\, \alpha = {}^{\cdot}\alpha$', or

$$`(x)(y)(z)(\langle x, z\rangle, \langle y, z\rangle \in \alpha \,.\!\supset\!.\, x = y) \,.\, \alpha = {}^{\cdot}\alpha'.$$

10.2 'arg α' for '$\{x\colon (\exists y)(\alpha``\{x\} = \{y\})\}$', or

$$`\{x\colon (\exists y)(z)(\langle z, x\rangle \in \alpha \,.\!\equiv\!.\, z = y)\}'.$$

Some obvious functions are Λ, I, and $\{\langle x, y\rangle\}$.

10.3 Func Λ.

Proof. $\Lambda \mid \breve{\Lambda} = \Lambda \subseteq I$. Further $\Lambda = {}^{\cdot}\Lambda$ by 9.7.

10.4 Func I, arg $I = \mathcal{V}$. *Proofs* evident from definitions.

10.5 Func $\{\langle x, y\rangle\}$.

Proof. By 2.1 and 7.1,

$$\langle v, z\rangle, \langle w, z\rangle \in \{\langle x, y\rangle\} \,.\!\supset\!.\, \langle v, z\rangle = \langle x, y\rangle = \langle w, z\rangle$$

(by 9.2) $\qquad \supset.\ v = w.$

By definitions

$$
\begin{aligned}
& \{\langle x, y\rangle\} && = \{\langle z, w\rangle: \langle z, w\rangle = \langle x, y\rangle\} \\
& \text{(by 9.3)} && = \{\langle z, w\rangle: z = x \,.\, w = y\} \\
& \text{(by 9.4)} && = \{v: (\exists z)(\exists w)(v = \langle z, w\rangle \,.\, z = x \,.\, w = y)\} \\
& \text{(by 6.1, 7.1)} && = \{\langle x, y\rangle\}.
\end{aligned}
$$

Now six theorem schemata.

10.6 Func α . Func β .⊃ Func $\alpha \mid \beta$.

Proof. Consider any x, y, z such that

$$\langle x, z\rangle, \langle y, z\rangle \in \alpha \mid \beta. \qquad \text{[i]}$$

By definition, then, there are u and v such that

$$\langle x, u\rangle, \langle y, v\rangle \in \alpha, \qquad \text{[ii]}$$

$$\langle u, z\rangle, \langle v, z\rangle \in \beta. \qquad \text{[iii]}$$

By hypothesis and 10.1, we can infer from [iii] that $u = v$. So, by [ii], $\langle x, v\rangle$, $\langle y, v\rangle \in \alpha$. So, by hypothesis and 10.1, $x = y$. But x, y, and z were any things fulfilling [i]. So, by 10.1, Func $\alpha \mid \beta$.

10.7 Func α . $y \notin \breve{\alpha}``\mathcal{V}$.⊃ Func $\alpha \cup \{\langle x, y\rangle\}$.

Proof. Consider any u, v, w such that $\langle u, w\rangle$, $\langle v, w\rangle \in \alpha \cup \{\langle x, y\rangle\}$. If $w \neq y$, then $\langle u, w\rangle$ and $\langle v, w\rangle$ are both in α; and then, since Func α, $u = v$. If $w = y$, then, since $y \notin \breve{\alpha}``\mathcal{V}$, both $\langle u, w\rangle$ and $\langle v, w\rangle$ are in $\{\langle x, y\rangle\}$; and then $u = x$ and $v = x$, so that again $u = v$. The bit about the dot is left to the reader.

10.8 Func α ⊃ Func $\alpha \cap \beta$. *Proof* evident from 10.1.

10.9 $\arg \alpha \subseteq \breve{\alpha}``\mathcal{V}$.

Proof. By definitions,

$$x \in \arg\alpha \,.\supset (\exists y)(\{y\} \subseteq \alpha``\{x\})$$

(by 7.4) $$\supset (\exists y)(y \in \alpha``\{x\})$$

$$\supset (\exists y)(\langle y, x\rangle \in \alpha).$$

10.10 $$\text{Func}\,`\alpha \equiv. \breve{\alpha}``\mathcal{V} \subseteq \arg\alpha$$
$$\equiv. \breve{\alpha}``\mathcal{V} = \arg\alpha.$$

Proof. Suppose that Func $`\alpha$ and $x \in \breve{\alpha}``\mathcal{V}$. So there is something y such that $\langle y, x\rangle \in \alpha$. By 10.1, $\langle z, x\rangle \in \alpha \,.\supset.\, y = z$ for any z; and conversely, by 6.7. So

$$(z)(\langle z, x\rangle \in \alpha \,.\equiv.\, z = y),$$

and hence, by 10.2, $x \in \arg\alpha$. So

$$\text{Func}\,`\alpha \supset. \breve{\alpha}``\mathcal{V} \subseteq \arg\alpha. \quad (1)$$

Now suppose conversely that $\breve{\alpha}``\mathcal{V} \subseteq \arg\alpha$, and consider any $x, y, z$ such that $\langle x, z\rangle, \langle y, z\rangle \in \alpha$. Then $z \in \breve{\alpha}``\mathcal{V}$, and so $z \in \arg\alpha$, and so, by 10.2, there is something w such that

$$(u)(\langle u, z\rangle \in \alpha \,.\equiv.\, u = w).$$

But then, since $\langle x, z\rangle, \langle y, z\rangle \in \alpha$, we have $x = w$ and $y = w$ and so $x = y$. So, by 10.1, Func $`\alpha$. The converse of (1) is thus proved. Combining,

$$\text{Func}\,`\alpha \equiv. \breve{\alpha}``\mathcal{V} \subseteq \arg\alpha$$

(by 10.9) $$\equiv. \breve{\alpha}``\mathcal{V} = \arg\alpha.$$

10.10a $$\text{Func}\,\alpha \,.\, \breve{\alpha}``\mathcal{V} \subseteq \breve{\beta}``\mathcal{V} \,.\, \beta \subseteq \alpha \,.\supset.\, \alpha = \beta.$$

Proof. If $\langle x, z\rangle \in \alpha$ then, by second hypothesis, $\langle y, z\rangle \in \beta$ for some y. Then $\langle y, z\rangle \in \alpha$, since $\beta \subseteq \alpha$. Then $x = y$, since Func α. Then $\langle x, z\rangle \in \beta$. Thus, by 9.8, $`\alpha \subseteq \beta$; i.e., by 10.1, $\alpha \subseteq \beta$.

When $x \in \arg \alpha$, there is one and only one object y such that $\langle y, x \rangle \in \alpha$; and it will be referred to briefly as $\alpha`x$. Such is the notation of *function application*, definable thus:

10.11 '$\alpha`\beta$' for '$(\imath y)(\langle y, \beta \rangle \in \alpha)$'.

The notation '$\alpha`x$' may conveniently be read 'the $\alpha$ of $x$', since this is what it comes to in the interesting case where $x \in \arg \alpha$. In view of the familiar '$f(x)$' of mathematical usage, one is tempted to write rather '$\alpha(x)$'; but the form '$\alpha`x$', which comes down from Peano through Whitehead and Russell, is the more vivid of the two when there is no distinctively functional letter like 'f' to remind us of what is afoot.

Since '$\alpha`\beta$' has by definition the form '$(\imath x)Fx$', the practice that we have already established of substituting descriptions outright for variables applies in particular to expressions of the form '$\alpha`\beta$'.

Now to a string of theorem schemata. The proofs of 10.13 and 10.14 illustrate the above convention.

10.12 $w \in \arg \alpha \mathbin{.\supset:} \langle z, w \rangle \in \alpha \mathbin{.\equiv.} z = \alpha`w.$

Proof. By hypothesis and 10.2, there is something y such that

$$(x)(\langle x, w \rangle \in \alpha \mathbin{.\equiv.} x = y).$$

So, by 8.20,

$$\langle z, w \rangle \in \alpha \mathbin{.\equiv.} z = (\imath x)(\langle x, w \rangle \in \alpha),$$

q.e.d. (cf. 10.11).

10.13 $w \in \arg \alpha \mathbin{.\equiv.} \alpha``\{w\} = \{\alpha`w\}.$

Proof. By 10.12

$$w \in \arg \alpha \mathbin{.\supset} (z)(z \in \alpha``\{w\} \mathbin{.\equiv.} z = \alpha`w)$$
$$\supset. \alpha``\{w\} = \{\alpha`w\}.$$

Converse by 10.2.

10.14 $w \in \arg \alpha \mathrel{.\supset.} \langle \alpha \text{`} w, w \rangle \in \alpha.$

Proof: take z in 10.12 as $\alpha \text{`} w$.

10.15 $w \notin \arg \alpha \mathrel{.\supset.} \alpha \text{`} w = \Lambda.$

Proof. By hypothesis and 10.2,

$$\sim(\exists y)(x)(\langle x, w \rangle \in \alpha \mathrel{.\equiv.} x = y).$$

So, by 8.22 and 10.11, $\alpha \text{`} w = \Lambda$.

10.16 $\text{Func}\,\alpha \,.\, \langle z, w \rangle \in \alpha \mathrel{.\supset.} z = \alpha \text{`} w.$

Proof. By second hypothesis, $w \in \breve{\alpha} \text{``} \mho$. So, by first hypothesis and 10.10, $w \in \arg \alpha$. So, by second hypothesis and 10.12, $z = \alpha \text{`} w$.

In 10.13 we see a concise version of $\arg \alpha$. Here is something to go with it.[1]

10.17 $\text{Func}\, \cdot\alpha \equiv (x)(\alpha \text{``} \{x\} \subseteq \{\alpha \text{`} x\}).$

Proof. Suppose that $\text{Func}\, \cdot\alpha$. For any $x \in \breve{\alpha} \text{``} \mho$, by 10.10, $x \in \arg \alpha$ and so, by 10.13, $\alpha \text{``} \{x\} = \{\alpha \text{`} x\}$; and for any $x \notin \breve{\alpha} \text{``} \mho$, $\alpha \text{``} \{x\} = \Lambda$. Either way, $\alpha \text{``} \{x\} \subseteq \{\alpha \text{`} x\}$. Conversely, if

$$(x)(\alpha \text{``} \{x\} \subseteq \{\alpha \text{`} x\})$$

then

$$\begin{aligned} (x)(y)(z)(\langle y, x \rangle, \langle z, x \rangle \in \alpha \mathrel{.\supset.} y, z \in \{\alpha \text{`} x\}) \\ \mathrel{\supset.} y = \alpha \text{`} x = z) \\ \mathrel{\supset.} y = z), \end{aligned}$$

and so, by 10.1, $\text{Func}\, \cdot\alpha$.

Next some matters of decreasing generality.

10.18 $x \in \arg \beta \mathrel{.\supset.} (\alpha \mid \beta) \text{`} x = \alpha \text{`} (\beta \text{`} x).$

---

[1] It is due to William C. Waterhouse.

Proof. By 10.11,

$$(\alpha \mid \beta)`x = (\imath y)(\langle y, x\rangle \in \alpha \mid \beta)$$

(by 9.13, 9.5) $= (\imath y)(\exists z)(\langle y, z\rangle \in \alpha \,.\, \langle z, x\rangle \in \beta)$

(by hypothesis and 10.12) $= (\imath y)(\exists z)(\langle y, z\rangle \in \alpha \,.\, z = \beta`x)$

(by 6.1) $= (\imath y)(\langle y, \beta`x\rangle \in \alpha)$

(by 10.11) $= \alpha`(\beta`x)$.

10.19 $$I`x = x.$$

Proof. By 9.15 and 9.5, $\langle x, x\rangle \in I$. So, by 10.4 and 10.16, $x = I`x$.

10.20 $$\Lambda`\alpha = \Lambda.$$

Proof. By 6.14, $\langle y, \alpha\rangle \notin \Lambda$. So $\sim(x)(\langle x, \alpha\rangle \in \Lambda \,.\!\equiv\!.\, x = y)$. So, by 10.11 and 8.22, $\Lambda`\alpha = \Lambda$.

The device of singular description, on which that of function application depends, is not beyond the reach of the virtual theory of classes and relations. I did define it in terms of a notion that is beyond that reach: the notion of the union of the members of a class of classes. But it can also be defined contextually, within the terms of any theory that has so much as quantification, the truth functions, and identity at its disposal. How to do this was set forth by Russell in 1905, and is familiar to most logic students. I held out for the more expensive method of §8 because it works more simply, and the wherewithal was destined anyway. It is only on this account that function application got no advance notice in §3.

The notion to which we now turn was left out of §3 for a more solid reason: almost all cases of it would (as we shall presently see) have been meaningless for the virtual theory. It is the notion of *function abstraction*, which was perhaps first made explicit by Frege. Like quantification, description, and class abstraction, function abstraction uses a variable-binding prefix; I shall render the prefix 'λ_x', following Church. But whereas the prefixes of quantification attach to sentences to produce sentences, and those of description and class abstraction attach to sentences to produce terms, the prefix of function abstraction attaches to terms to produce terms.[2] Where '$\ldots x \ldots$' stands for some term containing 'x' as a free variable, $\lambda_x(\ldots x \ldots)$ is the function whose value for each argument x is $\ldots x \ldots$. Thus $\lambda_x(x^2)$ is the function "square of." In general,

10.21 '$\lambda_x(\ldots x \ldots)$' for '$\{\langle y, x\rangle : y = \ldots x \ldots\}$'.

Past definitions explain '$y =$' only when what comes after is a quantifiable variable or a class abstract. So 10.21 covers essentially three cases:

$$\lambda_x x = \{\langle y, x\rangle : y = x\} = I, \quad \lambda_x z = \{\langle y, x\rangle : y = z\} = \{z\} \times \mathcal{V},$$

and the generality:

$$\lambda_x\{z : Fxz\} = \{\langle y, x\rangle : y = \{z : Fxz\}\}.$$

This last of course covers most of the applications of the notation, and we see from it why the notation is introduced only now rather than in §3. At the stage of §3 no sense had been assigned to '$=$' between the variable 'y' and a class abstract.

The reason for the clumsy recourse to dots in conveying the general convention 10.21 is that if we had written rather:

$$\text{'}\lambda_x\alpha\text{' for '}\{\langle y, x\rangle : y = \alpha\}\text{'}$$

we would not have been entitled to take 'α' therein as a term containing 'x' as a free variable (cf. §1). As 10.21 stands, we can take '$\ldots x \ldots$' as a term containing 'x' (but still not 'y') as a free variable.

---

[2] For Frege and Church it attaches also to sentences, thereby doubling for class abstraction; but this happens only because these authors adopt a special approach to logic and set theory whereby sentences are assimilated to terms and classes to functions.

There follow a few theorem schemata.

10.22 Func $\lambda_x(\ldots x \ldots)$.

Proof. By 6.7,

$$(y)(z)(w)(y = \ldots w \ldots . z = \ldots w \ldots .\supset. y = z).$$

That is, by 10.21 and 9.5,

$$(y)(z)(w)(\langle y, w\rangle, \langle z, w\rangle \in \lambda_x(\ldots x \ldots) .\supset. y = z),$$

q.e.d. (cf. 10.1).

10.23 $\ldots y \ldots \in \mathfrak{V} .\equiv. y \in \arg \lambda_x(\ldots x \ldots)$.

Proof.[3] By 6.9,

$$\ldots y \ldots \in \mathfrak{V} .\equiv (\exists z)(z = \ldots y \ldots)$$

(by 10.21, 9.5) $\equiv (\exists z)(\langle z, y\rangle \in \lambda_x(\ldots x \ldots))$

$\equiv. y \in \breve{\lambda}_x(\ldots x \ldots)``\mathfrak{V}$

(by 10.22, 10.10) $\equiv. y \in \arg \lambda_x(\ldots x \ldots)$.

Disconcerting clusters of parentheses can be avoided if we keep this simple rule in mind: a singulary operator, e.g. the sign of negation or complement, the sign of converse, the dot of relational part, the 'λ_x' of functional abstraction, is usually to be understood as governing the least bit of ensuing text that it grammatically can. Thus, the long term in the next to last line of the above proof is to be understood as referring to the right field of the function $\lambda_x(\ldots x \ldots)$. All three of these terms differ in meaning:

$$\breve{\lambda}_x(\ldots x \ldots)``\mathfrak{V}, \qquad \breve{\lambda}_x((\ldots x \ldots)``\mathfrak{V}), \qquad \breve{}(\lambda_x(\ldots x \ldots)``\mathfrak{V}).$$

[3] Shortened by Charles L. Getchell.

The same rule governs the reading of the following theorem schema, which concerns applications of $\lambda_x(\ldots x \ldots)$ to y.

10.24 $\ldots y \ldots \in \mathcal{V} \,.\!\supset\!.\, \lambda_x(\ldots x \ldots)\text{‘}y = \ldots y \ldots .$

Proof. By hypothesis and 10.23,

$$y \in \arg \lambda_x(\ldots x \ldots).$$

So, by 10.14,

$$\langle \lambda_x(\ldots x \ldots)\text{‘}y, y\rangle \in \lambda_x(\ldots x \ldots).$$

That is, by 10.21 and 9.5,

$$\lambda_x(\ldots x \ldots)\text{‘}y = \ldots y \ldots .$$

A useful case of function abstraction, and perhaps the simplest case after $\lambda_x x$ ($=I$) and $\lambda_x z$ ($= \{z\} \times \mathcal{V}$), is the unit-class function:

10.25 ‘ι’ for ‘$\lambda_x\{x\}$’.

Here are some things about it.

10.26 $\iota\text{‘}x = \{x\} \neq \Lambda.$ *Proof* by 10.24, 7.12, 7.6.

10.27 $x \in \arg \iota.$ *Proof* by 10.23 and 7.12.

10.28 $\langle\{x\}, y\rangle \in \iota \,.\!\equiv\!.\, x = y.$

Proof. By 9.5 and the definitions 10.21 and 10.25,

$$\langle\{x\}, y\rangle \in \iota \,.\!\equiv\!.\, \{x\} = \{y\}$$

(by 7.7) $\equiv .\; x = y.$

10.29 $\breve{\iota}\text{‘}\{x\} = x.$

Proof. By definitions,

$$\breve{\iota}\text{‘}\{x\} = (\imath y)(\langle\{x\}, y\rangle \in \iota)$$

(by 10.28) $= (\imath y)(x = y)$

(by 8.21) $= x.$

IV | NATURAL NUMBERS

11. Numbers unconstrued

The utility of quantifying over classes—including classes of pairs—is illustrated with increasing frequency and urgency when we turn to the treatment of number. So insistent are the demands of number upon class that the modern history of set theory is largely a history of troubles over number. We shall now begin to consider how classes are exploited in the treatment of number.

By *numbers* in this chapter I shall mean just the natural numbers: 0 and the positive integers. Let us accept them for a while as things of an unspecified kind. Let us suppose that we are given 0 by name and that we are given the successor function S such that, for each number x, S‘x is $x + 1$. Let us suppose further that all the numbers are admitted as values of our variables of quantification, but not that the values of our variables are confined to numbers. Problem: to define the class N of the natural numbers.

Frege (1879, 1884) solved this problem with the help of the real theory of classes, after the manner of his formulation of ‘x is an ancestor of y’ which we noted early in §4. The ancestors of y were the common members of all classes z fulfilling the initial condition ‘$y \in z$’ and a closure condition amounting to ‘α“$z \subseteq z$’, where α is the parent relation. Now similarly the numbers are describable as the common members of all classes z fulfilling the initial condition ‘$0 \in z$’ and the closure condition ‘S“$z \subseteq z$’. N is

(i) $$\{x\colon (z)(0 \in z \,.\, \text{S}``z \subseteq z \,.\!\supset\!.\, x \in z)\},$$

or more concisely

$$\bigcap\{z\colon 0 \in z \,.\, S``z \subseteq z\}.$$

We are not yet saying that numbers are classes, unless in the sense in which everything may be said to be a class (individuals being reckoned as their own unit classes). Nor are we saying that N is a real class; it could be merely virtual under (i). But the point to notice is that we have rendered '$x \in$ N' by appealing to classes as values of the bound variable 'z'. Here again, as in the ancestor example and ordered pairs and much else, the real theory of classes gets us over a hump.

But the demands on classes here are heavy. If the formulation (i) is to achieve its purpose, infinite classes are required. If there are no infinite classes, then there is no z whatever such that $0 \in z$ and $S``z \subseteq z$ (for any such would be infinite) and so, vacuously, everything x will belong to all such classes z, there being none. The class described in (i) will be $\mathcal{V}$ ($=\bigcap\Lambda$; cf. 8.15), a poor try at N. The parallel difficulty does not arise in the ancestor example, granted the existence in general of finite classes, because the class of a man's ancestors is finite.

We shall see in §12 that the several natural numbers can themselves be construed as finite classes. The trouble is just that, if we do not assume infinite classes in addition, the version (i) of 'N' makes N contain the natural numbers and everything else too. Nor let it be protested that N is then itself an infinite class, for it is virtual. Naturally N $\notin \mathcal{V}$ if there are no infinite classes.

Happily this need of infinite classes can be circumvented. (There will be other needs of them that cannot be.) We have merely to invert (i) thus:

(ii) $$\{x\colon (z)(x \in z \,.\, \breve{S}``z \subseteq z \,.\supset.\, 0 \in z)\}.$$

For classes z to be relevant here they do not need to be infinite. Any class z as of (i), containing 0 and closed with respect to S, had to go on forever. But for any one natural number x a class z as of (ii) need not contain more than x positive members and 0, hence $x + 1$ members. If every natural number x is to find its way into N defined by (ii), certainly there are going to have to be larger and larger classes without end as values of 'z'; but they can all be finite.[1]

In proving theorems of arithmetic, the place where we encounter the question of existence of finite or infinite classes is in justifying the law of *mathematical induction.* If something is true of 0, and whenever it is true of a number it is true of the next, then it is true of all numbers: such is the law, which is the most important proof technique in the theory of natural numbers. Schematically:

$$\begin{array}{l} F0\,. \\ (y)(Fy \supset F(\mathrm{S}`y))\,. \\ x \in \mathrm{N}\,. \\ \quad \supset Fx. \end{array}$$

When, as usual, N is defined as in (i), the justification of the law is as follows. By the third premiss, $x \in \mathrm{N}$. So, by the definition (i), x is a member of every class z that contains 0 (as does $\{y: Fy\}$, by the first premiss) and is closed with respect to S (as is $\{y: Fy\}$, by the second premiss). So $x \in \{y: Fy\}$, q.e.d. But the argument depends on existence of $\{y: Fy\}$, and under the premisses $\{y: Fy\}$ is bound to be infinite.

See now, in contrast, how the same schema of mathematical induction is justified when N is defined by (ii). By the third premiss ('$x \in \mathrm{N}$') and (ii), 0 belongs to every class z such that $x \in z$ and $\breve{\mathrm{S}}``z \subseteq z$. Take z then as the *finite* class of those numbers y from 0 to x such that $\sim Fy$. The second premiss of the

---

[1] Various ways are known of getting number theory without infinite classes. The constructions of number theory by Martin and Myhill are perhaps marginal cases, for they assume the idea of the ancestral (§15) subject to laws that would usually be based on infinite classes. But the method indicated by Gödel, 1940, pp. 31f, clearly qualifies. So does Zermelo's method of 1909, as clarified by Grelling, pp. 12ff. So does Dummett's as set forth by Wang, 1958, p. 491. Of my present device of inversion I would say only that it seems simpler than these various alternatives. My published note of 1961 on it needs, by the way, a correction: in it I inadvertently represented as an axiom what was always an axiom schema, viz. 13.1 below.

induction schema implies that

$$(y)(\sim F(\mathrm{S}`y) \supset \sim Fy)$$

and hence implies of our newly chosen z that

$$(y)(\mathrm{S}`y \in z \mathrel{.\supset.} y \in z),$$

i.e., $\check{\mathrm{S}}``z \subseteq z$. So we must have $0 \in z$ if $x \in z$. But $0 \notin z$ by the first premiss ('$F0$'); so $x \notin z$, which is to say Fx, q.e.d. Finite classes thus suffice.

I have not yet defined S; I have only said that applied to any natural number it gives the next. Its eventual definition might give it supplementary interpretation outside the natural numbers in such a way as to make 0 or other natural numbers bear S to some things besides natural numbers. In this event the conclusion of the preceding paragraph would be unwarranted. But here the moral is simple: do not so define S as to make any natural number the successor of anything other than a natural number. And in fact the three best-known ways of construing S all do conform to this moral, even while explaining S in application to all sorts of things, numerical and otherwise. We shall see these versions in §12.

To define N by (ii) is needlessly special in one respect. If we use 'y' in place of '0', the quantified formula in (ii) serves to define '$\leq$' for natural numbers:

(iii) $$y \leqq x \mathrel{.\equiv} (z)(x \in z \mathrel{.} \check{\mathrm{S}}``z \subseteq z \mathrel{.\supset.} y \in z).$$

Then in particular

(iv) $$\mathrm{N} = \{x\colon 0 \leqq x\}.$$

Incidentally we can define '$y < x$' as '$\mathrm{S}`y \leqq x$' and then '$x \geqq y$' as '$y \leqq x$' and '$x > y$' as '$y < x$'.

The primary use of the natural numbers is as measures of multiplicity. This use of a number x is epitomized in the idiom

'α has x members'. Now the plan:

$$\alpha \text{ has } 0 \text{ members} \equiv . \; \alpha = \Lambda,$$
$$\alpha \text{ has } \mathrm{S}`x \text{ members} \equiv (\exists y)(y \in \alpha \,.\, \alpha \cap {}^{-}\{y\} \text{ has } x \text{ members}),$$

due to Frege, enables us step by step to translate 'α has S'0 members', 'α has S'(S'0) members', and so on up to each specific natural number; but it does not enable us to eliminate 'α has x members' with quantifiable variable 'x'. That can be eliminated too, as Frege knew, but only along other lines. One quick way is as follows.

Following Cantor, we can explain '$\alpha \lesssim \beta$', or 'α has no more members than β', as meaning that the members of α can be exhaustively assigned to those of β, no two to the same. That is,

11.1 '$\alpha \lesssim \beta$' for '$(\exists x)(\mathrm{Func}\, x \,.\, \alpha \subseteq x``\beta)$'.

To say that α and β are alike in size, then, is to say that $\alpha \lesssim \beta$ and vice versa.

11.2 '$\alpha \simeq \beta$' for '$\alpha \lesssim \beta \lesssim \alpha$'.

Now the remaining step to measuring class sizes by number is suggested by counting: a class has x members if it is just as big as the class of numbers $<x$. (The traditional pattern of counting to x is distorted, in this application, in the minor respect of beginning with 0 and so stopping just short of x.) So we have '$\alpha \simeq \{y: y < x\}$' as our rendering of '$\alpha$ has x members'.[2] Note that in this condensed rendering I depend again on the assumption that any definition of 'S' ultimately to be considered will be such as never to cause a natural number to bear S to anything but a natural number; otherwise I would need a clause '$y \in \mathrm{N}$' in '$\{y: y < x\}$' even though x itself be a natural number.

In achieving the formulation '$\alpha \simeq \{y: y < x\}$' of '$\alpha$ has x members' we have had to exploit the real theory of classes in

---

[2] So Dedekind, 1888, §14.

two ways. Reality of α itself is not required, nor is reality of the S that is used in defining '$<$'. But the definition of '$<$' uses also '$\leqq$', the definition of which does involve quantification over classes, in the manner seen in (iii); and the definition of '$\simeq$' uses also '$\lesssim$', whose definition depends on quantifying over classes of ordered pairs. Still, the classes thus required are only finite ones. This was seen in connection with (ii), and in the case of '$\lesssim$' it may be quickly seen too; for, in order that $\alpha \simeq \{y : y < x\}$ there are needed according to 11.1 and 11.2 only a function comprising x pairs $\langle a_1, 0\rangle$, $\langle a_2, 1\rangle$, $\ldots$, $\langle a_x, x-1\rangle$ such that a_1, $\ldots$, $a_x \in \alpha$, and a function comprising the x opposite pairs.

What now of sum, product, and power? There are the familiar so-called recursive definitions or *recursions:*

$$x + 0 = x, \qquad x + \text{S}`y = \text{S}`(x + y);$$
$$x \cdot 0 = 0, \qquad x \cdot (\text{S}`y) = x + x \cdot y;$$
$$x^0 = \text{S}`0\ (=1), \qquad x^{\text{S}`y} = x \cdot x^y.$$

The top pair of equations enables us to eliminate '$+$' completely from '$x + 3$', which is to say '$x + \text{S}`(\text{S}`(\text{S}`0))$', in four steps; the whole comes down to '$\text{S}`(\text{S}`(\text{S}`x))$'. Correspondingly for '$x +$' followed by any specific numeral. But it does not enable us to eliminate '$+$' from '$x + y$', with quantifiable variable 'y'. The second pair serves to eliminate '$\cdot$' completely from '$x \cdot 3$' in four steps, yielding '$x + (x + (x + 0))$', which reduces in turn to '$x + (x + x)$'; but there is then no eliminating the '$+$'. Nor will the second pair eliminate even '$\cdot$' from '$x \cdot y$'. These recursions are genuinely eliminative definitions insofar as the letters are thought of as schematic letters for numerals but not when they are thought of as quantifiable variables.

Genuine definitions in the latter vein can, however, be supplied once we define *iterates*, or *powers of relations.* I mean iterates in the sense in which the relation of great-grandparent is the third iterate of the parent relation. The zero iterate, $z^{|0}$, of any relation z is I; the first iterate, $z^{|1}$, is z itself; the second iterate, $z^{|2}$, is $z \mid z$; the third, $z^{|3}$, is $z \mid z \mid z$; and so on. Once this notion is at hand, we can reduce the above recursions to direct definitions thus:

$$\text{(v)} \qquad x + y = \mathrm{S}^{|y}\text{‘}x, \qquad x \cdot y = (\lambda_z(x + z))^{|y}\text{‘}0,$$
$$x^y = (\lambda_z(x \cdot z))^{|y}\text{‘}1.$$

But how to define iterates? I did so just now by a recursion in turn, in effect:

$$\text{(vi)} \qquad z^{|0} = I, \qquad z^{|\mathrm{S}\text{‘}y} = z \mid z^{|y}.$$

The notion of the iterate has enabled us to transform the recursions for arithmetical sum, product, and power into direct definitions, but what is going to enable us to transform the recursion for the iterate into a direct definition? Answer: the notion of a *finite sequence.*

What matters for a finite sequence is that it have a first (or say zeroth) thing, and a next, and a next, and so on to a last, not precluding repetitions. So we may picture the sequence simply as a function w whose arguments are the "serial numbers," from 0 up to some n, and whose values—$w\text{‘}0$, $w\text{‘}1$, . . . , $w\text{‘}n$—are the things "in" the sequence. Thus

$$\text{(vii)} \qquad \mathrm{Seq} = \{w\colon \mathrm{Func}\, w \,.\, (\exists y)(\breve{w}\text{“}\mathcal{V} = \{z\colon z \leqq y\})\}.$$

Sequences become finite classes of ordered pairs. Now we can define the general notion $z^{|y}$ of the yth iterate outright. It is the relation of h to k where, for some sequence w, h is $w\text{‘}y$ and k is $w\text{‘}0$ and each succeeding thing "in" the sequence w bears z to the thing before it. That is, succinctly,

$$\text{(viii)} \qquad z^{|y} = \{\langle h, k\rangle\colon (\exists w)(w \in \mathrm{Seq}\,.$$
$$\langle h, y\rangle, \langle k, 0\rangle \in w \,.\, w \mid \mathrm{S} \mid \breve{w} \subseteq z)\}.$$[3]

The definitions adumbrated in (iii)–(v), (vii), and (viii) will receive their final formulations in 12.1, 12.3, 16.1–3, 14.1–2.

---

[3] The whole construction (v)–(viii) is in Dedekind, 1888, §§9, 11–13, except that he breaks his steps differently, thus not singling out quite the concepts $z^{|y}$ and Seq along the way. This version of sequences is due to Whitehead, 1903, pp. 158f.

12. Numbers construed

Our firmly numbered definitions have introduced notations as abbreviations ultimately of expressions couched in a primitive notation comprising only quantification, truth functions, and the predicate 'ϵ'. Definitions in §11, stated with temporary Roman numerals, have rested on '0' and 'S' as undefined supplementary notation; and we have found them adequate to the arithmetical operations, the idea of number ('N'), and the idea of class size. What we shall see next is that these basic notations can be reduced to the extent of getting rid of '0' and 'S'.

We have been admitting the numbers into the range of values of our variables of quantification, but we have not yet considered what sorts of things numbers are to be. We did see how to define 'N' given '0' and 'S'; the construing in turn of '0' and 'S' is what is needed, now, to fix the idea of number.

Any objects will serve as numbers so long as the arithmetical operations are defined for them and the laws of arithmetic are preserved. It has sometimes been urged that more is wanted: it is not enough that we account for pure arithmetic, we must also account for the application of number in the measurement of multiplicity. But this position, insofar as it is thought of as contrary to the other, is wrong. We have seen how to define not only the arithmetical operations but also the *Anzahlbegriff*, 'α has x members', without having yet decided what numbers are.

We are free to take 0 as anything we like, and construe S as any function we like, so long merely as the function is one that, when applied in iteration to 0, yields something different on every further application. For example, we may, with Zermelo (1908), take 0 arbitrarily as Λ and then take S'x for each x as $\{x\}$. The numbers become Λ, $\{\Lambda\}$, $\{\{\Lambda\}\}$, and so on. Alternatively we may, with von Neumann (1923), take each natural number as the class of all earlier numbers; then 0 becomes Λ again, but S'x becomes not $\{x\}$ but $x \cup \{x\}$. In particular, then, 1 is again $\{\Lambda\}$ as with Zermelo, but 2 becomes $\{0, 1\}$, or $\{\Lambda, \{\Lambda\}\}$; 3 becomes $\{0, 1, 2\}$, or $\{\Lambda, \{\Lambda\}, \{\Lambda, \{\Lambda\}\}\}$; and so on. In general, for von Neumann, $x = \{y: y < x\}$, or $y < x \;.\!\equiv.\; y \in x$, for all natural numbers x.

Von Neumann's version of numbers is looked upon as more natural than Zermelo's because of its closer relation to counting. In counting the x members of α we associate them severally with the first x numbers; and these are, for von Neumann, simply the members of x. For von Neumann, to say that α has x members is to say that $\alpha \simeq x$. Note that this is in effect just the '$\alpha \simeq \{y: y < x\}$' of §11 again, since $x = \{y: y < x\}$ for von Neumann.

In 1884 Frege, preoccupied with numbers as measures of multiplicity, construed each number in effect as the class of all classes having that number of members.[1] For him, therefore, 0 is $\{\Lambda\}$ rather than Λ, and S'x is

$$\{z: (\exists y)(y \in z \,.\, z \cap {}^{-}\{y\} \in x)\}.$$

For Frege, as for anyone, 'α has x members' is adequately rendered by '$\alpha \simeq \{y: y < x\}$', but for Frege it can also be rendered more concisely as '$\alpha \in x$' so long as $\alpha \in \mathcal{V}$ (cf. 6.12).

Among the three versions of number we have only to obviate ambiguity by appropriate qualifiers. Any of the three can serve, we see, the purpose of number ordinarily so called; and the same may be said of any of infinitely many alternative versions.

In §11 we found need of quantifying over classes, finite ones anyway, in formulating 'N' given '0' and 'S'. The same need arose again in defining the iterate or relative power that was used in defining '$x + y$', '$x \cdot y$', and 'x^y'. Also we quantified over finite classes of pairs in formulating 'α has x members', for this depended on 11.1. But now we find that real classes, and indeed finite ones, are not just a needed auxiliary for the theory of numbers; they are adequate to the whole (unless we take numbers in Frege's way, which makes them infinite classes).

So our inventory of signs is now reduced again to the quantifiers and variables, the truth-function signs, and '$\in$'. Such is the

---

[1] It was only as simplified by Russell that Frege's version effected quite this. The added complication in Frege's version hinged only on general traits of his logical system, however, and fell away quite naturally; so I think we may fairly speak of this version still as Frege's. Russell did (1919, p. 11).

primitive notation of the theory of classes, and we have now seen how it serves the basic purposes also of arithmetic.

Let us begin organizing the definitions for reference. I shall use Zermelo's versions of 0 and S, viz., Λ and ι. Adapting then (iii), (iv), and their suite (§11), we have:

12.1 '$\beta \leqq \alpha$' or '$\alpha \geqq \beta$' for '$(z)(\alpha \in z \,.\, \breve{\iota}``z \subseteq z \,.\!\supset\!.\, \beta \in z)$',

12.2 '$\beta < \alpha$' or '$\alpha > \beta$' for '$\{\beta\} \leqq \alpha$',

12.3 'N' for '$\{x\colon \Lambda \leqq x\}$'.

Next we observe that the relation expressed by '$\leqq$' is reflexive and transitive.

12.4 $x \leqq x.$ *Proof* by 12.1.

12.5 $x \leqq y \leqq z \,.\!\supset\!.\, x \leqq z.$

Proof. By hypotheses and 12.1,

$$(w)(y \in w \,.\, \breve{\iota}``w \subseteq w \,.\!\supset\!.\, x \in w : z \in w \,.\, \breve{\iota}``w \subseteq w \,.\!\supset\!.\, y \in w).$$

So

$$(w)(\breve{\iota}``w \subseteq w \,.\!\supset\!: z \in w \,.\!\supset\!.\, y \in w : y \in w \,.\!\supset\!.\, x \in w)$$
$$\supset: z \in w \,.\!\supset\!.\, x \in w).$$

That is, by 12.1, $x \leqq z$.

The next says that x is no greater than S'x, which for us is $\{x\}$.

12.6 $x \leqq \{x\}.$

Proof. By definitions, $\langle x, \{x\}\rangle \in \breve{\iota}$. So

$$\{x\} \in z \,.\!\supset\!.\, x \in \breve{\iota}``z$$
$$\supset: \breve{\iota}``z \subseteq z \,.\!\supset\!.\, x \in z,$$

q.e.d. (cf. 12.1).

In fact it is less.

12.7 $x < \{x\}.$ *Proof*: '$\{x\}$' for 'x' in 12.4; cf. 12.2.

Further easy consequences:

12.8 $x < y \leqq z \,.\supset.\, x < z$. *Proof* similar from 12.5.

12.9 $x < y \,.\supset.\, x \leqq y$.

Proof. By 12.6 and 12.5, $\{x\} \leqq y \,.\supset.\, x \leqq y$, q.e.d. (cf. 12.2).

12.10 $x < y < z \,.\supset.\, x < z$. *Proof* by 12.8, 12.9.

A more substantial theorem is that if $x \leqq y$ then $x = y$ unless y is a successor (i.e., a unit class).

12.11 $x \leqq y \,.\supset:\, x = y \,.\vee\, (\exists z)(y = \{z\})$.

Proof. Suppose that $x \leqq y$ and $(z)(y \neq \{z\})$; to prove that $x = y$. By 12.1, since $x \leqq y$,

$$(w)(y \in w \,.\, \breve{\iota}``w \subseteq w \,.\supset.\, x \in w). \qquad \text{[i]}$$

Since $(z)(y \neq \{z\})$, y does not bear ι. So $\breve{\iota}``\{y\} = \Lambda$. So $\breve{\iota}``\{y\} \subseteq \{y\}$. But also $y \in \{y\}$. So, by [i], $x \in \{y\}$. That is, $x = y$.

Proceeding to theorems about N, it is convenient first of all to spell out both '$w \leqq x$' and '$x \in \mathrm{N}$' more fully:

12.12 $w \leqq x \,.\equiv\, (z)(x \in z \,.\, (y)(\{y\} \in z \,.\supset.\, y \in z) \,.\supset.\, w \in z)$.

Proof. By definitions,

$$w \leqq x \,.\equiv\, (z)(x \in z \,.\, (u)(y)(u = \{y\} \,.\, u \in z \,.\supset.\, y \in z) \,.\supset.\, w \in z).$$

By 6.2 this reduces to 12.12.

12.13 $x \in \mathrm{N} \,.\equiv\, (z)(x \in z \,.\, (y)(\{y\} \in z \,.\supset.\, y \in z) \,.\supset.\, \Lambda \in z))$.

Proof by 12.12, 12.3.

Then come theorems to the effect that 0 is a number and the successors of numbers are numbers and every number but 0 is a successor.

12.14 $\Lambda \epsilon \mathrm{N}$. *Proof.* By 12.4, $\Lambda \leqq \Lambda$, q.e.d. (cf. 12.3).

12.15 $x \epsilon \mathrm{N} .\supset. \{x\} \epsilon \mathrm{N}$ (i.e., $\iota``\mathrm{N} \subseteq \mathrm{N}$).

Proof.[2] By 12.5 and 12.6, $\Lambda \leqq x .\supset. \Lambda \leqq \{x\}$, q.e.d. (cf. 12.3).

12.16 $x \epsilon \mathrm{N} .\supset: x = \Lambda .\mathbf{v}\ (\exists y)(x = \{y\})$.

Proof by 12.11, 12.3.

More about 0:

12.17 $x \leqq \Lambda .\equiv. x = \Lambda$.

Proof. By 10.26, $\sim(\exists z)(\Lambda = \{z\})$. So, by 12.11, $x \leqq \Lambda .\supset. x = \Lambda$. Converse by 12.4.

12.18 $\sim(x < \Lambda)$.

Proof. By 12.17 and 12.2, $x < \Lambda .\equiv. \{x\} = \Lambda$. So, by 10.26, $\sim(x < \Lambda)$.

It will be convenient to have a compact notation for $\{x: x \leqq y\}$. Whether y is a number or not, this is by 12.1 the class comprising y, and the sole member of y if such there be, and its sole member if such there be, and so on down. When y is a number, which is the case of primary interest for us, $\{x: x \leqq y\}$ is the class of all numbers up through y. So I shall write '$\{,,,y\}$' for it; this is meant to be reminiscent of the schematic notation '$\{\ldots, y\}$' without being schematic.

12.19 '$\{,,,\alpha\}$' for '$\{x: x \leqq \alpha\}$'.

Immediately we can transcribe 12.4 and 12.17 thus:

12.20 $x \epsilon \{,,,x\}$,

12.21 $\{,,,\Lambda\} = \{\Lambda\}$.

---

[2] Shortened by Miss Joyce Friedman.

13. Induction

By inverting the definition of N we were able to dispense, for the time being, with infinite classes (§11). The reason was that whereas a class containing 0 and containing the successors of all its own members must be infinite, a class containing x and containing the predecessors of all its own members need have no more than $x + 1$ members. But it will have to have that many. So if there is any *finite* bound to how big a class can be, then even our inverted definition will fail of its purpose just as the usual definition fails of its purpose in the absence of infinite classes. Our meager axiom 7.10, which guarantees classes of up to two members only, will have to be supplemented to assure ever larger finite classes.

The need is first specifically felt in justifying mathematical induction. The justification, after inversion of the definition of N, depended on existence of the class of those numbers y from 0 to x such that $\sim Fy$ (cf. §11), in short, the existence of $\{,,,x\} \cap \{y\colon \sim Fy\}$. This class is indeed finite. But it will have to exist for every number x, and for every formula in the role of 'Fy', if the justification of induction is to be general. So what we need is:

$$x \in \mathrm{N} \mathbin{.\supset.} \{,,,x\} \cap \alpha \in \mathcal{V}$$

as axiom schema, or an axiom schema from which we can deduce this.

For elegance I shall drop the hypothesis '$x \in \mathrm{N}$'. For $\{,,,x\}$ may be expected to remain finite whether $x \in \mathrm{N}$ or not. It has as members only x and the sole member of x if any and the sole member of that if any and so on until we hit either Λ or a class of many members; and could there fail to be such an end? Yes, if x is an individual, i.e., $x = \{x\}$ (cf. §4); but in this case $\{,,,x\}$ is x and so is still finite, having but one member.

Or imagine that you can get from x around to x not in a single step of ι but still in a finite number of such steps; x is the unit class of the unit class of . . . of itself. All such implausibly cyclic cases are characterized, along with the case of individuals $x = \{x\}$, by the formula '$x < x$' (cf. 12.2, 12.1). And in all such cases $\{,,,x\}$ clearly still is finite. Infinity of $\{,,,x\}$ is rather the extraordinary situation where

$$x = \{y\}, \quad y = \{z\}, \quad z = \{w\}, \ldots$$

ad infinitum and $x, y, z, w, \ldots$ are all distinct. Succinctly, it is where $\{,,,x\} \subseteq \iota``\mathcal{V}$ and yet $\sim(x < x)$.

One could add an axiom denying that there is such an x. But this is not to my purpose. I desire no theorem that there are no infinite classes; on the contrary, we shall see in Chapter VI and beyond that infinite classes are needed for good purposes. I am merely concerned to get the foundations of number theory before positively assuming that there are infinite classes. Assumption of '$\{,,,x\} \cap \alpha \in \mathcal{V}$' as an axiom schema of comprehension is quite satisfactory on this score if we are once and for all content that there not be any bizarre x such that $\{,,,x\} \subseteq \iota``\mathcal{V}$ and $\sim(x < x)$; and we are indeed. There is no danger of being able to prove that there is such an x, and no purpose in an axiom that there is not.

The schema '$\{,,,x\} \cap \alpha \in \mathcal{V}$', thus far defended, is inadequate in another way. It gives classes of numbers only, where x is a number. Even if x is not a number, $\{,,,x\}$ and $\{,,,x\} \cap \alpha$ are classes of a very special sort, oddly ingrown classes with at most one member that is not a unit class. We shall need classes of other sorts, though finite still, to do the work of the sequences at the end of §11 and of some of the functions in 11.1. Consequently the axiom schema of comprehension that I shall adopt at this point is not '$\{,,,x\} \cap \alpha \in \mathcal{V}$' but:

13.1 *Axiom schema.* Func $\alpha \supset . \ \alpha``\{,,,x\} \in \mathcal{V}$.

This extended version still postulates no classes larger than $\{,,,x\}$; for α, being a function, assigns at most one thing to each member of $\{,,,x\}$. It will be recalled indeed that our very definition (11.1) of '$\beta \preceq \gamma$', following Cantor, was that $\beta \subseteq z``\gamma$ for some function z. Granted, there is no demand in 13.1 that anything z *be* α, that $\alpha \in \mathcal{V}$.

The axiom schema 13.1 is suggested by a well-known axiom schema of *replacement*, which says in effect that Func $\alpha \supset .$ $\alpha``y \in \mathcal{V}$.[1] Given any class y to begin with, this latter schema postulates the existence of the class that you get from y by replacing each member by an arbitrary thing, same or different; hence the name 'replacement'. We could get 13.1 by assuming the axiom schema of replacement and, to prime the pump, the axiom '$\{,,,x\} \in \mathcal{V}$'. But from 13.1 itself we get nothing like the strength of the axiom schema of replacement. The latter determines much, conditionally, about infinite classes: that if there is an infinite class y, there are also no end of others of that size. On this score 13.1 is more modest even than '$x \cup \{y\} \in \mathcal{V}$'.[2]

The part '$\Lambda \in \mathcal{V}$' of 7.10 can be proved from 13.1; just take α as Λ. '$\Lambda \in \mathcal{V}$' was assumed ahead of 13.1 only for expository convenience. The luxurious provision at p. 58, which allows free substitution of 'Λ', '$\{\alpha\}$', '$\{\alpha, \beta\}$', and '$(\imath x)Fx$' for variables, depends heavily on '$\Lambda \in \mathcal{V}$'; for note the role of Λ in 8.22 and in proving 7.12 and 7.13.

All of 7.10, thus '$\{x, y\} \in \mathcal{V}$' as well as '$\Lambda \in \mathcal{V}$', becomes redundant if instead of 13.1 we adopt its variant:

(i) $$\text{Func } R \supset . \; R``\{,,,x\} \in \mathcal{V}.$$

This has been pointed out to me by Brown and also by Wang.

[1] It was propounded by Fraenkel (1922) and independently by Skolem (1923 for 1922). The name (*Ersetzung*) is from Fraenkel. The idea was partly anticipated by Mirimanoff (1917), in an informal axiom to the effect that a class exists if it is of the same size as one that exists. An axiom like Mirimanoff's appeared also in an 1899 letter of Cantor, unpublished until 1932 (p. 444). However, in order to argue from it to the axiom schema of replacement one needs not only the principle of *Aussonderung* (which was likewise in Cantor's letter) but also the axiom of choice (which was not). Incidentally, it was only Fraenkel and Skolem, especially Skolem, who clearly defined the subtle status of their principle as an axiom *schema*—a point that is essential if existence is not to be imputed to what I have called α. Their versions were less concise than 'Func $\alpha \supset . \alpha``y \in \mathcal{V}$', for want of the method of virtual classes; but they were equivalent to it.

[2] Cf. p. xi. Still '$\{,,,x\} \in \mathcal{V}$' is not trivial. Brown has shown that it cannot be proved even when the axiom schema of replacement is supplemented by all of Zermelo's axioms as of §38; it must await the axiom schema of *Fundierung* (p. 286, below), whereupon, Brown shows, it is forthcoming.

In (i) we have the '*R*' of §3 instead of 'α'; so we read 'Func' and 'R" . . .' as in pp. 22f now rather than 64f, and we dissociate '$\{,,,x\}$' from pairs by rereading 'ι"z' in 12.1 as '$\{w: \{w\} \epsilon z\}$'.

To prove '$\Lambda \epsilon \mathcal{V}$' from (i), take *R* as the $\Lambda \times \Lambda$ of §3, or $\{zw: z \neq z\}$. Next prove '$\{\Lambda\} \epsilon \mathcal{V}$', by taking x and *R* in (i) as Λ and the *I* of §3, or $\{zw: z = w\}$. Finally prove '$\{x, y\} \epsilon \mathcal{V}$' by taking the x of (i) as $\{\Lambda\}$ and taking *R* as

$$\{zw: z = x \,.\, w = \Lambda \,.\mathbf{v}.\, z = y \,.\, w = \{\Lambda\}\}.$$

Parallel reasoning fails when we work from 13.1 itself, because we are then dependent on 9.5, and 9.5 depends on 7.13 and so on 7.10. 7.13 enters the proof of 9.5 tacitly with 2.1, under the convention that was adopted at the middle of p. 52.

From the point of view of axiomatic theory, therefore, our present rudimentary foundation for set theory is best seen as comprising just the axiom 4.1 of extensionality and the schema (i). Practically and pedagogically, on the other hand, since ordered pairs were to come anyway, we did well to settle early for relations as classes of ordered pairs and not pause further over virtual relations as of §3. Hence the working version 4.1, 7.10, 13.1.

Superficially the definition of '$\beta \preceq \gamma$' according to 11.1 is broader than that β is z"γ for some function z; it is that $\beta \subseteq z$"γ for some function z. A corresponding broadening of 13.1 is convenient, and can be established as follows.

13.2 $\quad$ Func $\alpha \,.\, \beta \subseteq \alpha$"$\{,,,x\}$ $.\supset.$ $\beta \epsilon \mathcal{V}$.

Proof. By 10.8, 9.17, and hypothesis, Func $\beta \upharpoonright \alpha$. So, by 13.1, $(\beta \upharpoonright \alpha)$"$\{,,,x\} \epsilon \mathcal{V}$. But $(\beta \upharpoonright \alpha)$"$\{,,,x\}$ is $\beta \cap \alpha$"$\{,,,x\}$ and hence, by hypothesis, β.

The schema contemplated before 13.1 is easily derived too:

13.3 $\quad \{,,,x\} \cap \alpha \epsilon \mathcal{V}$.

Proof. $\{,,,x\} \cap \alpha \subseteq \{,,,x\}$. So

$$\{,,,x\} \cap \alpha \subseteq I\text{"}\{,,,x\}.$$

So, by 10.4 and 13.2, $\{,,,x\} \cap \alpha \in \mathcal{V}$.

There is also this consequence regarding existence of functions.

13.4 $\quad$ $\text{Func}\,\alpha\,.\,\breve{\alpha}``\mathcal{V} \subseteq \{,,,x\}\ .\supset.\ \alpha \in \mathcal{V}$.

Proof. By second hypothesis,

$$(y)(z)(\langle y, z\rangle \in \alpha\ .\supset.\ z \in \{,,,x\}). \qquad (1)$$

By first hypothesis, there is for each z at most one y, and hence at most one $\langle y, z\rangle$, such that $\langle y, z\rangle \in \alpha$. So Func β where

$$\beta = \{\langle\langle y, z\rangle, z\rangle : \langle y, z\rangle \in \alpha\}.$$

So, by 13.1, $\beta``\{,,,x\} \in \mathcal{V}$. But

$$\beta``\{,,,x\} = \{\langle y, z\rangle : z \in \{,,,x\}\,.\,\langle y, z\rangle \in \alpha\}$$

(by (1)) $\quad = \{\langle y, z\rangle : \langle y, z\rangle \in \alpha\}$

(by 9.6) $\quad = {}^{\cdot}\alpha$.

So ${}^{\cdot}\alpha \in \mathcal{V}$. But, by hypothesis and 10.1, ${}^{\cdot}\alpha = \alpha$.

The following is the form in which the law of mathematical induction is most directly provided by 13.1.

13.5 $\quad$ $x \in \alpha\,.\,(y)(\{y\} \in \alpha\ .\supset.\ y \in \alpha)\ .\supset.\ \{,,,x\} \subseteq \alpha$.

Proof. By first hypothesis and 12.20,

$$x \in \{,,,x\} \cap \alpha. \qquad (1)$$

By 12.9 and definitions,

$$\{y\} \in \{,,,x\}\ .\supset.\ y \in \{,,,x\};$$

so, by second hypothesis,

$$(y)(\{y\} \in \{,,,x\} \cap \alpha\ .\supset.\ y \in \{,,,x\} \cap \alpha). \qquad (2)$$

For any $w \in \{,,,x\}$, by 12.19, $w \leqq x$ and so, by 12.12,

$$(z)(x \in z\,.\,(y)(\{y\} \in z\ .\supset.\ y \in z)\ .\supset.\ w \in z).$$

Taking z here as $\{,,,x\} \cap \alpha$ on the strength of 13.3 and 6.11, then, we can conclude from (1) and (2) that $w \in \{,,,x\} \cap \alpha$ and so $w \in \alpha$.

Switching from the schematic class-abstract letter 'α' to the schematic predicate letter 'F', we can put the matter thus:

13.6 $Fx \,.\, (y)(F\{y\} \supset Fy) \,.\, w \leqq x \,.\!\supset Fw.$

Proof. Putting '$\{z\colon Fz\}$' for 'α' in 13.5 and reducing by 2.1, we can conclude from our first two hypotheses that $\{,,,x\} \subseteq \{z\colon Fz\}$. But, by last hypothesis and 12.19, $w \in \{,,,x\}$. So Fw.

The law of induction in the usual or upward direction follows thus:

13.7 $Fw \,.\, (y)(Fy \supset F\{y\}) \,.\, w \leqq x \,.\!\supset Fx.$

Proof. Substituting in 13.6,

$$\sim Fx \,.\, (y)(\sim F\{y\} \supset \sim Fy) \,.\, w \leqq x \,.\!\supset \sim Fw.$$

This is equivalent to 13.7.

We can lengthen but weaken the second premiss of 13.7 to get the stronger form of induction:

13.8 $Fw \,.\, (y)(w \leqq y \,.\, Fy \,.\!\supset F\{y\}) \,.\, w \leqq x \,.\!\supset Fx.$

Proof. By 12.4–12.6, $w \leqq w$ and $w \leqq y \,.\!\supset\!.\, w \leqq \{y\}$. So, by first two hypotheses,

$$w \leqq w \,.\, Fw, \qquad (y)(w \leqq y \,.\, Fy \,.\!\supset\!.\, w \leqq \{y\} \,.\, F\{y\}).$$

From these and the final hypothesis '$w \leqq x$' it follows by induction according to 13.7 that $w \leqq x \,.\, Fx$.

From 13.7 and 13.8 we get the expressly numerical forms:

13.9 $F\Lambda \,.\, (y)(Fy \supset F\{y\}) \,.\, x \in \mathrm{N} \,.\!\supset Fx,$

13.10 $F\Lambda \,.\, (y)(y \in \mathrm{N} \,.\, Fy \,.\!\supset F\{y\}) \,.\, x \in \mathrm{N} \,.\!\supset Fx$

of mathematical induction by taking w as Λ and looking to 12.3.

Peano's famous five axioms for S and N are forthcoming as theorems and a theorem schema.[2] His first two are that each number has a successor and only one; and where S is ι we are told these things in 10.27 ($x \in \arg \iota$). His third is that for all numbers x and y if $\mathrm{S}`x = \mathrm{S}`y$ then $x = y$; and we are told this in 7.7. His fourth is that there is a number that is not a successor; this we have in 10.26 and 12.14 ($\{x\} \neq \Lambda \in \mathrm{N}$). His fifth is induction, 13.10. So we have got all this without infinite classes.

The compilation of classical arithmetical laws of '$\leqq$', begun in §12, will now be continued with the help of mathematical induction.

13.11 $$x \leqq y \,.{\equiv}{:}\, x = y \,.\mathrm{v}.\, x < y.$$

Proof. By 12.7, $z < \{z\}$. So $x = z \,.{\supset}.\, x < \{z\}$ and also, by 12.10, $x < z \,.{\supset}.\, x < \{z\}$. Combining,

$$(z)(x = z \,.\mathrm{v}.\, x < z \,{:}{\supset}.\, x < \{z\})$$
$$\supset{:}\, x = \{z\} \,.\mathrm{v}.\, x < \{z\}). \qquad (1)$$

Further $x = x \,.\mathrm{v}.\, x < x$, since $x = x$. From this and (1) it follows by induction according to 13.7 that

$$x \leqq y \,.{\supset}{:}\, x = y \,.\mathrm{v}.\, x < y.$$

Converse by 12.4 and 12.9.

13.12 $$x < \{y\} \,.{\equiv}.\, x \leqq y.$$

Proof.[3] By 12.9 and 12.2,

$$\{x\} \leqq z \,.{\supset}.\, x \leqq z.$$

---

[2] Peano, 1889. They were also in Dedekind, 1888, §6, a work that Peano cites in his preface; but the name of Peano is now inseparable from them. See further Wang, 1957.

[3] Shortened by Graham Roupas.

So, *a fortiori*,

$$(z)(\{x\} \leqq z \,.\, x \leqq \iota`z \,.\supset.\, x \leqq z)$$

(by 10.29) $$\supset.\, x \leqq \iota`\{z\}).$$

But also, by 10.29 and 12.4, $x \leqq \iota`\{x\}$. From these two results it follows by induction according to 13.8 (taking the $w$ and $x$ of 13.8 as $\{x\}$ and $\{y\}$, and the '$Fz$' as '$x \leqq \iota`z$') that

$$\{x\} \leqq \{y\} \,.\supset.\, x \leqq \iota`\{y\}.$$

That is, by 12.2 and 10.29, $x < \{y\} \,.\supset.\, x \leqq y$. Conversely, by 12.7 and 12.10,

$$(u)(x < \{u\} \,.\supset.\, x < \{\{u\}\}),$$

from which and 12.7 we can infer by induction according to 13.7 that $x \leqq y \,.\supset.\, x < \{y\}$.

13.13 $x \leqq \{y\} \,.\equiv:\, x = \{y\} \,.\mathsf{v}.\, x \leqq y$

(i.e., $\{,\,,\,\{y\}\} = \{,\,,\,y\} \cup \{\{y\}\}$).

Proof. By 13.11,

$$x \leqq \{y\} \,.\equiv:\, x = \{y\} \,.\mathsf{v}.\, x < \{y\}$$

(by 13.12) $$\equiv:\, x = \{y\} \,.\mathsf{v}.\, x \leqq y.$$

13.14 $z \leqq x \,.\, z \leqq y \,.\supset:\, x \leqq y \,.\mathsf{v}.\, y \leqq x.$

Proof. By 13.11 and 12.2,

$$w \leqq x \,.\supset:\, w = x \,.\mathsf{v}.\, \{w\} \leqq x$$

(by 12.6) $$\supset:\, x \leqq \{w\} \,.\mathsf{v}.\, \{w\} \leqq x.$$

Also, by 12.5 and 12.6, $x \leqq w \,.\supset.\, x \leqq \{w\}$. Combining,

$$(w)(x \leqq w \,.\mathsf{v}.\, w \leqq x \,:\supset:\, x \leqq \{w\} \,.\mathsf{v}.\, \{w\} \leqq x).$$

By first hypothesis, $x \leqq z$ .v. $z \leqq x$. From these two results and the second hypothesis ('$z \leqq y$') we can infer by induction according to 13.7 that $x \leqq y$ .v. $y \leqq x$.

Despite our use of induction, the theorems 13.11–13.14 hold not just for numbers but, like 12.4–12.12, for any objects. They are general laws of '$\leqq$' in the sense of iterated $\breve{\iota}$, the sense defined in 12.1. They were proved with the help not of the peculiarly numerical induction laws 13.9 and 13.10, but of the induction laws 13.7 and 13.8 which govern '$\leqq$' or iterated $\breve{\iota}$ generally. We are suddenly reminded of this generality by the need of the hypothesis in 13.14. Connexity fails for '$\leqq$' in the general sense; we cannot get from every class to every class by iterating ι or $\breve{\iota}$. The needed hypothesis in 13.14 is taken care of when we adhere to numbers, since zero or Λ then plays the role of z, thus:

13.15 $x, y \in \mathrm{N} \,.\supset:\, x \leqq y \,.\mathsf{v}.\, y \leqq x.$

Proof by 13.14, 12.3.

Some further theorems special to numbers are as follows.

13.16 $x \in \mathrm{N} \,.\equiv:\, x = \Lambda \,.\mathsf{v}.\, \Lambda < x.$

Proof by 13.11, 12.3.

13.17 $x \in \mathrm{N} \,.\supset:\, \Lambda < x \,.\equiv.\, x \neq \Lambda.$

Proof. By hypothesis and 13.16, $x \neq \Lambda \,.\supset.\, \Lambda < x$. Conversely, by 12.18, $\sim(\Lambda < \Lambda)$ and so $\Lambda < x \,.\supset.\, x \neq \Lambda$.

13.18 $x \leqq y \in \mathrm{N} \,.\supset.\, x \in \mathrm{N}.$

Proof.[3] By 13.16,

$(z)(\{z\} \in \mathrm{N} \,.\supset:\, \{z\} = \Lambda \,.\mathsf{v}.\, \Lambda < \{z\})$

(by 10.26) $\supset.\, \Lambda < \{z\})$

(by 13.12, 12.3) $\supset.\, z \in \mathrm{N})$.

[3] Shortened by David Hemmendinger.

From this and the hypotheses it follows by mathematical induction according to 13.6 that $x \in \mathrm{N}$.

13.19 $$x \in \mathrm{N} \mathrel{.{\equiv}.} \{x\} \in \mathrm{N}.$$

Proof. By 12.6 and 13.18, $\{x\} \in \mathrm{N} \mathrel{.{\supset}.} x \in \mathrm{N}$. Converse by 12.15.

Early in the section we reflected on '$x < x$'. Individuals fulfill it, if such there be; and, for aught we can prove, other things may too. But we now prove by induction that numbers do not.

13.20 $$x \in \mathrm{N} \mathrel{.{\supset}} \sim(x < x).$$

Proof. By 13.12 and 12.2, $\{y\} < \{y\} \mathrel{.{\supset}.} y < y$. That is,

$$(y)(\sim(y < y) \supset \sim(\{y\} < \{y\})).$$

Also, by 12.18, $\sim(\Lambda < \Lambda)$. So 13.20 follows by induction according to 13.9.

The chapter concludes with two consequences of 13.20.

13.21 $$x \in \mathrm{N} \mathrel{.{\supset}:} x \leqq y \leqq x \mathrel{.{\equiv}.} x = y.$$

Proof. By 12.8, $x < y \leqq x \mathrel{.{\supset}.} x < x$. So, by hypothesis and 13.20, $\sim(x < y \leqq x)$. But, by 13.11,

$$x \leqq y \leqq x \mathrel{.{\supset}:} x = y \mathrel{.{\vee}.} x < y \leqq x.$$

So $x \leqq y \leqq x \mathrel{.{\supset}.} x = y$. Converse by 12.4.

13.22 $$x, y \in \mathrm{N} \mathrel{.{\supset}:} x \leqq y \mathrel{.{\equiv}} \sim(y < x).$$

Proof. By 13.11 and 12.4,

$$y \leqq x \mathrel{.{\supset}:} x \leqq y \mathrel{.{\vee}.} y < x.$$

By hypothesis and 13.15, $x \leqq y \mathrel{.{\vee}.} y \leqq x$. As in the preceding proof, $\sim(y < x \leqq y)$. These three results imply by truth-functional logic that $x \leqq y \mathrel{.{\equiv}} \sim(y < x)$.

V | ITERATION AND ARITHMETIC

14. Sequences and iterates

Pressing on now toward the definitions of sum, product, and power contemplated in (v) of §11, we activate the definitions of Seq and $z^{|w}$ contemplated in (vii) and (viii) of that section.

14.1 'Seq' for '$\{x\colon \text{Func}\, x \,.\, (\exists y)(\breve{x}``\mho = \{,,, y\})\}$',

14.2 '$\alpha^{|\beta}$' for '$\{\langle x, y\rangle\colon (\exists z)(z \in \text{Seq} \,.\, \langle x, \beta\rangle, \langle y, \Lambda\rangle \in z \,.\, z \mid \iota \mid \breve{z} \subseteq \alpha)\}$'.

The two basic laws of iterates were seen in the recursion (vi) of §11.

14.3 $$\alpha^{|\Lambda} = I.$$

Proof. Consider any x, y such that $\langle x, y\rangle \in \alpha^{|\Lambda}$. By 14.2, there is a sequence z such that $\langle x, \Lambda\rangle$, $\langle y, \Lambda\rangle \in z$. By 14.1, Func z. So $x = y$. Thus $\alpha^{|\Lambda} \subseteq I$. Conversely, let $z = \{\langle x, \Lambda\rangle\}$. Then Func z by 10.5 and $\breve{z}``\mho = \{\Lambda\} = \{,,, \Lambda\}$ by 12.21 and so, by 14.1, $z \in$ Seq. Further, since $(x)(\Lambda \neq \iota`x)$ by 10.26, $z \mid \iota = \Lambda$; so $z \mid \iota \mid \breve{z} = \Lambda$; so $z \mid \iota \mid \breve{z} \subseteq \alpha$. Further, $\langle x, \Lambda\rangle$, $\langle x, \Lambda\rangle \in z$. These things add up to saying that $\langle x, x\rangle \in \alpha^{|\Lambda}$; cf. 14.2. So $I \subseteq \alpha^{|\Lambda}$.

The other law will be proved in halves.

14.4 $$\alpha^{|\{x\}} \subseteq \alpha \mid \alpha^{|x}.$$

Proof. Consider any y, z such that $\langle y, z\rangle \in \alpha^{|\{x\}}$. By 14.2, there is a sequence w such that

$$\langle y, \{x\}\rangle, \langle z, \Lambda\rangle \in w, \qquad [i]$$

$$w \mid \iota \mid \breve{w} \subseteq \alpha. \qquad [ii]$$

By 14.1,

$$\text{Func}\, w \qquad [iii]$$

and there is something v such that

$$\breve{w}``\mathcal{V} = \{,\,,\,, v\}. \qquad [iv]$$

By [i], $\{x\} \in \breve{w}``\mathcal{V}$. So, by [iv] and definitions, $x < v$. So, by 12.9 and definition, $x \in \{,\,,\,, v\}$. So, by [iv], there is something u such that

$$\langle u, x\rangle \in w. \qquad [v]$$

So, in view again of [i], our sequence w meets the condition '$\langle u, x\rangle$, $\langle z, \Lambda\rangle \in w$' which, along with [ii], constitutes $\langle u, z\rangle$ a member of $\alpha^{|x}$ according to 14.2. Moreover, by [i] and [v], $\langle y, u\rangle \in w \mid \iota \mid \breve{w}$, and so, by [ii], $\langle y, u\rangle \in \alpha$. So, combining, $\langle y, z\rangle \in \alpha \mid \alpha^{|x}$. But $\langle y, z\rangle$ was any member of $\alpha^{|\{x\}}$.

Now to the converse of 14.4, with which I combine 14.4 itself. The proof is long, and the schema which it proves covers considerable territory. From it in a step or two we get each of the familiar recursion laws:

$$x + \text{S}`y = \text{S}`(x + y), \qquad x\cdot(\text{S}`y) = x + x\cdot y, \qquad x^{\text{S}`y} = x\cdot x^{y}$$

for all $y \in \text{N}$; see 16.6, 16.8, and 16.10 on pp. 107f.

14.6 $\qquad \alpha^{|\{x\}} = \alpha \mid \alpha^{|x}.$

Proof. Consider any y, z such that $\langle y, z\rangle \in \alpha \mid \alpha^{|x}$. That is, there is something u such that

$$\langle y, u\rangle \in \alpha \qquad [i]$$

and $\langle u, z\rangle \in \alpha^{|x}$, i.e., there is a sequence w such that

$$\langle u, x\rangle, \langle z, \Lambda\rangle \in w, \qquad \text{[ii]}$$

$$w \mid \iota \mid \breve{w} \subseteq \alpha. \qquad \text{[iii]}$$

By 14.1,

$$\text{Func } w \qquad \text{[iv]}$$

and there is something v such that

$$\breve{w}``\mathcal{V} = \{,,,v\}. \qquad \text{[v]}$$

By [v] and [ii], $x, \Lambda \in \{,,,v\}$. That is, by definitions,

$$x \leqq v \in \text{N}. \qquad \text{[vi]}$$

So, by 13.18,

$$x \in \text{N}. \qquad \text{[vii]}$$

That is, by definitions,

$$\Lambda \in \{,,,x\}. \qquad \text{[viii]}$$

By [vi], 12.5, and definition, $\{,,,x\} \subseteq \{,,,v\}$. That is, by [v],

$$\{,,,x\} \subseteq \breve{w}``\mathcal{V}. \qquad \text{[ix]}$$

By [iv] and 10.8, Func $w\restriction\{,,,x\}$. Further, by [vii] and 13.20,

$$\sim(x < x), \qquad \text{[x]}$$

i.e., by definitions, $\{x\} \notin \{,,,x\}$. So, by 10.7,

$$\text{Func } w\restriction\{,,,x\} \cup \{\langle y, \{x\}\rangle\}.$$

Moreover, by [ix], the right field of this function is $\{,,,x\} \cup \{\{x\}\}$, i.e., by 13.13, $\{,,,\{x\}\}$. So, by 13.4, the function is something t. So

$$t = w\restriction\{,,,x\} \cup \{\langle y, \{x\}\rangle\}. \qquad \text{[xi]}$$

As observed, Func t and $\breve{t}``\mathfrak{V} = \{, , , \{x\}\}$. So, by 14.1,

$$t \in \mathrm{Seq}. \qquad \text{[xii]}$$

By [ii] and [viii], $\langle z, \Lambda\rangle \in w \upharpoonright \{, , , x\}$. So, by [xi],

$$\langle y, \{x\}\rangle, \langle z, \Lambda\rangle \in t. \qquad \text{[xiii]}$$

Consider finally any q and s such that $\langle q, s\rangle \in t \mid \iota \mid \breve{t}$. By [xi], there are four possibilities to consider:

Case 1: $\langle q, s\rangle \in w \upharpoonright \{, , , x\} \mid \iota \mid \breve{\ }(w \upharpoonright \{, , , x\})$.

Then $\langle q, s\rangle \in w \mid \iota \mid \breve{w}$. Then, by [iii], $\langle q, s\rangle \in \alpha$.

Case 2: $\langle q, s\rangle \in w \upharpoonright \{, , , x\} \mid \iota \mid \{\langle \{x\}, y\rangle\}$.

Then q bears $w \upharpoonright \{, , , x\}$ to $\{\{x\}\}$. Then $\{\{x\}\} \in \{, , , x\}$. That is, by definitions, $\{x\} < x$. Then, by 12.9 and definition, $x < x$, contrary to [x]. So Case 2 is out.

Case 3: $\langle q, s\rangle \in \{\langle y, \{x\}\rangle\} \mid \iota \mid \breve{\ }(w \upharpoonright \{, , , x\})$.

Then $q = y$ and $\langle s, x\rangle \in w$. Then, by [ii] and [iv], $s = u$. So, by [i], $\langle q, s\rangle \in \alpha$.

Case 4: $\langle q, s\rangle \in \{\langle y, \{x\}\rangle\} \mid \iota \mid \{\langle \{x\}, y\rangle\}$.

Then $\langle \{x\}, \{x\}\rangle \in \iota$. Then, by 10.28, $x = \{x\}$, and so, by 12.7, $x < x$, contrary to [x]. So Case 4 is out.

So, in the two possible cases of $\langle q, s\rangle \in t \mid \iota \mid \breve{t}$, $\langle q, s\rangle \in \alpha$. So $t \mid \iota \mid \breve{t} \subseteq \alpha$. This and [xii] and [xiii] add up to saying, in view of 14.2, that $\langle y, z\rangle \in \alpha^{|\{x\}}$. But $\langle y, z\rangle$ was any member of $\alpha \mid \alpha^{|x}$. So $\alpha \mid \alpha^{|x} \subseteq \alpha^{|\{x\}}$. So, by 14.4, $\alpha^{|\{x\}} = \alpha \mid \alpha^{|x}$.

From 14.6 and 14.3 we have in particular that $\alpha^{|\{\Lambda\}} = \alpha \mid I$. So

14.7 $$\alpha^{|\{\Lambda\}} = {}^{\cdot}\alpha.$$

From this in turn we have by 14.6 that

14.8 $$\alpha^{|\{\{\Lambda\}\}} = \alpha \mid \alpha,$$

and so on.

Next let us dispose of the empty case.

14.9 $$x \notin \mathrm{N} \; .\supset. \; \alpha^{|x} = \Lambda.$$

Proof. Suppose $\langle y, z\rangle \in \alpha^{|x}$. Then, by definitions, there are v and w such that $\langle y, x\rangle, \langle z, \Lambda\rangle \in w$ and $\breve{w}``\mathcal{V} = \{,,,v\}$. Then $x, \Lambda \in \{,,,v\}$. That is, by definitions, $x \leqq v \in \mathrm{N}$. But then, by 13.18, $x \in \mathrm{N}$, contrary to hypothesis.

Since the composition of relations into a resultant $\alpha \mid \beta$ is an associative operation, $\alpha^{|y}$ should be $\alpha \mid \alpha \mid \ldots \mid \alpha$, to y occurrences, independently of any particular grouping. Therefore $\alpha^{|\{x\}}$ should be as well $\alpha^{|x} \mid \alpha$ as $\alpha \mid \alpha^{|x}$. This will now be proved.

14.10 $$\alpha^{|\{x\}} = \alpha^{|x} \mid \alpha.$$

Proof. By 14.6, $\alpha^{|\{\{y\}\}} = \alpha \mid \alpha^{|\{y\}}$. So

$$(y)(\alpha^{|\{y\}} = \alpha^{|y} \mid \alpha \; .\supset. \; \alpha^{|\{\{y\}\}} = \alpha \mid \alpha^{|y} \mid \alpha)$$

(by 14.6) $$= \alpha^{|\{y\}} \mid \alpha).$$

By 14.7,

$$\alpha^{|\{\Lambda\}} = {}^{\cdot}\alpha = I \mid \alpha$$

(by 14.3) $$= \alpha^{|\Lambda} \mid \alpha.$$

From these two results it follows by induction according to 13.9 that $\alpha^{|\{x\}} = \alpha^{|x} \mid \alpha$ if $x \in \mathrm{N}$. If $x \notin \mathrm{N}$, then $\alpha^{|x} = \Lambda$ by 14.9 and so $\alpha^{|x} \mid \alpha = \Lambda$; also $\{x\} \notin \mathrm{N}$ by 13.19 and so $\alpha^{|\{x\}} = \Lambda$ by 14.9.

We conclude with some laws about iterates of functions.

14.11 $$x \in \mathrm{N} \,.\, \arg \alpha = \mathcal{V} \; .\supset. \; \arg \alpha^{|x} = \mathcal{V}.$$

Proof. If $\arg \alpha^{|w} = \mathcal{V}$, then to anything z exactly one thing y bears $\alpha^{|w}$. But to y in turn, by hypothesis, exactly one thing bears α; so this thing alone will bear $\alpha \mid \alpha^{|w}$ to z. So

$$(w)(\arg \alpha^{|w} = \mathcal{V} \; .\supset. \; \arg(\alpha \mid \alpha^{|w}) = \mathcal{V})$$

(by 14.6) $$\supset. \; \arg \alpha^{|\{w\}} = \mathcal{V}).$$

But also, by 14.3 and 10.4, $\arg \alpha^{|\Lambda} = \mathcal{V}$. So we may conclude by induction according to 13.9 that $\arg \alpha^{|x} = \mathcal{V}$, since $x \in \mathrm{N}$.

14.12 $$\text{Func } \alpha \supset \text{Func } \alpha^{|x}.$$

Proof, where $x \in \mathrm{N}$, is the preceding proof with 'exactly' changed to 'at most' and 'arg . . . = $\mathcal{V}$' to 'Func . . .'. Where $x \notin \mathrm{N}$ the proof is by 14.9 and 10.3.

14.13 $$I^{|x} \text{`}\Lambda = \Lambda.$$

Proof. By 14.6, $I^{|\{y\}} = I \,|\, I^{|y} = I^{|y}$. So $I^{|y} = I \,.\!\supset\!.\, I^{|\{y\}} = I$. Further, by 14.3, $I^{|\Lambda} = I$. So, by 13.9, $I^{|x} = I$ for $x \in \mathrm{N}$. Where $x \notin \mathrm{N}$, $I^{|x} = \Lambda$ by 14.9. Both give 14.13.

15. The ancestral

We are now ready to proceed to sums, products, and powers of natural numbers. But I shall stop for an interlude on the *ancestral* of a relation. This is not a notion that will be used anywhere in the continuing treatment of natural numbers, nor even of real numbers. But it is an important notion. We shall use it at later points (§§22, 24, 29), and it is usually used in the foundations of the theory of natural numbers. I insert the development at this point because it rests immediately upon iterates.

The notion has already confronted us in two of its instances: the definition of ancestor in terms of parent, early in §4, and the definition of '$\geqq$' in terms of S (or of '$\in$ N' in terms of S and 0). In general, the ancestral of a relation w is meant to be the relation $*w$ that anything x bears to anything y if and only if x is y or bears w to y or bears w to something that bears w to y or so on. Thus, where w is the parent relation, $*w$ is the ancestor relation. Where w is the successor function, $*w$ is $\{\langle x, y\rangle : x \geqq y\}$ and N is $*w\text{``}\{0\}$. The classical way of defining $*w$, due to Frege,[1] we

[1] The method is persistently credited to Dedekind (1888) under the name of "chains"; but Frege set it forth earlier (1879, §§26, 29). He there defined both the ordinary ancestral and what I call, a few pages hence, the *proper* ancestral. In 1884 (p. 94) he defined the ordinary ancestral again. Dedekind acknowledges Frege's priority in a letter of 1890 which appears in translation in Wang's paper of 1957.

have already seen in the two illustrations; in general,

(i) $*\alpha = \{\langle x, y\rangle: (z)(y \in z \,.\, \alpha``z \subseteq z \,.\!\supset.\, x \in z)\}.$

But we also saw (§11) that when α was the successor function this expedient depended for its success on there being infinite classes. And we saw how that dependence could be obviated, in the successor example, by an inversion.

This inversion owed its success to a special trait of successor: the trait of giving rise to a series that has, though no end, a beginning. Classes that are closed with respect to successor are infinite when not trivial; not so the classes that are closed with respect to predecessor. But the switch would have availed us nothing if we had been dealing rather with the successor function among integers generally, including the negative ones. A class with integers in it has to be infinite if it is to be closed with respect to successor *or* predecessor in this domain.

But a general solution is at hand. After all, $*\alpha$ is simply the relation of x to y such that x bears an iterate of α to y. The ancestral is the union of all iterates.

15.1 '$*\alpha$' for '$\{w: (\exists z)(w \in \alpha^{|z})\}$'.[2]

Under the usual order of development, the general theory of the ancestral is developed first and N is got afterward by applying the general notion of the ancestral to S in particular. Under this usual approach the general definition of the ancestral is (i), and the theorems governing it depend largely on there being infinite classes of appropriate sorts. We found how the special case of the ancestral wanted for N could, thanks to a special trait of the successor function, be managed without assuming infinite classes. And now through the definitions 14.1, 14.2, and 15.1 we have derived from that favored special case of the ancestral a version of the general notion that is equivalent to the classical version granted the infinite classes, but that does not itself require the infinite classes. Instead of being, as usual, a prolegomenon to

---

[2] An improvement on my '$\{\langle x, y\rangle: (\exists z)(\langle x, y\rangle \in \alpha^{|z})\}$' by Miss Constance Leuer.

arithmetic, the theory of the ancestral is for us an application of arithmetic.

Let us derive now the various classical laws of the ancestral.

15.2 $\langle x, x\rangle \in {*\alpha}$ (i.e., $I \subseteq {*\alpha}$).[3]

Proof. By 14.3, $\langle x, x\rangle \in \alpha^{|\Lambda}$. So $(\exists z)(\langle x, x\rangle \in \alpha^{|z})$, q.e.d.

15.3 $\langle x, y\rangle \in \alpha \,.\!\supset\!.\, \langle x, y\rangle \in {*\alpha}$ (i.e., $`\alpha \subseteq {*\alpha}$).

Proof similar from 14.7.

15.4 $\langle x, y\rangle \in {*\alpha} \,.\, \langle y, z\rangle \in \alpha \,.\!\supset\!.\, \langle x, z\rangle \in {*\alpha}$
(i.e, ${*\alpha} \mid \alpha \subseteq {*\alpha}$).

Proof. By first hypothesis and 15.1, there is something w such that $\langle x, y\rangle \in \alpha^{|w}$. So, by second hypothesis, $\langle x, z\rangle \in \alpha^{|w} \mid \alpha$. So, by 14.10, $\langle x, z\rangle \in \alpha^{|\{w\}}$. So, by 15.1, $\langle x, z\rangle \in {*\alpha}$.

15.5 $\langle x, y\rangle \in \alpha \,.\, \langle y, z\rangle \in {*\alpha} \,.\!\supset\!.\, \langle x, z\rangle \in {*\alpha}$
(i.e., $\alpha \mid {*\alpha} \subseteq {*\alpha}$).

Proof similar from 14.6.

15.6 $\alpha \mid {*\alpha} = {*\alpha} \mid \alpha$.

Proof. By 14.6 and 14.10, $\alpha \mid \alpha^{|w} = \alpha^{|w} \mid \alpha$. That is,

$$(\exists y)(\langle x, y\rangle \in \alpha \,.\, \langle y, z\rangle \in \alpha^{|w}) \equiv (\exists y)(\langle x, y\rangle \in \alpha^{|w} \,.\, \langle y, z\rangle \in \alpha).$$

The rest is evident from the definitions.

15.7 $\alpha``\beta \subseteq \beta \,.\!\equiv\!.\, {*\alpha}``\beta = \beta$.

Proof. The right-to-left conditional is immediate from 15.3 ($`\alpha \subseteq {*\alpha}$). So assume conversely that $\alpha``\beta \subseteq \beta$; to prove that

---

[3] On this point my version of the ancestral agrees with Frege's and departs from that of Whitehead and Russell, for whom $\langle x, x\rangle$ does not stand in the ancestral of α unless x is in the field of α. They secure this restriction by inserting a clause in (i). Also they restrict their version of $\alpha^{|0}$ to match.

$*\alpha``\beta = \beta$. Since $\alpha``\beta \subseteq \beta$, we can argue that $\gamma``(\alpha``\beta) \subseteq \gamma``\beta$ and so in particular

$$\alpha^{|x}``(\alpha``\beta) \subseteq \alpha^{|x}``\beta.$$

That is, by 14.10, $\alpha^{|\{x\}}``\beta \subseteq \alpha^{|x}``\beta$. So

$$(x)(\alpha^{|x}``\beta \subseteq \beta \;.\supset.\; \alpha^{|\{x\}}``\beta \subseteq \beta).$$

But also, by 14.3, $\alpha^{|\Lambda}``\beta \subseteq \beta$. So, by induction according to 13.9, we have for any $z \in \mathrm{N}$ that $\alpha^{|z}``\beta \subseteq \beta$. But also, by 14.9, $\alpha^{|z}``\beta \subseteq \beta$ for any $z \notin \mathrm{N}$. So $(z)(\alpha^{|z}``\beta \subseteq \beta)$, i.e.,

$$(z)(x)(y)(\langle x, y\rangle \in \alpha^{|z} \,.\, y \in \beta \;.\supset.\; x \in \beta),$$

i.e., by 15.1, $*\alpha``\beta \subseteq \beta$. Conversely, $\beta = I``\beta \subseteq *\alpha``\beta$ by 15.2.

As a companion to 15.7 we have further that

15.8 $$\alpha \mid \beta \subseteq \beta \;.\equiv.\; *\alpha \mid \beta = \beta.$$

Proof. Substituting in 15.7,

$$\alpha``(\beta``\{y\}) \subseteq \beta``\{y\} \;.\equiv.\; *\alpha``(\beta``\{y\}) = \beta``\{y\}.$$

That is,

$$(\alpha \mid \beta)``\{y\} \subseteq \beta``\{y\} \;.\equiv.\; (*\alpha \mid \beta)``\{y\} = \beta``\{y\}.$$

So

$$(x)(y)(\langle x, y\rangle \in \alpha \mid \beta \;.\supset.\; \langle x, y\rangle \in \beta) \equiv$$
$$(x)(y)(\langle x, y\rangle \in *\alpha \mid \beta \;.\equiv.\; \langle x, y\rangle \in \beta).$$

By 9.8 and 9.9 this reduces to 15.8.

The transitivity of $*\alpha$ follows quickly.

15.9 $\langle x, y\rangle, \langle y, z\rangle \in *\alpha \;.\supset.\; \langle x, z\rangle \in *\alpha$ (indeed $*\alpha \mid *\alpha = *\alpha$).

Proof. By 15.5, $\alpha \mid *\alpha \subseteq *\alpha$. That is, by 15.8, $*\alpha \mid *\alpha = *\alpha$.

The hard core of 15.7 is '$\alpha``\beta \subseteq \beta \;.\!\supset\!.\; *\alpha``\beta \subseteq \beta$'. It encapsulates the general law of *ancestral induction*:

15.10 $$Fz \,. \quad (x)(y)(\langle y, x\rangle \in \alpha \,.\, Fx \,.\!\supset Fy) \,. \quad \langle w, z\rangle \in *\alpha \,. \quad \supset Fw.$$

Proof. By second hypothesis,

$$\alpha``\{x\colon Fx\} \subseteq \{x\colon Fx\}.$$

So, by 15.7,

$$*\alpha``\{x\colon Fx\} = \{x\colon Fx\}. \tag{1}$$

By first premiss, $z \in \{x\colon Fx\}$. So, by third premiss,

$$w \in *\alpha``\{x\colon Fx\}.$$

So, by (1), Fw.

Mathematical induction in its familiar form 13.9 is a specialization of this law, by taking α as successor. But we, contrary to custom, have derived the general from the special; note the use of 13.9 in proving 15.7.

It was remarked that the definition in §4 in terms of parent gave 'ancestor' an extended sense: everything became its own ancestor. Correspondingly we have 15.2: $I \subseteq *\alpha$. But it is easy to derive what corresponds to ancestor in the proper sense, and it in its general formulation is called the *proper* ancestral of α. It is the relation of x to y where x bears some *positive* iterate of α to y, not just $\alpha^{|\Lambda}$ $(=I)$. It is simply $\alpha \mid *\alpha$, or, what is the same by 15.6, $*\alpha \mid \alpha$. As is not to be wondered at, $*\alpha$ is the union of I and the proper ancestral. This will now be proved.

15.11 $$*\alpha = I \cup (\alpha \mid *\alpha).$$

Proof.[4] Let

$$\beta = I \cup (\alpha \mid *\alpha). \tag{1}$$

[4] Shortened by William C. Waterhouse.

By 15.2 and 15.5, then,

$$\beta \subseteq {*\alpha}. \tag{2}$$

So $\alpha \mid \beta \subseteq \alpha \mid {*\alpha}$. So, by (1), $\alpha \mid \beta \subseteq \beta$. That is, by 15.8,

$$*\alpha \mid \beta = \beta. \tag{3}$$

By (1), $I \subseteq \beta$. So $*\alpha \mid I \subseteq {*\alpha} \mid \beta$. That is, $*\alpha \subseteq {*\alpha} \mid \beta$. That is, by (3), $*\alpha \subseteq \beta$. So, by (2), $*\alpha = \beta$.

One more law worth adding is that

15.12 $$*\breve{\alpha} = \breve{}{*\alpha}.$$

Proof. By 15.4,

$$(z)(y)(\langle y, z\rangle \in \breve{\alpha} \,.\, \langle x, z\rangle \in {*\alpha} \,.\supset.\, \langle x, y\rangle \in {*\alpha}).$$

From this and 15.2 we can infer by ancestral induction according to 15.10, for any w such that $\langle w, x\rangle \in {*\breve{\alpha}}$, that $\langle x, w\rangle \in {*\alpha}$; hence that $\langle w, x\rangle \in \breve{}{*\alpha}$. But x was anything. So

$$*\breve{\alpha} \subseteq \breve{}{*\alpha}. \tag{1}$$

That is, $\breve{}{*\breve{\alpha}} \subseteq {*\alpha}$. Similarly, with '$\breve{\alpha}$' for '$\alpha$', $\breve{}{*\alpha} \subseteq {*\breve{\alpha}}$. So, by (1), $*\breve{\alpha} = \breve{}{*\alpha}$.

Finally let us close the circuit by showing that $\{\langle x, y\rangle : x \geqq y\}$ is after all the ancestral of the successor function, or ι, and that N is $*\mathrm{S}``\{0\}$, or $*\iota``\{\Lambda\}$.

15.13 $$x \geqq y \,.\equiv.\, \langle x, y\rangle \in {*\iota}.$$

Proof. $\langle\{z\}, z\rangle \in \iota$. So, by 15.5,

$$(z)(\langle z, y\rangle \in {*\iota} \,.\supset.\, \langle\{z\}, y\rangle \in {*\iota}).$$

Also, by 15.2, $\langle y, y\rangle \in {*\iota}$. So, by induction according to 13.7,

$$y \leqq x \,.\supset.\, \langle x, y\rangle \in {*\iota}. \tag{1}$$

Conversely,

$$(z)(w)(\langle z, w\rangle \in \iota \ .\supset.\ z = \{w\})$$

(by 12.6) $\supset.\ z \geqq w)$

(by 12.5) $\supset\colon w \geqq y \ .\supset.\ z \geqq y).$

Also, by 12.4, $y \geqq y$. So, by induction according to 15.10,

$$\langle x, y\rangle \in {}^*\iota \ .\supset.\ x \geqq y.$$

This and (1) add up to 15.13.

15.14 $$\mathrm{N} = {}^*\iota``\{\Lambda\}.$$

Proof. By 12.3 and 15.13, N is $\{x\colon \langle x, \Lambda\rangle \in {}^*\iota\}$, q.e.d.
More specifically, indeed,

15.15 $$x \in \mathrm{N} \ .\supset.\ \langle x, \Lambda\rangle \in \iota^{|x}.$$

Proof. $\langle\{y\}, y\rangle \in \iota$. So

$$(y)(\langle y, \Lambda\rangle \in \iota^{|y} \ .\supset.\ \langle\{y\}, \Lambda\rangle \in \iota \mid \iota^{|y})$$

(by 14.6) $\supset.\ \langle\{y\}, \Lambda\rangle \in \iota^{|\{y\}}).$

Also, by 14.3, $\langle\Lambda, \Lambda\rangle \in \iota^{|\Lambda}$. So, by induction according to 13.9, we have 15.15.

The interlude on the ancestral is over, and we return to the theory of natural numbers, in which no use will be made of the ancestral.

16. Sum, product, power

Now to the definitions of sum, product, and power that were anticipated in §11.

16.1 '$\alpha + \beta$' for '$\iota^{|\beta}`\alpha$'.

16.2 '$\alpha\cdot\beta$' for '$(\lambda_x(\alpha + x))^{|\beta}`\Lambda$'.

16.3 'α^{β}' for '$(\lambda_x(\alpha\cdot x))^{|\beta}`\{\Lambda\}$'.

Since these expressions are all defined ultimately as singular descriptions, they come under the convenient practice that already holds for descriptions: free substitution for variables.

Now to disposing of the empty cases.

16.4 $$x \notin \mathrm{N} \;.\!\supset.\; \alpha + x = \alpha \cdot x = \alpha^{x} = \Lambda.$$

Proof. By hypothesis and 14.9 the three expressions as defined in 16.1–16.3 reduce respectively to:

$$\Lambda\text{‘}\alpha, \quad \Lambda\text{‘}\Lambda, \quad \Lambda\text{‘}\{\Lambda\}.$$

By 10.20, all are Λ.

Next we prove the familiar recursions.

16.5 $$x + \Lambda = x.$$

Proof. By 14.3 and 16.1, $x + \Lambda = I\text{‘}x = x$.

16.6 $$y \in \mathrm{N} \;.\!\supset.\; x + \{y\} = \{x + y\}.$$

Proof. From hypothesis and 10.27 we have by 14.11 that $\arg \iota^{|y} = \mathcal{V}$. So, by 10.18 and 10.26,

$$(\iota \mid \iota^{|y})\text{‘}x = \{\iota^{|y}\text{‘}x\}.$$

That is, by 14.6, $\iota^{|\{y\}}\text{‘}x = \{\iota^{|y}\text{‘}x\}$. That is, by 16.1, $x + \{y\} = \{x + y\}$.

16.7 $$x \cdot \Lambda = \Lambda.$$

Proof. By 14.3 and 16.2, $x \cdot \Lambda = I\text{‘}\Lambda = \Lambda$.

16.8 $$y \in \mathrm{N} \;.\!\supset.\; x \cdot \{y\} = x + x \cdot y.$$

Proof. Let $\alpha = \lambda_z(x + z)$. By 10.23, then, since $(z)(x + z \in \mathcal{V})$, $\arg \alpha = \mathcal{V}$. So, by 14.11, $\arg \alpha^{|y} = \mathcal{V}$. So $\Lambda \in \arg \alpha^{|y}$. So, by 10.18,

$$(\alpha \mid \alpha^{|y})\text{‘}\Lambda = \alpha\text{‘}(\alpha^{|y}\text{‘}\Lambda).$$

So, by 14.6, $\alpha^{|\{y\}|}`\Lambda = \alpha`(\alpha^{|y|}`\Lambda)$. That is, by 16.2, $x \cdot \{y\} = \alpha`(x \cdot y)$. That is, by 10.24, $x \cdot \{y\} = x + x \cdot y$.

16.9 $$x^{\Lambda} = \{\Lambda\}.$$

16.10 $$y \in \mathrm{N} \;.\supset.\; x^{\{y\}} = x \cdot x^{y}.$$

Proofs similar.

We see next that sums, products, and powers of natural numbers are natural numbers.

16.11 $$x \in \mathrm{N} \;.\supset.\; x + y \in \mathrm{N}.$$

Proof. By 12.15,

$$(z)(x + z \in \mathrm{N} \;.\supset.\; \{x + z\} \in \mathrm{N}).$$

So, by 16.6,

$$(z)(z,\, x + z \in \mathrm{N} \;.\supset.\; x + \{z\} \in \mathrm{N}).$$

Also, by hypothesis and 16.5, $x + \Lambda \in \mathrm{N}$. So we conclude by induction in the strong form 13.10 that, if $y \in \mathrm{N}$, $x + y \in \mathrm{N}$. But if $y \notin \mathrm{N}$ then $x + y = \Lambda$ by 16.4, so that again $x + y \in \mathrm{N}$.

16.12 $$x \in \mathrm{N} \;.\supset.\; x \cdot y \in \mathrm{N}.$$

Proof. Case 1: $y \notin \mathrm{N}$ or $y = \Lambda$. By 16.4 or 16.7, $x \cdot y = \Lambda$. So $x \cdot y \in \mathrm{N}$.

Case 2: $\Lambda \neq y \in \mathrm{N}$. By 12.16, $y = \{z\}$ for some z. By 13.19, $z \in \mathrm{N}$. So, by 16.8, $x \cdot y = x + x \cdot z$. But, by 16.11 and hypothesis, $x + x \cdot z \in \mathrm{N}$. So $x \cdot y \in \mathrm{N}$.

16.13 $$x \in \mathrm{N} \;.\supset.\; x^{y} \in \mathrm{N}.$$ *Proof* similar.

The next two theorems relate '$\leqq$' to '$+$'.

16.14 $$y \in \mathrm{N} \;.\supset.\; x \leqq x + y.$$

Proof. By 16.6,

$$z \in \mathrm{N} \mathbin{.\supset.} \{x + z\} = x + \{z\}$$

(by 12.6) $\qquad \supset. \; x + z \leqq x + \{z\}$

(by 12.5) $\qquad \supset: x \leqq x + z \mathbin{.\supset.} x \leqq x + \{z\}. \qquad (1)$

By 16.5 and 12.4, $x \leqq x + \Lambda$. From these two results and the hypothesis, we infer by induction according to 13.10 that $x \leqq x + y$.

16.15 $\qquad x \leqq y \mathbin{.\equiv} (\exists z)(z \in \mathrm{N} \,.\, x + z = y).$

Proof. By 16.6,

$$z \in \mathrm{N} \mathbin{.\supset.} x + \{z\} = \{x + z\}$$

$$\supset: x + z = w \mathbin{.\supset.} x + \{z\} = \{w\}.$$

So, by 12.15,

$$z \in \mathrm{N} \,.\, x + z = w \mathbin{.\supset.} \{z\} \in \mathrm{N} \,.\, x + \{z\} = \{w\}.$$

So

$$(w)((\exists z)(z \in \mathrm{N} \,.\, x + z = w) \supset (\exists z)(z \in \mathrm{N} \,.\, x + z = \{w\})).$$

Also, by 16.5 and 12.14,

$$(\exists z)(z \in \mathrm{N} \,.\, x + z = x).$$

From these two results it follows by induction according to 13.7 that

$$x \leqq y \mathbin{.\supset} (\exists z)(z \in \mathrm{N} \,.\, x + z = y).$$

Conversely, by 16.14, $z \in \mathrm{N} \mathbin{.\supset.} x \leqq x + z$ for any z, so that

$$(\exists z)(z \in \mathrm{N} \,.\, x + z = y) \supset. \; x \leqq y.$$

What is called *elementary number theory* comprises the theory that can be expressed using only the notations of zero, successor, sum, product, power, identity, the truth functions, and quantification over natural numbers. A shorter list would suffice; one can omit the first four items just now listed, or the first two and the fifth, and show how to paraphrase them in terms of the remainder. But the redundant list is a natural one in that the classical axiom system fits it pretty directly: the Peano axioms and the recursions for sum, product, and power. They are not a complete axiomatization; Gödel's celebrated discovery of 1931 was that elementary number theory admits no such. But they go a long way. The derivation of classical laws of elementary number theory from this standard basis is a standard business, and the remainder of the chapter will go mostly to illustrating it, now that the recursions as well as the Peano axioms are at hand among our theorems.

The range of our own variables of quantification of course goes beyond numbers, to which the variables of elementary number theory are limited. But we have the form of clause '$x \in \mathrm{N}$' by which to limit our variables where it matters. Since the only values of the variables that interest us in this section are natural numbers, I shall simplify the remaining proofs of the section by omitting clauses of the type '$x \in \mathrm{N}$', '$\{x\} \in \mathrm{N}$', '$x + y \in \mathrm{N}$', '$x \cdot y \in \mathrm{N}$', keeping them in the theorems but skipping them in proofs. I shall omit reference here to the laws 12.14, 12.15, 16.11, and 16.12 that deliver such clauses. Even when new variables are introduced in the course of a proof, I shall leave the '$\in \mathrm{N}$' condition tacit. The reader can easily fill in these missing details, and might profitably try it for drill.

In recounting the vocabulary of elementary number theory I omitted '$\leqq$' (and its derivatives '$<$', '$\geqq$', '$>$'). It is redundant, since '$(\exists z)(x + z = y)$' serves; cf. 16.15. Where it enters the ensuing specimens of standard procedure, its properties are got via 16.15 from those of '$+$'.

16.16 $\qquad x \in \mathrm{N} \;.\supset.\; \Lambda + x = x.$

Proof. By 16.6, $\Lambda + \{y\} = \{\Lambda + y\}$. So

$$\Lambda + y = y \;.\supset.\; \Lambda + \{y\} = \{y\}.$$

But also, by 16.5, $\Lambda + \Lambda = \Lambda$. So, by induction, $\Lambda + x = x$.

16.17 $\quad x, y \in \mathrm{N} \,.\supset.\, \{x\} + y = \{x + y\}$.

Proof. By 16.5, $x + \Lambda = x$ and $\{x\} + \Lambda = \{x\}$. So

$$\{x\} + \Lambda = \{x + \Lambda\}. \tag{1}$$

By 16.6, $x + \{z\} = \{x + z\}$. So

$$\begin{aligned}(z)(\{x\} + z = \{x + z\} \,.\supset.\, x + \{z\} &= \{x\} + z) \\ \supset.\, \{x + \{z\}\} &= \{\{x\} + z\}) \\ \text{(by 16.6)} \qquad &= \{x\} + \{z\}) \\ \supset.\, \{x\} + \{z\} &= \{x + \{z\}\}).\end{aligned}$$

From this and (1) we have by induction that $\{x\} + y = \{x + y\}$.

16.18 $\quad x, y \in \mathrm{N} \,.\supset.\, x + y = y + x$.

Proof. By 16.6 and 16.17, $x + \{z\} = \{x + z\}$ and $\{z\} + x = \{z + x\}$. So

$$x + z = z + x \,.\supset.\, x + \{z\} = \{z\} + x.$$

Also, by 16.16 and 16.5, $x + \Lambda = \Lambda + x$. So, by induction, $x + y = y + x$.

16.19 $\quad x, y, z \in \mathrm{N} \,.\supset.\, (x + y) + z = x + (y + z)$.

Proof. By 16.6,

$$(x + y) + \{w\} = \{(x + y) + w\}.$$

So

$$\begin{aligned}(x + y) + w = x + (y + w) \,.\supset.& \\ (x + y) + \{w\} &= \{x + (y + w)\} \\ \text{(by 16.6)} \qquad &= x + \{y + w\} \\ \text{(by 16.6)} \qquad &= x + (y + \{w\}).\end{aligned}$$

By 16.5, $(x + y) + \Lambda = x + y$ and $y + \Lambda = y$. So

$$(x + y) + \Lambda = x + (y + \Lambda).$$

From these two results we have by induction that

$$(x + y) + z = x + (y + z).$$

16.20 $x, y, z \in \mathrm{N} \,.\, x + z = y + z \,.\supset.\, x = y.$

Proof. By 7.7,

$$x + w = y + w \,.\equiv.\, \{x + w\} = \{y + w\}$$

(by 16.6) $\qquad \equiv.\, x + \{w\} = y + \{w\}.$

So

$$(w)(x + w \neq y + w \,.\supset.\, x + \{w\} \neq y + \{w\}).$$

From this and '$x + \Lambda \neq y + \Lambda$' it would follow by induction that $x + z \neq y + z$, contrary to hypothesis; so $x + \Lambda = y + \Lambda$, i.e., by 16.5, $x = y$.

16.21 $x, y \in \mathrm{N} \,.\, x + y = x \,.\supset.\, y = \Lambda.$

Proof. By hypothesis and 16.18, $y + x = x$. So, by 16.16, $y + x = \Lambda + x$. So, by 16.20, $y = \Lambda$.

16.22 $x, y \in \mathrm{N} \,.\, x + y = \Lambda \,.\supset.\, x = \Lambda.$

Proof. By hypothesis and 16.14, $x \leqq \Lambda$. So, by 12.17, $x = \Lambda$.

16.23 $\Lambda \cdot x = \Lambda.$

Proof. By 16.8 and 16.16, $\Lambda \cdot \{y\} = \Lambda \cdot y$. So $\Lambda \cdot y = \Lambda .\supset. \Lambda \cdot \{y\} = \Lambda$. By 16.7, $\Lambda \cdot \Lambda = \Lambda$. So, by 13.10, $x \in \mathrm{N} \,.\supset.\, \Lambda \cdot x = \Lambda$. So, by 16.4, $\Lambda \cdot x = \Lambda$.

16.24 $x, y \in \mathrm{N} \,.\supset.\, \{x\} \cdot y = x \cdot y + y.$

Proof. By 16.17,

$$\{x\} + (x{\cdot}z + z) = \{x + (x{\cdot}z + z)\}$$

(by 16.19) $$= \{(x + x{\cdot}z) + z\}$$

(by 16.6) $$= (x + x{\cdot}z) + \{z\}.$$

So

$$\{x\}{\cdot}z = x{\cdot}z + z \mathrel{.\supset.} \{x\} + \{x\}{\cdot}z = (x + x{\cdot}z) + \{z\}$$

(by 16.8) $$\supset. \{x\}{\cdot}\{z\} = x{\cdot}\{z\} + \{z\}. \qquad (1)$$

By 16.7, $\{x\}{\cdot}\Lambda = x{\cdot}\Lambda$. So, by 16.5, $\{x\}{\cdot}\Lambda = x{\cdot}\Lambda + \Lambda$. From this and (1) we infer by induction that $\{x\}{\cdot}y = x{\cdot}y + y$.

16.25 $$x \in \mathrm{N} \mathrel{.\supset.} \{\Lambda\}{\cdot}x = x.$$

Proof. By 16.24, $\{\Lambda\}{\cdot}x$ is $\Lambda{\cdot}x + x$, which, by 16.23 and 16.16, is x.

16.26 $$x, y \in \mathrm{N} \mathrel{.\supset.} x{\cdot}y = y{\cdot}x.$$

Proof. By 16.8 and 16.18, $x{\cdot}\{z\} = x{\cdot}z + x$. By 16.24, $\{z\}{\cdot}x = z{\cdot}x + x$. So

$$x{\cdot}z = z{\cdot}x \mathrel{.\supset.} x{\cdot}\{z\} = \{z\}{\cdot}x.$$

By 16.7 and 16.23, $x{\cdot}\Lambda = \Lambda{\cdot}x$. So, by induction, $x{\cdot}y = y{\cdot}x$.

16.27 $$x, y, z \in \mathrm{N} \mathrel{.\supset.} x{\cdot}(y + z) = x{\cdot}y + x{\cdot}z.$$

Proof.

$$w{\cdot}(y + z) = w{\cdot}y + w{\cdot}z \mathrel{.\supset.} w{\cdot}(y + z) + (y + z)$$

$$= (w{\cdot}y + w{\cdot}z) + (y + z)$$

(by 16.19, 16.18) $$= (w{\cdot}y + y) + (w{\cdot}z + z)$$

(by 16.24) $$\supset. \{w\}{\cdot}(y + z)$$

$$= \{w\}{\cdot}y + \{w\}{\cdot}z. \qquad (1)$$

By 16.5, $\Lambda = \Lambda + \Lambda$. So, by 16.23,

$$\Lambda \cdot (y + z) = \Lambda \cdot y + \Lambda \cdot z.$$

From this and (1) it follows by induction that

$$x \cdot (y + z) = x \cdot y + x \cdot z.$$

16.28 $\quad x, y, z \in \mathrm{N} \mathbin{.\supset.} (x \cdot y) \cdot z = x \cdot (y \cdot z).$

Proof. By 16.27 and 16.26,

$$(w \cdot y + y) \cdot z = (w \cdot y) \cdot z + y \cdot z.$$

So

$$(w \cdot y) \cdot z = w \cdot (y \cdot z) \mathbin{.\supset.} (w \cdot y + y) \cdot z = w \cdot (y \cdot z) + y \cdot z$$

(by 16.24) $\quad \supset. (\{w\} \cdot y) \cdot z = \{w\} \cdot (y \cdot z).$

Also, by 16.23,

$$(\Lambda \cdot y) \cdot z = \Lambda \cdot (y \cdot z).$$

So, by induction,

$$(x \cdot y) \cdot z = x \cdot (y \cdot z).$$

16.29 $\quad x, y \in \mathrm{N} \mathbin{.\supset:.} x \cdot y = \Lambda \mathbin{.\equiv:} x = \Lambda \mathbin{.\vee.} y = \Lambda.$

Proof. If $y = \{z\}$ for some z, then

$$x \cdot y = \Lambda \mathbin{.\supset.} x \cdot \{z\} = \Lambda$$

(by 16.8) $\quad \supset. x + x \cdot z = \Lambda$

(by 16.22) $\quad \supset. x = \Lambda.$

If on the other hand $y = \{z\}$ for no z, then, by 12.16, $y = \Lambda$. Conversely, $x = \Lambda \mathbin{.\supset.} x \cdot y = \Lambda$ by 16.23 and $y = \Lambda \mathbin{.\supset.} x \cdot y = \Lambda$ by 16.7.

16.30 $\quad x, y \in \mathrm{N} \mathbin{.} y \neq \Lambda \mathbin{.\supset.} x < x + y.$

Proof. By hypothesis and 16.21, $x + y \neq x$. But, by 16.14, $x \leqq x + y$. So, by 13.11, $x < x + y$.

16.31 $x, y, z \in \mathrm{N} \,.\, x \leqq y \,.\!\supset\!.\, x{\cdot}z \leqq y{\cdot}z.$

Proof. By 16.26 and 16.27,

$$(x + w){\cdot}z = x{\cdot}z + w{\cdot}z.$$

So

$$\begin{aligned}(\exists w)(x + w = y) &\supset (\exists w)(x{\cdot}z + w{\cdot}z = y{\cdot}z)\\ &\supset (\exists u)(x{\cdot}z + u = y{\cdot}z).\end{aligned}$$

So, by 16.15,

$$x \leqq y \,.\!\supset\!.\, x{\cdot}z \leqq y{\cdot}z.$$

16.32 $x, y, z \in \mathrm{N} \,.\, x{\cdot}z < y{\cdot}z \,.\!\supset\!.\, x < y.$

Proof. By 16.31 and 13.22,

$$\sim(x < y) \supset \sim(x{\cdot}z < y{\cdot}z).$$

16.33 $x, y, z \in \mathrm{N} \,.\, z \neq \Lambda \,.\, x < y \,.\!\supset\!.\, x{\cdot}z < y{\cdot}z.$

Proof. By last hypothesis and definition, $\{x\} \leqq y$. So, by 16.31, $\{x\}{\cdot}z \leqq y{\cdot}z$. But also, by hypothesis and 16.30, $x{\cdot}z < x{\cdot}z + z$, i.e., by 16.24, $x{\cdot}z < \{x\}{\cdot}z$. So, by 12.8, $x{\cdot}z < y{\cdot}z$.

16.34 $x, y \in \mathrm{N} \,.\, x{\cdot}x < y{\cdot}y \,.\!\supset\!.\, x < y.$

Proof. By 16.31 and 16.26,

$$y \leqq x \,.\!\supset\!.\, y{\cdot}y \leqq x{\cdot}y \leqq x{\cdot}x.$$

So, by 13.22,

$$\sim(x < y) \supset \sim(x{\cdot}x < y{\cdot}y).$$

For an exercise the reader might try his hand at the laws of exponents:

$$x^{y+z} = x^y{\cdot}x^z, \qquad x^{y\cdot z} = (x^y)^z.$$

PART TWO

HIGHER FORMS OF NUMBER

VI | REAL NUMBERS

17. Program. Numerical pairs

We have seen how the notation of the theory of classes suffices for the arithmetic of natural numbers. It also suffices for the further sorts of numbers. Let us turn our consideration to ratios (excluding, for present convenience, negative ones).

The use of ratios to express proportion between natural numbers does not require us to recognize ratios as additional objects at all. To say that x is u/v of y, or that $x/y = u/v$, is simply to say what can be said within natural number theory thus: $x \cdot v = y \cdot u$. To say that $x/y < u/v$, again, is merely to say that $x \cdot v < y \cdot u$. Indeed we can even express proportion *between* ratios within natural number theory; for, to say that x/z is u/v of y/w is merely to say that $x \cdot v \cdot w = y \cdot u \cdot z$. Nor are matters altered when addition and multiplication are extended to ratios; for, '$(x/z) \cdot (y/w)$' and '$(x/z) + (y/w)$' are merely variant ways of writing '$(x \cdot y)/(z \cdot w)$' and '$(x \cdot w + z \cdot y)/(z \cdot w)$'. Thus far a virtual theory of ratios, reducing to a real theory of natural numbers, is sufficient.

Exponentiation of ratios is a very different thing. There is no easy dismissal of $(u/v)^{z/w}$. But here the difficulty is that we are carried beyond the rational domain (for most choices of natural numbers u, v, z, w) and into irrational numbers.

As long as we move merely from natural numbers to ratios, our move is one that can be explained away as the merest stylistic variation. It is when we proceed to take in the real numbers generally, thus interlarding the ratios with irrationals, that there arises a serious question what sort of things all these numbers are to be. Let us consider first what serial structure this interlarding of irrationals is supposed to achieve.

A number is an (upper) *bound* of a class α of numbers if no member of α exceeds it. It may or may not be a member of α; if it is, it is of course the highest. A class of real numbers may be at once bounded and infinite; an example is the class of the ratios between 1/3 and 2/3, for it has infinitely many ratios and yet is bounded, e.g., by 3/4. There is, moreover, a least ratio that bounds it: 2/3. Next consider the class rather of those ratios whose squares are less than 2; this class again has bounds, e.g. 3/2, but it has no ratio as its least bound. There is no least ratio x/y whose square $(x \cdot x)/(y \cdot y)$ exceeds 2, nor any greatest whose square does not. Now what distinguishes the full domain of reals from that of just the ratios is that the various least bounds that are missing from the domain of ratios—the so-called irrational numbers—are thrown in. For instance, whereas the class of ratios whose squares are less than 2 was seen to have no rational least bound, it has an irrational one: $\sqrt{2}$. In general,

(i) For each class of ratios that is bounded by ratios at all there is a real number that is its least bound.

There is, as remarked, little purpose in objectifying ratios save as a step toward construing real numbers in general. Let us then seek a version of ratios which invites interpolation of irrationals as required by (i).

It would be unsatisfactory to construe a ratio x/y in general simply as $\langle x, y\rangle$, since we want $2/3 = 4/6$, whereas $\langle 2, 3\rangle \neq \langle 4, 6\rangle$. We could accommodate this point by taking the ratio always as the corresponding ordered pair "in lowest terms": thus

$$2/3 = 4/6 = \langle 2, 3\rangle \neq \langle 4, 6\rangle.$$

Another way would be to take 2/3 as the class of all the pairs $\langle 2, 3\rangle$, $\langle 4, 6\rangle$, $\langle 6, 9\rangle$, etc.; this would mean defining x/y in general as

$$\{\langle z, w\rangle : z, w \in \mathrm{N} \,.\, x \cdot w = z \cdot y\}.$$

Such was Peano's version (1901). But neither of these versions prepares the way for any very natural interpolation of irrationals.

A further evident fault of these versions is that they distinguish $x/1$ from x. But it is convenient and customary in foundational studies to acquiesce in this inelegance, thus accepting an artificial distinction between the natural numbers and the corresponding integral ratios.

The desideratum of preparing the way for interpolation of irrationals, however, does favor a third version of x/y, namely:

$$\{\langle z, w\rangle : z, w \in \mathrm{N} \,.\, z \cdot y < x \cdot w\}.$$

Under this version—to put it intuitively in a circular way—x/y is the class of those pairs of natural numbers z and w such that $z/w < x/y$. In particular the ratio $0/1$ becomes Λ, hence 0 indeed; while the ratio one or $1/1$ turns out to be the relation of less to greater among natural numbers.

That this version of ratios is congenial to interpolation of irrationals can be sensed as follows. Just as x/y comprises the pairs $\langle z, w\rangle$ such that $z/w < x/y$, so we may fit $\sqrt{2}$ in as comprising the pairs $\langle z, w\rangle$ such that $z/w < \sqrt{2}$. This characterization decircularizes to:

$$\sqrt{2} = \{\langle z, w\rangle : z, w \in \mathrm{N} \,.\, z^2 < 2w^2\}.$$

The pairs of natural numbers can be pictured as intersections in a grid covering a quadrant of the plane. The pair $\langle x, y\rangle$ is x places over and y places down. Then x/y, as we are now construing it, is the class of all intersections falling beneath ("southwest of") the ray that runs from the origin $\langle 0, 0\rangle$ through $\langle x, y\rangle$. Thus $\frac{2}{3}$ is the class of all intersections beneath the ray shown in the diagram. Irrational numbers are marked off by rays in the same way, but by rays that miss all intersections other than the origin.

The ratios (except 0) and the irrational numbers, so conceived, are infinite classes of ordered pairs of natural numbers. We may therefore count on having, somewhere along the way, to add some appropriate existence axioms; for our axioms up to now give only finite classes. Actually there is a way of readjusting our

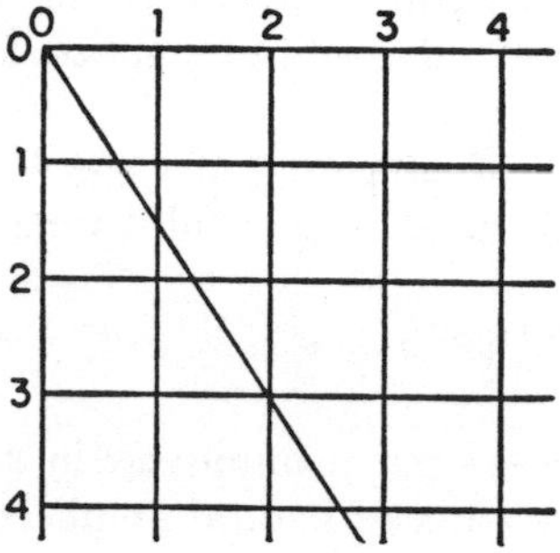

contemplated definitions that will superficially simplify these further existence requirements a bit, though not rendering them finite. Namely, we can reconstrue the ratios and irrationals as classes simply of natural numbers, rather than of pairs of natural numbers. For the ordered pairs of natural numbers can be unequivocally represented by single natural numbers, $x + (x + y)^2$ representing $\langle x, y\rangle$.

That this is an adequate way of representing pairs of natural numbers is seen by reflecting that, where z is a natural number, we can uniquely recover the respective natural numbers x and y (if such there be) such that $z = x + (x + y)^2$. For $(x + y)^2$ is the largest square $\leqq z$; x is z minus that square; and y is the root of that square minus x.

Let us utilize the nineteenth-century ordered-pair notation, '$x;y$', to refer to the corresponding number $x + (x + y)^2$. Thus

17.1 '$\alpha;\beta$' for '$\alpha + (\alpha + \beta)\cdot(\alpha + \beta)$'.

That this arithmetical function serves the purpose of the ordered pair, so far as natural numbers are concerned, is the content of the next two theorems.

17.2 $x, y, z, w \in \mathrm{N} \,.\, x;y = z;w \,.\!\supset\!.\, x = z \,.\, y = w.$

Proof. By 10.26, $\Lambda \neq \{x + y\}$. So, by 16.30,

$$
\begin{aligned}
& & x;y &< x;y + \{x + y\} \\
&\text{(by 16.14)} & &\leqq (x;y + \{x + y\}) + y \\
&\text{(by 17.1)} & &= ((x + (x + y)\cdot(x + y)) + \{x + y\}) + y \\
&\text{(by 16.18, 16.19)} & &= \{x + y\} + ((x + y) + (x + y)\cdot(x + y)) \\
&\text{(by 16.8)} & &= \{x + y\} + (x + y)\cdot\{x + y\} \\
&\text{(by 16.26, 16.8)} & &= \{x + y\}\cdot\{x + y\}. \qquad (1)
\end{aligned}
$$

By 16.14 and 17.1, $(z + w)\cdot(z + w) \leqq z;w$. So

$$
\begin{aligned}
& & x;y = z;w \,.\!\supset\!.\, (z + w)\cdot(z + w) &\leqq x;y \\
&\text{(by (1))} & &< \{x + y\}\cdot\{x + y\} \\
&\text{(by 16.34)} & \supset.\, z + w &< \{x + y\} \\
&\text{(by 13.12)} & \supset.\, z + w &\leqq x + y.
\end{aligned}
$$

Similarly

$$z;w = x;y \,.\!\supset\!.\, x + y \leqq z + w.$$

So, combining,

$$
\begin{aligned}
& & x;y = z;w \,.\!\supset\!.\, & x + y \leqq z + w \leqq x + y \\
&\text{(by 13.21)} & \supset.\, & x + y = z + w \qquad (2) \\
&\text{(by 17.1)} & \supset.\, & z;w = z + (x + y)\cdot(x + y).
\end{aligned}
$$

But then

$$
\begin{aligned}
& x;y = z;w \,.\!\supset\!.\, x;y = z + (x + y)\cdot(x + y) \\
&\text{(by 17.1)} \quad \supset.\, x + (x + y)\cdot(x + y) = z + (x + y)\cdot(x + y) \\
&\text{(by 16.20)} \quad \supset.\, x = z.
\end{aligned}
$$

But then, by (2),

$$x;y = z;w \,.\!\supset.\; x + y = x + w$$

(by 16.18, 16.20) $\supset.\; y = w.$

17.3 $x, y, z, w \in \mathrm{N} \,.\!\supset\!: x;y = z;w \,.\!\equiv.\; x = z \,.\, y = w.$

Proof evident from 17.2.

Corresponding to the law of concretion for relations, 9.5, we have now:

17.4 $z, w \in \mathrm{N} \,.\!\supset\!: z;w \in \{x;y\colon x, y \in \mathrm{N} \,.\, Fxy\} \,.\!\equiv Fzw.$

Proof. By 9.4,

$z;w \in \{x;y\colon x, y \in \mathrm{N} \,.\, Fxy\}$

$.\!\equiv\; (\exists x)(\exists y)(x, y \in \mathrm{N} \,.\, Fxy \,.\, z;w = x;y)$

(by hyp. and 17.3) $\equiv\; (\exists x)(\exists y)(x, y \in \mathrm{N} \,.\, Fxy \,.\, z = x \,.\, w = y)$

(by 6.1) $\equiv.\; z, w \in \mathrm{N} \,.\, Fzw$

(by hypothesis) $\equiv\; Fzw.$

18. Ratios and reals construed

Thus armed, let us return to x/y. We can now define it as a class directly of natural numbers:

18.1 'α/β' for '$\{z;w\colon z, w \in \mathrm{N} \,.\, z{\cdot}\beta < \alpha{\cdot}w\}$'.

From this definition and 17.4 we have that

18.2 $z, w \in \mathrm{N} \,.\!\supset\!: z;w \in x/y \,.\!\equiv.\; z{\cdot}y < x{\cdot}w.$

It follows that

18.3 $x, y \in \mathrm{N} \,.\!\supset.\; x;y \notin x/y.$

Proof. By hypothesis, 16.12, and 13.20, $\sim(x{\cdot}y < x{\cdot}y)$. So, by hypothesis and 18.2, $x;y \notin x/y$.

Our diagrammatic representation of ratios and irrational numbers stands unchanged, except that we now cease to see the intersections as ordered pairs $\langle x, y\rangle$ and come to see them as the corresponding natural numbers $x;y$. Natural numbers are now assigned to the vertical and horizontal lines of the grid *and* to their intersections; see the diagram. Thus $\frac{2}{3}$ is now the class whose members are 1, 4, 9, 10, 16, 17, 25, 26, 36, 37, 38, 49, etc.

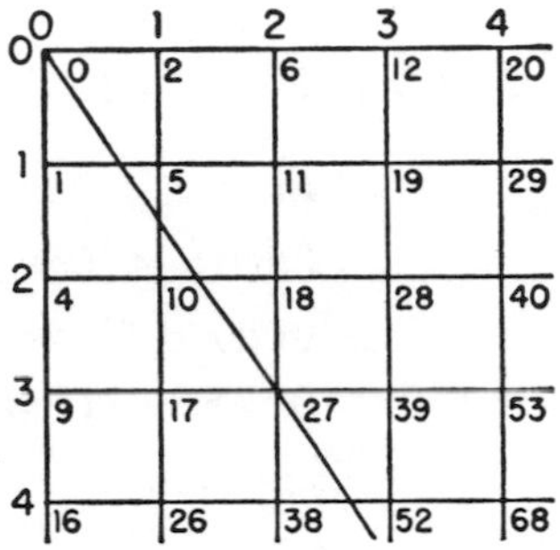

Ratios, and indeed real numbers generally as we are construing them, are clearly *nested* classes: each is a subclass of each further one. The connective '$\subseteq$' itself serves the purpose, among our real numbers, of the classical '$\leqq$'. We must remember that the sign '$\leqq$' as we have defined it orders the natural numbers and not the reals (or ratios). We defined it indeed not just for natural numbers but quite generally, in effect as $*\iota$; but it is only among the natural numbers, and not the reals, that $*\iota$ does the work of the classical '$\leqq$'. And it is among the reals, not the natural numbers, that '$\subseteq$' does the work of the classical '$\leqq$'.

The classical law:

$$x, y, z, w \in \mathrm{N} \,.\, w \neq 0 \,.\!\supset\!:\, x/y \leqq z/w \,.\!\equiv\!.\, x \cdot w \leqq z \cdot y$$

is therefore reflected in the following theorems, which serve to coordinate the ordering of the real numbers with that of the natural numbers.

18.4 $\quad x, y, z, w \in \mathrm{N} \,.\, x/y \subseteq z/w \,.\!\supset\!.\, x \cdot w \leqq z \cdot y.$

Proof. By 18.3, $z;w \notin z/w$. But, by hypothesis, $x/y \subseteq z/w$. So

$z;w \notin x/y$. So, by 18.2, $\sim(z \cdot y < x \cdot w)$. So, by 13.22, $x \cdot w \leqq z \cdot y$.

18.5 $x, y, z, w \in \mathrm{N} \,.\, w \neq \Lambda \,.\, x \cdot w \leqq z \cdot y \;.\supset.\; x/y \subseteq z/w.$

Proof. By hypotheses and 16.31, for any $v \in \mathrm{N}$,

$$(x \cdot w) \cdot v \leqq (z \cdot y) \cdot v. \tag{1}$$

By hypotheses and 16.33, for any $u, v \in \mathrm{N}$,

$$u \cdot y < x \cdot v \;.\supset.\; (u \cdot y) \cdot w < (x \cdot v) \cdot w$$

(by 16.28, 16.26) $\supset.\; (u \cdot w) \cdot y < (x \cdot w) \cdot v$

(by (1), 12.8) $\supset.\; (u \cdot w) \cdot y < (z \cdot y) \cdot v$

(by 16.28, 16.26) $\supset.\; (u \cdot w) \cdot y < (z \cdot v) \cdot y$

(by 16.32) $\supset.\; u \cdot w < z \cdot v.$

So, by 18.2,

$$u;v \in x/y \;.\supset.\; u;v \in z/w.$$

But, by 18.1, any member of x/y is $u;v$ for some $u, v \in \mathrm{N}$. So $x/y \subseteq z/w$.

We could use '$z \neq \Lambda$' instead of '$w \neq \Lambda$' in 18.5. I.e.,

18.6 $x, y, z, w \in \mathrm{N} \,.\, z \neq \Lambda \,.\, x \cdot w \leqq z \cdot y \;.\supset.\; x/y \subseteq z/w.$

Proof. If $w \neq \Lambda$, 18.5 serves; so suppose $w = \Lambda$. By 12.18,

$$u \cdot y < x \cdot v \;.\supset.\; x \cdot v \neq \Lambda$$

(by 16.7) $\supset.\; v \neq \Lambda$

(by hyp., 16.29) $\supset.\; z \cdot v \neq \Lambda$

(by 13.16) $\supset.\; \Lambda < z \cdot v$

(by 16.7) $\supset.\; u \cdot \Lambda < z \cdot v$

(since $w = \Lambda$) $\supset.\; u \cdot w < z \cdot v.$

The proof concludes like that of 18.5.

Combining 18.4–18.6,

18.7 $x, y, z, w \in \mathrm{N} \,.\, {\sim}(z = w = \Lambda) \,.\!\supset\!:\, x/y \subseteq z/w$
$.\!\equiv\!.\; x{\cdot}w \leqq z{\cdot}y.$

Thence in turn we have the corollary.

18.8 $x, y, z, w \in \mathrm{N} \,.\, {\sim}(z = w = \Lambda) \,.\!\supset\!:\, x/y \subseteq z/w$
$.\!\equiv\!.\; z;w \notin x/y.$

Proof. By hypothesis and 18.7,

$$x/y \subseteq z/w \;.\!\equiv\!.\; x{\cdot}w \leqq z{\cdot}y$$

(by 13.22) $\equiv \; {\sim}(z{\cdot}y < x{\cdot}w)$

(by 18.2) $\equiv. \; z;w \notin x/y.$

As remarked, the integral ratios are in general distinct from the corresponding natural numbers. The integral ratio is $x/1$, or $x/\{\Lambda\}$, where the natural number is x. Coincidence occurs only at 0; we readily see from 18.1 that $0/1$, or $\Lambda/\{\Lambda\}$, is simply Λ, or 0. Indeed, it is clear from 18.1 that $\Lambda/x = \Lambda$ for every natural number x, even Λ, and that $x/\Lambda = \{\Lambda\}/\Lambda$ only for natural numbers $x \neq \Lambda$. Thus the traditionally enigmatic $0/0$ happens on our constructions to come out 0. In terms of the grid, $0/1$ or Λ comprises the intersections left of the vertical ray, hence none, while at the other extreme $1/0$ or $\{\Lambda\}/\Lambda$ comprises all the intersections below the horizontal ray, hence all intersections except those at the top edge. This last remark is the burden of the following theorem.

18.9 $\{\Lambda\}/\Lambda = \{x;y\colon x, y \in \mathrm{N} \,.\, y \neq \Lambda\}.$

Proof. By 16.7 and 16.25,

$$x{\cdot}\Lambda < \{\Lambda\}{\cdot}y \;.\!\equiv\!.\; \Lambda < y.$$

So, by 13.17,

$$y \in \mathrm{N} \,.\!\supset\!:\, x{\cdot}\Lambda < \{\Lambda\}{\cdot}y \;.\!\equiv\!.\; y \neq \Lambda.$$

So by 18.1 we get our theorem.

But when we define the class of ratios we make the standard exception of 1/0, thus:

18.10 'Rat' for '$\{x/y\colon x, y \in \mathrm{N} \,.\, y \neq \Lambda\}$'.

That 1/0 is thereby excluded takes still a bit of proving, thus:

18.11 $\{\Lambda\}/\Lambda \notin \mathrm{Rat}$.

Proof. Suppose that $\{\Lambda\}/\Lambda \in \mathrm{Rat}$. Then, by 18.10, there are $x, y \in \mathrm{N}$ such that $y \neq \Lambda$ and $x/y = \{\Lambda\}/\Lambda$. But then $\{\Lambda\}/\Lambda \subseteq x/y$ and so, by 18.7, $\{\Lambda\}\cdot y \leqq x\cdot\Lambda$, i.e., by 16.7 and 16.25, $y \leqq \Lambda$, i.e., by 12.17, $y = \Lambda$, a contradiction.

The real numbers, next, were to comprise the ratios and, in addition, the least bounds of bounded classes of ratios (cf. §17). But this phrasing is redundant; any ratio w is itself the least bound of a bounded class, viz. $\{w\}$, of ratios. So we may say simply that the real numbers are to be the least bounds of the bounded classes of ratios. Now an explicit formulation of this lies ready to hand. Since '$\subseteq$' is playing the role of the classical '$\leqq$' for real numbers, a bound of a class z of ratios is describable simply as any y such that

$$(x)(x \in z \,.\supset.\, x \subseteq y),$$

or, in short, such that $\mathsf{U}z \subseteq y$ (cf. 8.5). Hence in particular $\mathsf{U}z$ is itself a bound of z, and, being $\subseteq$ each bound, it is the least. So a real number is to be anything that is $\mathsf{U}z$ for some $z \subseteq \mathrm{Rat}$ that is bounded by some ratio. Now for z to be bounded by some ratio is for there to be some ratio x/y such that

$$(v)(v \in z \,.\supset.\, v \subseteq x/y),$$

i.e., by 18.8, such that

$$(v)(v \in z \,.\supset.\, x;y \notin v),$$

i.e., such that $x;y \notin \mathsf{U}z$. It merely excludes the case where $\mathsf{U}z$ contains $x;y$ for *all* ratios x/y—the case, in short, where $\mathsf{U}z$ is

$\{\Lambda\}/\Lambda$ (cf. 18.9). So

18.12 'Real' for '$\{\mathsf{U}z\colon z \subseteq \text{Rat}\} \cap {}^{-}\{\{\Lambda\}/\Lambda\}$'.

A step in the reasoning that just now brought us to 18.12 was the recognition that ratios would count as reals without special provision. Let us make a theorem of this.

18.13 $\text{Rat} \subseteq \text{Real}$.

Proof. Consider any $u \in \text{Rat}$. Then $\{u\} \subseteq \text{Rat}$; further, by 8.2, $u = \mathsf{U}\{u\}$; so $u \in \{\mathsf{U}z\colon z \subseteq \text{Rat}\}$. Further, by 18.11, $u \neq \{\Lambda\}/\Lambda$. So, by 18.12, $u \in \text{Real}$.

The basic idea underlying my version of real numbers goes back to Dedekind, who in 1872 pointed out how each real number corresponds to a certain *cut* in the series of ratios: a cut separating the ratios that are less than the real number from those that are not. Looking just to the respective classes of ratios below the several cuts and not to the cuts as such, we get each real into correlation with a certain class of ratios: a class that is *solid* in the sense of containing all ratios that are less than members, and *open* in the sense of having no highest member, and *inexhaustive* of the ratios.

Whitehead and Russell (*310, *314) systematically developed two versions of the real numbers. In one version the real numbers were identified with these last-mentioned classes of ratios. Thus each real number x became, intuitively speaking, the class z of all ratios $< x$. In the other version x became rather $\mathsf{U}z$: thus, intuitively speaking, the union of all ratios $< x$. So my version of real numbers follows this second version of Whitehead and Russell's in an important particular: reals are on a par with ratios, they are not classes of ratios but unions of ratios, they are classes of the things that ratios are classes of. Still my version differs from even the second Whitehead-Russell version in another important particular: for me the ratios are themselves real numbers, for Whitehead and Russell not. The reason not is that Whitehead and Russell's ratios were still mutually exclusive, like Peano's (cf. §17), whereas their real numbers were nested.

For me, as in general for writers on these matters, the natural numbers are not integral ratios; they are only aped by the integral ratios. For Whitehead and Russell, similarly, in either of their versions, the ratios are not rational reals; they are only aped by the rational reals. For me, on the other hand, the ratios are reals. And the essential reason, in the terms of the above historical sketch, is just that I contrived to construct the reals of Whitehead and Russell's second version without using the name and notation of ratios, and so could reserve that name and notation to the rational reals themselves.

In an effort to clarify this historical relationship I have slurred over differences. One is that Whitehead and Russell's ratios were relations not between numbers, as Peano's were, but between relations. Another is my use of numbers $x;y$ instead of pairs $\langle x, y\rangle$, so as to get real numbers down to the category of classes of natural numbers.[1] The two important points of theory that this move illustrates come down from Cantor: that the real numbers can be correlated with classes of natural numbers and that the pairs of natural numbers can be correlated with natural numbers.

19. Existential needs. Operations and extensions

In §17 we noted a law (i) of least bound, whose realization was a primary purpose of developing a concept of real number. Our eventual definition 18.12 of real number may seem to have accomplished that purpose, for we saw that 18.12 makes everything a real number that either is a ratio or is the least bound $\mathsf{U}z$ of some class z of ratios that is bounded by some ratio. Actually this is not enough to assure (i) of §17, for we have no assurance that $\mathsf{U}z$ exists for every such z. This existence assumption is the residual content of (i) of §17, and I shall so number it anew:

(i) $$z \subseteq \text{Rat} \,.\, \mathsf{U}z \neq \{\Lambda\}/\Lambda \,.\supset.\, \mathsf{U}z \in \mathcal{V}.$$

[1] My version of the ratios and reals appeared in "Element and number," §4, footnote, without this feature.

It has to be added as a comprehension axiom or covered by broader comprehension axioms if the classical theory of real numbers is to be obtained on the basis of our definitions. Alternative definitions are known, but I know none that enable us to obtain the classical theory from palpably weaker existence assumptions.

Actually (i) of itself is compatible with there being nothing beyond the finite classes that we have already posited in our axiom 7.10 and our axiom schema 13.1. For any ratio x/y is an infinite class of natural numbers, except where x is Λ, in which case x/y is Λ. So, if there are only finite classes, Rat $= \{\Lambda\}$. But then, for all $z \subseteq$ Rat, $\cup z = \Lambda$ and so $\cup z \in \mathcal{V}$, in fulfillment of (i).

This reflection, however, is less a reassurance than a reminder that for purposes of a satisfactory theory of real numbers we need another existence assumption over and above (i). We need also to provide for the existence of every ratio x/y, thus:

(ii) $$x, y \in \mathrm{N} \,.\, y \neq \Lambda \,.\!\supset\!.\, x/y \in \mathcal{V}.$$

This does assert the existence of infinite classes; and (i), when supported by (ii), then asserts the existence of further infinite classes. (ii) asserts the existence of all ratios in the sense of 18.1, and so makes Rat as of 18.10 the class of all such ratios, which it would not otherwise be. Then (i) goes on to assert the existence also of all the irrationals, and so makes Real as of 18.12 the class really of all the real numbers. The law of least bound is simply the law of existence of all irrationals, when supported by (ii). Of course there is no presumption, even granted (ii) and (i), that Rat $\in \mathcal{V}$ or Real $\in \mathcal{V}$.

I am not yet declaring (i) and (ii) as axioms. I exhibit them only as laws that we would want ultimately to provide for.

The classical theory of real numbers includes a law of least bounds that is yet more general than (i). It speaks of classes not just of ratios but of reals generally, thus:

> For each class of real numbers that is bounded by a ratio at all there is a real number that is its least bound.

In lieu then of (i) we should have:

$$\text{(iii)} \qquad z \subseteq \text{Real} \,.\, \mathsf{U}z \neq \{\Lambda\}/\Lambda \,.\!\supset\!.\, \mathsf{U}z \in \mathcal{V}.$$

It is usual to remark that this version of the law of least bound adds nothing to the other. The reason given is that the least bound of any class of real numbers is at the same time the least bound of a class purely of ratios. In fact we can prove, independently of (i) or (ii) or other special assumptions, that

$$\textbf{19.1} \qquad \alpha \subseteq \text{Real} \,.\!\supset\!.\, \mathsf{U}\alpha = \mathsf{U}(\text{Rat} \cap \{w\colon w \subseteq \mathsf{U}\alpha\}).$$

Proof. By definition of $\mathsf{U}\alpha$,

$$
\begin{array}{lrl}
 & x \in \mathsf{U}\alpha \,.\!\supset & (\exists u)(x \in u \in \alpha) \\
\text{(by hypothesis)} & \supset & (\exists u)(x \in u \in \alpha \,.\, u \in \text{Real}) \\
\text{(by 18.12)} & \supset & (\exists z)(x \in \mathsf{U}z \in \alpha \,.\, z \subseteq \text{Rat}) \\
\text{(by def. of } \mathsf{U}z\text{)} & \supset & (\exists z)(\exists w)(x \in w \in z \subseteq \text{Rat} \,.\, \mathsf{U}z \in \alpha) \\
\text{(by 8.6)} & \supset & (\exists z)(\exists w)(x \in w \subseteq \mathsf{U}z \subseteq \mathsf{U}\alpha \,.\, w \in \text{Rat}) \\
 & \supset & (\exists w)(x \in w \subseteq \mathsf{U}\alpha \,.\, w \in \text{Rat}) \\
\text{(by def. of `}\mathsf{U}\text{')} & \supset. & x \in \mathsf{U}(\text{Rat} \cap \{w\colon w \subseteq \mathsf{U}\alpha\}).
\end{array}
$$

Conversely, by definition of 'U',

$$
\begin{array}{rl}
x \in \mathsf{U}(\text{Rat} \cap \{w\colon w \subseteq \mathsf{U}\alpha\}) \,.\!\supset & (\exists w)(x \in w \subseteq \mathsf{U}\alpha) \\
\supset. & x \in \mathsf{U}\alpha.
\end{array}
$$

The classical point is, in short, that classes of real numbers determine no limits, or least bounds, not already determined by the classes of ratios.

But actually (i) is not known to imply (iii), despite 19.1. How would we argue (iii) from (i) and 19.1? We would begin by substituting 'Rat $\cap \{w\colon w \subseteq \mathsf{U}z\}$' for '$z$' in (i). But this substitution presupposes that

$$\text{(iv)} \qquad \text{Rat} \cap \{w\colon w \subseteq \mathsf{U}z\} \in \mathcal{V},$$

at least for all z fulfilling the antecedent of (iii).

Instead of supplementing (i) with (iv) to secure (iii), it is more to the point to fix upon (iii) in the first place in lieu of (i). Obviously (iii) implies (i), in view of 18.13.

Another way of securing (iii) is by adopting, in lieu of the sentence (i), the corresponding schema:

(v) $$\alpha \subseteq \mathrm{Rat} \,.\, \mathsf{U}\alpha \neq \{\Lambda\}/\Lambda \;.\supset.\; \mathsf{U}\alpha \in \mathcal{V}.$$

For we can make our desired substitution on 'α' here without regard to existence, and so derive (iii) without benefit of (iv).

So an eventual set of comprehension axioms adequate to the theory of real numbers as we have defined them must either include (ii) and (iii) or imply them as theorems; and one way in which they can provide them as theorems is by providing (ii) as a theorem and (v) as a theorem schema.

Comparison of the schema (v) with the sentence (i) suggests, by analogy, the further schema:

(vi) $$\alpha \subseteq \mathrm{Real} \,.\, \mathsf{U}\alpha \neq \{\Lambda\}/\Lambda \;.\supset.\; \mathsf{U}\alpha \in \mathcal{V},$$

which is related to the sentence (iii) as (v) is related to (i). This, however, adds nothing to (v). Substitution in (v) gives:

$$\mathsf{U}(\mathrm{Rat} \cap \{w\colon w \subseteq \mathsf{U}\alpha\}) \neq \{\Lambda\}/\Lambda \;.\supset.\; \mathsf{U}(\mathrm{Rat} \cap \{w\colon w \subseteq \mathsf{U}\alpha\}) \in \mathcal{V},$$

whence, by 19.1, we have (vi).

So just the two types of eventual provision for the theory of real numbers emerge: strong provision, affording (ii) and (v) and therewith implicitly (vi), and weak provision, affording (ii) and (iii).

All these—(ii), (iii), (v), and their consequences—affirm the existence only of subclasses of N. So these needs could be met by assuming simply that $\alpha \subseteq \mathrm{N} \;.\supset.\; \alpha \in \mathcal{V}$, or indeed

(vii) $$\alpha \subset \mathrm{N} \;.\supset.\; \alpha \in \mathcal{V}.$$

But this is stronger than necessary for (ii) and (v), let alone (iii).

What is achieved by interlarding the series of ratios with the least bounds is called *continuity*. The original weaker property is called *density*: the property merely of there being always further numbers between any two. In general a relation x, e.g. that of less to greater among the ratios or the reals, is called dense if $x \subseteq x \mid x$. It is called continuous if, further, every class that has a bound (with respect to the ordering x) has one that is least (with respect to x). So the relation of less to greater among reals is continuous, but not when limited to the ratios. The real numbers are said to constitute a *continuum*.

A word follows on sums and products. These and power were defined in 16.1–16.3 for purposes of natural numbers. The definitions made sense also as applied to things other than natural numbers, but trivial sense; they gave Λ (cf. 16.4). The three operations need of course to be defined anew for real numbers, and, in principle if not in practice, should be rendered by signs distinct from those expressing the corresponding operations on natural numbers. Temporarily let us then write '$x \oplus y$' and '$x \odot y$' for the sum and product of x and y in the senses appropriate to real numbers. I shall pursue the subject only long enough to show how to define these.

Where the real numbers x and y happen both to be ratios, h/k and m/n, there is no difficulty; we know that $x \oplus y$ and $x \odot y$ in the desired senses are $(h \cdot n + m \cdot k)/(k \cdot n)$ and $(h \cdot m)/(k \cdot n)$. But now consider the general case, where x or y may be irrational. Let us first address the problem of $x \odot y$. We want $x \odot y$ to be the class of all natural numbers $z;w$ such that, intuitively speaking, z/w is less than $x \odot y$ (cf. 18.8). But z/w will be thus, in classical arithmetic, just in case z/w can itself be expressed as a product of ratios h/k and m/n which are less respectively than x and y. But h/k is less than x just in case $h;k \in x$; correspondingly for m/n; and their product is, we saw, $(h \cdot m)/(k \cdot n)$. So we may define $x \odot y$ as

$$\{(h \cdot m);(k \cdot n) \colon h, k, m, n \in \mathrm{N} \,.\, h;k \in x \,.\, m;n \in y\}.$$

Parallel reasoning issues in definition of $x \oplus y$ as

$$\{(h \cdot n + m \cdot k);(k \cdot n) \colon h, k, m, n \in \mathrm{N} \,.\, h;k \in x \,.\, m;n \in y\},$$

except that this version breaks down where x or y is 0/1, or Λ. For, where x or y is Λ, obviously this version reduces irretrievably to Λ, whereas what we want is that $x \oplus \Lambda = x$ and $\Lambda \oplus y = y$. However, these cases can be accommodated by appending '$\cup x \cup y$' to the above formulation; this emendation saves the two wayward cases and has no effect on other cases.

We have provided a *model* of arithmetic in set theory when we have provided a way of so reinterpreting arithmetical notations in set-theoretic terms as to carry the truths of arithmetic into truths of set theory. Now what more than such formal simulation is demanded in actually *reducing* numbers to set theory? Seemingly there is also a question of their application; thus, in the case of natural numbers, class measurement. But we noticed at the beginning of §12 that for natural numbers this posed no added demand; any version of the natural numbers would be suited to class measurement if it fulfilled the formal laws. Now much the same can be said of the real numbers: when they are applied, say by assignment to sundry continuous magnitudes in the physical world, any model could be applied as well. Modeling again proves tantamount to reduction because all traits relevant to application carry over into the model.

In the next three chapters it will become apparent that the same is true of the infinite ordinal and infinite cardinal numbers: any model is a tenable version, lending itself to all the applications. And, to speak of more immediate concerns, the same is true of the familiar addenda to our real-number system, namely, the negative and imaginary numbers. I shall train the next few paragraphs on these.

We can get a model of the arithmetic of the signed reals, or positive and negative real numbers, by construing the positive real $+x$ and the negative real $-x$, for each real number x, arbitrarily as the ordered pairs $\langle x, 0\rangle$ and $\langle 0, x\rangle$. This gives $+x = -x$ when and only when x is 0, as desired. A new definition of '$<$' suited to signed reals can then be built on this idea:

$$\langle x, y\rangle < \langle z, w\rangle \;.\!\equiv:\; x \subset z \;.\mathbf{v}.\; x = 0 \,.\, w \subset y,$$

the '$\subset$' on the right being the '$<$' of unsigned reals. Appropriate senses of sum, product, and power can be tricked up in the same spirit.

Another way, Peano's,[1] is to take the signed reals as difference relations of unsigned reals, hence $+x$ as the relation of y to z where $y = z \oplus x$, and $-x$ as the relation of z to y where $y = z \oplus x$. Succinctly, $+x = \lambda_z(z \oplus x)$ and $-x = \breve{\ } +x$. For signed reals u and v in this sense, '$<$' and '$+$' become neatly definable;

$$u < v .\equiv (\exists z)(u`z < v`z), \qquad u + v = (u \mid v) \cup (v \mid u).$$

Product and power are more elaborate.

Neither version identifies the positive reals with the unsigned reals, as might have been wished. One acquiesces in their distinctness, as one has in the distinctness of the whole ratios from the natural numbers and in the distinctness of the rational reals from the ratios. Actually we, unlike others, did not acquiesce in this last; we got the rational reals to be the ratios. And we can arrange as well for the positive reals. Instead of adopting either of the above versions of the signed reals, we can dispense with the notation '$+x$' and introduce negative reals $-x$ as a direct supplement to the reals hitherto so called. The method may be seen most clearly if for a little while we think of the reals again as classes of actual pairs $\langle y, z\rangle$ of natural numbers, as in §17, instead of as classes of the corresponding natural numbers $y;z$. When x is a real number in that sense, hence a relation of natural numbers, we can take $-x$ simply as $\breve{x}$. Thus since the real number one or 1/1 is the relation of less to greater among natural numbers (cf. §17), $-(1/1)$ becomes the relation of greater to less. We get $x = -x$ when and only when $x = 0$, as desired; $\breve{\Lambda} = \Lambda$. The more general effect can be seen by looking to 2/3, which consisted of the pairs $\langle y, z\rangle$ of natural numbers such that $y/z < 2/3$; its negation $-(2/3)$ or $\breve{\ }(2/3)$ can be seen to consist of the pairs $\langle y, z\rangle$ such that $3/2 < y/z$.

---

[1] 1901, pp. 48f. He cites Maclaurin and Cauchy.

Corrected to suit our actual version of real numbers as classes of numbers $y;z$ rather than as classes of pairs $\langle y, z\rangle$, our definition of $-x$ of course becomes not $\breve{x}$ but $\{y;z\colon z;y \in x\}$.

Identification of the positive reals thus with the ordinary reals, and of $-x$ with the converse $\breve{x}$ or the simulated converse $\{y;z\colon z;y \in x\}$, leaves little to be desired in the way of elegance. The appropriate accompanying definitions of '<', '+', etc. leave more, and will be left to the reader, so that we may turn in conclusion to the imaginary numbers.

The imaginary numbers form a series just like the reals except that the unit which takes the place of the real number 1 is called i and looked upon as $\sqrt{-1}$. Adoption of the imaginary numbers extends the domain of reals to that of the *complex numbers* $x + yi$; here x and y are real numbers in an already extended sense, allowing negatives. It has long been a commonplace that the complex numbers are adequately modeled by taking $x + yi$ as $\langle x, y\rangle$. Again the arithmetical operations call for redefinition, and the keys to two of them are these:

$$\langle x, y\rangle + \langle z, w\rangle = \langle x + z, y + w\rangle,$$
$$\langle x, y\rangle\cdot\langle z, w\rangle = \langle x\cdot z - y\cdot w, x\cdot w + y\cdot z\rangle,$$

as one sees by thinking of $\langle x, y\rangle$ stubbornly as $x + yi$ and of $i\cdot i$ as -1.

The version of $x + yi$ as $\langle x, y\rangle$ does not identify the complex real number $x + 0\cdot i$ or $\langle x, 0\rangle$ with the real number x as might have been wished. But again we can provide an alternative definition that accomplishes the desired identification. We have merely to pick an arbitrary correspondence α relating things other than natural numbers to all the natural numbers; then we can explain $x + yi$ as $x \cup \alpha``y$. As desired, this reduces to $x$ when $y$ is 0 (i.e., $\Lambda$). Also, as required, the real numbers $x$ and $y$ are each uniquely recoverable from $x \cup \alpha``y$. For, inasmuch as a real number (even when negative) is in our final version a class of natural numbers,

$$x = \mathrm{N} \cap (x \cup \alpha``y), \qquad y = \breve{\alpha}``(x \cup \alpha``y).$$

Given our adoption of the Zermelo version of natural number, a correspondence that meets the requirement on α is $\lambda_z\{z, \{z\}\}$. So we may set

$$x + yi = x \cup \{\{z, \{z\}\} : z \in y\},$$

leaving the detail of formal definitions again to the reader.

VII | ORDER AND ORDINALS

20. Transfinite induction

We followed the theme of mathematical induction through a number of minor variations in §§13 and 15. But there is also a major variation of it, called *course-of-values induction*,[1] that I have deferred until now. As applied to natural numbers, the law of course-of-values induction says that anything is true of all natural numbers if, when it is true of all up to any one, it is true always of the next. So the schema is:

20.1 $(y)((x)(x < y \mathbin{.\supset} Fx) \supset Fy) \mathbin{.} z \in \mathrm{N} \mathbin{.\supset} Fz.$

Proof. By hypothesis,

$$(x)(x < y \mathbin{.\supset} Fx) \supset. (x)(x < y \mathbin{.\supset} Fx) \mathbin{.} Fy$$
$$\supset (x)(x < y \mathbin{.\supset} Fx : x = y \mathbin{.\supset} Fx)$$
$$\supset (x)(x < y \mathbin{.\mathrm{v}.} x = y :\supset Fx)$$

(by 13.11) $\supset (x)(x \leqq y \mathbin{.\supset} Fx)$

(by 13.12) $\supset (x)(x < \{y\} \mathbin{.\supset} Fx).$

By 12.18, vacuously, $(x)(x < \Lambda \mathbin{.\supset} Fx)$. From these two results and the hypothesis '$z \in \mathrm{N}$' it follows by induction according to 13.9 that $(x)(x < z \mathbin{.\supset} Fx)$. So, by the long hypothesis, Fz.

---

[1] Kleene, p. 22.

Another way of looking at course-of-values induction is as a *law of first exception*: for every $z \in \mathrm{N}$ it must be true that Fz, unless there is a first $y \in \mathrm{N}$ for which $\sim Fy$. This version is the merest restatement of 20.1. For, the long first hypothesis in 20.1 simply says of each y that it is not the first such that $\sim Fy$, but that, on the contrary, if $\sim Fy$ then also $\sim Fx$ for some $x < y$.

The varieties of induction noted earlier were, in their application to natural numbers, specializations of laws of ancestral induction that held as well with an unspecified 'α' in place of '$\breve{\iota}$' (cf. 15.10, 15.13, 15.14). With 20.1 the matter is otherwise. 20.1 depends on a special trait of $\breve{\iota}$, invoked through 13.12, and cannot validly be extended to relations generally. Let us see how 20.1 would look with 'α' for '$\breve{\iota}$'. Since the clause '$x < y$' amounts (for numbers) to '$\langle x, y\rangle \in \breve{\iota} \mid *\breve{\iota}$' and to '$\langle x, y\rangle \in *\breve{\iota} \cap {}^{-}I$', there is a question which way to generalize that part. Let us try both ways.

(i) $(y)((x)(\langle x, y\rangle \in \alpha \mid *\alpha \mathbin{.{\supset}} Fx) \supset Fy) \mathbin{.} \langle \Lambda, z\rangle \in *\alpha \mathbin{.{\supset}} Fz,$

(ii) $(y)((x)(\langle x, y\rangle \in *\alpha \cap {}^{-}I \mathbin{.{\supset}} Fx) \supset Fy) \mathbin{.} \langle \Lambda, z\rangle \in *\alpha \mathbin{.{\supset}} Fz.$

To see how (i) and (ii) can fail, take α as the subclass relation $\{\langle s, t\rangle : s \subseteq t\}$. On this interpretation $\alpha = *\alpha = \alpha \mid *\alpha$, by reflexivity and transitivity of the subclass relation; further '$\Lambda \subseteq z$' may be dropped. So (i) and (ii) become:

(iii) $(y)((x)(x \subseteq y \mathbin{.{\supset}} Fx) \supset Fy) \supset Fz,$

(iv) $(y)((x)(x \subset y \mathbin{.{\supset}} Fx) \supset Fy) \supset Fz.$

Now since

$$(y)((x)(x \subseteq y \mathbin{.{\supset}} Fx) \supset: y \subseteq y \mathbin{.{\supset}} Fy) \\ \supset Fy),$$

(iii) reduces outright to 'Fz', which could be anything. To discredit (iv) is less trivial; we must go further and interpret 'F'—say as finitude: the having finitely many members. Clearly if a class is infinite, dropping a member leaves it infinite; hence if rather every proper subclass of a class y is finite, so is y; i.e.,

$$(y)((x)(x \subset y \mathbin{.{\supset}} Fx) \supset Fy).$$

So (iv) reduces to 'Fz', meaning 'z is finite', where z could be any class at all.

We can best appreciate why course-of-values induction fails for the general theory of the ancestral if we think of course-of-values induction again as a law of first exception. The trouble then is simply that among the exceptions, among the objects z such that $\sim Fz$, there might be none that are *minimal* with respect to $*\alpha \cap {}^{-}I$; instead there might be an infinite descent in which each exception has $*\alpha \cap {}^{-}I$ borne to it by further exceptions. This is why (iv) failed for 'F' as finitude: no infinite class is minimal with respect to '$\subset$', each has a proper subclass that is infinite in turn.

It thus becomes evident that while we need not expect course-of-values induction to apply solely to the ordering of the natural numbers by '$<$', we may expect it to work in general only for relations which, like that one, assure that a class containing any of the related objects always contains minimal ones.

Such a relation is said to be *founded*. Thus α is founded if there is no class (but Λ) to whose every member α is borne in turn by a member of the class. More briefly, α is founded if there is no class $x \neq \Lambda$ whose every member is in $\breve{\alpha}``x$; no class $x \neq \Lambda$ such that $x \subseteq \breve{\alpha}``x$. So

20.2 'Fnd α' for '$(x)(x \subseteq \breve{\alpha}``x \;.\!\supset\!.\; x = \Lambda)$'.

A relation like that of less to greater among natural numbers, briefly $\{\langle x, y\rangle : \Lambda \leqq x < y\}$, determines a linear order among its objects and is called an *ordering*. The relation

$$\{\langle x, y\rangle : x, y \in \text{Real} \,.\, x \subset y\}$$

of less to greater among real numbers is likewise an ordering. The more general relation $\{\langle x, y\rangle : x \subset y\}$ of proper subclass is not an ordering, for there are x and y such that neither $x \subset y$ nor $y \subset x$ nor $x = y$; *connexity* fails (§3). Similarly for the relation $\{\langle x, y\rangle : x \prec y\}$ of smaller to larger among classes, where

20.3 '$\alpha \prec \beta$' or '$\beta \succ \alpha$' for '$\sim(\beta \preceq \alpha)$'

(cf. 11.1); for there are x and y such that neither $x \prec y$ nor $y \prec x$ nor $x = y$. Now a point worth noting at this juncture is that being founded has nothing to do with being an ordering. The ordering $\{\langle x, y\rangle: \Lambda \leqq x < y\}$ is founded: every class of natural numbers but Λ boasts a minimal member with respect to that relation. The relation of less to greater among ratios or reals, on the other hand, though an ordering, is not founded; the class of ratios above 1/1, e.g., or of reals above 1/1, has no minimal members with respect to that relation. Again $\{\langle x, y\rangle: x \prec y\}$, though not an ordering, is founded; every class $z \neq \Lambda$ has minimal members with respect to $\{\langle x, y\rangle: x \prec y\}$, viz., those members of z than which no smaller classes belong to z. They will be alike in size, but there may be many of them. Finally $\{\langle x, y\rangle: x \subset y\}$, again not an ordering, is not founded; the class of all infinite classes, e.g., supposing that it exists and is not empty, has no minimal members with respect to $\{\langle x, y\rangle: x \subset y\}$.

When a founded relation is an ordering, it is called a *well-ordering.*[2] Even a well-ordering can depart significantly from the structure of our prime example $\{\langle x, y\rangle: \Lambda \leqq x < y\}$. Thus take the relation of earlier to later among

$$0;0,\ 0;1,\ 0;2, \ldots, 1;0,\ 1;1,\ 1;2, \ldots, 2;0,\ 2;1,\ 2;2, \ldots, 3;0, \ldots,$$

which is to say, according to 17.1,

(v) $\quad 0, 1, 4, \ldots, 2, 5, 10, \ldots, 6, 11, 18, \ldots, 12, \ldots .$

Trailing off as it does into an infinite succession at each of infinitely many places, this arrangement is structurally unlike what $\{\langle x, y\rangle: \Lambda \leqq x < y\}$ gives; yet it is a well-ordering too.

One little thing that can be said categorically about founded relations is that they are irreflexive.

20.4 $\qquad \text{Fnd}\ \alpha \supset.\ \langle x, x\rangle \notin \alpha.$

---

[2] The concept of a well-ordering goes back to Cantor. In defining foundedness and ordering separately I follow Whitehead and Russell (vol. 2, p. 529; vol. 3, p. 6) except in terminology. A founded relation, an ordering, and a well-ordering were in their terminology a well-ordered relation, a series, and a well-ordered series respectively.—Formal definition of ordering and well-ordering is deferred to 21.2 and 21.4.

Proof. By 10.26, $\{x\} \neq \Lambda$. So, by hypothesis and 20.2, $\sim(\{x\} \subseteq \breve{\alpha}``\{x\})$. That is, by 7.4, $x \notin \breve{\alpha}``\{x\}$. That is, $\langle x, x\rangle \notin \alpha$.

Now to the law of course-of-values induction for founded relations in general. The approximate pattern is before us in 20.1. We have merely to change '$x < y$' therein to '$\langle x, y\rangle \in \alpha$' and assume that Fnd α. The clause '$z \in$ N', oddly enough, can be dropped without replacement. But a premiss of comprehension is needed.

20.5 $\{x: \sim Fx\} \in \mathcal{V} \,.\, \text{Fnd}\,\alpha \,.\, (y)((x)(\langle x, y\rangle \in \alpha \,.\!\supset Fx) \supset Fy)$
$.\!\supset Fz.$

Proof. Contraposing the long last hypothesis,

$$(y)(\sim Fy \supset (\exists x)(\sim Fx \,.\, \langle x, y\rangle \in \alpha))$$
$$\supset.\ y \in \breve{\alpha}``\{x: \sim Fx\}).$$

That is,

$$\{x: \sim Fx\} \subseteq \breve{\alpha}``\{x: \sim Fx\}.$$

But, by hypothesis and 20.2, $w \subseteq \breve{\alpha}``w$ only where $w = \Lambda$. So, taking w as $\{x: \sim Fx\}$ on the strength of the comprehension premiss, we conclude that $\{x: \sim Fx\} = \Lambda$. So Fz.

One may wonder why '$z \in$ N' was needed in 20.1, seeing no analogue of it in 20.5. The answer is that $\{\langle x, y\rangle: x < y\}$ in general, as against its numerical specialization $\{\langle x, y\rangle: \Lambda \leqq x < y\}$, is not known to be founded. It might not even be irreflexive; cf. §13.

20.5 is startling in that there are no strings on z. The explanation is that the long last hypothesis is very strong, implying of itself that Fy for all y outside $\breve{\alpha}``\mathcal{V}$. Sometimes 20.5 finds its use through its more cluttered corollary:

20.6 $\{x: x \in (\alpha \cup \breve{\alpha})``\mathcal{V} \,.\, \sim Fx\} \in \mathcal{V} \,.\, \text{Fnd}\,\alpha \,.$
$(y)((x)(\langle x, y\rangle \in \alpha \,.\!\supset Fx) \,.\, y \in (\alpha \cup \breve{\alpha})``\mathcal{V} \,.\!\supset Fy) \,.$
$z \in (\alpha \cup \breve{\alpha})``\mathcal{V} \,.\!\supset Fz.$

Proof. By first hypothesis,

$$\{x: \sim(x \in (\alpha \cup \breve{\alpha})``\mathcal{V} \,.\supset Fx)\} \in \mathcal{V}.$$

By the long third hypothesis, since '$\langle x, y\rangle \in \alpha$' implies '$x \in (\alpha \cup \breve{\alpha})``\mathcal{V}$',

$$(y)((x)(\langle x, y\rangle \in \alpha \,.\supset\colon x \in (\alpha \cup \breve{\alpha})``\mathcal{V} \,.\supset Fx) \supset\colon y \in (\alpha \cup \breve{\alpha})``\mathcal{V} \,.\supset Fy).$$

From these two results and the hypothesis 'Fnd α' it follows according to 20.5 that $z \in (\alpha \cup \breve{\alpha})``\mathcal{V} \,.\supset Fz$.

We saw that course-of-values induction does not always work where ancestral induction works. The converse can also be said. Thus take the ordering of numbers depicted in (v), and suppose some condition represented by 'Fz'. We may know that $F0$, and we may know, whenever x is a number and y is the next in the order (v), that $Fx \supset Fy$; but we cannot conclude that Fz for every such number z. Ancestral induction is inadequate to such a situation because, where β is the relation of each number to its predecessor in the order (v), not all those numbers bear $*\beta$ to 0; even 2 does not. On the other hand if α is the relation of every number in the order (v) to every later one in that order, and if we know that

$$(y)((x)(\langle x, y\rangle \in \alpha \,.\supset Fx) \supset Fy),$$

then by 20.5 or 20.6 we can conclude at once for *every* number z in (v) that Fz (granted the comprehension premiss). There being infinitely many numbers short of 2 in (v) is no longer an obstacle.

Thus course-of-values induction in the general form 20.5 or 20.6 may be contrasted with ordinary or ancestral induction as carrying us not merely throughout an infinite sequence but beyond into continuations prior to which there are infinitely many intervening things. For this reason, course-of-values induction as of 20.5 or 20.6 is called *transfinite* induction.

The transfinite character here concerned is a question not of quantity but of arrangement. The numbers in (v) can be reordered thus:

$$0, 1, 2, 4, 5, 6, 9, 10, 11, 12, 16, \ldots$$

and this order is indeed accessible to ordinary ancestral induction. Where γ is the relation of each number to its predecessor in this order, each of these numbers does bear $*\gamma$ to 0—unlike the $*\beta$ of two paragraphs back. The relation $*\gamma$, like the α of that paragraph and unlike the $*\beta$, holds forward or backward between each two numbers occurring in (v). Still even $*\gamma$ and α are decidedly different relations, and ancestral induction is suited to the one, transfinite to the other.

There is also such a thing as difference of sizes of infinite classes, and transfinite induction does have its uses also in covering totalities that cannot be covered by ancestral induction under any arrangement. But these are matters for Chapters IX and X.

Before we get farther from the topic, this law about founded relations should be set down for reference.

20.7 $\alpha \subseteq \beta \,.\, \text{Fnd}\,\beta \,.\!\supset \text{Fnd}\,\alpha.$

Proof. Since $\alpha \subseteq \beta$, $\breve{\alpha}``x \subseteq \breve{\beta}``x$. So $x \subseteq \breve{\alpha}``x \,.\!\supset\!.\, x \subseteq \breve{\beta}``x$. So, by 20.2, $\text{Fnd}\,\beta \supset \text{Fnd}\,\alpha$.

21. Order

Founded relations are notable both for transfinite induction, above, and as well-orderings. These, as remarked, are ordering relations that are founded. Well-orderings are notable for their exemplary behavior in connection with isomorphisms, as will be explained at the end of this section.

An ordering relation is a relation that puts all the objects of its field into a linear order, each earlier or later than each other. The main example in §20 was $\{\langle x, y\rangle \colon \Lambda \leqq x < y\}$. In general, what makes α an ordering relation is that it relates each two objects in its field, one to the other and not vice versa, and if it relates x to y and y to z then it relates x to z rather than vice versa. So an ordering relation is *connected*,

21.1 'Connex α' for
$$`(x)(y)(x, y \in (\alpha \cup \breve{\alpha})``\mathcal{V} \;.\supset.\; \langle x, y\rangle \in \alpha \cup \breve{\alpha} \cup I)';$$

transitive ($\alpha \mid \alpha \subseteq \alpha$), and *asymmetric* ($\alpha \subseteq {}^{-}\breve{\alpha}$). Also it is irreflexive ($\alpha \subseteq {}^{-}I$), but that follows from asymmetry. Or, better, stipulate the irreflexivity and derive the asymmetry, thus:

21.2 'Ordg α' for '$\alpha \mid \alpha \subseteq \alpha \subseteq {}^{-}I$. Connex α',

21.3 Ordg $\alpha \;\supset.\; \alpha \subseteq {}^{-}\breve{\alpha}$.

Proof. If $\langle x, y\rangle \in \alpha \cap \breve{\alpha}$ then $\langle x, y\rangle$, $\langle y, x\rangle \in \alpha$ and so, since $\alpha \mid \alpha \subseteq \alpha$, $\langle x, x\rangle \in \alpha$; but this is contrary to '$\alpha \subseteq {}^{-}I$'.

There is considerable variety in ordering relations. The relation of earlier to later in (v) of §20 qualifies despite its observed divergence in structure from $\{\langle x, y\rangle: \Lambda \leqq x < y\}$. Also the relation of less to greater in the ratios or reals qualifies, despite there being no immediate successors or predecessors. Also the relation of less to greater in negative numbers qualifies, despite there being no bottom. Of course these last two orderings are not founded, and hence not *well-orderings*; for,

21.4 'Wellord α' for 'Fnd α . Ordg α'.

Finally $\{\langle x, y\rangle: x \subset y\}$ and $\{\langle x, y\rangle: x \prec y\}$ are not ordering relations at all, for they fail of connexity. But they are called *partial orderings*, because of meeting the condition '$\alpha \mid \alpha \subseteq \alpha \subseteq {}^{-}I$' of transitivity and irreflexivity. Partial orderings are asymmetric too; for the proof of 21.3 does not use connexity.

Arbitrarily I have been identifying the ordering relation with the relation of each ordered object to each later one. We could identify it instead with the relation of each ordered object to itself *and* each later one, since either relation suffices to fix the order of the objects. Indeed each relation is expressible in terms of the other; it is only a question of the best place for a handle.

The second alternative has some advantages. Under the first or "strong" version, the field of an ordering cannot be a unit class; under the second or "weak" version there is no such exception, and some theorems and proofs turn out simpler in consequence. If we had chosen the weak version, our prime example of an ordering relation would have been not $\{\langle x, y\rangle : \Lambda \leqq x < y\}$ but $\{\langle x, y\rangle : \Lambda \leqq x \leqq y\}$; and our examples of partial orderings would have been $\{\langle x, y\rangle : x \subseteq y\}$ and $\{\langle x, y\rangle : x \lesssim y\}$. Other properties than connexity and irreflexivity would have been called for in 21.2. Transitivity would have remained, but instead of irreflexivity there would have been antisymmetry (cf. §3) and instead of connexity in the sense of 21.1 there would have been a strong connexity, defined by 21.1 without the '$\cup I$'.

There are further alternatives, each with its advantages. Thus we might identify the ordering not with a relation at all but with a nest of classes, one class corresponding to each of the ordered objects and consisting of it and all earlier objects.[1] Each such alternative would call for a different definition in place of 21.2.

But I am holding to the first alternative, for it is more intuitive and has also some formal advantages of its own, e.g., in formulating transfinite induction.

Let us now prove a few things about ordering relations.

21.5 $\quad \text{Ordg}\, \alpha \,.\, x, y \in (\alpha \cup \breve{\alpha})``\mathcal{V} \,.\, \alpha``\{x\} = \alpha``\{y\} \,.\supset.\, x = y.$

Proof. By 21.2, since Ordg α, $\alpha \subseteq {}^{-}I$. So $x \notin \alpha``\{x\}$. So, by last hypothesis, $x \notin \alpha``\{y\}$. That is, $\langle x, y\rangle \notin \alpha$. Similarly $\langle y, x\rangle \notin \alpha$. But, by 21.2, Connex α and so, by second hypothesis, $\langle x, y\rangle \in \alpha \cup \breve{\alpha} \cup I$. So $\langle x, y\rangle \in I$.

It is not true in general that if Ordg α and $\gamma \subseteq \alpha$ then Ordg γ. Connexity could fail for γ. For instance, if from our proverbial ordering $\{\langle x, y\rangle : \Lambda \leqq x < y\}$ we drop even the single pair $\langle 5, 6\rangle$, the remaining class of pairs is not an ordering. One accustomed to talking of order in the widespread mathematical

[1] The idea comes from Hessenberg (1906), with successive improvements by Kuratowski (1920) and Sierpiński (1921).

idiom of "ordered set" would rightly say, to the seeming contrary, that any subset of an ordered set is an ordered set; but this statement is not really to the contrary, and has its proper analysis rather in the following:

21.6 $\qquad \text{Ordg}\,\alpha \supset \text{Ordg}\,\alpha \cap (\beta \times \beta).$

Proof. By hypothesis and definition,

$$\alpha \mid \alpha \subseteq \alpha \subseteq {}^{-}I, \qquad (1) \qquad \text{Connex}\,\alpha. \qquad (2)$$

Whenever

$$\langle x, y\rangle, \langle y, z\rangle \in \alpha \cap (\beta \times \beta)$$

we have x, $z \in \beta$ and also $\langle x, y\rangle$, $\langle y, z\rangle \in \alpha$, whence, by (1), $\langle x, z\rangle \in \alpha$ and thus $\langle x, z\rangle \in \alpha \cap (\beta \times \beta)$. So

$$\alpha \cap (\beta \times \beta) \text{ is transitive.} \qquad (3)$$

Further, by (1),

$$\alpha \cap (\beta \times \beta) \subseteq {}^{-}I. \qquad (4)$$

Any x and y in the field of $\alpha \cap (\beta \times \beta)$ are in the field of α and in β. So, by (2),

$$\langle x, y\rangle \in \alpha \cup \breve{\alpha} \cup I, \qquad x, y \in \beta.$$

That is, $x = y$ or x bears $\alpha \cap (\beta \times \beta)$ to y or y to x. So

$$\text{Connex}\,\alpha \cap (\beta \times \beta).$$

So, by (3), (4), and definition, $\text{Ordg}\,\alpha \cap (\beta \times \beta)$.

Let us write '$x 1 \alpha$' to mean that x comes first under the ordering α.

21.7 $\qquad$ '$\beta 1 \alpha$' for '$\beta \in \alpha``\mathcal{V} \,.\, \beta \notin \breve{\alpha}``\mathcal{V}$'.

We prove that an order has one beginning at most.

21.8 $\qquad \text{Ordg}\,\alpha \,.\, x 1 \alpha \,.\, y 1 \alpha \,.\!\supset\!.\; x = y.$

Proof. By hypotheses and 21.7,

$$x, y \notin \breve{\alpha}``\mathcal{V}, \qquad (1) \qquad x, y \in \alpha``\mathcal{V}. \qquad (2)$$

By (1), $\alpha``\{x\} = \Lambda = \alpha``\{y\}$. From this and (2) and the first hypothesis, it follows according to 21.5 that $x = y$.

Finally one law about well-ordering.

21.9 Wellord $\alpha \supset$ Wellord $\alpha \cap (\beta \times \beta)$.

Proof by 21.4, 20.7, 21.6.

Two finite orderings can be compared in point of length by pairing the first thing of the one ordering with the first of the other, the next with the next, and so on, until one ordering is exhausted; the other is then the longer. A similar method of coordination can often be applied also to infinite orderings. Sameness of length, in general, is a matter of there being an *isomorphism* between the two orderings, that is, an order-preserving correspondence of the field of the one ordering to the field of the other. By "order-preserving" I mean that anything x will precede anything y in the one ordering if and only if, in the other ordering, the correspondent of x precedes that of y.

For example, the successor function as applied to odd numbers constitutes an isomorphism between the standard ordering of odds and that of evens; for, whenever x and y are odds such that $x < y$, and only then, we have for the correlated evens that $S`x < S`y$. The existence of this isomorphism may be said to make the ordering of the odds and the ordering of the evens equal in length, even though both orderings are infinite.

When on the other hand one ordering z is in this sense equal in length only to an initial segment of another ordering w, finite or infinite, we speak of w as longer than z.

In finite cases the longer ordering is of course simply the one that orders more things. But in the infinite case we can come out with the verdict that the one ordering is longer than the other even when the shorter ordering orders all the things that the longer one does and more. Thus compare the standard ordering $\{\langle x, y\rangle : \Lambda \leqq x < y\}$ of the natural numbers with the ordering α

depicted in (v) of §20. The first thing under the ordering α can be paired with 0, the next with 1, the third with 2, and so on. This principle of pairing reaches everything ordered by $\{\langle x, y\rangle: \Lambda \leqq x < y\}$—every natural number— without ever getting as far as 2 in the ordering α. So the ordering α is, by the criterion, longer than $\{\langle x, y\rangle: \Lambda \leqq x < y\}$ despite the fact that all the things ordered by α, and more, are ordered by $\{\langle x, y\rangle: \Lambda \leqq x < y\}$.

Some infinite orderings are incomparable by such means. Thus take the arithmetical ordering of the natural numbers and the arithmetical ordering of the ratios; i.e.,

$$\{\langle x, y\rangle: \Lambda \leqq x < y\}, \quad \{\langle x, y\rangle: x, y \in \text{Rat} \,.\, x \subset y\}.$$

Undertaking to compare them, we begin by pairing the first natural number with the first ratio; both are Λ. But with what ratio shall we pair the next natural number, 1? There is no next ratio, and so the plan of progressive pairing breaks down without potentially exhausting either the natural numbers or the ratios.

But well-orderings are always comparable. (Always, anyway, apart from possible technical failures of class existence at crucial points.) This, the exemplary behavior of well-orderings that I already alluded to, will emerge in the *enumeration theorem* in §27.

22. Ordinal numbers

Because of the general comparability of well-orderings, we can adopt measures for them—numbers of a sort, called *ordinal numbers*. Not limited to finite cases, these length measures will constitute a transfinite extension of the natural number series. For finite well-orderings they will be simply the natural numbers, or might as well be; for, as remarked, the lengths of finite orderings compare as the quantity of things ordered. But the lengths of infinite well-orderings can differ, we saw, even when the things ordered do not. Consequently the transfinite ordinals cannot be looked upon as extending the class-size business of natural numbers to infinite classes. The size of a class is one matter (resumed in Chapter IX) and the length of a well-ordering is another.

We observed (§11) that the purpose of measuring finite classes is served by any version of the natural numbers as long as their order is assured. Their order of itself enables them to measure class size, since a class's having n members can always be explained as likeness in size to the class of numbers $< n$. Now a parallel remark proves to apply to the ordinals: construe them anyhow, suitably ordered, and they can be used to measure the lengths of well-orderings. For a well-ordering's being of length p can always be explained as likeness in length to the series of ordinals $< p$.

So we shall want, first of all, some progression 0, 1, 2, . . . of finite ordinals. (I temporarily dissociate these numerals from the Zermelo interpretation that they received in §12.) Each finite ordinal p measures the length of the series of ordinals $< p$. Then we shall want also a first transfinite ordinal, to measure the length of the whole infinite progression 0, 1, 2, ... This ordinal is called ω, following Cantor. It in turn must have some sort of successor, call it $S`\omega$, to measure the transfinite ordering $0, 1, 2, \ldots, \omega$. Next comes $S`(S`\omega)$, as measuring the ordering $0, 1, 2, \ldots, \omega, S`\omega$. And so on. After the whole doubly infinite ordering $0, 1, 2, \ldots, \omega, S`\omega, S`(S`\omega), \ldots$, we shall want an ordinal number to measure all that; it is called $\omega + \omega$, or $\omega \cdot 2$, according to a transfinite generalization by Cantor of '+' and '·' that we shall look into presently. Then come $S`(\omega \cdot 2)$, $S`(S`(\omega \cdot 2))$, and so on, and, exceeding all these, $\omega \cdot 3$; then $S`(\omega \cdot 3)$, and so on. To measure the ordering of all such numbers of the form $S`(\ldots(S`(\omega \cdot n))\ldots)$, we want the still further number $\omega^2$; then $S`\omega^2$, $S`(S`\omega^2), \ldots, \omega^2 \cdot 2, \ldots, \omega^2 \cdot 3, \ldots$, $\omega^\omega, \ldots, \omega^{\omega^\omega}$, and so on. How far this goes—whether, for that matter, it stopped short of ω—is a question of eventual definitions and comprehension axioms. While they last, anyway, each ordinal number measures the series of all earlier ordinal numbers.

The ordinals divide conspicuously into two kinds: the *successors*, or ordinals of the form $S`x$, and the so-called *limit ordinals*, viz. $0, \omega, \omega \cdot 2, \omega \cdot 3, \omega^2$, etc., which have no immediate predecessors. An ordering measured by a successor may be infinite, but still it will have a last place; an ordering measured by a limit ordinal will have no last place.

Since we may construe the ordinals in any way that assures the required order, the best counsel is to construe them conveniently; and for convenience there is nothing to match the transfinite extension of von Neumann's way of generating the natural numbers. For von Neumann, each natural number was the class of all the earlier ones; and the beauty of this idea is that it still makes sense beyond the finite. Thus, take the finite ordinals as von Neumann's natural numbers. Thereupon the merest wish for a number ω beyond the series of natural numbers carries with it the definition: the new number can be construed, after the manner of the natural numbers themselves, as the class of all its predecessors, hence simply as N (but N now in the von Neumann sense). Then a next number recommends itself as the class of all *its* predecessors—hence $\omega \cup \{\omega\}$. This is $S`\omega$ according to the general definition of S for von Neumann (cf. §12). Similarly we get $S`(S`\omega)$, $S`(S`(S`\omega))$, and so on. Similarly we get $\omega \cdot 2$ as the class of all of $0, 1, 2, \ldots, \omega, S`\omega, S`(S`\omega), \ldots$. And so for the rest; each ordinal, meant to measure the series of all earlier ordinals, is now simply the class of all earlier ordinals.

This way of taking the ordinals, also the transfinite ones, is von Neumann's own.[1] Its adequacy for the purpose rests of course on its meeting the following requirement, which takes some proving: any well-ordering is, in length, like the series of ordinals $< p$ for some ordinal p. This *enumeration theorem* will be proved in §27 on certain existence assumptions.

There was an earlier version of the ordinals, analogous rather to the Frege version of the natural numbers. Just as each natural number under the Frege version was the class of all classes having that many members, so each ordinal number was the class of all well-orderings of that length. More explicitly the definition is twofold: first the ordinal number of a well-ordering x is defined as the class of all the well-orderings that are isomorphic to x (i.e., such that there are isomorphisms between them and x; cf. §21) and then an ordinal number is defined as anything that

---

[1] 1923. According to Bernays, 1941, pp. 6, 10, it was anticipated by Zermelo in unpublished work of 1915.

is the ordinal number of a well-ordering. This was the line taken by Whitehead and Russell and hinted at by Cantor.

It had the virtue of subsuming the ordinal numbers under the wider category of what Cantor called *order types*. Orderings that are isomorphic one to another are said to have the same order type. So the order type of x may be defined as the class of all orderings isomorphic to x. Ordinal numbers were the order types of well-orderings.

Converses of well-orderings need not be well-orderings, but converses of orderings are orderings; and, where y is the order type of x, the order type of $\breve{x}$ has come to be called $y*$ (by Cantor $*y$). Thus, ω being the ordinal number or order type of the relation of less to greater among natural numbers, $\omega*$ is the order type of the relation of less to greater among the negative integers. The order type of the relation of less to greater among ratios is called η, provided that we either exclude 0 or include 0 and the negatives. The corresponding order type for real numbers is called λ. These order types $\omega*$, η, and λ are not ordinal numbers.

Further generalization is immediate: we may entertain the class of all relations isomorphic to x whether x is an ordering or not. Such is Whitehead and Russell's concept of the *relation number* of x. Order types are relation numbers of orderings, and ordinal numbers, for Whitehead and Russell, are relation numbers of well-orderings. Only the ordinals arrange themselves in a natural order of magnitude.

Von Neumann's ordinals are handier and more elegant than Whitehead and Russell's, largely because of the remarkable fact that '$<$' there is given simply by 'ϵ', and '$\leqq$' by '$\subseteq$'. So I shall take ordinals in von Neumann's sense rather than as relation numbers of well-orderings. Order types or relation numbers generally, if wanted, would independently be defined still as above. I shall not be wanting them.

Since no purpose is served by making finite ordinals differ from natural numbers, one could regret that in Chapter IV we did not prepare for the present phase of development by taking the natural numbers in von Neumann's way. However, there was a reason there for preferring Zermelo's way: I have not seen how to do the other as neatly. Brown finds indeed that the only change needed in our axioms would be the covert change wrought in 13.1 by adjusting an underlying definition: von Neumann's successor function would supplant ι in 12.1, which underlies 12.19 and so 13.1. But ι is simpler, and the difference shows in proofs. So, while I recommend exploring the other course as a source for exercises, the natural numbers remain Zermelo's in this book and the ordinals von Neumann's. This plan pays anyway in familiarizing the reader with both approaches.

The correlation between the natural numbers in the sense adopted from Zermelo and the finite ordinals in the sense that we are now adopting from von Neumann is readily formulated.

22.1 'Ś' for '$\lambda_x(x \cup \{x\})$',

22.2 'C' for '$\lambda_x(\text{Ś}^{|x}\text{‘}\Lambda)$'.

Ś is the successor function for ordinals, and C is the correlation of the finite ordinals to the natural numbers. (C also assigns Λ to non-numbers.) For any $x \in$ N, C‘x is the corresponding ordinal.

There follow five rudimentary points about Ś and C.

22.3 Ś‘$\Lambda = \{\Lambda\}$.

Proof. Since $\Lambda \cup \{\Lambda\} = \{\Lambda\}$, we have $\Lambda \cup \{\Lambda\} \in \mathcal{V}$ and so, by 10.24, Ś‘$\Lambda = \Lambda \cup \{\Lambda\}$.

22.4 C‘x = $\text{Ś}^{|x}$‘Λ.

22.5 arg C = $\mathcal{V}$.

Proofs by 10.24 and 10.23, since $\text{Ś}^{|x}$‘$\Lambda \in \mathcal{V}$.

22.6 C‘$\Lambda = \Lambda$. *Proof:* 22.4, 14.3.

22.7 C‘$\{\Lambda\} = \{\Lambda\}$.

Proof. By 22.4, C‘$\{\Lambda\}$ = $\text{Ś}^{|\{\Lambda\}}$‘Λ
(by 14.7) = Ś‘Λ
(by 22.3) = $\{\Lambda\}$.

Since an ordinal is the class of all earlier ordinals, the class of all finite ordinals will be, if it exists, the first infinite ordinal. So we may write

22.8 $\quad$ 'ω' for '$*\acute{S}``\{\Lambda\}$'.

Accordingly, by 15.2 and 15.5,

22.9 $\quad \Lambda \in \omega,$

22.10 $\quad \acute{S}``\omega \subseteq \omega.$

This last says that the successors of finite ordinals are, what there are of them, finite ordinals. The next theorem assures, further, that each finite ordinal has a successor.

22.11 $\quad x \in \omega \;.\supset.\; x \cup \{x\} \in \mathcal{V}.$

Proof. By hypothesis and definitions, there is y such that $\langle x, \Lambda\rangle \in \acute{S}^{|y}$. By 14.9, then,

$$y \in \mathrm{N}. \tag{1}$$

By 22.1 and 10.22, Func $\acute{S}$. So, by 14.12, Func $\acute{S}^{|y}$. So

$$x = \acute{S}^{|y}`\Lambda \tag{2}$$

By 12.21,

$$\begin{aligned} C``\{,,,\Lambda\} &= C``\{\Lambda\} \\ \text{(by 22.5)} \qquad &= \{C`\Lambda\} \\ \text{(by 22.6)} \qquad &= \Lambda \cup \{\Lambda\} \\ \text{(by 14.3)} \qquad &= \acute{S}^{|\Lambda}`\Lambda \cup \{\acute{S}^{|\Lambda}`\Lambda\}. \end{aligned} \tag{3}$$

Suppose $z \in \mathrm{N}$ such that

$$C``\{,,,z\} = \acute{S}^{|z}`\Lambda \cup \{\acute{S}^{|z}`\Lambda\}. \qquad \text{[i]}$$

Then, by 13.1 and 22.5, $\acute{S}^{|z}`\Lambda \cup \{\acute{S}^{|z}`\Lambda\} \in \mathcal{V}$. So, by 10.24 and 22.1,

$$\acute{S}^{|z}`\Lambda \cup \{\acute{S}^{|z}`\Lambda\} = \acute{S}`(\acute{S}^{|z}`\Lambda). \qquad \text{[ii]}$$

Case 1: $z \neq \Lambda$. Then, by 13.17, since $z \in \mathrm{N}$, $\Lambda < z$. I.e., by definitions, $\{\Lambda\} \in \{,,,z\}$. Then, by 22.5, $C`\{\Lambda\} \in C``\{,,,z\}$.

But, by 22.7, $C`\{\Lambda\} \neq \Lambda$. So $C``\{,,,z\} \neq \{\Lambda\}$. So, by [i], $\check{S}^{|z`}\Lambda \neq \Lambda$. So, by 10.15, $\Lambda \in \arg \check{S}^{|z}$.

Case 2: $z = \Lambda$. Then again, by 14.3 and 10.4, $\Lambda \in \arg \check{S}^{|z}$.

Both cases: $\Lambda \in \arg \check{S}^{|z}$. So, by 10.18 and 14.6,

$$\check{S}`(\check{S}^{|z`}\Lambda) = \check{S}^{|\{z\}`}\Lambda. \qquad [iii]$$

By 13.13,

$$
\begin{aligned}
C``\{,,,\{z\}\} &= C``\{,,,z\} \cup C``\{\{z\}\} \\
\text{(by 22.5)} \quad &= C``\{,,,z\} \cup \{C`\{z\}\} \\
\text{(by 22.4)} \quad &= C``\{,,,z\} \cup \{\check{S}^{|\{z\}`}\Lambda\} \\
\text{(by [i]–[iii])} \quad &= \check{S}^{|\{z\}`}\Lambda \cup \{\check{S}^{|\{z\}`}\Lambda\}.
\end{aligned}
$$

Since this follows from '$z \in N$' and [i], we have from (1) and (3) by mathematical induction according to 13.10 that

$$C``\{,,,y\} = \check{S}^{|y`}\Lambda \cup \{\check{S}^{|y`}\Lambda\}.$$

So, by (2), $C``\{,,,y\} = x \cup \{x\}$. So, by 22.5 and 13.1, $x \cup \{x\} \in \mathcal{V}$.

We can now strengthen 22.10 on the existential point.

22.12 $$x \in \omega \,.\supset.\, x \cup \{x\} \in \omega.$$

Proof. By hypothesis and 22.11,

$$x \cup \{x\} \in \mathcal{V}. \qquad (1)$$

So, by definitions, $\langle x \cup \{x\}, x\rangle \in \check{S}$. So, by hypothesis and (1), $x \cup \{x\} \in \check{S}``\omega$. So, by 22.10, $x \cup \{x\} \in \omega$.

Our next task is to encompass the adopted notion of ordinal number, finite and infinite, in a formal definition. What are the distinguishing traits? For one thing, each ordinal number x is the class of the earlier ones. Each of these being the class in turn of the ones earlier than it, we see that all members of members of x must be members of x; i.e., $\bigcup x \subseteq x$. For another thing, the members of x are ordered by the membership relation; for they are ordinals, and each smaller is a member of each larger. A third and less obvious trait is that x harbors no endless descents in respect of membership. Essentially the reason is that, though there are infinitely many ordinals between one limit ordinal and the next, there are only finitely many ordinals between one limit ordinal and any ordinal short of the next limit ordinal. Counting upward, there is always a next and there are thus endless ascents in respect of membership. Counting downward, we necessarily tumble past infinitely many ordinals each time we pass below a limit ordinal, and we reach bottom in finitely many steps however perversely taken.

In the sharp formulation the symbol '$\mathfrak{E}$' for the membership relation will be useful.

22.13 '$\mathfrak{E}$' for '$\{\langle y, z\rangle: y \in z\}$'.

In particular $\mathfrak{E} \upharpoonright \beta$ is $\mathfrak{E}$ with its whole *field* confined to β, in case $\bigcup \beta \subseteq \beta$.

22.14 $\bigcup \beta \subseteq \beta \mathrel{.\supset.} \mathfrak{E} \upharpoonright \beta = \mathfrak{E} \cap (\beta \times \beta)$.

Proof. By hypothesis, $x \in y \in \beta \mathrel{.\supset.} x \in \beta$. That is,

$$x \in y \in \beta \mathrel{.\equiv.} x \in y \,.\, x, y \in \beta.$$

So, by definitions, $\mathfrak{E} \upharpoonright \beta = \mathfrak{E} \cap (\beta \times \beta)$.

Let us return now to the three traits of an ordinal number x. The first was that $\bigcup x \subseteq x$. The second was that the members of x are ordered by $\mathfrak{E}$, i.e., that Ordg $\mathfrak{E} \cap (x \times x)$, or, in view of 22.14, that Ordg $\mathfrak{E} \upharpoonright x$. The third was that Fnd $\mathfrak{E} \upharpoonright x$. Combining,

22.15 'NO' for '$\{x: \bigcup x \subseteq x \,.\, \text{Wellord}\ \mathfrak{E} \upharpoonright x\}$'.[2]

---

[2] Von Neumann's formulation was more devious. Zermelo's unpublished formulation of 1915, as reported by Bernays, 1941, pp. 6, 10, amounts to the following (if we drop Bernays's first clause, which is obviously implied by his third): NO is

$$\{x: (y)(y \in x \mathrel{.\supset.} y \cup \{y\} \in x \cup \{x\} : y \subseteq x \mathrel{.\supset.} \bigcup y \in x \cup \{x\})\}.$$

The formulation in 22.15 comes from Gödel's formulation (1940, foot p. 22) by an obvious simplification. See also Suppes, p. 131. The earliest formulation akin to 22.15 was provided by Robinson, 1937; the difference was just that he got by with 'Connex' instead of 'Wellord' by leaning on the axiom of *Fundierung* (see below, §39). If we accept that axiom, indeed, as I do not, we can formulate NO as $\{x: (y)(y \in x \mathrel{.\supset.} \bigcup y \subseteq y \subseteq x)\}$. This is obtainable by elementary transformations from a formulation which Bernays attributes to Gödel's lectures of 1937. Indeed $\{x: (y)(x \in y \mathrel{.\supset} (\exists z)(z \in y \,.\, \bigcup z \subseteq z \subseteq \bar{y}))\}$ will serve, Brown has proved, without *Fundierung*. See also Quine and Wang, where a related version is linked to the trick of inversion that we saw in (ii) of p. 75.

The arithmetical operations were applied to ordinal numbers in an expository way a few pages back. Let us now look into this extension. The ordinal sum $x + y$ is meant to measure the length of a well-ordering z that has a *segment* (meaning an initial segment; such is the usage) of length x and a remainder of length y. For example, $\omega + 2$ (for ordinal 2) is the length of:

$$0, 1, 2, \ldots, a, b.$$

In transfinite cases addition fails of commutativity; thus $2 + \omega$, unlike $\omega + 2$, is the length merely of:

$$a, b, 0, 1, 2, \ldots,$$

which is clearly isomorphic to:

$$0, 1, 2, 3, 4, \ldots$$

and so of length ω.

The ordinal product $x \cdot y$ is meant to measure the length of a well-ordering obtained from a well-ordering of length y by inserting, in place of each single one of its ordered things, a whole string of length x. For example, $\omega \cdot 2$ is the length of:

$$0, 1, 2, \ldots, a, b, c, \ldots$$

while $2 \cdot \omega$ is the length of:

$$0, a, 1, b, 2, c, \ldots .$$

Again, thus, commutativity fails; $\omega = 2 \cdot \omega \neq \omega \cdot 2 = \omega + \omega$.

These concepts of sum and product work as well for order types generally as for ordinal numbers. Thus $\omega^* + \omega$ is the order type of the relation of less to greater among the integers, negatives included. However, I shall disregard this extra coverage and allow the concepts of sum and product to shrink conveniently away from it under further belaboring.

The arithmetical operations on ordinals should in theory, if not in practice, be distinguished notationally from those defined for natural numbers in §16. Alternatively, indeed, once the operations for ordinals are strictly defined, their definitions could be made to supersede the old; the content of the definitions of the operations in natural number theory could be recovered in theorems governing the special case where the ordinals concerned are finite. But this suggestion neglects a complication incidental to the plan of this book: the fact that the natural numbers as of §§12–16 are not the finite ordinals as of 22.15. Anyway, it is perhaps as well to leave the theory of natural numbers neutral as between this transfinite ordinal extension and a different transfinite extension, in cardinals, that awaits us in §30.

Working toward a formal definition of the ordinal sum, we might be expected to begin with a formal definition of segment. A segment $\mathrm{seg}_w\, z$, cut off from an ordering z just before some one w of the ordered objects, is clearly the ordering

$$\{\langle u, v\rangle\colon \langle u, v\rangle, \langle v, w\rangle \in z\}.$$

More generally, we may speak of an ordering as a segment of z when it is either z or $\mathrm{seg}_w\, z$ for some w. Of the notion of remainder, also used in the above brief characterization of the ordinal sum, the definition is again evident: where s is a segment of z, and t is the field of s, the remainder of z is $\bar{t}\rceil z$. Finally $x + y$ is to be the length of z where z has a segment of length x and a remainder of length y.

But rather than press on with the formalization of this, we may note that the matter can be put more simply by taking advantage of special traits of the von Neumann ordinals. The members of x are themselves, taken in order, an ordering of length x; and the rest of the members of $x + y$, taken in order, are an ordering of length y. So we can describe $x + y$ simply as the ordinal v such that the ordering of $v \cap \bar{x}$ is of length y. "*The* ordering" of $v \cap \bar{x}$ is, of course, the relation of less to greater among ordinals belonging as members to $v \cap \bar{x}$. Less to greater among ordinals being $\mathfrak{E}$, that ordering of $v \cap \bar{x}$ is $\mathfrak{E} \cap (\bar{x} \times v)$. So our ordinal sum $x + y$ is now describable as the ordinal v such that $\mathfrak{E} \cap (\bar{x} \times v)$ is of length y, i.e., isomorphic to $\mathfrak{E}\restriction y$. How to formalize this phrase may be quickly perceived from things said in §21, or observed in ponderous practice in the course of §27. (Incidentally, the fact that the field of an ordering cannot be a unit class requires adjustment of the definition for $x + 1$; cf. §21. Also provision must be made for uniqueness of $x + 0$.)

But I stop short of the final definition of ordinal sum because there are advantages in another approach, using transfinite recursion (§25). The ordinal product is more easily defined by transfinite recursion than by trying to formalize the sketchy explanation of $x \cdot y$ that I gave above; ordinal power, which I have not tried to sketch here, is likewise best defined by transfinite recursion; so we gain unity and systematic connection by defining all three operations in that way. Also an analogy then becomes visible between these operations and their counterparts for natural numbers as defined by iteration (§16) or recursive definition.

23. Laws of ordinals

In the reasoning that led to the definition 22.15 of NO it was less than apparent that NO so defined covered all ordinals in the intended sense—viz., Λ and, as a single new ordinal, each accumulation of ordinals from Λ on (barring skipping). This we shall want to establish. The one point, $\Lambda \in \text{NO}$, is proved below in 23.1. The other takes some formulating. To say of a class x of ordinals that it skips past none is to say that every ordinal less than a member of x is in x; i.e., since '$<$' for ordinals is 'ϵ', that every member of a member of x is in x; i.e., that $\bigcup x \subseteq x$. So the assurance wanted is that $\bigcup x \subseteq x \subseteq \text{NO} \;.\supset.\; x \in \text{NO}$. It will be proved in 24.5.

What assurance have we, conversely, that NO as of 22.15 takes in nothing but the ordinals as intended? We shall see in 24.3 that NO is well-ordered by membership. Hence, if there are any unwelcome members, there must be a first with respect to this ordering. (Granted, such reasoning from well-ordering needs a comprehension premiss.) But that first unwelcome member x of NO is then a class purely of intended ordinals. Moreover, x skips past none of them along the way; this we are assured, again, by the fact that NO is ordered by membership, together with the fact that all the intended ordinals are in NO. But then x itself meets the requirement of an intended ordinal.

Nothing but intuitive understanding hinges on our thus showing that 22.15 conforms to our intuitive intent. The desideratum in any version of ordinal numbers is the enumeration theorem, which shows that the ordinals serve their purpose of measuring well-orderings; and this is forthcoming, for 22.15, in §27.

Let us press on with the elementary laws of von Neumann's ordinals.

23.1 $\Lambda, \{\Lambda\} \in \mathrm{NO}.$

Proof. By definitions, Wellord Λ. But $\mathfrak{E}{\restriction}\Lambda = \mathfrak{E}{\restriction}\{\Lambda\} = \Lambda$. Further $\mathsf{U}\Lambda = \Lambda$ and $\mathsf{U}\{\Lambda\} = \Lambda \subseteq \{\Lambda\}$. So, by 22.15, Λ, $\{\Lambda\} \in \mathrm{NO}$.

23.2 $\Lambda \neq x \in \mathrm{NO} \;.\supset.\; \Lambda \in x.$

Proof. By hypothesis and definitions, Fnd $\mathfrak{E}{\restriction}x$. So

$$x \subseteq \breve{}(\mathfrak{E}{\restriction}x)``x \;.\supset.\; x = \Lambda.$$

So, by hypothesis, $x \nsubseteq \breve{}(\mathfrak{E}{\restriction}x)``x$, i.e., there is something $z \in x$ that is not in $\breve{}(\mathfrak{E}{\restriction}x)``x$. Then

$$(w)(w \in x \;.\supset.\; \langle w, z\rangle \notin \mathfrak{E}{\restriction}x)$$

(since $z \in x$) $\qquad\qquad \supset.\; w \notin z).$ (1)

By hypothesis and definition, $\mathsf{U}x \subseteq x$. So, by 8.5, since $z \in x$, $z \subseteq x$. So, by (1), $z = \Lambda$. So $\Lambda \in x$.

The successor of an ordinal x being $x \cup \{x\}$, the predecessor, if any, is $\mathsf{U}x$. For,

23.3 $x \in \mathrm{NO} \;.\supset.\; x = \mathsf{U}(x \cup \{x\}).$

Proof. $\mathsf{U}\{x\} = x$ by 8.2. So $\mathsf{U}(x \cup \{x\}) = \mathsf{U}x \cup x$ by 8.3. But $\mathsf{U}x \cup x = x$, since $\mathsf{U}x \subseteq x$ by hypothesis and 22.15.

Since it is $\mathfrak{E}$ that is to order the ordinals, the next two theorems were to be hoped for.

23.4 $x \in \mathrm{NO} \;.\supset.\; x \notin x.$

Proof. By hypothesis and definitions, $\mathfrak{E}\restriction x \subseteq {}^{-}I$. So, by definitions, $x \notin x$.

23.5 $x \in \text{NO} \;.\supset \sim(x \in^2 x)$.

Proof. By hypothesis and definition, $\mathsf{U}x \subseteq x$. So, by 23.4, $x \notin \mathsf{U}x$.

The next theorem begins to equate the two ways of saying that one ordinal is less than another: '$\in$' and '$\subset$'.

23.6 $x \in y \in \text{NO} \;.\supset.\; x \subset y$.

Proof. By 22.15, since $y \in \text{NO}$, $\mathsf{U}y \subseteq y$. So, by 8.5, since $x \in y$, $x \subseteq y$. But, by hypothesis and 23.4, $x \neq y$.

One law after another that holds for each ordinal turns out to hold also for the class NO of all ordinals. Thus take 23.2, which says that $\Lambda \in x$ for each nonempty ordinal x; we have also $\Lambda \in \text{NO}$, as seen in 23.1. The next three theorems correspond similarly to 23.4, 23.6, and the '$\mathsf{U}x \subseteq x$' of 22.15.

23.7 $\text{NO} \notin \text{NO}$.

Proof. If $\text{NO} \in \text{NO}$ then $\text{NO} \in \mathcal{V}$ and we can take x in 23.4 as NO, concluding that $\text{NO} \notin \text{NO}$.

23.8 $x \in \text{NO} \;.\supset.\; x \subset \text{NO}$.

Proof By hypothesis and definition,

$$\text{Wellord}\ \mathfrak{E}\restriction x. \tag{1}$$

So, by definitions,

$$\mathfrak{E}\restriction x \mid \mathfrak{E}\restriction x \subseteq \mathfrak{E}. \tag{2}$$

Consider any $w \in x$. By hypothesis and 23.6,

$$w \subset x. \qquad \text{[i]}$$

Consider next any $y \in \mathsf{U}w$. There is something z, then, such that $y \in z \in w$. Since $z \in w$, we have by [i] that $z \in x$. Gathering these results, we have $y \in z \in w$ and $z, w \in x$; i.e.,

$$\langle y, z\rangle, \langle z, w\rangle \in \mathfrak{E}{\restriction}x.$$

So, by (2), $y \in w$. But y was any member of $\mathsf{U}w$. So

$$\mathsf{U}w \subseteq w. \qquad [ii]$$

By (1) and 21.9,

$$\text{Wellord } \mathfrak{E}{\restriction}x \cap (w \times w),$$

i.e., by [i] and 9.16, Wellord $\mathfrak{E} \cap (w \times w)$, i.e., by 22.14 and [ii], Wellord $\mathfrak{E}{\restriction}w$. So, by [ii] and 22.15, $w \in$ NO. But w was any member of x. So $x \subseteq$ NO. But, by hypothesis and 23.7, $x \neq$ NO. So $x \subset$ NO.

23.9 UNO $\subseteq$ NO. *Proof* by 23.8, 8.5.

When $z \in$ NO, we know from our definitions that $\mathfrak{E}{\restriction}z$, or $\mathfrak{E} \cap (z \times z)$, is connected. This is not quite as much as to say that $\mathfrak{E}$ connects each two members of z. But this can be proved too.

23.10 $x, y \in z \in \text{NO} \;.\supset:\; x \in y \;.\mathsf{v}.\; y \in x \;.\mathsf{v}.\; x = y.$

Proof. By hypothesis and definitions,

$$\mathsf{U}z \subseteq z, \quad (1) \qquad \text{Connex } \mathfrak{E}{\restriction}z. \quad (2)$$

By hypothesis, $x, y \in z$; so, by 9.16,

$$(u)(v)(u \in x \,.\, v \in y \;.\supset.\; \langle u, x\rangle, \langle v, y\rangle \in \mathfrak{E}{\restriction}z)$$

(by (2)) $\supset:\; x \in y \;.\mathsf{v}.\; y \in x \;.\mathsf{v}.\; x = y).$

That is,

$$x \neq \Lambda \neq y \;.\supset:\; x \in y \;.\mathsf{v}.\; y \in x \;.\mathsf{v}.\; x = y. \qquad (3)$$

By hypothesis and 23.8, $x \in z \subset$ NO. So $x \in$ NO. So, by 23.2, $\Lambda \neq x \;.\supset.\; \Lambda \in x$. So $x \neq \Lambda = y \;.\supset.\; y \in x$. Similarly, $x =$

$\Lambda \neq y \mathrel{.\supset.} x \in y$. Finally, $x = \Lambda = y \mathrel{.\supset.} x = y$. These three conclusions combine with (3) to show that, in every case,

$$x \in y \mathrel{.\mathrm{v}.} y \in x \mathrel{.\mathrm{v}.} x = y.$$

If α has members and they all are ordinals, then their intersection $\bigcap\alpha$ is the least of them. That $\bigcap\alpha \in \alpha$ will be proved only in 23.25, but we can prove now that there is no smaller ordinal in α. Since '$\in$' expresses 'less', the point can be put thus:

23.11 $\alpha \subseteq \mathrm{NO} \mathrel{.\supset.} \alpha \cap \bigcap\alpha = \Lambda.$

Proof. If $x \in \alpha$ then, by hypothesis, $x \in \mathrm{NO}$, and so, by 23.4, $x \notin x \in \alpha$ and so $x \notin y \in \alpha$ for some y; i.e., by 8.9, $x \notin \bigcap\alpha$.

Further laws of ordinals will depend increasingly upon existence provisions beyond the reach of our meager assumptions 7.10 and 13.1. An added axiom schema that will carry us far is an analogue of 13.1 for ordinals. 13.1 said, for all $x \in \mathrm{N}$, that if Func α then there exists the class of all values of α for arguments $\leqq x$. (13.1 figured also where $x \notin \mathrm{N}$, but that was by the way.) Now our new axiom schema will say the same of all $x \in \mathrm{NO}$, with adjustments. It will say for all $x \in \mathrm{NO}$ that if Func α then there exists the class of all values of α for arguments less than x. But 'less than' now means '$\in$'. So

23.12 *Axiom schema.* Func $\alpha \,.\, x \in \mathrm{NO} \mathrel{.\supset.} \alpha``x \in \mathcal{V}.$

Like 13.1, and more directly, this illustrates the principle of replacement. 13.1 assured us of all classes up to any finite size. 23.12 assures us of all classes up to the size of any ordinal.

It was noted that 13.1 tells us nothing even conditionally about infinite classes. 23.12 is different. It still does not imply that there are infinite classes; however, if we are given certain ones, 23.12 tells us of other infinite classes that must accompany them.

Since the members of N can be correlated with the finite ordinals, we might expect 23.12 to supersede 13.1 and to imply it. Actually, however, there is no evident way of deriving 13.1 from 23.12. The obstacle is not just that 13.1 covers the waste cases where $x \notin \mathrm{N}$; we should be glad to waive those. Nor is the obstacle the use of Zermelo numbers in N as against von Neumann numbers in NO. If by revising §12 we were to convert N to von Neumann's line, it is not evident how to deduce even the thus reconstrued 13.1 from 23.12. For the definition of N would presumably run as in §11, with the von Neumann sense of 'S'; and the trouble would then come in proving that $\mathrm{N} \subseteq \mathrm{NO}$. Induction would be the natural means, and it rests on 13.1.

In an eventual strong system we would want to combine 13.1 and 23.12 under some single broader schema of replacement. But at the present stage there is a premium on weakness. In celebration of this trait we may note that until almost the end of the chapter (24.8) the consequences to be drawn from 23.12 will depend only on the second of the following three corollaries, an instance of the principle of *Aussonderung*.

23.13 $\mathrm{Func}\,\alpha\,.\,x \in \mathrm{NO}\,.\,\beta \subseteq \alpha``x \;.\supset.\; \beta \in \mathcal{V}$,

23.14 $x \in \mathrm{NO} \;.\supset.\; x \cap \alpha \in \mathcal{V}$,

23.15 $\mathrm{Func}\,\alpha\,.\,\breve{\alpha}``\mathcal{V} \subseteq x \in \mathrm{NO} \;.\supset.\; \alpha \in \mathcal{V}$.

Proofs from 23.12 like those of 13.2, 13.3, and 13.4 from 13.1.

Just as 13.3 supported the law 13.5 of mathematical induction over the natural numbers, so 23.14 supports the following law of transfinite induction over the ordinals.

23.16 $(y)((x)(x \in y \;.\supset Fx)\,.\,y \in \mathrm{NO} \;.\supset Fy)\,.\,z \in \mathrm{NO} \;.\supset Fz$.

Proof.[1] By 23.14, since $z \in \mathrm{NO}$, $z \cap \{x\colon \sim Fx\} \in \mathcal{V}$. I.e.,

$$\{x\colon \sim(x \in z \;.\supset Fx)\} \in \mathcal{V}. \qquad (1)$$

We have for all $y \in z$ that $y \in \mathrm{NO}$ by 23.8. So the long hypothesis gives:

$$(y)((x)(x \in y \;.\supset Fx) \supset\colon y \in z \;.\supset Fy).$$

We may redundantly recombine '$y \in z$', getting:

$$(y)((x)(x \in y \in z \;.\supset Fx) \supset\colon y \in z \;.\supset Fy).$$

[1] In this I am indebted to Natuhiko Yosida.

Since $z \in \mathrm{NO}$, we have by 23.6 that $x \in z$ whenever $x \in y \in z$. So we may redundantly insert '$x \in z$' thus:

$$(y)((x)(x \in y \in z \,.\!\supset\!:\, x \in z \,.\!\supset Fx) \supset\!:\, y \in z \,.\!\supset Fy),$$

i.e.,

$$(y)((x)(\langle x, y\rangle \in \mathfrak{E}\restriction z \,.\!\supset\!:\, x \in z \,.\!\supset Fx) \supset\!:\, y \in z \,.\!\supset Fy). \qquad (2)$$

Since $z \in \mathrm{NO}$, Fnd $\mathfrak{E}\restriction z$. From this and (1) and (2) we have by 20.5 that $u \in z \,.\!\supset Fu$ for any u. So $(x)(x \in z \,.\!\supset Fx)$. So, by hypothesis (with y as z), Fz.

There follow two corollaries. The first is merely 23.16 with a premiss strengthened.

23.17 $(y)((x)(x \in y \,.\!\supset Fx) \supset Fy) \,.\, z \in \mathrm{NO} \,.\!\supset Fz.$

23.18[2] $\alpha \subseteq \breve{\mathfrak{E}}``\alpha \,.\!\supset\!.\, \alpha \cap \mathrm{NO} = \Lambda.$

Proof. By hypothesis,

$$(y)(y \in \alpha \,.\!\supset (\exists x)(x \in \alpha \,.\, x \in y)).$$

I.e.,

$$(y)((x)(x \in y \,.\!\supset\!.\, x \notin \alpha) \supset\!.\, y \notin \alpha).$$

Then by 23.17, for any $z \in \mathrm{NO}$, $z \notin \alpha$. So $\alpha \cap \mathrm{NO} = \Lambda$.

The next theorem schema is converse to 23.6, thus rounding out the interchangeability of '$\in$' and '$\subset$' as applied to ordinals. This converse requires, unlike 23.6, the assumption that α as well as z is an ordinal—or at least shares the trait '$\mathsf{U}\alpha \subseteq \alpha$' of ordinals.[3]

23.19 $\mathsf{U}\alpha \subseteq \alpha \subset z \in \mathrm{NO} \,.\!\supset\!.\, \alpha \in z.$

Proof. By hypothesis, $z \cap \bar{\alpha} \neq \Lambda$. But, by hypothesis and

---

[2] In this I am indebted to Akira Ohe.

[3] In my use of 'α' here instead of 'x' I am indebted to Joseph Sukonick. In the proof I follow Robinson in essential respects.

23.8, $z \subset \text{NO}$. So $z \cap \bar{\alpha} \cap \text{NO} \neq \Lambda$. So, by 23.18,

$$z \cap \bar{\alpha} \not\subseteq \breve{\mathfrak{E}}``(z \cap \bar{\alpha}).$$

So there is w such that

$$w \in z, \quad (1) \qquad\qquad w \notin \alpha, \quad (2)$$

and $(v)(v \in z \,.\, v \notin \alpha \,.\!\supset\!.\, v \notin w)$, that is, $w \cap z \subseteq \alpha$. But $w \subset z$ by (1) and 23.6, since $z \in \text{NO}$. So

$$w \subseteq \alpha. \tag{3}$$

Consider any $x \in \alpha$. Then $x \subseteq \bigcup\alpha$. Then, by first hypothesis, $x \subseteq \alpha$. So, by (2),

$$w \notin x \,.\, w \neq x. \qquad \text{[i]}$$

By hypothesis, since $x \in \alpha$, $x \in z \in \text{NO}$. So, by (1) and 23.10,

$$w \in x \,.\!\vee\!.\, x \in w \,.\!\vee\!.\, w = x.$$

So, by [i], $x \in w$. But x was any member of α. So $\alpha \subseteq w$. So, by (3), $\alpha = w$. So, by (1), $\alpha \in z$.

The above theorem schema combines with its converse to give:

23.20 $\qquad x, y \in \text{NO} \,.\!\supset\!:\, x \in y \,.\!\equiv\!.\, x \subset y.$

Proof. By hypothesis and definition, $\bigcup x \subseteq x$. So, by hypothesis and 23.19, $x \subset y \,.\!\supset\!.\, x \in y$. Converse by 23.6.

NO is a nest; i.e., each ordinal is a subclass or a superclass of each.

23.21 $\qquad x, y \in \text{NO} \,.\!\supset\!:\, x \subseteq y \,.\!\vee\!.\, y \subseteq x.$

Proof. Consider any $w \in \text{NO}$ such that

$$(z)(z \in w \,.\!\supset\!:\, x \subseteq z \,.\!\vee\!.\, z \subseteq x). \qquad \text{[i]}$$

I.e.,

$$(z)(z \in w \,.\!\supset\!:\, x \subseteq z \,.\!\vee\!.\, z \subset x). \qquad \text{[ii]}$$

But, for any $z \in w$, we have $z \in \text{NO}$ by 23.8 and so $z \in x \,.\!\equiv\!.\, z \subset x$

by 23.20. So [ii] becomes:

$$(z)(z \in w \;.\supset:\; x \subseteq z \;.\mathrm{v}.\; z \in x). \qquad \text{[iii]}$$

Case 1: $x \subseteq z$ for some $z \in w$. Since $w \in$ NO, $z \subset w$ by 23.6. So $x \subseteq w$.

Case 2: $x \subseteq z$ for no $z \in w$. Then, by [iii], $z \in x$ for all $z \in w$. I.e., $w \subseteq x$.

Both cases: $x \subseteq w \;.\mathrm{v}.\; w \subseteq x$. But w was any ordinal fulfilling [i]. So

$$(w)((z)(z \in w \;.\supset:\; x \subseteq z \;.\mathrm{v}.\; z \subseteq x) \;.\; w \in \mathrm{NO} \;.\supset:\; x \subseteq w \;.\mathrm{v}.\; w \subseteq x).$$

From this it follows by transfinite induction according to 23.16, since $y \in$ NO, that $x \subseteq y \;.\mathrm{v}.\; y \subseteq x$.

There follow two corollaries.

23.22 $\quad x, y \in \mathrm{NO} \;.\supset:\; x \subseteq y \;.\mathrm{v}.\; y \in x.$

23.23 $\quad x, y \in \mathrm{NO} \;.\supset:\; x \in y \;.\mathrm{v}.\; y \in x \;.\mathrm{v}.\; x = y.$

Proofs by 23.21 and 23.20, since '$y \subseteq x$' in 23.21 is redundant for '$y \subset x$'.

We saw that various laws of ordinal numbers hold also for NO. The point is further illustrated now in 23.23, which affirms of NO itself what 23.10 affirmed of each ordinal, viz., that it is connected by $\mathfrak{E}$. The following law is similarly related to 23.19 or 23.20.

23.24 $\quad \mathsf{U}\alpha \subseteq \alpha \subset \mathrm{NO} \;.\equiv.\; \alpha \in \mathrm{NO}.$

Proof. By copying the proof of 23.19, but using NO and 23.23 instead of z and 23.10, we show that

$$\mathsf{U}\alpha \subseteq \alpha \subset \mathrm{NO} \;.\supset.\; \alpha \in \mathrm{NO}.$$

Converse by 23.8 and 22.15.

Another point about $\mathsf{U}\alpha$, for any class α of ordinals, is that it is itself an ordinal unless it is NO.

23.25 $\quad \alpha \subseteq \mathrm{NO} \;.\supset:\; \mathsf{U}\alpha \in \mathrm{NO} \;.\mathrm{v}.\; \mathsf{U}\alpha = \mathrm{NO}.$

Proof. By definitions, since $\alpha \subseteq \mathrm{NO}$, we have for any $y \in \alpha$ that $\mathsf{U}y \subseteq y$ and so $z \in w \in y \mathrel{.\supset.} z \in y$. Thus

$$(y)(z)(w)(z \in w \in y \in \alpha \mathrel{.\supset.} z \in y \in \alpha).$$

So $\mathsf{UU}\alpha \subseteq \mathsf{U}\alpha$. Also, since $\alpha \subseteq \mathrm{NO}$, we have $\mathsf{U}\alpha \subseteq \mathsf{U}\mathrm{NO}$ and then, by 23.9, $\mathsf{U}\alpha \subseteq \mathrm{NO}$. So $\mathsf{UU}\alpha \subseteq \mathsf{U}\alpha \subseteq \mathrm{NO}$. So either $\mathsf{U}\alpha = \mathrm{NO}$ or, by 23.24, $\mathsf{U}\alpha \in \mathrm{NO}$.

When we reflect that 'ϵ' is the '$<$' of ordinals, we see that the following theorem says in effect that $x \cup \{x\}$ is the next ordinal after x if there is an ordinal y after x at all.

23.26 $\quad x \in y \in \mathrm{NO} \mathrel{.\supset:} x \cup \{x\} \in y \mathrel{.\mathbf{v}.} x \cup \{x\} = y.$

Proof. By hypothesis and 23.9, $x \in \mathrm{NO}$. So, by 23.3, $x = \mathsf{U}(x \cup \{x\})$. So

$$\mathsf{U}(x \cup \{x\}) \subseteq x \cup \{x\}. \tag{1}$$

By hypothesis, $\{x\} \subseteq y$ and also, in view of 23.6, $x \subset y$. So $x \cup \{x\} \subseteq y$. So either $x \cup \{x\} = y$, q.e.d., or else $x \cup \{x\} \subset y$, in which event, by (1) and hypothesis,

$$\mathsf{U}(x \cup \{x\}) \subseteq x \cup \{x\} \subset y \in \mathrm{NO}$$

and so, by 23.19, $x \cup \{x\} \in y$.

In conclusion we return to the theme of the least member of a class of ordinals; cf. 23.11.

23.27 $\quad \Lambda \neq \alpha \subseteq \mathrm{NO} \mathrel{.\supset.} \bigcap\alpha \in \alpha.$

Proof. By hypothesis, $\alpha \cap \mathrm{NO} \neq \Lambda$. So, by 23.18, $\alpha \not\subseteq \breve{\mathfrak{C}}``\alpha$. So, for some $x \in \alpha$,

$$(y)(y \in \alpha \mathrel{.\supset.} y \notin x). \tag{1}$$

But $\alpha \subseteq \mathrm{NO}$, and so x, $y \in \mathrm{NO}$ for any x, $y \in \alpha$, whereupon $x \subseteq y \mathrel{.\mathbf{v}.} y \in x$ by 23.22. So, by (1), $(y)(y \in \alpha \mathrel{.\supset.} x \subseteq y)$. I.e., by 8.13, $x \subseteq \bigcap\alpha$. But also $\bigcap\alpha \subseteq x$ by 8.14, since $x \in \alpha$. So $x = \bigcap\alpha$. So $\bigcap\alpha \in \alpha$.

24. The order of the ordinals

The ordering of the ordinals, the relation of less to greater among them, is $\mathfrak{E} \cap (\mathrm{NO} \times \mathrm{NO})$. More compactly,

24.1 $\mathfrak{E} \upharpoonright \mathrm{NO} = \mathfrak{E} \cap (\mathrm{NO} \times \mathrm{NO})$. *Proof:* 22.14, 23.9.

Its field is NO.

24.2 $(\mathfrak{E} \upharpoonright \mathrm{NO} \cup \breve{}(\mathfrak{E} \upharpoonright \mathrm{NO}))``\mathcal{V} = \mathrm{NO}$.

Proof. By 23.1, $\{\Lambda\} \in \mathrm{NO}$ and so $\Lambda \in (\mathfrak{E} \upharpoonright \mathrm{NO})``\mathcal{V}$. By 23.2, $\langle \Lambda, x \rangle \in \mathfrak{E} \upharpoonright \mathrm{NO}$ and so $x \in \breve{}(\mathfrak{E} \upharpoonright \mathrm{NO})``\mathcal{V}$ for all $x \in \mathrm{NO}$ other than Λ. Converse inclusion by 24.1.

Now to the theorem that the ordinals are well-ordered.

24.3 Wellord $\mathfrak{E} \upharpoonright \mathrm{NO}$.

Proof. For any $w \in \mathrm{NO}$ we have $\bigcup w \subseteq w$ by 22.15. So

$$(u)(v)(w)(u \in v \in w \in \mathrm{NO} \;.\supset.\; u \in w \in \mathrm{NO}).$$

So $\mathfrak{E} \upharpoonright \mathrm{NO} \mid \mathfrak{E} \upharpoonright \mathrm{NO} \subseteq \mathfrak{E} \upharpoonright \mathrm{NO}$. Further, by 23.4, $\mathfrak{E} \upharpoonright \mathrm{NO} \subseteq \overline{I}$. Further, by 23.23, $\langle y, z \rangle \in \mathfrak{E} \upharpoonright \mathrm{NO} \cup \breve{}(\mathfrak{E} \upharpoonright \mathrm{NO}) \cup I$ for all y, $z \in \mathrm{NO}$; so, by 24.2, Connex $\mathfrak{E} \upharpoonright \mathrm{NO}$. Combining,

$$\text{Ordg } \mathfrak{E} \upharpoonright \mathrm{NO}. \tag{1}$$

Consider any x such that $x \subseteq \breve{}(\mathfrak{E} \upharpoonright \mathrm{NO})``x$. Clearly $x \subseteq \mathrm{NO}$. Also, by 23.18, $x \cap \mathrm{NO} = \Lambda$. So $x = \Lambda$. Thus, by 20.2, Fnd $\mathfrak{E} \upharpoonright \mathrm{NO}$. So, by (1) and 21.4, Wellord $\mathfrak{E} \upharpoonright \mathrm{NO}$.

We can almost say that everything true of each ordinal is true of NO; for NO itself satisfies the two conditions on 'x' in 22.15, as witness 23.9 and 24.3. Why can we not quite say it? One thing true of each ordinal and not of NO is that it is an ordinal. This is denied of NO in 23.7. But how can we deny it of NO when NO satisfies both defining conditions of ordinals? The answer is that $\mathrm{NO} \notin \mathcal{V}$. For belonging to a class, fulfilling the membership conditions is not enough; existence is required.

The proof of '$\mathrm{NO} \notin \mathcal{V}$' is before us: if NO existed, 23.9 and

24.3 would contradict 23.7.

24.4 $\text{NO} \notin \mathcal{V}$.

Essentially '$\text{NO} \notin \mathcal{V}$' is the tamed state of one of the famous paradoxes: Burali-Forti's, which argues that there must and must not be a greatest ordinal number. Historically this was the first of the paradoxes of set theory, dating from 1897.[1] At that time Burali-Forti saw the contradiction only as a *reductio ad absurdum* of the comparability of ordinals, not appreciating how well that comparability could be argued. Nowadays this paradox is accommodated like the others, by not supposing that all membership conditions determine classes; and so our '$\text{NO} \notin \mathcal{V}$'.

A less bizarre consequence of the well-ordering of the ordinals is the following corollary, which was mentioned early in §23.

24.5 $\text{U}x \subseteq x \subseteq \text{NO} .\equiv. x \in \text{NO}$.

Proof. Apart from the alternative '$x = \text{NO}$', which is precluded by 24.4, this is a case of 23.24.

An important structural trait of the ordering $\mathfrak{E} \restriction \text{NO}$ of the ordinals, besides the fact of its being a well-ordering (24.3), is that it has no last term. To prove this is the main remaining business of this section. It will be proved by proving that for every ordinal x there exists a successor $x \cup \{x\}$ which is a further ordinal.

It is easy to prove that whatever successors ordinals have are ordinals.

24.6 $\acute{\text{S}}``\text{NO} \subseteq \text{NO}$.

Proof. If $x \in \acute{\text{S}}``\text{NO}$, there is $y \in \text{NO}$ such that $x = y \cup \{y\}$. By 23.3, $y = \text{U}x$. So $\text{U}x \subseteq x$. Also, by 23.8, $y \subset \text{NO}$ and so $x \subseteq \text{NO}$. So, by 24.5, $x \in \text{NO}$.

It follows that finite ordinals are ordinals.

24.7 $\omega \subseteq \text{NO}$.

---

[1] In a biography published in Cantor's *Gesammelte Abhandlungen*, Fraenkel claims (p. 470) that Cantor was aware of this paradox by 1895 and that he communicated it to Hilbert in 1896.

Proof. By 23.1 and 22.8, $\omega \subseteq *\acute{S}``\mathrm{NO}$. But, by 24.6 and 15.7, $*\acute{S}``\mathrm{NO} = \mathrm{NO}$.

The next is the hard part.

24.8 $$x \in \mathrm{NO} \,.\!\supset.\, x \cup \{x\} \in \mathcal{V}.$$

Proof. 22.11 covers the case where $x \in \omega$. So assume

$$x \notin \omega. \tag{1}$$

When $y \cup \{y\} = z \cup \{z\}$ and $y, z \in \mathrm{NO}$, we get $y = z$ by 23.3. So Func $\breve{}(\acute{S}\restriction\mathrm{NO})$. So, by 24.7, Func $\breve{}(\acute{S}\restriction\omega)$. By 22.10, the field of this function lies within ω and so excludes the field of the function $I\restriction\bar{\omega}$. So

$$\mathrm{Func}\ \breve{}(\acute{S}\restriction\omega) \cup I\restriction\bar{\omega}. \tag{2}$$

By 7.6, $\Lambda \neq u \cup \{u\}$ for all u. So $\Lambda \notin \acute{S}``\mathcal{V}$. Nor, by 22.9, is Λ a member of the field of $I\restriction\bar{\omega}$. So Λ is foreign to the right field of the function described in (2). So, where

$$\alpha = \breve{}(\acute{S}\restriction\omega) \cup I\restriction\bar{\omega} \cup \{\langle x, \Lambda\rangle\}, \tag{3}$$

we have by (2) and 10.7 that

$$\mathrm{Func}\ \alpha. \tag{4}$$

By (1) and 22.9, $x \neq \Lambda$. So, by hypothesis and 23.2, $\Lambda \in x$. But, by (3), $\langle x, \Lambda\rangle \in \alpha$. So

$$x \in \alpha``x. \tag{5}$$

Consider any

$$y \in x. \tag{i}$$

Case 1: $y \in \omega$. Then, by 22.12, $y \cup \{y\} \in \omega$. So, by (1), $x \neq y \cup \{y\}$. So, by [i], hypothesis, and 23.26, $y \cup \{y\} \in x$. Moreover, by definitions, $\langle y, y \cup \{y\}\rangle \in \breve{}(\acute{S}\restriction\omega)$ and so, by (3), $\langle y, y \cup \{y\}\rangle \in \alpha$. So $y \in \alpha``x$.

Case 2: $y \notin \omega$. Then, by (3), $\langle y, y\rangle \in \alpha$. So, by [i], $y \in \alpha``x$.

Both cases: $y \in \alpha``x$, for all $y$ fulfilling [i]. So $x \subseteq \alpha``x$. So, by (5), $x \cup \{x\} \subseteq \alpha``x$. So, by hypothesis, (4), and 23.13, $x \cup \{x\} \in \mathcal{V}$.

From the above theorem and 24.6 there follows, as did 22.12 from 22.11 and 22.10, the desired corollary.

24.9 $x \in \text{NO} \ .\supset.\ x \cup \{x\} \in \text{NO}.$

Incidentally it follows from this and 23.9 that $\mathsf{U}\text{NO} = \text{NO}$.

I conclude the chapter by showing that, where α is any class of ordinals, the ordinal next larger than all in the class is always $\alpha \cup \mathsf{U}\alpha$ if this exists. First let us prove that $\alpha \cup \mathsf{U}\alpha$ is an ordinal if it exists.

24.10 $\alpha \subseteq \text{NO} \ .\supset:\ \alpha \cup \mathsf{U}\alpha \in \text{NO} \ .\text{v}.\ \alpha \cup \mathsf{U}\alpha = \text{NO}.$

Proof by 23.25 if $\alpha \cup \mathsf{U}\alpha = \mathsf{U}\alpha$. Otherwise there is $x \in \alpha$ such that $(y)(y \in \alpha \ .\supset.\ x \notin y)$. But then, by hypothesis and 23.22, $(y)(y \in \alpha \ .\supset.\ y \subseteq x)$. That is, by 8.5, $\mathsf{U}\alpha \subseteq x$. But also, by, 8.6, $x \subseteq \mathsf{U}\alpha$. So $x = \mathsf{U}\alpha$. But x was any member of $\alpha \cap \overline{}\mathsf{U}\alpha$, and there were such. So $\alpha \cap \overline{}\mathsf{U}\alpha = \{x\}$. So $\alpha \cup \mathsf{U}\alpha = \mathsf{U}\alpha \cup \{x\}$. That is, $\alpha \cup \mathsf{U}\alpha = x \cup \{x\}$. So, by 24.9, $\alpha \cup \mathsf{U}\alpha \in \text{NO}$.

The other thing to show was that this ordinal $\alpha \cup \mathsf{U}\alpha$ is the one next larger than all in α; impressionistically,

$$(x)(x < \alpha \cup \mathsf{U}\alpha \ .\equiv:\ x \in \alpha \ .\text{v}\ (\exists y)(x < y \in \alpha)).$$

Since '$<$' for ordinals is '$\in$', the formula runs rather:

$$(x)(x \in \alpha \cup \mathsf{U}\alpha \ .\equiv:\ x \in \alpha \ .\text{v}\ (\exists y)(x \in y \in \alpha)).$$

But this follows directly from definitions.

The class α may or may not have a highest member; these two cases detach themselves in the proof of 24.10. Either way, the ordinal $\alpha \cup \mathsf{U}\alpha$ is next larger than all in α. If α has a highest member x, then x is $\mathsf{U}\alpha$ and $\alpha \cup \mathsf{U}\alpha$ is its successor. If α has no highest member, then $\alpha \cup \mathsf{U}\alpha$ is simply $\mathsf{U}\alpha$, a limit ordinal, the limit of α. Here α might be the class of the odd finite ordinals, or of the prime finite ordinals; then $\mathsf{U}\alpha$, its limit, is ω.

VIII | TRANSFINITE RECURSION

25. Transfinite recursion

Recursion as a way of specifying a function is familiar from the classical cases of sum, product, and power. Thus take the recursion for product:

$$\text{(i)} \qquad x \cdot 0 = 0, \qquad x \cdot (\mathrm{S}`z) = x + x \cdot z.$$

We saw (§11) how to turn such a recursion into a genuine or direct definition:

$$\text{(ii)} \qquad x \cdot y = (\lambda_v(x + v))^{|y`}0.$$

The general pattern of (i) may be put thus:

$$\text{(iii)} \qquad \alpha`0 = k, \qquad \alpha`(\mathrm{S}`z) = \beta`(\alpha`z),$$

and the general pattern of the directification (ii) thus:

$$\text{(iv)} \qquad \alpha`y = \beta^{|y`}k \quad (\text{or } \alpha = \lambda_y(\beta^{|y`}k)).$$

Let us uncover more structure by looking to the definition ((viii), §11) of this notation of iterates of relations. We find $\beta^{|y`}k$ defined as $w`y$ where w is a sequence such that $\langle k, 0\rangle \in w$ and $w \mid \mathrm{S} \mid \breve{w} \subseteq \beta$. So (iv) has the net effect of identifying $\alpha`y$, for each natural number $y$, with $w`y$ for any such sequence w—provided of course that w, though finite, does not stop short of taking y as argument. The function α itself, admitting as it does every natural number y as argument, may be seen as an *infinite* sequence. It coincides with each of the described finite sequences w as far as each goes, but outruns each; indeed, it is the union of them all.

(v) $\alpha = \bigcup\{w\colon w \in \mathrm{Seq} \,.\, \langle k, 0\rangle \in w \,.\, w \mid \mathrm{S} \mid \breve{w} \subseteq \beta\}.$

Such is the force of (iv).

Our example of (iv) was (ii). The corresponding example of (v) is:

(vi) $\lambda_y(x{\cdot}y) = \bigcup\{w\colon w \in \mathrm{Seq} \,.\, \langle 0, 0\rangle \in w \,.$
$w \mid \mathrm{S} \mid \breve{w} \subseteq \lambda_v(x + v)\}.$

The forms (v) and (vi) are less perspicuous than (iv) and (ii), but I bring them in to prepare the way for two extensions.

Let us sum (v) up in an intuitive terminology: it identifies α with *the infinite sequence that is generated from k by* β. Thus (vi), in particular, explains the "x-times" function as the infinite sequence that is generated from 0 by the "x-plus" function. Similarly the "x-to-the-power" function, $\lambda_y(x^y)$, becomes describable as the infinite sequence that is generated from 1 by the "x-times" function; and the "x-plus" function is the infinite sequence that is generated from x by S.

Such, then, is the essence of recursion, at least as embodied in the classical recursions for sum, product, and power. What recursion defines is some infinite sequence α, or function over all natural numbers. It defines it by saying what α is generated by and what from: by β from k. How to express the α directly, in terms of those two data β and k that "recursively define" it, is shown in (v).

But this version of recursion, while adequate to sum, product, power, and other simple examples, is needlessly narrow in requiring β to determine each succeeding value of α in terms of just the preceding value. A properly liberal version of recursion would allow each succeeding value of α to depend rather on the whole course of prior values. Now this course of prior values—the course of values of α for arguments prior to a given argument y—is simply the stump of α that stops at that point; hence the sequence $\alpha \upharpoonright \{z\colon z < y\}$. What we want instead of β, therefore, by way of liberalization, is γ where, for each succeeding y,

$$\text{(vii)} \qquad \alpha`y = \gamma`(\alpha \upharpoonright \{z\colon z < y\})$$

(instead of just $\alpha`y = \beta`(\alpha`(\breve{S}`y))$; cf. (iii)). This γ generates the sequence α by specifying, for each stump of α as argument, what comes next.

Let us extend (v) accordingly. Instead of being the infinite union of the finite sequences w that begin with k and are such that $w \mid S \mid \breve{w} \subseteq \beta$, α is now to be the infinite union rather of the finite sequences w that begin with k and are such that

$$\text{(viii)} \qquad (y)(y \in \breve{w}``\mathcal{V} \,.\supset.\, w`y = \gamma`(w \upharpoonright \{z\colon z < y\}).$$

That is,

$$\alpha = \bigcup\{w\colon w \in \text{Seq} \,.\, \langle k, 0\rangle \in w \,.\, (y)(y \in \breve{w}``\mathcal{V} \,.\supset.\, \langle w`y, w \upharpoonright \{z\colon z < y\}\rangle \in \gamma)\}.$$

Actually the γ is sufficient datum without k; for k is to be the $w`0$ of (viii), hence $\gamma`\Lambda$. So our extended recursion schema comes to be:

$$\text{(ix)} \qquad \alpha = \bigcup\{w\colon w \in \text{Seq} \,.\, (y)(y \in \breve{w}``\mathcal{V} \,.\supset.\, \langle w`y, w \upharpoonright \{z\colon z < y\}\rangle \in \gamma)\}.$$

Such, then, is the essence of recursion as liberalized: course-of-values recursion. It defines an infinite sequence, or function over all natural numbers, simply by saying what function γ generates it—in a reformed sense of generation. Generation of α now means specification of successive values of α not in terms of the respective single values just preceding, but in terms of however much of α has thus far been generated.

It was course-of-values induction (§20) that clamored for extension to well-orderings and indeed to founded relations generally, and emerged as transfinite induction. A parallel development is forthcoming in recursion: our course-of-values recursion admits immediately of transfinite extension. Our α is an infinite sequence, but only in the sense of taking all natural numbers as arguments. We can go on to transfinite sequences: functions admitting both finite and transfinite ordinals as arguments.

A definition is wanted, to begin with, of sequences in this extended sense. We may define them as functions whose right fields comprise all the ordinals less than some ordinal—hence simply as functions whose right fields are ordinals. Also we throw in the case where the right field is NO; these extreme sequences are not expected to exist, but they make good virtual classes. On their account the extended notion of sequence is best rendered not by a class term, like 'Seq', but by a predicate.

25.1 'SEQ α' for 'Func α : $\breve{\alpha}$"$\mathcal{V}$ ϵ NO .v. $\breve{\alpha}$"$\mathcal{V}$ = NO'.

Now to extend the course-of-values recursion schema (ix) to the transfinite we have merely to change '$w \epsilon$ Seq' to 'SEQ w', and incidentally simplify '$\{z: z < y\}$' to 'y' in recognition of the fact that we are now working not with natural numbers in Zermelo's sense but with ordinals in von Neumann's sense. The α that (ix) as thus emended describes will be called Aγ, following Bernays.

25.2 'Aγ' for '$\bigcup\{w$: SEQ w .
$(y)(y \epsilon \breve{w}$"$\mathcal{V}$.⊃. $\langle w‘y, w\restriction y\rangle \epsilon \gamma)\}$'.

Here γ is the function—the *sequence function*, as Halmos calls it—that specifies each succeeding value of a desired sequence by reference to the course of prior ones. Aγ is the sequence that γ thus generates. We may speak of Aγ as the *accumulate* of γ; for it is the total sequence that is accumulated by applying γ to each interim accumulation.[1]

---

[1] Bernays intended 'Aγ' to stand for the words 'the adaptor of γ'. Finding 'adaptor' unsuggestive, I have been at pains to fit a more suggestive word to the same initial. I wanted at least to keep his notation, for his concept is recognizably that defined in 25.2 once the differences in approach are sorted out. See Bernays and Fraenkel, pp. 100ff. In its essentials the idea goes back to von Neumann, "Ueber die Definition" and even "Zur Einführung," note 4.

Transfinite recursion is for us embodied in the above definition. A desired sequence has been specified by transfinite recursion when the sequence function γ has been given whose accumulate $A\gamma$ is the desired sequence.

Let us try transfinite recursion as a means of redefining the ordinal sum $x + y$ (cf. §22). The sequence here to be defined by transfinite recursion is $\lambda_y(x + y)$: the sequence α whose yth (from 0th) value $\alpha`y$ for each y is $x + y$. Wanted: the sequence function γ such that $A\gamma$ is α, or $\lambda_y(x + y)$. The sequence α is a class of pairs comprising

$$\langle x, 0\rangle, \langle \acute{S}`x, 1\rangle, \ldots, \langle x + y, y\rangle, \ldots,$$

and the sequence function γ should be such that $\gamma`z$ turns out to be the left number in such a pair whenever $z$ is the class of all prior pairs. So, since the desired left numbers are just the ordinals from $x$ on in normal order, what we want $\gamma`z$ to be is simply the number next larger than all left numbers in z; next larger, in other words, than all members of $z``\mathcal{V}$. But there is an exception where $z = \Lambda$: we want $\gamma`\Lambda$ to be $x$. Now we can combine the rule and the exception by saying that we want $\gamma`z$ to be the number that is next larger than all left numbers in z *and* all numbers less than x. But the class of all left numbers in z is $z``\mathcal{V}$, and the class of all numbers less than $x$ is $x$: so we want $\gamma`z$ to be the number next larger than all in $z``\mathcal{V} \cup x$. So, in view of the end of §24, what we want is that

$$\begin{aligned} \gamma`z &= z``\mathcal{V} \cup x \cup \mathsf{U}(z``\mathcal{V} \cup x) \\ \text{(by 8.3)} \quad &= z``\mathcal{V} \cup x \cup \mathsf{U}(z``\mathcal{V}) \cup \mathsf{U}x \\ &= z``\mathcal{V} \cup \mathsf{U}(z``\mathcal{V}) \cup x \end{aligned}$$

(since $\mathsf{U}x \subseteq x$ by 22.15). So we can take γ as

$$\lambda_z(z``\mathcal{V} \cup \mathsf{U}(z``\mathcal{V}) \cup x)$$

and then $x + y$ as $A\gamma`y$.

To define $x \cdot y$ by transfinite recursion we must specify for each x a sequence function γ such that $A\gamma$ turns out to be $\lambda_y(x \cdot y)$, which is the transfinite sequence α whose yth (from 0th) value $\alpha`y$ for each y is $x \cdot y$. Now this desired α or $\lambda_y(x \cdot y)$ is a class of pairs comprising

$$\langle 0, 0\rangle, \langle x, 1\rangle, \langle x + x, 2\rangle, \ldots, \langle x \cdot y, y\rangle, \ldots.$$

The sequence function γ should be such that $\gamma`z$ turns out to be the left number in such a pair whenever $z$ is the class of all prior pairs. So we want $\gamma`z$ always to be the highest number in $z``\mathcal{V}$, if highest there be, plus $x$. When $z``\mathcal{V}$ has no highest but consists rather of an unending ascent of multiples of x, then we want the pair next after the infinite pair-class z to have as its left number the limit or least bound of all those ascending multiples of x. The least bound of $z``\mathcal{V}$ being $\bigcup(z``\mathcal{V})$, we see that $\gamma`z$ is to be $\bigcup(z``\mathcal{V})$ when $z``\mathcal{V}$ has no highest member.

So we define γ by an alternation, making $\gamma`z$ the highest member of $z``\mathcal{V}$, if such there be, plus $x$, and otherwise $\bigcup(z``\mathcal{V})$. How may we express this? We reflect that $z``\mathcal{V}$ has a highest member if and only if $\breve{z}``\mathcal{V}$ does; also that $\breve{z}``\mathcal{V}$, unlike $z``\mathcal{V}$, is itself an ordinal; also that an ordinal has a highest member if and only if it is a successor, $u \cup \{u\}$, rather than a limit ordinal; and finally that when $\breve{z}``\mathcal{V}$ is $u \cup \{u\}$, the highest member of $z``\mathcal{V}$ is $z`u$. So

$$\gamma = \{\langle w, z\rangle : (\exists u)(\breve{z}``\mathcal{V} = u \cup \{u\} \,.\, w = z`u + x)$$
$$\mathbf{v}.\ (u)(\breve{z}``\mathcal{V} \neq u \cup \{u\}) \,.\, w = \bigcup(z``\mathcal{V})\}.$$

Finally $x \cdot y = \mathrm{A}\gamma`y$.

We can define x^y almost like $x \cdot y$. Instead of '$z`u + x$' we would here use '$(z`u) \cdot x$'. But also we must provide especially for x^0 to be 1 rather than 0, if such is our wish. This effect can be got by changing the '$\bigcup(z``\mathcal{V})$' to '$\bigcup(z``\mathcal{V}) \cup \{\Lambda\}$'.

Transfinite recursion can be further illustrated by defining the summation $\sum\beta$ of a sequence β. If in particular β is simply $\{x\} \times y$—hence, intuitively, the sequence $x, x, x, \ldots$ to y places—then $\sum\beta$ is $x \cdot y$. So we may find our way to a general definition of $\sum\beta$ by generalizing the above construction of $x \cdot y$. Now each successive value of the sequence α or $\mathrm{A}\gamma$ of that construction issued from its predecessor by the adding of x. In the new $A\gamma$ of the more general construction we want each successive value, say the vth (from 0th), to issue from its predecessor by the adding of $\beta`v$. To gain this effect we have only to change the above formulation of $\gamma$ to the extent of changing the '$x$' to '$\beta`u$'. For γ thus modified, $A\gamma$ is the sequence that cumulatively adds up the sequence β. It is the sequence whose vth (from 0th) value $A\gamma`v$, for each v up to the length of β, is the sum of the first v values of the sequence β. $\sum\beta$ itself, then, is the last value of the sequence $A\gamma$—the highest member of $A\gamma``\mathcal{V}$—if such there be, and otherwise the limit. Either way, $\sum\beta = \bigcup(A\gamma``\mathcal{V})$. So we have the definition of $\sum\beta$.

Given this, we could of course have defined product more briefly: $x \cdot y = \sum(\{x\} \times y)$.

Then we can define productation, $\prod\beta$, analogously to summation (but arranging that $\prod\Lambda = 1$). Finally $x^y = \prod(\{x\} \times y)$.

26. Laws of transfinite recursion[1]

We want $A\gamma$ to be the grand sequence whose value for each argument y is γ of its stump up to y; hence $\gamma`(A\gamma \restriction y)$. So we must show that SEQ $A\gamma$ and that $A\gamma`y$ in general is $\gamma`(A\gamma \restriction y)$. Finally we must show that $A\gamma$ goes as far as such a sequence can: that $\gamma$ cannot apply to *it* to append anything further, $\gamma`A\gamma$, to the end of the sequence $A\gamma$. Such are the agenda for this section.

The following lemma goes a long way toward one of those agenda, viz., toward showing that $A\gamma`y$ is $\gamma`(A\gamma \restriction y)$.

26.1 $\quad$ Func $A\gamma \restriction y \,.\, \langle x, y\rangle \in A\gamma \;.\supset.\; \langle x, A\gamma \restriction y\rangle \in \gamma \,.\, A\gamma \restriction y \in \mathcal{V}$.

Proof. By second hypothesis and 25.2, there is w such that

$$w \subseteq A\gamma, \quad (1) \qquad \langle x, y\rangle \in w, \quad (2) \qquad \text{SEQ}\, w, \quad (3)$$

$$(z)(z \in \breve{w}``\mathcal{V} \;.\supset.\; \langle w`z, w \restriction z\rangle \in \gamma). \quad (4)$$

---

[1] This section departs markedly from the first edition. The central improvement is due to Parsons, q.v.

By (2),

$$y \in \breve{w}``\mathcal{V}. \tag{5}$$

By (3) and 25.1, $\breve{w}``\mathcal{V} \in \mathrm{NO}$ or $\breve{w}``\mathcal{V} = \mathrm{NO}$. Either way, by (5), 23.6, and 23.8,

$$y \in \mathrm{NO}, \quad (6) \qquad\qquad y \subset \breve{w}``\mathcal{V}. \quad (7)$$

By (7), $y = \breve{\ }(w{\upharpoonright}y)``\mathcal{V}$. But

$$\breve{\ }(\mathrm{A}\gamma{\upharpoonright}y)``\mathcal{V} \subseteq y. \tag{8}$$

So $\breve{\ }(\mathrm{A}\gamma{\upharpoonright}y)``\mathcal{V} \subseteq \breve{\ }(w{\upharpoonright}y)``\mathcal{V}$. Also, by (1), $w{\upharpoonright}y \subseteq \mathrm{A}\gamma{\upharpoonright}y$. So, by first hypothesis and 10.10a,

$$\mathrm{A}\gamma{\upharpoonright}y = w{\upharpoonright}y. \tag{9}$$

By (3), Func w. So, by (2),

$$x = w`y. \tag{10}$$

By (4) and (5), $\langle w`y, w{\upharpoonright}y\rangle \in \gamma$. So, by (9) and (10), $\langle x, \mathrm{A}\gamma{\upharpoonright}y\rangle \in \gamma$, q.e.d. Also, from first hypothesis and (6) and (8), we have by 23.15 that $\mathrm{A}\gamma{\upharpoonright}y \in \mathcal{V}$.

The next two lemmas go toward another of the agenda, viz., toward showing that SEQ $\mathrm{A}\gamma$.

26.2 $\qquad \bigcup(\breve{\mathrm{A}}\gamma``\mathcal{V}) \subseteq \breve{\mathrm{A}}\gamma``\mathcal{V} \subseteq \mathrm{NO}.$

Proof. Consider any $z \in \breve{\mathrm{A}}\gamma``\mathcal{V}$. By 25.2 there is w such that

$$w \subseteq \mathrm{A}\gamma, \quad [\mathrm{i}] \qquad z \in \breve{w}``\mathcal{V}, \quad [\mathrm{ii}] \qquad \mathrm{SEQ}\ w. \quad [\mathrm{iii}]$$

By [ii] and [iii], as in (6) and (7) of preceding proof,

$$z \in \mathrm{NO}, \quad [\mathrm{iv}] \qquad\qquad z \subset \breve{w}``\mathcal{V}. \quad [\mathrm{v}]$$

By [v] and [i], $z \subset \breve{\mathrm{A}}\gamma``\mathcal{V}$. But $z$ was any member of $\breve{\mathrm{A}}\gamma``\mathcal{V}$. So, by 8.5, $\bigcup(\breve{\mathrm{A}}\gamma``\mathcal{V}) \subseteq \breve{\mathrm{A}}\gamma``\mathcal{V}$. Also, by [iv], $\breve{\mathrm{A}}\gamma``\mathcal{V} \subseteq \mathrm{NO}$.

26.3 $\qquad \breve{\mathrm{A}}\gamma``\mathcal{V} \in \mathrm{NO}\ .\mathrm{v}.\ \breve{\mathrm{A}}\gamma``\mathcal{V} = \mathrm{NO}.$

Proof. Either $\breve{\mathrm{A}}\gamma``\mathcal{V} = \mathrm{NO}$ or else, by 26.2 and 23.24, $\mathrm{A}\gamma``\mathcal{V} \in \mathrm{NO}$.

Now to the rest of the proof that SEQ $\mathrm{A}\gamma$. It requires the assumption that γ is a function.

26.4 $\qquad \mathrm{Func}\ \gamma \supset \mathrm{SEQ}\ \mathrm{A}\gamma.$

Proof. Suppose $\sim \mathrm{Func}\ \mathrm{A}\gamma$. I.e., $\breve{\mathrm{A}}\gamma``\mathcal{V} \cap {}^{-}\mathrm{arg}\ \mathrm{A}\gamma \neq \Lambda$. This class is comprised of ordinals, by 26.2. So, by 23.27, there is something z such that

$$z = \bigcap(\breve{\mathrm{A}}\gamma``\mathcal{V} \cap {}^{-}\mathrm{arg}\ \mathrm{A}\gamma), \qquad [i]$$

$$z \in \breve{\mathrm{A}}\gamma``\mathcal{V}, \quad [ii] \qquad z \notin \mathrm{arg}\ \mathrm{A}\gamma. \quad [iii]$$

By 26.2 and [ii],

$$z \subseteq \breve{\mathrm{A}}\gamma``\mathcal{V}. \qquad [iv]$$

But, by [i] and 23.11, z shares no member with $\breve{\mathrm{A}}\gamma``\mathcal{V}$ and ${}^{-}\mathrm{arg}\ \mathrm{A}\gamma$. So

$$z \subseteq \mathrm{arg}\ \mathrm{A}\gamma. \qquad [v]$$

By [ii] and [iii] there are x and y such that

$$x \neq y, \quad [vi] \qquad \langle x, z\rangle, \langle y, z\rangle \in \mathrm{A}\gamma. \quad [vii]$$

By [v], Func $\mathrm{A}\gamma{\upharpoonright}z$. From this and [vii] it follows according to 26.1 that

$$\langle x, \mathrm{A}\gamma{\upharpoonright}z\rangle, \langle y, \mathrm{A}\gamma{\upharpoonright}z\rangle \in \gamma, \qquad \mathrm{A}\gamma{\upharpoonright}z \in \mathcal{V}.$$

Then, since Func γ by hypothesis, $x = y$. But this contradicts [vi]. So the assumption '$\sim$ Func $\mathrm{A}\gamma$' is disproved. So, by 26.3 and 25.1, SEQ $\mathrm{A}\gamma$.

One of our agenda was to show, for each argument y of $\mathrm{A}\gamma$, that $\mathrm{A}\gamma`y$ is $\gamma`(\mathrm{A}\gamma{\upharpoonright}y)$. We take up the tale from 26.1.

26.5 $\qquad \mathrm{Func}\ \gamma \,.\, y \in \breve{\mathrm{A}}\gamma``\mathcal{V} \,.\supset.\, \langle \mathrm{A}\gamma`y, \mathrm{A}\gamma{\upharpoonright}y\rangle \in \gamma.$

Proof. By first hypothesis and 26.4, Func $\mathrm{A}\gamma$. So Func $\mathrm{A}\gamma{\upharpoonright}y$. But also, by second hypothesis, $\langle \mathrm{A}\gamma`y, y\rangle \in \mathrm{A}\gamma$. So, by 26.1, $\langle \mathrm{A}\gamma`y, \mathrm{A}\gamma{\upharpoonright}y\rangle \in \gamma$.

The last of our three agenda was to show that $A\gamma$ is not an argument of γ. This will now be shown, subject to exception only in the unlikely case where $A\gamma \in \mathcal{V}$ though $\breve{A\gamma}``\mathcal{V} \notin \mathcal{V}$.

26.6 $\quad \text{Func}\,\gamma\,.\,\breve{A\gamma}``\mathcal{V} \in \mathcal{V}\ .\supset.\ A\gamma \notin \breve{\gamma}``\mathcal{V}.$

Proof. By first hypothesis and 26.4,

$$\text{Func}\, A\gamma. \tag{1}$$

By second hypothesis, 26.3, and 24.4,

$$\breve{A\gamma}``\mathcal{V} \in \text{NO}. \tag{2}$$

So, by 23.4 and 23.5,

$$\breve{A\gamma}``\mathcal{V} \notin \breve{A\gamma}``\mathcal{V}, \quad (3) \qquad\qquad \sim(\breve{A\gamma}``\mathcal{V} \in^2 \breve{A\gamma}``\mathcal{V}). \quad (4)$$

Let

$$\alpha = A\gamma \cup \{\langle \gamma`A\gamma, \breve{A\gamma}``\mathcal{V}\rangle\}. \tag{5}$$

So

$$\breve{\alpha}``\mathcal{V} = \breve{A\gamma}``\mathcal{V} \cup \{\breve{A\gamma}``\mathcal{V}\}. \tag{6}$$

So, by (3) and second hypothesis, $\breve{A\gamma}``\mathcal{V}$ is a member not of $\breve{A\gamma}``\mathcal{V}$ but of $\breve{\alpha}``\mathcal{V}$. So

$$A\gamma = \alpha\upharpoonright(\breve{A\gamma}``\mathcal{V}), \quad (7) \qquad\qquad \alpha \not\subseteq A\gamma, \quad (8)$$

and also, by (1) and 10.7,

$$\text{Func}\,\alpha. \tag{9}$$

By(2), (6), and 24.9,

$$\breve{\alpha}``\mathcal{V} \in \text{NO}. \tag{10}$$

So, by (9) and 25.1,

$$\text{SEQ}\,\alpha. \tag{11}$$

By (9), (10), and 23.15,

$$\alpha \in \mathcal{V}. \tag{12}$$

By (5), (9), and second hypothesis,

$$\gamma\text{‘}\mathrm{A}\gamma = \alpha\text{‘}({}^{\smile}\mathrm{A}\gamma\text{“}\mathcal{V}). \tag{13}$$

Now suppose, *per impossibile*, that

$$\mathrm{A}\gamma \in \breve{\gamma}\text{“}\mathcal{V}. \qquad \text{[i]}$$

By first hypothesis, then, $\langle \gamma\text{‘}\mathrm{A}\gamma, \mathrm{A}\gamma\rangle \in \gamma$. I.e., by (13) and (7),

$$\langle \alpha\text{‘}({}^{\smile}\mathrm{A}\gamma\text{“}\mathcal{V}), \alpha\upharpoonright({}^{\smile}\mathrm{A}\gamma\text{“}\mathcal{V})\rangle \in \gamma. \qquad \text{[ii]}$$

Consider any $y \in {}^{\smile}\mathrm{A}\gamma\text{“}\mathcal{V}$. By first hypothesis and 26.5,

$$\langle \mathrm{A}\gamma\text{‘}y, \mathrm{A}\gamma\upharpoonright y\rangle \in \gamma. \qquad \text{[iii]}$$

By (3), $y \neq {}^{\smile}\mathrm{A}\gamma\text{“}\mathcal{V}$; so, by (5), $\mathrm{A}\gamma\text{‘}y = \alpha\text{‘}y$. By (4), ${}^{\smile}\mathrm{A}\gamma\text{“}\mathcal{V} \notin y$; so, by (5), $\mathrm{A}\gamma\upharpoonright y = \alpha\upharpoonright y$. Substituting in [iii] according to these two equations, we have $\langle \alpha\text{‘}y, \alpha\upharpoonright y\rangle \in \gamma$. This is for any $y \in {}^{\smile}\mathrm{A}\gamma\text{“}\mathcal{V}$. But it holds also when $y = {}^{\smile}\mathrm{A}\gamma\text{“}\mathcal{V}$, by [ii]. So, by (6),

$$(y)(y \in \breve{\alpha}\text{“}\mathcal{V} \;.\supset.\; \langle \alpha\text{‘}y, \alpha\upharpoonright y\rangle \in \gamma).$$

So, by (11) and (12), we see that α is something w fulfilling the condition in 25.2. So $\alpha \subseteq \mathrm{A}\gamma$, contrary to (8). So '$\mathrm{A}\gamma \in \breve{\gamma}\text{“}\mathcal{V}$' has led to contradiction.

27. Enumeration

Ordinal numbers measure the lengths of well-orderings. An ordinal number p is meant to measure the length of the ordering of the ordinals less than p (see §22). To say that a well-ordering α has p as its ordinal number, then, or that it is of length p, is to say that there is an isomorphism between α and the ordering of the ordinals less than p (see §21). But the ordering of the ordinals less than p is the relation $\mathcal{E}$ among the ordinals less than p; hence $\mathcal{E}$ among the members of p; hence $\mathcal{E} \cap (p \times p)$; hence, by 22.14, $\mathcal{E}\upharpoonright p$. The isomorphism in question, then, is an isomorphism between α and $\mathcal{E}\upharpoonright p$; hence a correspondence between $(\alpha \cup \breve{\alpha})\text{“}\mathcal{V}$ and p under which the ordering α on the one hand runs parallel to $\mathcal{E}$ on the other. Clearly this correspondence qualifies as a sequence in the sense of 25.1. Moreover, it is unique; only one correspondence between $(\alpha \cup \breve{\alpha})``\mho$ and an ordinal can keep the order. I shall call it *the enumeration of* $\alpha$, briefly e$\alpha$. Once this is defined, we have a compact expression for the ordinal number of the well-ordering $\alpha$; it is simply the right field of the enumeration, hence $\breve{\text{e}}\alpha``\mho$.

Informally one might be inclined to speak of the "series" of all the prime numbers, or the infinite "sequence" of them, or the "ordering" of them, without intending any technical distinction. Technically we have a somewhat arbitrary distinction between the latter two phrases; the sequence of the primes is by 25.1 the relation of 1 to 0, 2 to 1, 3 to 2, 5 to 3, etc., whereas the ordering of the primes is the relation of 1 to 2, 3, 5, etc., and of 2 to 3, 5, 7, etc., and of 3 to 5, 7, 11, etc. Now where α is the ordering in this technical sense, eα is the corresponding sequence in this technical sense; this is all the idea of enumeration amounts to. Indeed, eα'y for each ordinal y is simply the yth thing in the ordering α (after the initial one, which counts as 0th). What more natural?

Even so, eα has still to be defined. Since it is to be a sequence, the way to define it is by transfinite recursion. So what we need to define it is its generating sequence function—the relation of each next value x of the sequence eα to the whole (call it z) of eα up to there. But the relation of x to z each time is simply that what are earlier than x under the ordering α are the things in the sequence z, the values of the function z; succinctly, $\alpha``\{x\} = z``\mho$. So the sequence function, call it Φ_α, that generates eα is apparently

$$\{\langle x, z\rangle : \alpha``\{x\} = z``\mho\},$$

and eα is A of it. Just this refinement is wanted: lest any and every $x \notin (\alpha \cup \breve{\alpha})``\mho$ bear Φ_α to Λ, we insert the stipulation '$z = \Lambda \,.\!\supset x \mathrm{l} \alpha$'. So these are our definitions:

27.1 'Φ_α' for '$\{\langle x, z\rangle : \alpha``\{x\} = z``\mho : \cdot z = \Lambda \,.\!\supset x \mathrm{l} \alpha\}$',[1]

27.2 'eα' for 'AΦ_α'.

---

[1] Corrected by Colin Godfrey.

One use for eα, as remarked, is in expressing the ordinal number of α, viz., as $\breve{\text{e}}\alpha``\mathfrak{V}$. But there are further uses too. Since eα'y is the yth thing (plus one) in the ordering α, the device offers a particularly lucid variety of transfinite recursion. Thus take again the ordinal sum $x + y$. It is the yth ordinal after x, hence the yth thing in the ordering of the ordinals from x on, counting x as 0th. But the ordinals from x on are the ordinals other than members of x; and the ordering of them is $\mathfrak{E} \cap (\bar{x} \times \text{NO})$. So

$$x + y = \text{e}(\mathfrak{E} \cap (\bar{x} \times \text{NO}))`y.$$

This is somewhat briefer and much more intuitive than the transfinite recursion to the same purpose that we arrived at late in §25 The reader might try proving them equivalent.

There were allusions in §21 and §23 to an *enumeration theorem* according to which there is an isomorphism between any well-ordering and the ordering of the ordinals up to a point. Now where α is the well-ordering, eα is that isomorphism. So the enumeration theorem will for us take the form of a string of theorem schemata that attribute the desired properties to eα. One is that eα is a *correspondence*, or one-one relation; let us at last record the obvious definition of this term.

27.3 'Cor β' for 'Func β . Func $\breve{\beta}$'.

One is that its left field is the field of α. One is that its right field, $\breve{\text{e}}\alpha``\mathfrak{V}$, is the class of ordinals up to a point—hence simply that it is either an ordinal or NO. And one is, finally, that eα preserves order; i.e., eα'x bears α to eα'y when and only when the ordinal x is less than the ordinal y (i.e., $x \in y$).

The third of these four properties can be established immediately.

27.4 $\breve{\text{e}}\alpha``\mathfrak{V} \in \text{NO} \,.\text{v}.\, \breve{\text{e}}\alpha``\mathfrak{V} = \text{NO}$. *Proof:* 26.3, 27.2.

The next one to aim for is number one: that eα is a correspondence. Two lemmas precede it.

27.5 Ordg $\alpha \supset$ Func Φ_α.

Proof. Consider any u, v, w such that

$$\langle u, w\rangle, \langle v, w\rangle \in \Phi_\alpha. \qquad [i]$$

To show $u = v$. If ${}^{\cdot}w = \Lambda$, [i] and 27.1 give $u 1 \alpha$ and $v 1 \alpha$ and so, by 21.8 and hypothesis, $u = v$. If on the other hand ${}^{\cdot}w \neq \Lambda$, then we have from [i] and 27.1 that

$$\alpha``\{u\} = \alpha``\{v\} = w``\mho \neq \Lambda,$$

in which event $u, v \in \breve{\alpha}``\mho$ and so, by hypothesis and 21.5, $u = v$.

27.6 $\quad \text{Ordg}\, \alpha \,.\, y \in \breve{}\text{e}\alpha``\mho \;.\supset.\; \alpha``\{\text{e}\alpha`y\} = \text{e}\alpha``y.$

Proof. By first hypothesis and 27.5, Func Φ_α. So, by 26.4 and definitions, Func eα. So Func $\text{e}\alpha\restriction y$ and also, by second hypothesis, $\langle \text{e}\alpha`y, y\rangle \in \text{e}\alpha$. So, by 26.1 and definition, $\langle \text{e}\alpha`y, \text{e}\alpha\restriction y\rangle \in \Phi_\alpha$ and $\text{e}\alpha\restriction y \in \mho$. So, by 27.1, $\alpha``\{\text{e}\alpha`y\} = (\text{e}\alpha\restriction y)``\mho$, q.e.d.

Now to the proof that the enumeration of an ordering is a correspondence.

27.7 $\quad \text{Ordg}\, \alpha \supset \text{Cor}\, \text{e}\alpha.$

Proof. As in preceding proof,

$$\text{Func e}\alpha. \qquad (1)$$

Consider any y, z such that

$$y, z \in \breve{}\text{e}\alpha``\mho, \quad [i] \qquad \text{e}\alpha`y = \text{e}\alpha`z. \quad [ii]$$

By (1) and [i],

$$y, z \in \arg \text{e}\alpha. \qquad [iii]$$

By [i], hypothesis, and 27.6,

$$\alpha``\{\text{e}\alpha`y\} = \text{e}\alpha``y, \quad [iv] \qquad \alpha``\{\text{e}\alpha`z\} = \text{e}\alpha``z. \quad [v]$$

By 27.4 and 23.8, $\breve{}\text{e}\alpha``\mho \subseteq \text{NO}$. So, by [i], $y, z \in \text{NO}$. So, by 23.23,

$$y \in z \,.\text{v}.\, z \in y \,.\text{v}.\, y = z. \qquad [vi]$$

Suppose $y \in z$. Then, by [iii], $\mathrm{e}\alpha`y \in \mathrm{e}\alpha``z$. Then, by [v], $\mathrm{e}\alpha`y \in \alpha``\{\mathrm{e}\alpha`z\}$, i.e., $\langle \mathrm{e}\alpha`y, \mathrm{e}\alpha`z\rangle \in \alpha$. But this conflicts with [ii] and the hypothesis that Ordg α. So $y \notin z$. Similarly $z \notin y$. So, by [vi], $y = z$. But y and z were any members of $\breve{\mathrm{e}\alpha}``\mathcal{V}$ fulfilling [ii]. So Func $\breve{\mathrm{e}\alpha}$. So, by (1), Cor $\mathrm{e}\alpha$.

Now we prove the fourth desideratum: that $\mathrm{e}\alpha$ preserves order.

27.8 $\quad$ $\mathrm{Ordg}\,\alpha \,.\, x, y \in \breve{\mathrm{e}\alpha}``\mathcal{V} \;.\supset\!:\; \langle \mathrm{e}\alpha`x, \mathrm{e}\alpha`y\rangle \in \alpha \;.\!\equiv\!.\; x \in y.$

Proof. By first hypothesis and 27.7, Cor $\mathrm{e}\alpha$. So, by second hypothesis,

$$(z)(\langle \mathrm{e}\alpha`x, z\rangle \in \mathrm{e}\alpha \;.\!\equiv\!.\; x = z). \tag{1}$$

By hypotheses and 27.6, $\alpha``\{\mathrm{e}\alpha`y\} = \mathrm{e}\alpha``y$. So

$$\begin{aligned} \langle \mathrm{e}\alpha`x, \mathrm{e}\alpha`y\rangle \in \alpha \;.\!\equiv\!.\; & \mathrm{e}\alpha`x \in \mathrm{e}\alpha``y \\ \equiv\; & (\exists z)(z \in y \,.\, \langle \mathrm{e}\alpha`x, z\rangle \in \mathrm{e}\alpha) \\ \text{(by (1))} \qquad \equiv\; & (\exists z)(z \in y \,.\, x = z) \\ \equiv\!.\; & x \in y. \end{aligned}$$

Finally we take up the remaining one of the four desired properties of $\mathrm{e}\alpha$: that its left field be the field of α. It will be convenient to prove the identity in halves.

27.9 $\quad$ $\mathrm{e}\alpha``\mathcal{V} \subseteq (\alpha \cup \breve{\alpha})``\mathcal{V}.$

Proof. Consider any $x \in \mathrm{e}\alpha``\mathcal{V}$. There is something y such that $\langle x, y\rangle \in \mathrm{e}\alpha$. By 27.2 and 25.2, then, there is something w such that

$$\langle x, y\rangle \in w, \quad \text{[i]} \qquad (z)(z \in \breve{w}``\mathcal{V} \;.\supset.\; \langle w`z, w\restriction z\rangle \in \Phi_\alpha), \quad \text{[ii]}$$

and SEQ w, i.e.,

$$\mathrm{Func}\, w, \quad \text{[iii]} \qquad \breve{w}``\mathcal{V} \in \mathrm{NO} \;.\mathrm{v}.\; \breve{w}``\mathcal{V} = \mathrm{NO}. \quad \text{[iv]}$$

By [i] and [iii],

$$y \in \breve{w}``\mathcal{V}, \quad \text{[v]} \qquad x = w`y. \quad \text{[vi]}$$

By [v], [iv], and 23.8, $y \in \mathrm{NO}$; also, by [iii], Func $w\restriction y$; so, by 23.15,

$$w\restriction y \in \mathcal{V}. \quad \text{[vii]}$$

By [v] and [ii], $\langle w`y, w \upharpoonright y\rangle \in \Phi_\alpha$. I.e., by [vi], $\langle x, w \upharpoonright y\rangle \in \Phi_\alpha$. I.e., by 27.1 and [vii],

$$\alpha``\{x\} = (w\upharpoonright y)``\mathfrak{V}, \qquad w\upharpoonright y = \Lambda \,.\!\supset x1\alpha.$$

Thus if $w\upharpoonright y = \Lambda$ then $x \in \alpha``\mathfrak{V}$, and if $w\upharpoonright y \neq \Lambda$ then $\alpha``\{x\} \neq \Lambda$ and so $x \in \breve{\alpha}``\mathfrak{V}$.

For the converse inclusion, substantial premisses are wanted.

27.10 $\quad$ $\text{Wellord}\,\alpha \,.\, \check{}\,\text{e}\alpha``\mathfrak{V} \in \mathfrak{V} \,.\, (\alpha \cup \breve{\alpha})``\mathfrak{V} \cap {}^{-}(\text{e}\alpha``\mathfrak{V}) \in \mathfrak{V}$
$\qquad .\!\supset\!. \text{e}\alpha``\mathfrak{V} = (\alpha \cup \breve{\alpha})``\mathfrak{V}.$

Idea of proof. Since we have 27.9, what needs to be shown is just that $(\alpha \cup \breve{\alpha})``\mathfrak{V} \subseteq \text{e}\alpha``\mathfrak{V}$; i.e., that all the things that are ordered by the well-ordering α are in $\text{e}\alpha``\mathfrak{V}$. Let $y$ be anything, among the things ordered by $\alpha$, such that all earlier things are in $\text{e}\alpha``\mathfrak{V}$. Then we show at length that $y \in \text{e}\alpha``\mathfrak{V}$. It follows by transfinite induction that everything ordered by $\alpha$ is in $\text{e}\alpha``\mathfrak{V}$.

Details of proof.[2] From the first two hypotheses, we have by 27.7 and 27.4 respectively that

$$\text{Cor}\,\text{e}\alpha, \quad (1) \qquad\qquad \check{}\,\text{e}\alpha``\mathfrak{V} \in \text{NO}. \quad (2)$$

So, by 23.15,

$$\text{e}\alpha \in \mathfrak{V}. \tag{3}$$

By first hypothesis and 27.5, Func Φ_α. So, by second hypothesis and 26.6 and the definition 27.2,

$$\text{e}\alpha \notin \check{}\,\Phi_\alpha``\mathfrak{V}. \tag{4}$$

Consider anything y such that

$$y \in (\alpha \cup \breve{\alpha})``\mathfrak{V}, \quad [\text{i}] \qquad\qquad \alpha``\{y\} \subseteq \text{e}\alpha``\mathfrak{V}. \quad [\text{ii}]$$

By [i] and 21.7,

$$\alpha``\{y\} = \Lambda \,.\!\supset y1\alpha. \qquad [\text{iii}]$$

By (4) and (3), $\langle y, \text{e}\alpha\rangle \notin \Phi_\alpha$. So, by 27.1 and (3),

$$\sim(\alpha``\{y\} = \text{e}\alpha``\mathfrak{V} :\text{e}\alpha = \Lambda \,.\!\supset y1\alpha),$$

---

[2]Much shortened by Joseph Ullian.

i.e.,

$$\sim(\alpha``\{y\} = \mathrm{e}\alpha``\mathcal{V} : \mathrm{e}\alpha``\mathcal{V} = \Lambda \mathbin{.\supset} y1\alpha),$$

i.e., by 6.7,

$$\sim(\alpha``\{y\} = \mathrm{e}\alpha``\mathcal{V} : \alpha``\{y\} = \Lambda \mathbin{.\supset} y1\alpha),$$

i.e., by [iii], $\alpha``\{y\} \neq \mathrm{e}\alpha``\mathcal{V}$. So, by [ii], there is w such that

$$w \in \mathrm{e}\alpha``\mathcal{V}, \quad \text{[iv]} \qquad \langle w, y\rangle \notin \alpha. \quad \text{[v]}$$

By [iv] and (1) there is x such that

$$x \in \breve{\ }\mathrm{e}\alpha``\mathcal{V}, \quad \text{[vi]} \qquad w = \mathrm{e}\alpha`x. \quad \text{[vii]}$$

From [vi] and first hypothesis we have by 27.6 that $\alpha``\{\mathrm{e}\alpha`x\} = \mathrm{e}\alpha``x$. That is, by [vii], $\alpha``\{w\} = \mathrm{e}\alpha``x$. So

$$\alpha``\{w\} \subseteq \mathrm{e}\alpha``\mathcal{V}. \qquad \text{[viii]}$$

By [iv] and 27.9, $w \in (\alpha \cup \breve{\alpha})``\mathcal{V}$; also, by first hypothesis, Connex $\alpha$; so, by [i] and [v], $w = y$ or $\langle y, w\rangle \in \alpha$. Hence $y \in \mathrm{e}\alpha``\mathcal{V}$, by [iv] in the one case and by [viii] in the other. But y was anything fulfilling [i] and [ii]. So

$$(y)(\alpha``\{y\} \subseteq \mathrm{e}\alpha``\mathcal{V} \,.\, y \in (\alpha \cup \breve{\alpha})``\mathcal{V} \mathbin{.\supset.} y \in \mathrm{e}\alpha``\mathcal{V}),$$

i.e.,

$$(y)((z)(\langle z, y\rangle \in \alpha \mathbin{.\supset.} z \in \mathrm{e}\alpha``\mathcal{V}) \,.\, y \in (\alpha \cup \alpha)``\mathcal{V} \mathbin{.\supset.} y \in \mathrm{e}\alpha``\mathcal{V}).$$

From this and the hypotheses it follows by transfinite induction according to 20.6 that $w \in \mathrm{e}\alpha``\mathcal{V}$ for any $w \in (\alpha \cup \breve{\alpha})``\mathcal{V}$. So, by 27.9, $(\alpha \cup \breve{\alpha})``\mathcal{V} = \mathrm{e}\alpha``\mathcal{V}$.

So the enumeration theorem is now at hand, in the scattered form comprising 27.4, 27.7, 27.8, and 27.10.

From the enumeration theorem we can prove that any two well-orderings are comparable, in the sense of §21. We can show, where Wellord x and Wellord y, that $\mathrm{e}x \mid \breve{\ }\mathrm{e}y$ (if it exists) is an isomorphism between x and y, or between x and a segment of y, or between a segment of x and y. More simply, we can compare well-orderings x and y by comparing their respective ordinal numbers, $\breve{\text{e}}x``\mho$ and $\breve{\text{e}}y``\mho$. The comparability of the ordinals themselves goes back to 23.23.

IX | CARDINAL NUMBERS

28. Comparative size of classes

We saw in 11.1 how to compare classes as larger or no larger one than another. Some simple laws governing such comparisons are quickly proved.

28.1 $\alpha \subseteq \beta \precsim \gamma \,.\supset.\, \alpha \precsim \gamma.$

Proof. By hypothesis and 11.1 there is a function x such that $\alpha \subseteq \beta \subseteq x``\gamma$, whence, by 11.1, $\alpha \precsim \gamma$.

28.2 $\alpha \precsim \beta \subseteq \gamma \,.\supset.\, \alpha \precsim \gamma.$ *Proof* equally easy.

28.3 $\Lambda \precsim \alpha.$ *Proof:* Func Λ and $\Lambda \subseteq \Lambda``\alpha$.

28.4 $\{x\} \precsim \{y\}.$

Proof: Func $\{\langle x, y\rangle\}$ and $\{x\} \subseteq \{\langle x, y\rangle\}``\{y\}$.

28.5 $\alpha \precsim \{x\} \,.\!\equiv:\, \alpha = \Lambda \,.\mathsf{v}\, (\exists y)(\alpha = \{y\}).$

Proof. If $\alpha \precsim \{x\}$, then $\alpha \subseteq z``\{x\}$ by 11.1 for some function z and so $\alpha \subseteq \{z`x\}$ by 10.17 and so $\alpha$ is $\Lambda$ or $\{z`x\}$. Converse by 28.3 and 28.4.

But the limit of what can be proved on this topic without comprehension premisses is quickly reached. Even '$\alpha \precsim \alpha$' is beyond us. It says that $\alpha \subseteq x``\alpha$ for some function x; and we cannot prove this by citing the function I, or the function $I \restriction \alpha$, unless under comprehension assumptions implying that $I \in \mathcal{V}$ or that

$I \upharpoonright \alpha \in \mathcal{V}$ or at any rate that something x exists between, so that $I \upharpoonright \alpha \subseteq x \subseteq I$. Let us give a number to one of these guarded statements.

28.6 $$I \upharpoonright \alpha \in \mathcal{V} \mathrel{.\supset.} \alpha \precsim \alpha.$$

Proof by 11.1, since $\alpha = (I \upharpoonright \alpha)``\alpha$.

Transitivity needs a comprehension premiss too. If $\alpha \precsim \beta \precsim \gamma$, there are, by 11.1, functions x and y such that $\alpha \subseteq x``\beta$ and $\beta \subseteq y``\gamma$ and so $\alpha \subseteq (x \mid y)``\gamma$; and certainly Func $x \mid y$, moreover, by 10.6. But, unless $x \mid y \in \mathcal{V}$, this is no proof that $\alpha \precsim \gamma$.

These obstacles do not arise in finite cases. As long as we can show of α that $\alpha \precsim \{, , , x\}$ for some x, we can exploit our modest present comprehension axioms to prove that $\beta``\alpha \precsim \alpha$ whenever Func β; here we can ignore '$\beta \in \mathcal{V}$'.

28.7 $$\alpha \precsim \{, , , x\} \,.\, \text{Func}\, \beta \mathrel{.\supset.} \beta``\alpha \precsim \alpha.$$

Proof. By first hypothesis and 11.1, there is y such that

$$\text{Func}\, y, \quad (1) \qquad\qquad \alpha \subseteq y``\{, , , x\}. \quad (2)$$

Let

$$\gamma = \{\langle\langle u, v\rangle, w\rangle \colon \langle u, v\rangle \in \beta \,.\, \langle v, w\rangle \in y\}. \tag{3}$$

By hypothesis, Func β. So, by (1) and (3), Func γ. So, by 13.1, there is something z such that

$$\begin{aligned} z &= \gamma``\{, , , x\} \\ \text{(by (3))} \quad &= \{\langle u, v\rangle \colon \langle u, v\rangle \in \beta \,.\, v \in y``\{, , , x\}\} \\ &= \beta \upharpoonright (y``\{, , , x\}). \end{aligned} \tag{4}$$

By (2), then, $z``\alpha = \beta``\alpha$. Further, since Func β, Func z. So, by 11.1, $\beta``\alpha \precsim \alpha$.

So we can adjoin to 28.6 the poor supplement:

28.8 $\alpha \precsim \{, , , x\} \mathrel{.\supset.} \alpha \precsim \alpha.$ *Proof:* 28.7 with β as I.

Similarly for transitivity.

28.9 $\alpha \lesssim \beta \lesssim \gamma \lesssim \{,,,x\} \;.\supset.\; \alpha \lesssim \gamma.$

Proof. By hypothesis, as lately noted, there are y and z such that Func $y \mid z$ and $\alpha \subseteq (y \mid z)``\gamma$. By last hypothesis and 28.7, $(y \mid z)``\gamma \lesssim \gamma$. So, by 28.1, $\alpha \lesssim \gamma$.

The condition of *firm finitude* of α, as we might call it, is:

$$(\exists x)(x \in \mathrm{N} \,.\, \alpha \lesssim \{,,,x\}).$$

In contrast '$(\exists x)(\alpha \lesssim \{,,,x\})$' alone might be called the condition of *provisional* finitude, since it is compatible with infinitude of α if endless noncyclic sole-member descents are to be had; cf. the discussion preceding 13.1. But provisional finitude does assure finitude barring that silly twist to the universe. This much assurance has sufficed for 28.8 and 28.9, and suffices similarly for many other laws of class comparison which, like '$\alpha \lesssim \alpha$' and '$\alpha \lesssim \beta \lesssim \gamma \;.\supset.\; \alpha \lesssim \gamma$', would otherwise require comprehension premisses. The reason provisional finitude can thus supplant comprehension premisses is simply that provisional finitude is the condition of the following comprehension schema.

28.10 $\alpha \lesssim \{,,,x\} \;.\supset.\; \alpha \in \mathcal{V}.$ *Proof* by 13.2, 11.1.

Under this head of provisional finitude let me set down here just three more laws for future reference.

28.11 $\{,,,x\} \lesssim \{,,,x\}.$

Proof. By 13.4, since $\breve{}(I \restriction \{,,,x\})``\mathcal{V}$ is $\{,,,x\}$, $I \restriction \{,,,x\} \in \mathcal{V}$. So, by 28.6, $\{,,,x\} \lesssim \{,,,x\}$.

28.12 $\alpha \lesssim \beta \lesssim \{,,,x\} \;.\supset.\; \alpha \lesssim \{,,,x\}.$

Proof: 28.9, with γ as $\{,,,x\}$, and 28.11.

28.13 $\alpha \lesssim \{,,,\{x\}\} \;.\supset\; (\exists y)(\alpha \cap \overline{\{y\}} \lesssim \{,,,x\}).$

Proof. By hypothesis and 11.1, there is z such that

$$\text{Func } z, \quad (1) \qquad \alpha \subseteq z``\{,,, \{x\}\}. \quad (2)$$

By (2) and 13.13,

$$\alpha \subseteq z``\{,,, x\} \cup z``\{\{x\}\}.$$

But, by (1) and 10.17, $z``\{\{x\}\} \subseteq \{y\}$ for some y. So

$$\alpha \subseteq z``\{,,, x\} \cup \{y\}.$$

So

$$\alpha \cap {}^{-}\{y\} \subseteq z``\{,,, x\}.$$

So, by (1) and 11.1, $\alpha \cap {}^{-}\{y\} \lesssim \{,,, x\}$.

Besides the laws of class comparison based on premisses of provisional finitude, there are ones requiring firm finitude. Typically this need arises when the law is proved by mathematical induction. Mathematical induction can be adapted directly to firmly finite classes, instead of to numbers, thus: if $F\Lambda$, and $F(y \cap {}^{-}\{z\}) \supset Fy$ for all y and z, and α is firmly finite, then $F\alpha$.

28.14 $\quad F\Lambda \,.\, (y)(z)(F(y \cap {}^{-}\{z\}) \supset Fy) \,.\, x \in \mathrm{N} \,.\, \alpha \lesssim \{,,, x\} \;.\!\supset F\alpha.$

Proof. Consider any y and w such that

$$(v)(v \lesssim \{,,, w\} \;.\!\supset Fv), \quad [\text{i}] \qquad y \lesssim \{,,, \{w\}\}. \quad [\text{ii}]$$

By [ii] and 28.13, there is something z such that $y \cap {}^{-}\{z\} \lesssim \{,,, w\}$. So, by 28.10, $y \cap {}^{-}\{z\}$ is something v such that $v \lesssim \{,,, w\}$. So, by [i], $F(y \cap {}^{-}\{z\})$. So, by second hypothesis, Fy. But y and w were any things fulfilling [i] and [ii]. So

$$(w)((v)(v \lesssim \{,,, w\} \;.\!\supset Fv) \supset (v)(v \lesssim \{,,, \{w\}\} \;.\!\supset Fv)). \quad (1)$$

By hypothesis, $F\Lambda$. So, for any u, $F(\{u\} \cap {}^{-}\{u\})$. But then, by second hypothesis, $F\{u\}$. By 12.21,

$$(v)(v \precsim \{,\,,\,\Lambda\} \;.\supset.\; v \precsim \{\Lambda\})$$

(by 28.5) $\supset: v = \Lambda \,.\mathbf{v}\, (\exists u)(v = \{u\}))$

(since $F\Lambda$ and $F\{u\}$) $\supset Fv)$.

From this and (1) and the hypothesis '$x \in \mathrm{N}$', it follows by induction according to 13.9 that

$$(v)(v \precsim \{,\,,\,x\} \;.\supset Fv).$$

But, by last hypothesis and 28.10, α is something v such that $v \precsim \{,\,,\,x\}$. So $F\alpha$.

This version of induction brings to mind, indeed, that we could define firm finitude itself more directly by just paralleling the definition of N instead of using N. A class u is finite if it belongs to every class w such that $\Lambda \in w$ and

$$(y)(z)(y \cap {}^{-}\{z\} \in w \;.\supset.\; y \in w).$$[1]

Or, inverting as we did in the case of N to avoid depending on infinite w, we may say rather that u is finite if Λ belongs to every class w such that $u \in w$ and

$$(y)(z)(y \in w \;.\supset.\; y \cap {}^{-}\{z\} \in w).$$

The version 28.14 of induction admits of a longer and stronger variant, corresponding to 13.10.

28.15 $F\Lambda \,.\, (y)(z)(y \precsim \{,\,,\,x\} \,.\, F(y \cap {}^{-}\{z\}) \;.\supset Fy) \,.$
$x \in \mathrm{N} \,.\, \alpha \precsim \{,\,,\,x\} \;.\supset F\alpha.$

Proof. By 28.1,

$$y \precsim \{,\,,\,x\} \;.\supset.\; y \cap {}^{-}\{z\} \precsim \{,\,,\,x\}.$$

So, if further

---

[1] So Whitehead and Russell, *120·24.

$$y \cap {}^{-}\{z\} \precsim \{,,,x\} \;.\supset F(y \cap {}^{-}\{z\}),$$

it will follow that $y \precsim \{,,,x\} \;.\supset F(y \cap {}^{-}\{z\})$ and hence that

$$y \precsim \{,,,x\} \;.\supset.\; y \precsim \{,,,x\} \;.\; F(y \cap {}^{-}\{z\})$$

(by 2d hypothesis) $\qquad \supset Fy.$

To sum up,

$$(y)(z)(y \cap {}^{-}\{z\} \precsim \{,,,x\} \;.\supset F(y \cap {}^{-}\{z\}) \;:\supset:\; y \precsim \{,,,x\} \;.\supset Fy).$$

By first hypothesis, $\Lambda \precsim \{,,,x\} \;.\supset F\Lambda$. From these two results and the last two hypotheses, it follows by induction according to 28.14 that $\alpha \precsim \{,,,x\} \;.\supset F\alpha$. So, by last hypothesis, $F\alpha$.

One typical law that can be proved by such induction is:

(i) $\qquad x \in \mathrm{N} \;.\; \alpha \cup \{y\} \precsim \alpha \precsim \{,,,x\} \;.\supset.\; y \in \alpha,$

which says that a firmly finite α must be smaller than $\alpha \cup \{y\}$ unless y is in it. Another is:

(ii) $\qquad x \in \mathrm{N} \;.\; \alpha \precsim \{,,,x\} \;.\; \alpha \precsim \beta \;.\supset (\exists x)(\alpha \simeq x \subseteq \beta).$

which says that a firmly finite α must be of the same size as some subclass of β if $\alpha \precsim \beta$. I omit the proofs. The reader curious to see a long inductive proof of a humdrum theorem on finite classes may turn instead to 31.3; and he might try (i) and (ii) as exercises.

Laws proved from provisional finitude generally hold for infinite classes too, granted some reasonable comprehension premisses, since provisional finitude itself generally operates merely through 13.1. In fact 28.7–28.12 have analogues relating to ordinals and based on 23.12 instead of 13.1, thus:

$$\alpha \precsim x \in \mathrm{NO} \;.\; \mathrm{Func}\,\beta \;.\supset.\; \beta``\alpha \precsim \alpha,$$
$$\alpha \precsim x \in \mathrm{NO} \;.\supset.\; \alpha \precsim \alpha,$$
$$\alpha \precsim \beta \precsim \gamma \precsim x \in \mathrm{NO} \;.\supset.\; \alpha \precsim \gamma,$$
$$\alpha \precsim x \in \mathrm{NO} \;.\supset.\; \alpha \in \mathcal{V},$$
$$x \in \mathrm{NO} \;.\supset.\; x \precsim x,$$
$$\alpha \precsim \beta \precsim x \in \mathrm{NO} \;.\supset.\; \alpha \precsim x.$$

The proofs are obtainabke from those of 28.7–28.12 simply by citing 23.12, 23.13, and 23.15 instead of 13.1, 13.2, and 13.4.

Laws proved from firm finitude by induction, on the other hand, sometimes prove false—and not just indemonstrable—in infinite cases. Such is the way of (i); '$\alpha \cup \{y\} \preceq \alpha \,.\!\supset\!.\, y \in \alpha$' can fail for infinite α, as will be evident when, in the next few pages, we have begun to explore the oddities of size comparisons of infinite classes. In (ii) yet another situation is illustrated: (ii) presumably holds without its firm finitude premisses, but its proof for infinite cases requires a special premiss, of other than comprehension form, which we shall encounter in the next chapter under the name of the axiom of choice.

Before Cantor it was not clear that we might significantly compare infinite multiplicities in point of greater and less. When α has only finitely many members, we assign them one by one to members of β in an arbitrary order, and if we exhaust β and still have some members of α left over then we conclude that α had more members than β. (Or we may assign the members of α to numbers, as in counting, and similarly for β, and compare afterward.) But when classes are infinite, we begin to observe curious variations which hint that such comparisons have lost their significance. Thus, suppose we try assigning the infinitely numerous natural numbers to the infinitely numerous even numbers. One procedure, that of assigning each number to its equal, leaves the odd numbers over and thus suggests that there were more numbers altogether than evens; but another procedure, that of assigning each number x to $x + x$, disposes of everything and thus suggests that there were no more numbers than even ones.

Cantor resolved such dilemmas by declaring α no larger than β as long as there is *some* function that assigns all the members of α to members of β. Such is the definition that we have had before us since 11.1. Adherence to it settles the above question how to compare N and the class of evens. Thanks to the favorable function (x assigned to $x + x$) and despite the unfavorable one (identity), we reckon N no larger than the class of evens.

Anyway this settles the question if the function *exists*; i.e., if

$$\{\langle x, x + x\rangle : x \in \mathrm{N}\} \in \mathcal{V}.$$

Comparisons of infinite classes will generally turn thus upon comprehension assumptions, because of the quantified variable for functions in 11.1.

What makes Cantor's criterion significant is that in some cases, though not in the case of N versus the class of evens, it does register differences in size and shows (on generally accepted comprehension assumptions) that a class may have more members than N does. Cantor established, for example, that under his criterion there are more real numbers than natural numbers. That is, N $\prec$ Real.

We may quickly appreciate this by thinking again of the diagram in §17, and of real numbers as rays. Where x is any function, a ray $r \notin x``\text{N}$ is specifiable by infinite approximation as follows. r is to lie in the lower half of the right angle at $\langle 0, 0\rangle$ unless the ray $x`0$ lies there, in which case $r$ is to lie in the upper half. Whichever half $r$ lies in, $r$ is to lie in the lower half *of* that half unless the ray $x`1$ lies there, in which case r is to lie in the other half of its half of the right angle. Whichever quarter r lies in, r is to lie in the lower half of its quarter unless $x`2$ lies there; and so on. So $r$ differs from $x`y$ for each $y \in \text{N}$. So Real $\not\subseteq x``\text{N}$. But x was any function. So, by the definitions 11.1 and 20.3, N $\prec$ Real.

One is perhaps not surprised that N $\prec$ Real, since there are infinitely many reals between each integer and the next. But this is a bad reason for not being surprised; for the same reason would lead us wrongly to suppose that N $\prec$ Rat. Actually we do have a function that assigns all ratios to natural numbers, viz., the function mentioned in §3 that consists of all pairs of the form $\langle y/z, 2^y \cdot 3^z\rangle$.

Again this last remark is subject to a comprehension premiss:

$$\{\langle y/z, 2^y \cdot 3^z\rangle : y, z \in \text{N}\} \in \mathcal{V}.$$

It is only on this assumption that the citing of this function shows that Rat $\preceq$ N.

Talking of gaps, there are of course various in the preceding argument that N $\prec$ Real. Rigorously presented, that argument would treat arithmetically of sums of powers of $\frac{1}{2}$. The real number r would be got as the least bound of an appropriate class of sums of powers of $\frac{1}{2}$, and our argument would depend on a comprehension premiss affirming the existence of that class. I am glad to say, however, that we do not need the example '$\mathrm{N} \prec \mathrm{Real}$' to show that there are classes larger than the class N. We can turn to another example, due also to Cantor, which combines the virtues of being more general and sparing us further development of classical arithmetic.

For Cantor has shown that $\mathrm{N} \prec \{x: x \subseteq \mathrm{N}\}$, and, more generally, that $\alpha \prec \{x: x \subseteq \alpha\}$, i.e., that any class has more subclasses than members. For us this theorem schema needs a comprehension premiss. First I prove, for convenience of separate reference later, the lemma:

28.16 $\quad \alpha \cap \{y: y \notin \beta\text{‘}y\} \in \mathcal{V} \,.\, \mathrm{Func}\,\beta \,.\!\supset\!.\, \{x: x \subseteq \alpha\} \nsubseteq \beta\text{“}\alpha.$

Proof. By first hypothesis, there is something w such that

$$w = \{y: y \in \alpha \,.\, y \notin \beta\text{‘}y\}. \tag{1}$$

Then

$$(y)(y \in \alpha \,.\!\supset\!:\, y \in w \,.\!\equiv\!.\, y \notin \beta\text{‘}y)$$

$$\supset.\ w \neq \beta\text{‘}y)$$

(by second hypothesis) $\quad \supset.\ \langle w, y\rangle \notin \beta).$

That is, $w \notin \beta\text{“}\alpha$. But, by (1), $w \subseteq \alpha$. So $\{x: x \subseteq \alpha\} \nsubseteq \beta\text{“}\alpha$.

Now Cantor's law, with our comprehension premiss.

28.17 $\quad (w)(\alpha \cap \{y: y \notin w\text{‘}y\} \in \mathcal{V}) \supset.\ \alpha \prec \{x: x \subseteq \alpha\}.$

Proof. By 28.16 and hypothesis,

$$(w)(\mathrm{Func}\, w \supset.\ \{x: x \subseteq \alpha\} \nsubseteq w\text{“}\alpha).$$

That is, by 11.1 and 20.3, $\alpha \prec \{x: x \subseteq \alpha\}$.

According to this law, far from there being only one infinite size, there is no end to them except as the comprehension assumptions give out.

We must beware, however, of dissociating Cantor's law from its comprehension premiss. Some theorems that carry comprehension premisses can reasonably be contemplated in abstraction from those premisses, because the premisses are ones that would eventually be sustained, in general or in typical cases, by any body of comprehension axioms that we are likely to settle for. But Cantor's law falls immediately into paradox except as held in check by comprehension failures. Unhedged, '$\alpha \prec \{x: x \subseteq \alpha\}$' gives '$\mathcal{V} \prec \{x: x \subseteq \mathcal{V}\}$', briefly '$\mathcal{V} \prec \mathcal{V}$', which is known as Cantor's paradox.

28.18 $(w)(\{y: y \notin w`y\} \in \mathcal{V}) \supset . \mathcal{V} \prec \mathcal{V}.$

Proof: $\mathcal{V}$ for α in 28.17.

It was indeed through this channel that Russell first came upon his famous simpler paradox.[2] To bring out the connection, let us go back to 28.16 and take α as $\mathcal{V}$ there, instead of in 28.17. We get, with the obvious reductions, that

28.19 $\{y: y \notin \beta`y\} \in \mathcal{V} . \text{Func}\,\beta . \supset . \beta``\mathcal{V} \neq \mathcal{V}.$

Now what is paradoxical about this (comprehension premiss aside) is that patently, to the contrary, Func I and $I``\mathcal{V} = \mathcal{V}$. But, with β as I, the comprehension premiss '$\{y: y \notin \beta`y\} \in \mathcal{V}$' itself becomes '$\{y: y \notin y\} \in \mathcal{V}$', whose falsity is familiar from Russell's paradox.

Along with the corollary 28.19 which came of 28.16 by taking α as $\mathcal{V}$, it is worthwhile to record also the corollary that comes rather by taking β as I:

28.20 $\alpha \cap \{y: y \notin y\} \in \mathcal{V} . \supset . \{x: x \subseteq \alpha\} \nsubseteq \alpha.$

Taking α here as $\mathcal{V}$ turns the consequent into the falsehood '$\mathcal{V} \nsubseteq \mathcal{V}$', and the antecedent into the falsehood '$\{y: y \notin y\} \in \mathcal{V}$' again.

---

[2] Cf. *Principles*, pp. 101, 362.

'$\mathcal{V} < \mathcal{V}$' itself does not have to be viewed as false. If we so frame our comprehension assumptions that $I \notin \mathcal{V}$ and more generally

$$\sim(\exists x)(\text{Func } x \,.\, x``\mathcal{V} = \mathcal{V}),$$

we thereby count '$\mathcal{V} < \mathcal{V}$' as true and become free even to adopt the comprehension premiss of 28.18 as true too.

29. The Schröder-Bernstein theorem

From among the network of laws that are meant to govern '$\lesssim$' and '$\simeq$', we might have chosen others than:

(i) $\alpha \lesssim \beta \,.{\equiv}\, (\exists x)(\text{Func } x \,.\, \alpha \subseteq x``\beta)$,

(ii) $\alpha \simeq \beta \,.{\equiv}.\, \alpha \lesssim \beta \lesssim \alpha$

for defining '$\alpha \lesssim \beta$' and '$\alpha \simeq \beta$'. We might have used '$=$' instead of '$\subseteq$' in (i), for purposes of definition, and then derived the actual (i) rather as a theorem schema, subject to a comprehension premiss. Or, deviating more widely, we might have defined '$\alpha \simeq \beta$' rather as any of:

(iii) $(\exists x)(\text{Cor } x \,.\, \alpha \subseteq x``\beta \,.\, \beta \subseteq \breve{x}``\alpha)$,

(iv) $(\exists x)(\text{Cor } x \,.\, \alpha = x``\beta \,.\, \beta = \breve{x}``\alpha)$,

(v) $(\exists x)(\text{Cor } x \,.\, \alpha = x``\mathcal{V} \,.\, \beta = \breve{x}``\mathcal{V})$

and then '$\alpha \lesssim \beta$' as '$(\exists y)(\alpha \simeq y \subseteq \beta)$' or even, independently of '$\simeq$', as either of:

(vi) $(\exists x)(\text{Cor } x \,.\, \alpha \subseteq x``\beta)$,

(vii) $(\exists x)(\text{Cor } x \,.\, \alpha = x``\beta)$.

Equivalences corresponding to all such definitions are wanted as theorems, but my choice of (i) and (ii) as starting point had the advantage of demanding less elaborate comprehension premisses at early stages than would have been demanded under alternative approaches.

We are in a domain where proofs can suddenly turn difficult, and the demands on comprehension premisses exorbitant, out of all keeping with the seeming slightness of the law to be proved. Thus take (ii) with '$\simeq$' and '$\lesssim$' reconstrued according to (iii) and (vi). It equates (iii) with:

$$\text{(viii)} \qquad (\exists x)(\text{Cor}\ x \,.\, \alpha \subseteq x``\beta) \,.\, (\exists x)(\text{Cor}\ x \,.\, \beta \subseteq x``\alpha).$$

Clearly (iii) implies (viii), granted that $(x)(\breve{x} \in \mathcal{V})$. But that (viii) implies (iii) takes a lot of proving and a weighty comprehension premiss. It is called the *Schröder–Bernstein theorem.*

It is much the same theorem whether we take its antedecent as (viii) as it stands or with '$\subseteq$' strengthened to '$=$' (cf. (vii)), and whether we take its consequent as (iii) or (iv) or (v). I shall take the least favorable combination: (viii) as antecedent, (v) as consequent. (Obviously (v) implies (iv) and (iv) implies (iii), even without comprehension premisses.)

In comprehension premisses here I shall, for brevity, accept more generality than is strictly needed, but little that is likely to conflict with otherwise attractive set theories. An exception is '$(x)(y)(x \cup y \in \mathcal{V})$', which, though assumed in many set theories, conflicts with some; it conflicts with theories in which some classes are allowed to belong to smaller classes only (cf. §§7, 44).

The following abbreviations will be used in the comprehension premisses.

29.1 'C_1' for '$(x)(y)(x \cap \bar{y},\ \breve{x},\ x``\mathcal{V},\ x{\upharpoonright}y \in \mathcal{V})$',

29.2 'C_2' for '$(x)(y)(x \mid y,\ {}^{-}(*x``\bar{y}),\ x \cup y \in \mathcal{V})$'.[1]

There is this to observe about 'C_1'.

29.3 $C_1 \supset (x)(y)(x \cap y,\ x``y \in \mathcal{V})$.

Proof. By 'C_1', $x \cap \bar{y} \in \mathcal{V}$ and so, by 'C_1' again, $x \cap {}^{-}(x \cap \bar{y}) \in \mathcal{V}$, i.e., $x \cap y \in \mathcal{V}$. Further, by 'C_1', $x{\upharpoonright}y \in \mathcal{V}$ and so, by 'C_1' again, $(x{\upharpoonright}y)``\mathcal{V} \in \mathcal{V}$, i.e., $x``y \in \mathcal{V}$.

---

[1] If the $-(*x``\bar{y})$ seems extravagant, note that in view of 15.2 it is always a subclass of y.

And here is the Schröder–Bernstein theorem. I have subdued the 'α' and 'β' of (viii) and (v) to 'y' and 'z', thus assuming further existence.

29.4 $\quad C_1 \,.\, C_2 \,.\, (\exists x)(\text{Cor}\, x \,.\, y \subseteq x``z) \,.\, (\exists x)(\text{Cor}\, x \,.\, z \subseteq x``y) \,.\!\supset (\exists x)(\text{Cor}\, x \,.\, y = x``\mathcal{V} \,.\, z = \breve{x}``\mathcal{V})$.

Idea of proof.[2] By hypothesis there is a correspondence x such that $y \subseteq x``z$. Switching and trimming it, we get a correspondence $u$ such that $y = \breve{u}``\mathcal{V}$ and $u``\mathcal{V} \subseteq z$. By the other hypothesis, similarly, there is a correspondence $v$ such that $z = \breve{v}``\mathcal{V}$ and $v``\mathcal{V} \subseteq y$. Thus $v \mid u$ is *borne to* each member of $y$ by some member or other of $y$. But a given member of $y$ still, conceivably, need not *bear* $v$ in its turn; it can fall outside $v``\mathcal{V}$. Let w be the class of just those members of y from which you can not get out of $v``\mathcal{V}$ by steps of $v \mid u$. Now define a new relation thus: members of w bear it to whatever they bear v to, while other things bear it to whatever they bear $\breve{u}$ to. This relation is shown at length to be a correspondence whose left and right fields are y and z.

Details of proof. By hypothesis there is a correspondence x such that $y \subseteq x``z$. But then members of $y$ bear $x$ to nothing but members of $z$ (since Cor $x$); i.e., $\breve{x}``y \subseteq z$. By '$C_1$', there is something u such that $u = \breve{x}\restriction y$. It follows, since Cor x and $y \subseteq x``z$ and $\breve{x}``y \subseteq z$, that

$$\text{Cor}\, u, \quad (1) \qquad y = \breve{u}``\mathcal{V}, \quad (2) \qquad u``\mathcal{V} \subseteq z. \quad (3)$$

By the last hypothesis we are assured similarly of a v such that

$$\text{Cor}\, v, \quad (4) \qquad z = \breve{v}``\mathcal{V}, \quad (5) \qquad v``\mathcal{V} \subseteq y. \quad (6)$$

By 'C_2', $v \mid u \in \mathcal{V}$. Also, by 'C_1', $v``\mathcal{V} \in \mathcal{V}$. So, by '$C_2$', there is something w such that

[2] The general idea of this proof was propounded in 1906 independently by König, Peano, and Zermelo. Earlier proofs, one of them wrong, go back to 1898. See Fraenkel, *Einleitung*, pp. 75f; also note 9 in Zermelo's 1908 paper.

$$w = {}^{-}({*}(v \mid u)``{}^{-}(v``\mathcal{V})) \qquad (7)$$

$$= \{h\colon (k)(\langle h, k\rangle \in {*}(v \mid u) \mathbin{.\supset.} k \in v``\mathcal{V})\}. \qquad (8)$$

By 15.2, anything h bears any ancestral to itself. So, by (8), if $h \in w$ then $h \in v``\mathcal{V}$. So

$$w \subseteq v``\mathcal{V}. \qquad (9)$$

By 15.5,

$$(v \mid u)``({*}(v \mid u)``{}^{-}(v``\mathcal{V})) \subseteq {*}(v \mid u)``{}^{-}(v``\mathcal{V}).$$

That is, by (7), $(v \mid u)``\overline{w} \subseteq \overline{w}$. That is, $v``(u``\overline{w}) \subseteq \overline{w}$. That is, no members of $w$ bear $v$ to members of $u``\overline{w}$. That is,

$$\breve{v}``w \cap u``\overline{w} = \Lambda. \qquad (10)$$

By iterated use of 'C_1' we have successively that $y \cap \overline{w} \in \mathcal{V}$ and $u \restriction (y \cap \overline{w}) \in \mathcal{V}$, which is to say, by (2), $u \restriction \overline{w} \in \mathcal{V}$. Also from '$C_1$' we have more quickly that $\breve{v} \restriction w \in \mathcal{V}$. So there are r and s such that

$$r = \breve{v} \restriction w, \quad (11) \qquad\qquad s = u \restriction \overline{w}. \quad (12)$$

So

$$r``\mathcal{V} = \breve{v}``w, \quad (13) \qquad\qquad s``\mathcal{V} = u``\overline{w}, \quad (14)$$

$\breve{r}``\mathcal{V} = w \cap v``\mathcal{V}$, and $\breve{s}``\mathcal{V} = \overline{w} \cap \breve{u}``\mathcal{V}$. So, by (9) and (2),

$$\breve{r}``\mathcal{V} = w, \quad (15) \qquad\qquad \breve{s}``\mathcal{V} = \overline{w} \cap y. \quad (16)$$

By (1), (4), (11), and (12), r and s are correspondences; by (15) and (16), their right fields are mutually exclusive; by (10), (13), and (14), their left fields are too; so

$$\text{Cor}\ r \cup s. \qquad (17)$$

By (13) and (5), $r``\mathcal{V} \subseteq z$. By (14) and (3), $s``\mathcal{V} \subseteq z$. So

$$(r \cup s)``\mathcal{V} \subseteq z. \qquad (18)$$

By (15) and (16), $\breve{}(r \cup s)``\mathcal{V} = w \cup y$. By (9) and (6), $w \subseteq y$. So

$$\breve{}(r \cup s)``\mathcal{V} = y. \tag{19}$$

Consider any

$$q \in z. \qquad [\text{i}]$$

By (5), there is something p such that

$$\langle p, q \rangle \in v, \qquad [\text{ii}]$$

Case 1: $p \in w$. Then, by [ii], $q \in \breve{v}``w$. So, by (13), $q \in r``\mathcal{V}$.
Case 2: $p \notin w$. That is, by (8), there is something k such that

$$\langle p, k \rangle \in *(v \mid u), \quad [\text{iii}] \qquad\qquad k \notin v``\mathcal{V}. \quad [\text{iv}]$$

By [ii], $p \in v``\mathcal{V}$. So

$$k \neq p. \qquad [\text{v}]$$

By 15.11,

$$*(v \mid u) = I \cup (v \mid u \mid *(v \mid u)).$$

So, by [iii] and [v],

$$\langle p, k \rangle \in v \mid u \mid *(v \mid u).$$

That is, p bears v to something that bears $u \mid *(v \mid u)$ to k. But that something is q, by [ii] and (4). So

$$\langle q, k \rangle \in u \mid *(v \mid u).$$

That is, there is something h such that

$$\langle q, h \rangle \in u, \quad [\text{vi}] \qquad\qquad \langle h, k \rangle \in *(v \mid u). \quad [\text{vii}]$$

By [iv] and [vii], h bears $*(v \mid u)$ to something in $^{-}(v``\mathcal{V})$. That is, by (7), $h \notin w$. So, by [vi], $q \in u``\overline{w}$. So, by (14), $q \in s``\mathcal{V}$.

Both cases: $q \in (r \cup s)``\mathcal{V}$. But $q$ was anything fulfilling [i]. So, by (18), $(r \cup s)``\mathcal{V} = z$. Also, by '$C_1 . C_2$', $x = \breve{}(r \cup s)$ for some x. So $\breve{x}``\mathcal{V} = z$ and also, by (19) and (17), $x``\mathcal{V} = y$ and Cor x.

It was our reflections on the interrelations among (i)–(viii) that brought us up against the Schröder–Bernstein theorem. There is more to be said of those interrelations. Thus take the proverbial '$x \leq y$ .v. $y \leq x$', called the *law of comparability* or *trichotomy*. It owes the latter name to the version:

$$x \prec y \text{ .v. } x \simeq y \text{ .v. } y \prec x,$$

which, under our definitions 11.2 and 20.3, is a triviality of the form '$\sim p \vee qp \vee \sim q$'. If we had defined '$x \simeq y$' and '$x \leq y$' in any of the alternative ways noted in (iii)–(vii), and then '$y \prec x$' as '$\sim(x \leq y)$' again as usual, then the law of comparability in the trichotomic version above would not have been trivial, but would have amounted to the Schröder–Bernstein theorem.

And what of the law of comparability in the previous version '$x \leq y$ .v. $y \leq x$'? Or the seemingly stronger version '$x \prec y$ .v. $y \leq x$'? This last is for us trivial again, in view of 20.3; it has the form '$\sim p \vee p$'. But '$x \leq y$ .v. $y \leq x$', remarkably, is on our definition less readily established even than the Schröder–Bernstein theorem. It requires the axiom of choice, which was mentioned in §28 and will be faced in §31. (See 33.1.)

Accidents of definition aside, there are three distinct things here: the axiom of choice, the Schröder–Bernstein theorem, and triviality. The law of comparability or trichotomy in one or another plausible form may become any of the three in the course of the shell game of redefinition. Defining one way or another obviates neither the burden of assuming the axiom of choice nor the burden of proving the Schröder–Bernstein theorem and assuming its comprehension premisses. My choice of definitions had the virtue only of postponing these eventualities conveniently.

Within (i)–(viii) themselves also there are links that require the axiom of choice. It is needed to show that '$\alpha \leq \beta$' in the sense of (i), our sense, implies (vi). (See 33.2.)

30. Infinite cardinal numbers

Numbers as measures of multiplicity are called *cardinal numbers*. Thus the natural numbers are adequate as finite cardinals. Besides them there is to be, for each infinite class, an infinite cardinal number—the cardinal numbers of classes z and w being identical if and only if $z \simeq w$.

We saw in §11 how to do a good deal about natural numbers without adjudicating among Zermelo, von Neumann, and Frege as to what sorts of things the natural numbers were to be, but simply proceeding from '0' and 'S' as undefined. Let us now adopt for a while a similarly neutral attitude toward cardinal numbers generally, just taking as undefined a notation '$\bar{\bar{z}}$' for the cardinal number of z and demanding of it that $\bar{\bar{z}} = \bar{\bar{w}} \,.{\equiv}.\, z \simeq w$. Such was Cantor's procedure.[1] The arithmetical comparisons and operations can thereupon be fitted to cardinals by the following definitions, again essentially Cantor's.

$$
\begin{aligned}
x \leq y \,.{\equiv}\, & (\exists z)(\exists w)(x = \bar{\bar{z}} \,.\, y = \bar{\bar{w}} \,.\, z \preceq w),\\
x < y \,.{\equiv}\, & (\exists z)(\exists w)(x = \bar{\bar{z}} \,.\, y = \bar{\bar{w}} \,.\, z \prec w),\\
x + y = {} & (\imath v)(\exists z)(\exists w)(x = {}^{=}(z \cap w) \,.\, y = {}^{=}(z \cap \bar{w}) \,.\, v = \bar{\bar{z}}),\\
x \cdot y = {} & (\imath v)(\exists z)(\exists w)(x = \bar{\bar{z}} \,.\, y = \bar{\bar{w}} \,.\, v = {}^{=}(z \times w)),\\
x^{y} = {} & (\imath v)(\exists z)(\exists w)(x = \bar{\bar{z}} \,.\, y = \bar{\bar{w}} \,.\\
& \qquad v = {}^{=}\{u\colon \mathrm{Func}\, u \,.\, u``\mathcal{V} \subseteq z \,.\, \breve{u}``\mathcal{V} = w\}).
\end{aligned}
$$

The idea behind this last is that if you are to assign members of z to all members of w, no two to the same, then for each member of w there are $\bar{\bar{z}}$ choices of what to assign to it; thus there are $\bar{\bar{z}}^{\bar{\bar{w}}}$ ways of doing the whole job. The ideas behind the definitions of $x + y$ and $x \cdot y$ are more obvious. Of course these ideas are rooted in the finite; in using them to define sums, products, and powers of infinite cardinals we are arbitrarily assigning a sense to the infinite cases of these operations by extrapolation from the finite.

Unlike ordinal addition and multiplication, cardinal addition and multiplication as above defined are commutative (granted modest comprehension assumptions). But still we must not expect all of familiar arithmetic to carry over.

Thus let $\alpha = \mathrm{N} \cap {}^{-}\{\Lambda\}$. Then $\mathrm{N} = \breve{\iota}``\alpha$ and so $\mathrm{N} \preceq \alpha$ (granted that $\breve{\iota} \restriction \alpha \in \mathcal{V}$) and so $\alpha \cup \{\Lambda\} \preceq \alpha$ even though $\Lambda \notin \alpha$.

---

[1] See also Suppes, pp. 111–125.

This gives $\bar{\bar{\alpha}} + 1 \leqq \bar{\bar{\alpha}}$, contrary to familiar arithmetic. More generally any infinite cardinal remains unchanged when we add any not greater cardinal, or multiply it by any such.

Rather less lethargy is to be observed on the part of the exponential function. Thus consider 2^y. By the above definition, 2^y is how many functions u there are such that $u``\mathcal{V} \subseteq \{s, t\}$ and $\breve{u}``\mathcal{V} = w$, where $s \neq t$ and w has y members. Now there is precisely one such function u for each subclass of w. For, corresponding to each subclass of w, there is the function that assigns s to the members of the subclass and t to the other members of w; and conversely, corresponding to each such function, there is the subclass whose members are the things to which the function assigns s. Thus 2^y is $\overline{\overline{\{z: z \subseteq w\}}}$, where w has y members. But we have by Cantor's law, 28.17, that $w \prec \{z: z \subseteq w\}$. So $y < 2^y$.

This argument turns on tacit comprehension premisses at several points, notably in the appeal to 28.17, whose comprehension premiss must fail in some cases on pain of paradox. But $y < 2^y$ within such limits. And yet there is lethargy here too; for we get $2^y = 3^y$ for infinite y, and even $2^y = y^y$.[2]

The first infinite cardinal was called $\aleph_0$ (aleph zero) by Cantor. To have this as its cardinal number, a class x must be as small as any infinite class but not as small as any finite one.

$$\aleph_0 = \bar{\bar{x}} .\equiv (y)(x \preceq y .\equiv (z)(z \in \text{N} .\supset. \{,,,z\} \prec y)).$$

The next he called $\aleph_1$; and so on. Thus

$$\aleph_1 = \bar{\bar{x}} .\equiv (y)(x \preceq y .\equiv (z)(\aleph_0 = \bar{\bar{z}} .\supset. z \prec y)).$$

Using little more than the reflexivity of '$\preceq$' we easily assure ourselves that $\aleph_0 = \bar{\bar{w}}$ and $\aleph_0 = \bar{\bar{x}}$, on the above formulation, only when $w \simeq x$; and similarly for $\aleph_1$ and the rest.

After $\aleph_0, \aleph_1, \ldots$, *ad infinitum*, comprehension permitting, there is $\aleph_\omega$. It is the cardinal number of classes that are bigger than all having any of the cardinal numbers $\aleph_0, \aleph_1, \ldots$, but are

---

[2] See e.g. Bachmann, p. 120. Proof of this, as well as of the lethargic laws of sum and product, depends on the axiom of choice.

no bigger than any that are in turn bigger than all those. Then comes $\aleph_{S`\omega}$, and eventually $\aleph_{\omega \cdot 2}$, and so on. What we are getting is an enumeration of the infinite cardinals as ordered by the '$<$' relation, i.e., by $\{\langle \overline{\overline{x}}, \overline{\overline{y}} \rangle : x \prec y\}$. We may exclude the finite cardinals by expressing the ordering relation as $\beta =$

$$\{\langle \overline{\overline{x}}, \overline{\overline{y}} \rangle : (u)(u \in \mathrm{N} \ .\supset.\ \{,,,u\} \prec x \prec y)\}.$$

Then $\aleph_z$ is definable as $e\beta`z$ for all ordinals z.

Questions crowd in. Can we show that every infinite cardinal is an aleph—that $\overline{\overline{x}}$ for every infinite class x is $\aleph_z$ for some $z \in \mathrm{NO}$? Can we show that some or all of $\aleph_0, \aleph_1, \ldots$ are not vacuous? They might be vacuous not from lack of large classes, but from an excess: instead of there being any just next larger infinite classes there might be an endless descent. In showing the contrary, that β above is a well-ordering, the axiom of choice is needed. For that matter, it is needed even to assure comparability, as remarked—hence even to show that β is an ordering.

When we grant the axiom of choice, on the other hand, we get with it a theorem that is a great boon to the theory of cardinals: the numeration theorem, which says that there is a correspondence between the members of any class x and the ordinals up to some ordinal.[3] (The ordinals up to an ordinal are just the members of the ordinal in von Neumann's version, but for a while we can stay aloof from versions.) Thus every cardinal comes to be $^{=}\{y: y <_o u\}$ for some ordinal u, where '$<_o$' is '$<$' in the ordinal sense ('ϵ' for von Neumann).

No infinite ordinal has fewer predecessors than ω has, since the predecessors of ω precede all infinite ordinals. So $\{y: y <_o \omega\}$ is as small as an infinite class $\{y: y <_o u\}$, with $u \in \mathrm{NO}$, can be. So, since every cardinal is $^{=}\{y: y <_o u\}$ for some $u \in \mathrm{NO}$, $\aleph_0$ is $^{=}\{y: y <_o \omega\}$. $\aleph_0$ is how many finite ordinals there are. Then also $\aleph_0 = {}^{=}\mathrm{N}$. A class x of this size is called *denumerable*, in allusion to the fact that its members can all be assigned natural numbers; $x \simeq \mathrm{N}$.

---

[3] §32. The extreme case where the members of x are in correspondence with all the ordinals is excluded, in most set theories, by failure of such an x to exist; after all, $\mathrm{NO} \notin \mathcal{V}$.

If $\aleph_0 = {}^{=}\{y\colon y <_o u\}$ for every infinite ordinal u, then, by the numeration theorem, $\aleph_0$ is the only infinite cardinal. If not, then, since the ordinals are well ordered, there is a least ordinal u such that $\aleph_0 < {}^{=}\{y\colon y <_o u\}$. This least u is called ω_1. Then $\{y\colon y <_o \omega_1\}$ is as small as a class $\{y\colon y <_o u\}$, with $u \in$ NO, can be and still exceed the size $\aleph_0$. So, since every cardinal is ${}^{=}\{y\colon y <_o u\}$ for some $u \in$ NO, $\aleph_1$ is ${}^{=}\{y\colon y <_o \omega_1\}$.

The ordinal number ω_1 lies far beyond $\omega \cdot 2$, ω^ω, ω^{ω^ω}, far beyond even ϵ (which is $\omega^{\omega^{\omega^{\cdots}}}$). This may be seen as follows. All the ordinals that we can ever reach in the manner of S'ω, $\omega \cdot 2$, ω^ω, ω^{ω^ω}, and the like are specifiable in this systematic notation, and there are no intervening ordinals but what are similarly specifiable. Now what makes this uninterrupted notational accessibility relevant is that the class of all expressions constructible in given notation is always denumerable, as follows. The shortest expressions will be finite in number, the alphabet being finite; number them 0, 1, 2, . . . , m in alphabetical order. The next to shortest expressions will be finite in number too; number them $m + 1, \ldots, n$ in alphabetical order. And so on.[4] So we conclude that each of S'ω, $\omega \cdot 2$, ω^ω, ω^{ω^ω}, ϵ, etc. has only denumerably many predecessors. But each is the class of its predecessors. So each is a denumerable class. So ω_1, the first ordinal that is not a denumerable class, lies beyond all those. In Cantor's terminology the intervening ordinals from ω on comprise, as against the finite ordinals, the *second number class.*

Similarly $\aleph_2$ is ${}^{=}\{y\colon y <_o \omega_2\}$ where ω_2 is the least ordinal u, if any there be, such that $\aleph_1 < {}^{=}\{y\colon y <_o u\}$. The ordinals from ω_1 on, short of ω_2, comprise the third number class. Among them are S'ω_1, S'(S'ω_1), $\omega_1 + \omega$, $\omega_1 +$ S'ω, $\omega_1 \cdot 2$, $\omega_1 \cdot \epsilon$, $\omega_1{}^\omega$, $\omega_1{}^{\omega_1}$. But most of them of course defy any preassigned notation.

Similarly $\aleph_3$ is ${}^{=}\{y\colon y <_o \omega_3\}$, and so on. Further $\aleph_\omega$ is ${}^{=}\{y\colon y <_o \omega_\omega\}$ where ω_ω is the least ordinal u, if any there be, such that $\aleph_i < {}^{=}\{y\colon y <_o u\}$ for all finite i. And so in general: $\aleph_z$ is ${}^{=}\{y : y <_o \omega_z\}$.

---

[4] This method, called lexicographic ordering, was used by both König and Richard in 1905.

The defining trait of ω_z is that it is the least ordinal that has $\aleph_z$ ordinals below it. Thus ω_z is what is called an *initial* ordinal: an infinite ordinal that is preceded by more ordinals than is any preceding ordinal. Conversely it can be shown by transfinite induction that any initial ordinal is ω_z for some z.

The recent question can then be answered: every infinite cardinal $\bar{\bar{x}}$ is an aleph. For, by the numeration theorem, $\bar{\bar{x}}$ is $^=\{y: y <_o u\}$ for some infinite ordinal u, in fact many. Since the ordinals are well ordered, there will be a least such u. It will be an initial ordinal, hence ω_z for some z. So $\bar{\bar{x}} = {}^=\{y: y <_o \omega_z\} = \aleph_z$.

The alephs play a role also in studies where the axiom of choice is held in abeyance. But then they are seen as cardinals only of a special sort: the cardinal numbers of fields of infinite well-orderings.

Cantor's law told us that the infinite cardinals go on and on; $y < 2^y$. The numeration theorem provided further that they are all alephs, so that there is always a *just* next. The question remains: is the just next between y and 2^y, or is it 2^y? The question comes down from Cantor. That 2^y just exceeds y is known as the *generalized continuum hypothesis.* Its special case '$2^{\aleph_0} = \aleph_1$' is the continuum hypothesis simply so called.[5] On these matters intuition seems to have no verdict; about all we can say for the hypothesis is that it is evidently a simpler assumption than the contrary. (Cf. further §33.)

Some further concepts call for mention. An ordinal x has, since Cantor, been called an *epsilon number* when $\omega^x = x$. Thus ϵ above is the first epsilon number. Also each of ω_1, ω_2, etc. is an epsilon number.[6] One sees here a contrast between ordinal and cardinal exponents. In cardinals we never have $z^x = x$ unless $z = x = 1$.

Of the cardinals, like the ordinals, some have immediate prede-

---

[5] So called because $2^{\aleph_0}$ is called the power of the continuum, meaning the cardinal number of the class of all real numbers. 'Power' here, by the way, is for *Mächtigkeit*, Cantor's term for cardinal number. The 'power' in 'power set' is for *Potenz*, power in the exponential sense. See §38.

[6] Sierpiński, 1958, p. 395.

cessors and some not. The latter, e.g. $\aleph_0$ and $\aleph_\omega$, are called *limit* cardinals. Now a limit cardinal is more particularly an *inaccessible number*, in Tarski's terminology (1938), if every cardinal sum of fewer than x cardinals, each less than x, is itself less than x.

Since any sum of finitely many finite numbers is finite, $\aleph_0$ qualifies as inaccessible. It is not evident that there are further inaccessible numbers beyond $\aleph_0$.

Note that the definition of inaccessible number presupposes a definition of cardinal summation over a perhaps transfinite sequence of cardinals. But we saw late in §25 how to define that. Just give '$+$' the cardinal sense this time instead of the ordinal.

An inaccessible number x is more particularly a *Grenzzahl* for Zermelo,[7] or *inaccessible in the narrower sense* for Tarski, if it meets the further condition that y^z in the cardinal sense is less than x for all cardinals y and z less than x. Thus $\aleph_0$ qualifies again. Tarski shows that this added condition follows from the other if we assume the generalized continuum hypothesis.

We still have to construe $\bar{\bar{x}}$. Whitehead and Russell's version, essentially Frege's (1884, §72), is parallel to their version of the ordinals (p. 153 above) and a direct extension of the Frege version of the natural numbers (p. 82). According to it $\bar{\bar{x}}$ is $\{y: y \simeq x\}$. To say that a class y has z members is, for infinite as for finite z, to say that $y \in z$.

The arithmetical definitions that were formulated above for the purposes of unconstrued cardinals tend to boil down when the peculiarities of any particular version of the cardinals are brought into play. In particular the definition of $x + y$ now condenses to:

$$\{z: (\exists w)(z \cap w \in x \,.\, z \cap \overline{w} \in y)\}.$$

The reader might try his hand at the others.

---

[7] 1930. He was treating of initial ordinals rather than cardinals, but on von Neumann's version they are the same, as we are about to see. For more on inaccessible numbers and related matters see references in pp. 325 and 328 below; also Bachmann; Kreider and Rogers; Mendelson, pp. 202–205.

We turn now to von Neumann's version of the cardinals, which is preferable for its economies. We have already seen that $\aleph_z = {}^{=}\{y\colon y <_o \omega_z\}$; if therefore we take ordinals in our regular way, which is von Neumann's, so that '$<_o$' becomes 'ϵ', we have simply $\aleph_z = {}^{=}\omega_z$. Now we get von Neumann's version of the infinite cardinals by taking the further step of construing ${}^{=}\omega_z$ as ω_z. Each aleph, $\aleph_z$, is thus construed as a certain class of $\aleph_z$ members, viz., the initial ordinal ω_z itself. Since (under the axiom of choice) all infinite cardinals are alephs, this accounts for the infinite cardinals. The finite cardinals he simply takes as the finite ordinals (or natural numbers in his sense). So now every cardinal number x, finite or infinite, is at once an ordinal and a class of x ordinals. To say on von Neumann's version that y has x members is, for infinite as for finite x, to say that $y \simeq x$.

We were able to say of von Neumann's finite numbers that each, x, is the class of the first x ordinals. We could say the same of his infinite cardinals, but for the fact that uniqueness lapses; e.g., you have just $\aleph_0$ numbers if you stop anywhere in the second number class. But we can say of his cardinals that each, x, is the bottom class of x ordinals.

To our definitions. Which ordinal for von Neumann is $\overline{\overline{\alpha}}$? The first ordinal $\simeq \alpha$. Or, since an ordinal is the class of all earlier ones, it is the class of all ordinals $\prec \alpha$.

30.1 '$\overline{\overline{\alpha}}$' or '${}^{=}\alpha$' for '$\{x\colon x \epsilon \text{NO} \,.\, x \prec \alpha\}$'.

A cardinal number *simpliciter* is, on any approach, anything that is $\overline{\overline{x}}$ for some x. But on von Neumann's approach it will be the cardinal number of itself among other things, so

30.2 'NC' for '$\{x\colon x = \overline{\overline{x}}\}$'.

Before construing $\overline{\overline{x}}$ we saw how to define $\aleph_z$ by enumeration, and how then, nearly enough, to define ω_z from $\aleph_z$. But on the present approach definition of $\aleph_z$ *is* definition of ω_z. What then was our old definition of $\aleph_z$? It was $\mathrm{e}\beta\text{‘}z$ where β was the ordering of the infinite cardinals. Now that the cardinals are ordinals, the ordering wanted is $\mathfrak{E}$ within the infinite cardinals. Now the class of the finite cardinals is ω; so the class of the infinite cardinals is NC $\cap\ \bar{\omega}$; so the ordering of the infinite cardinals is $\mathfrak{E} \cap ((\mathrm{NC} \cap \bar{\omega}) \times \mathrm{NC})$; so

30.3 'ω_α' for 'e$(\mathfrak{E} \cap ((\mathrm{NC} \cap \bar{\omega}) \times \mathrm{NC}))$'$\alpha$'.

The definitions advanced earlier for cardinal '$\leqq$' and '$<$' of course lapse for the von Neumann cardinals; '$\subseteq$' and 'ϵ' suffice, as they do for his ordinals generally. Those for sum and product can for the von Neumann cardinals be put more compactly thus:

$$x + y = {}^{=}(x \cup (y \times \{\Lambda\})), \qquad x \cdot y = {}^{=}(x \times y).$$

The point of the $y \times \{\Lambda\}$ is that like y it has y members but unlike y it shares no members with x (so long as $x, y \in \mathrm{NO}$).

It was remarked in §22 that the operations of ordinal arithmetic should in theory, if not in practice, be distinguished notationally from those of §16. So should these of cardinal arithmetic. Also these must be distinguished from those of ordinal arithmetic, even when, following von Neumann, we do not distinguish the cardinal numbers from the initial ordinals. On this approach the operations of ordinal and cardinal arithmetic coincide in the finite, certainly; but they diverge in the transfinite. We already noticed this in the case of exponents, and it is true also of sum and product. For example, the cardinal sum or product $\omega + \omega = 2 \cdot \omega = \omega \cdot 2$ is simply ω, while the ordinal sum or product $\omega + \omega = \omega \cdot 2 \neq 2 \cdot \omega$ as of §22 is not a cardinal at all, but an ordinal intermediate between the cardinals ω and ω_1.

In terms of ordinal sum and product the cardinal sum and product of ordinals in von Neumann's sense can indeed be defined simply as ${}^{=}(x + y)$ and ${}^{=}(x \cdot y)$. I owe this observation to A. T. Tymoczko.

X | THE AXIOM OF CHOICE

31. Selections and selectors

Two small platitudes regarding size comparisons of classes were noted at the end of §29 and said to depend upon an *axiom of choice* which I did not there formulate. This premiss or axiom goes back to Zermelo (1904), and what it says is that, given any class of mutually exclusive classes, there exists a *selection* from it, i.e., a class containing exactly one member from each of those mutually exclusive classes (except Λ). Let us adopt a brief notation for 'β is a selection from α':

31.1 'β Sln α' for '$(y)(y \in \alpha \,.\, y \neq \Lambda \,.\!\supset (\exists x)(\beta \cap y = \{x\}))$'.

The condition that the classes belonging to α be mutually exclusive can be put succinctly thus: Func $\breve{}(\mathfrak{E}{\restriction}\alpha)$. So, writing

31.2 'Ch α' for 'Func $\breve{}(\mathfrak{E}{\restriction}\alpha) \supset (\exists w)(w$ Sln $\alpha)$',

we may package the axiom of choice for convenient reference as '(z) Ch z'.

Intuitively the principle seems reasonable, even obvious. The trouble is just that it is not as simple and elementary a statement as could be desired as a starting point, and no way is known of deducing it strictly from anything simpler. For this reason it is common practice to distinguish between results that depend on the axiom of choice and those that do not. Accordingly I shall not adopt the principle as axiom or axiom schema, but shall merely use it as premiss where needed. I shall thus treat it as I have been treating comprehension assumptions, beyond 7.10, 13.1, and 23.12.

The axiom of choice is not itself a comprehension assumption, though it is an assumption of class existence. For there is no general way of specifying the selection w relative to α (or z) by means of a membership condition with 'α' (or 'z') as parameter. Generally the axiom of choice has to be assumed, if wanted, even after one's full stock of comprehension axioms is laid in.

I adopted the comprehension axioms 7.10, 13.1, and 23.12 because they posit no infinite classes. Just the infinite existences have been held in abeyance by deferring further comprehension axioms. Now the situation of the axiom of choice is in fact similar: in not adopting it as axiom we are really only holding its infinite cases in abeyance. For where α is (firmly) finite we can prove that Ch α. The proof runs longer than it otherwise would because of our niggardliness over comprehension axioms. No special comprehension premisses are added, nor is 23.12 involved.

31.3 $x \in \text{N} \,.\, \alpha \preceq \{,\,,\,, x\} \;.\!\supset \text{Ch}\,\alpha.$

Idea of proof. If y is a class of $n + 1$ exclusive classes one of which is z, and if s Sln $y \cap {}^{-}\{z\}$, then we have also $(s \cap \bar{z}) \cup \{w\}$ Sln y for all $w \in z$ if $z \neq \Lambda$, and simply s Sln y if $z = \Lambda$. Thus every class of $n + 1$ exclusive classes has a selection if every class of n exclusive classes does. But Λ Sln Λ by 31.1. So, by induction, every finite class of exclusive classes has a selection.

Details of proof. Consider any things y and z such that

$$y \preceq \{,\,,\,, x\}, \quad \text{[i]} \qquad \text{Ch}\, y \cap {}^{-}\{z\}. \quad \text{[ii]}$$

Case 1: $z \notin y$. Then $y \cap {}^{-}\{z\} = y$. Then, by [ii], Ch y.
Case 2: $\sim$ Func $\breve{}(\mathfrak{E}\upharpoonright y)$. By 31.2, then, vacuously, Ch y.
Case 3: Func $\breve{}(\mathfrak{E}\upharpoonright y)$ and $z \in y$. Then

$$\text{Func}\,\breve{}(\mathfrak{C}\upharpoonright(y \cap {}^{-}\{z\})).$$

So, by [ii] and 31.2, there is something s such that

$$s \text{ Sln } y \cap {}^{-}\{z\}. \qquad \text{[iii]}$$

Case 3a: $z = \Lambda$. In view of the '$\neq\Lambda$' in 31.1, then, [iii] amounts to 's Sln y'. So, by 31.2, Ch y.

Case 3b: $z \neq \Lambda$. Then there is something

$$w \in z. \qquad \text{[iv]}$$

By the Case-3 hypothesis, no members of y overlap; so, since $z \in y$,

$$z \cap \mathsf{U}(y \cap {}^{-}\{z\}) = \Lambda. \qquad \text{[v]}$$

What [iii] says of s remains true, in view of 31.1, when s is diminished or augmented by things not in $\mathsf{U}(y \cap {}^{-}\{z\})$. So $s \cap \bar{z}$ Sln $y \cap {}^{-}\{z\}$ by [v], or for that matter, by [iv],

$$(s \cap \bar{z}) \cup \{w\} \text{ Sln } y \cap {}^{-}\{z\},$$

i.e., by 31.1,

$$(t)(t \in y \,.\, \Lambda \neq t \neq z \,.\!\supset (\exists r)(((s \cap \bar{z}) \cup \{w\}) \cap t = \{r\})). \qquad \text{[vi]}$$

But

$$((s \cap \bar{z}) \cup \{w\}) \cap z = \{w\} \cap z$$

(by [iv]) $\qquad = \{w\}$

and thus the caution '$t \neq z$' in [vi] is needless. Dropping it, we can condense [vi] by 31.1 to:

$$(s \cap \bar{z}) \cup \{w\} \text{ Sln } y. \qquad \text{[vii]}$$

So $(s \cap \bar{z}) \cup \{w\}$ shares at most one member with each member of y. That is,

$$\text{Func } \{\langle u, v\rangle : u \in (s \cap \bar{z}) \cup \{w\} \,.\, u \in v \in y\}.$$

Call this function β. By [i] and 28.7, $\beta``y \preceq y$. So, by [i] and 28.12, $\beta``y \preceq \{,,,x\}$. But clearly

$$((s \cap \bar{z}) \cup \{w\}) \cap \mathsf{U}y \subseteq \beta``y.$$

So, by 28.1,

$$((s \cap \bar{z}) \cup \{w\}) \cap \mathsf{U}y \preceq \{,,,x\}.$$

So, by 28.10,

$$((s \cap \bar{z}) \cup \{w\}) \cap \mathsf{U}y \in \mathcal{V}. \qquad \text{[viii]}$$

As remarked, any selection from y remains such when diminished by things not in $\mathsf{U}y$. So, by [vii],

$$((s \cap \bar{z}) \cup \{w\}) \cap \mathsf{U}y \text{ Sln } y.$$

So, by [viii], $(\exists u)(u \text{ Sln } y)$. So, by 31.2, Ch y.

All cases (1, 2, 3a, 3b): 'Ch y' has been proved from [i] and [ii]. So

$$(y)(z)(y \preceq \{,,,x\} \mathbin{.} \text{Ch } y \cap {}^{-}\{z\} \mathbin{.\supset} \text{Ch } y).$$

But also $(s)(s \text{ Sln } \Lambda)$ by 31.1, and so, by 31.2, Ch Λ. From these we infer 31.3 by 28.15.

So we have seen that the axiom of choice is needed only for its infinite cases.

There is a variant version of the axiom of choice which says that for any class of classes there is a *selector:* a function selecting a member from each member (except Λ). Succinctly defined,

31.4 'β Slr α' for '$\beta \subseteq \mathfrak{E} \mathbin{.} \alpha \cap {}^{-}\{\Lambda\} \subseteq \arg \beta$'.

So the law in question, which can on reasonable comprehension premisses be shown equivalent to the axiom of choice '(z) Ch z', is '$(z)(\exists w)(w \text{ Slr } z)$'.

We may for the added generality address ourselves not to '$(z)(\exists w)(w \text{ Slr } z)$' but to the corresponding schema '$(\exists w)(w \text{ Slr } \alpha)$'. Now, however, special care is needed in talking of equivalence.

For '$(\exists w)(w \text{ Slr } \alpha)$' is not equivalent to '$\text{Ch } \alpha$', even under appropriate comprehension premisses. The relation is rather as follows. We can indeed specify a selection from α (if, of course, the members of α are mutually exclusive) in terms of a selector from α itself; but in order conversely to specify a selector from α we make use of a selection, not from α itself, but from

$$\{y \times \{y\} : y \in \alpha\}$$

—a class of mutually exclusive relations. The details are set forth in the following two theorem schemata.

31.5 $\beta \text{ Slr } \alpha \,.\, \text{Func } \breve{}(\mathfrak{E} \restriction \alpha) \,.\!\supset\!.\, \beta``\alpha \text{ Sln } \alpha.$

Proof. By first hypothesis and 31.4,

$$\beta \subseteq \mathfrak{E}, \quad (1) \qquad\qquad \alpha \cap {}^{-}\{\Lambda\} \subseteq \arg \beta. \quad (2)$$

Consider anything x such that

$$x \in \alpha \cap {}^{-}\{\Lambda\}. \qquad [\text{i}]$$

Then, by (2), there is something y such that

$$\beta``\{x\} = \{y\}. \qquad [\text{ii}]$$

Then, by (1), $y \in x$; also, by [ii] and [i], $y \in \beta``\alpha$; so

$$y \in x \cap \beta``\alpha. \qquad [\text{iii}]$$

For any member v of $x \cap \beta``\alpha$ there is a $u \in \alpha$ such that $\langle v, u\rangle \in \beta$ and so, by (1), $v \in u$. Thus

$$\langle v, u\rangle \in \beta, \qquad v \in x \in \alpha, \qquad v \in u \in \alpha.$$

The last two give $u = x$, by the second hypothesis, and so '$\langle v, u\rangle \in \beta$' becomes '$\langle v, x\rangle \in \beta$', which, with [ii], gives $v = y$. So we see that any member of $x \cap \beta``\alpha$ is $y$. So, by [iii], $x \cap \beta``\alpha = \{y\}$. But x was anything fulfilling [i]. So

$$(x)(x \in \alpha \cap {}^{-}\{\Lambda\} \,.\!\supset (\exists y)(x \cap \beta``\alpha = \{y\})).$$

That is, by 31.1, $\beta``\alpha$ Sln α.

31.6 β Sln $\{y \times \{y\} : y \in \alpha\}$.⊃. $\beta \cap \mathfrak{E}$ Slr α.[1]

Proof. By hypothesis and 31.1,

$$(z)(z \in \{y \times \{y\} : y \in \alpha\} \cap {}^{-}\{\Lambda\} \;.\!\supset (\exists w)(\beta \cap z = \{w\})),$$

i.e.,

$$(y)(y \in \alpha \cap {}^{-}\{\Lambda\} \;.\!\supset (\exists w)(\beta \cap (y \times \{y\}) = \{w\})).$$

That is, where y is any member of $\alpha \cap {}^{-}\{\Lambda\}$, $\beta \cap (y \times \{y\})$ has exactly one member. That member will have to be $\langle v, y\rangle$ where v is the one and only member of y that bears β to y; hence where v is the one and only thing that bears $\beta \cap \mathfrak{E}$ to y. So we have found that, where y is any member of $\alpha \cap {}^{-}\{\Lambda\}$, one and only one thing will bear $\beta \cap \mathfrak{E}$ to y. That is,

$$\alpha \cap {}^{-}\{\Lambda\} \subseteq \arg(\beta \cap \mathfrak{E}).$$

So, by 31.4, $\beta \cap \mathfrak{E}$ Slr α.

It is evident how on the basis of 31.5 and 31.6 to prove the equivalence of the versions '(z) Ch z' and '$(z)(\exists w)(w$ Slr $z)$' of the axiom of choice, subject to appropriate comprehension premisses.

Next consider the comprehension premiss '$(w)(\arg w \in \mathcal{V})$'. It holds in any set theory one is likely to settle for. Another comprehension premiss of which this may be said is '$(x)(x \cup \{\Lambda\} \in \mathcal{V})$'. Now observe that

$$(\exists w)(w \text{ Slr } \mathcal{V}) \supset. \mathcal{V} \in \mathcal{V}$$

granted those two premisses. For, where w Slr $\mathcal{V}$, we have by 31.4 that $\arg w \cup \{\Lambda\} = \mathcal{V}$. Furthermore, $\arg w \in \mathcal{V}$. So, since $(x)(x \cup \{\Lambda\} \in \mathcal{V})$, we have $\mathcal{V} \in \mathcal{V}$.

---

[1] β itself would have qualified as a selector of α if we had defined 'β Slr α' simply as '$\alpha \cap {}^{-}\{\Lambda\} \subseteq \arg(\beta \cap \mathfrak{E})$', or again as '$(x)(\Lambda \neq x \in \alpha \;.\!\supset. \beta`x \in x)$'; and so we could, granted some adjustments of phrasing in 31.5 and elsewhere.

The moral of this is that a kind of strengthening which the version '$(z)(\exists w)(w \text{ Slr } z)$' of the axiom of choice invites is spurious. Whereas '$(z)(\exists w)(w \text{ Slr } z)$' postulates for each class a selector, '$(\exists w)(w \text{ Slr } \mathcal{V})$' postulates a universal selector. But the foregoing reasoning shows, granted the two mild comprehension assumptions, that '$(\exists w)(w \text{ Slr } \mathcal{V})$' is either untenable or covered already by '$(z)(\exists w)(w \text{ Slr } z)$' according as $\mathcal{V} \notin \mathcal{V}$ or $\mathcal{V} \in \mathcal{V}$.

In our axiom '$\{x, y\} \in \mathcal{V}$' (7.10) we took our stand against ultimate classes. For set theories admitting ultimate classes, on the other hand, the question can be raised of there being a certain pale counterpart of the universal selector last contemplated, viz., a selector that takes a member merely from every set (but Λ), possibly neglecting ultimate classes. In brief this proposition is that $(\exists w)(w \text{ Slr } \bigcup\mathcal{V})$. But our foregoing reasoning still applies: the proposition is untenable if $\bigcup\mathcal{V} \notin \mathcal{V}$, and already covered by '$(z)(\exists w)(w \text{ Slr } z)$' if $\bigcup\mathcal{V} \in \mathcal{V}$.[2]

Turning our backs again upon set theories that assume ultimate classes, let us return to the question of a universal selector for the space of a further comment. '$(\exists w)(w \text{ Slr } \mathcal{V})$', we saw, is out when $\mathcal{V} \notin \mathcal{V}$. Still we can postulate a good part of its intended force if we add a primitive selector predicate '$\mathfrak{S}$'. For we can then adopt:

$$\text{(i)} \qquad \{\langle x, y\rangle : \mathfrak{S}xy\} \text{ Slr } \mathcal{V}$$

as axiom without hinting that $\{\langle x, y\rangle : \mathfrak{S}xy\} \in \mathcal{V}$ or $\mathcal{V} \in \mathcal{V}$ or $(\exists w)(w \text{ Slr } \mathcal{V})$. More directly, giving our added primitive notation the form not of a two-place selector predicate '$\mathfrak{S}$' but of a selector operator 'σ', we could postulate simply that

$$\text{(ii)} \qquad (x)(x \neq \Lambda \;.\!\supset\!.\; \sigma x \in x).$$

[2] Axiom E of Gödel, 1940, p. 6, comes in our notation precisely to '$(\exists w)(w \text{ Slr } \bigcup\mathcal{V})$'. But for his system this was a mere equivalent of '$(z)(\exists w)$ $(w \text{ Slr } z)$', since '$\bigcup\mathcal{V} \in \mathcal{V}$' issues from his other axioms. When he called it "a very strong form of the axiom of choice" he was contrasting it with the following two, which, by his 5.19, are again equivalent to each other:

$$(z)(z \in \bigcup\mathcal{V} \;.\!\supset (\exists w)(w \text{ Slr } z)), \qquad (z)(z \in \bigcup\mathcal{V} \;.\!\supset (\exists w)(w \in \bigcup\mathcal{V} \,.\, w \text{ Slr } z)).$$

On this approach we would have also to adjust the underlying logic of quantification to admit 'σx' in positions of variables.

The expedient (ii) is due to Skolem (1929). And it can be liberalized yet a bit by schematization:

$$\text{(iii)} \qquad \alpha \neq \Lambda \mathrel{.\supset.} \sigma\alpha \in \alpha.$$

This phase is due essentially to Hilbert.[3]

But (i)–(iii) are drastic departures. They add to the primitive notation, and what they add we do not even know how to translate into intuitive terms.

32. Further equivalents of the axiom

Another equivalent of the axiom of choice says that every function harbors a correspondence whose values are the same. That is,

$$\text{(i)} \qquad (y)(\text{Func}\, y \supset (\exists x)(\text{Cor}\, x \,.\, x \subseteq y \,.\, x``\mathcal{V} = y``\mathcal{V})).$$

For, if Func y, then

$$\{z\colon (\exists w)(z = \breve{y}``\{w\})\}$$

is a class of mutually exclusive classes and therefore has a selection, u, according to the axiom of choice; and then $y{\restriction}u$ meets the condition on 'x' in (i), as the following theorem schema shows.

$$\textbf{32.1} \qquad \text{C}_1 \,.\, \text{Func}\, y \,.\, \beta\ \text{Sln}\ \{z\colon (\exists w)(z = \breve{y}``\{w\})\} \mathrel{.\supset.} \text{Cor}\ y{\restriction}\beta \,.\, (y{\restriction}\beta)``\mathcal{V} = y``\mathcal{V}.$$

Proof. By last hypothesis and 31.1,

$$(z)(w)(z = \breve{y}``\{w\} \neq \Lambda \mathrel{.\supset} (\exists x)(\beta \cap z = \{x\})). \qquad (1)$$

By 'C_1', $\breve{y} \in \mathcal{V}$. So, by '$\text{C}_1$' and 29.3, $\breve{y}``\{w\} \in \mathcal{V}$. So we may put '$\breve{y}``\{w\}$' for 'z' in (1). Thus

---

[3] So formulated and attributed by Bernays and Fraenkel, p. 197. The allusion is to the Hilbert ϵ-operator; cf. Hilbert and Bernays, vol. 2, pp. 9ff.

$$(w)(\breve{y}``\{w\} \neq \Lambda \,.\supset (\exists x)(\beta \cap \breve{y}``\{w\} = \{x\})).$$

That is,

$$(w)(w \in y``\mathcal{V} \,.\supset (\exists x)(\breve{\ }(y \restriction \beta)``\{w\} = \{x\})).$$

That is, by 10.2,

$$y``\mathcal{V} \subseteq \arg \breve{\ }(y \restriction \beta). \qquad (2)$$

So, by 10.10, Func $\breve{\ }(y \restriction \beta)$. So, by second hypothesis, Cor $y \restriction \beta$. But also, by (2), $(y \restriction \beta)``\mathcal{V} = y``\mathcal{V}$.

So much for (i) as a consequence of the axiom of choice. To get the axiom of choice conversely from (i), take the y of (i) as $\{\langle y, w\rangle : w \in y \in z\}$. Thereupon the antecedent in (i) becomes precisely that of 'Ch z' according to 31.2, while the consequent comes to say that some correspondence x is a subclass of $\{\langle y, w\rangle : w \in y \in z\}$ and has the same left field. It is then quickly seen that $\breve{x}``\mathcal{V}$ Sln z, establishing 'Ch z'. The comprehension premisses implicit in this reasoning are easily uncovered.

Another law that classically is equated to the axiom of choice is superficially more general than (i), and says that every relation harbors a function with the same right field. That is,

$$\text{(ii)} \qquad (y)(\exists x)(\text{Func}\, x \,.\, x \subseteq y \,.\, \breve{x}``\mathcal{V} = \breve{y}``\mathcal{V}).$$

From among the equivalents of the axiom of choice that we have heretofore noted, the one to which we can most easily equate (ii) is:

$$(z)(\exists w)(w \text{ Slr } z).$$

We can derive this from (ii) by taking y in (ii) as $\mathfrak{E} \restriction z$; for the x that exists according to (ii) thereupon turns out to be a function w fulfilling 'w Slr z', as is readily seen from 31.4. Conversely, to derive (ii) we take

$$z = \{u: (\exists v)(u = y``\{v\})\}$$

and then observe that, where w Slr z, (ii) is fulfilled by

$$x = \{\langle u, v\rangle : \langle u, y``\{v\}\rangle \in w\}.$$

The comprehension premisses involved are apparent.

A more startling equivalent of the axiom of choice is the *numeration theorem*, to the effect that any class z is the left field of a sequence (in the sense SEQ). More particularly, z is the left field of a sequence without repetitions, hence a sequence that is a correspondence. So there is a correspondence between the members of z and the ordinals up to some ordinal. In a word, the members of any class can be numbered.

In fact, where β Slr $\{x\colon x \subseteq z\}$, a particular numeration w of z is specifiable in intuitive terms as follows. The selector β selects from each subclass x (but Λ) of z a representative member $\beta`x$. Now the numeration $w$ assigns to the ordinal $\Lambda$ the representative member $\beta`z$ of z itself; it assigns to the next ordinal, $\{\Lambda\}$, the representative member $\beta`(z \cap {}^{-}\{\beta`z\})$ of $z \cap {}^{-}\{\beta`z\}$; and in general it assigns to each ordinal $y$ the representative member $\beta`(z \cap {}^{-}(w``y))$ of the leavings of z, if any, not assigned to ordinals up to y.

The way to specify this sequence w formally is by transfinite recursion. To do so, look for its generating function. Given the class u of all the value-and-argument pairs of the sequence w up to and excluding the argument y, what is $w`y$? It is $\beta$ of the leavings of $z$; hence $\beta$ of $z$-minus-all-those-prior-values; hence $\beta`(z \cap {}^{-}(u``\mathcal{V}))$. So the generating function required is

$$\{\langle y, u\rangle\colon \langle y, z \cap {}^{-}(u``\mathcal{V})\rangle \in \beta\},$$

or briefly $\Psi_{\beta z}$ if we write

32.2 '$\Psi_{\beta\gamma}$' for '$\{\langle y, x\rangle\colon \langle y, \gamma \cap {}^{-}(x``\mathcal{V})\rangle \in \beta\}$'.

The desired numeration w of z is then $\mathrm{A}\Psi_{\beta z}$.

Accordingly the substance of the numeration theorem that wants proving is that, where β Slr $\{x\colon x \subseteq z\}$, $\mathrm{A}\Psi_{\beta z}$ is a correlation whose left field is z and whose right is an ordinal. Complete with comprehension premisses, the law is this:

32.3 $\mathrm{C}_1 \,.\, \beta \text{ Slr } \{x\colon x \subseteq z\} \,.\, w = \mathrm{A}\Psi_{\beta z}$
$\qquad .\supset.\ \text{Cor } w \,.\, w``\mathcal{V} = z \,.\, \breve{w}``\mathcal{V} \in \text{NO}.$

Proof. By 'C_1',

$$\breve{w}``\mathcal{V} \in \mathcal{V}. \qquad (1)$$

By second hypothesis and definition,

$$\beta \subseteq \mathfrak{E}, \qquad (2) \qquad\qquad \{x\colon \Lambda \neq x \subseteq z\} \subseteq \arg \beta. \qquad (3)$$

To any subclass of z at most one thing bears β: nothing, by (2), if the subclass is Λ, and one thing, by (3), otherwise. So, by 32.2,

$$\text{Func}\ \Psi_{\beta z}. \qquad (4)$$

So, by 26.4 and last hypothesis, SEQ w. I.e.,

$$\text{Func}\ w \qquad (5)$$

and $\breve{w}``\mathfrak{V} \in \text{NO}$ or $\breve{w}``\mathfrak{V} = \text{NO}$. So, by (1) and 24.4,

$$\breve{w}``\mathfrak{V} \in \text{NO}. \qquad (6)$$

By 'C_1' and 29.3, $(v)(w``v \in \mathfrak{V})$. So, by '$C_1$',

$$(v)(z \cap {}^{-}(w``v) \in \mathfrak{V}). \qquad (7)$$

Consider any $\langle u, v\rangle \in w$. By (5), $u = w`v$. Further $v \in \breve{w}``\mathfrak{V}$, and from this and (4) we can infer, by 26.5 and the last hypothesis, that $\langle w`v, w{\restriction}v\rangle \in \Psi_{\beta z}$, i.e., $\langle u, w{\restriction}v\rangle \in \Psi_{\beta z}$, i.e., by 32.2 (since $w{\restriction}v \in \mathfrak{V}$ by 'C_1'),

$$\langle u, z \cap {}^{-}((w{\restriction}v)``\mathfrak{V})\rangle \in \beta,$$

i.e., $\langle u, z \cap {}^{-}(w``v)\rangle \in \beta$, and so, by (2) and (7), $u \in z \cap {}^{-}(w``v)$. But $\langle u, v\rangle$ was any member of w. So

$$(u)(v)(\langle u, v\rangle \in w \,.\!\supset\!.\, u \in z \,.\, u \notin w``v). \qquad (8)$$

Consider next any u, v, v' such that $\langle u, v\rangle$, $\langle u, v'\rangle \in w$. Then $u \notin w``v$ by (8) and so, since $\langle u, v'\rangle \in w$, $v' \notin v$. Similarly $v \notin v'$. Yet $v, v' \in \breve{w}``\mathfrak{V}$ and so, by (6) and 23.10, $v \in v'$ or $v' \in v$ or $v = v'$. So $v = v'$. Thus Func $\breve{w}$. So, by (5),

$$\text{Cor}\ w. \qquad (9)$$

By (8)

$$w``\mathcal{V} \subseteq z. \qquad (10)$$

By 'C_1', $z \cap {}^-(w``\mathcal{V}) \in \mathcal{V}$. So

$$z \cap {}^-(w``\mathcal{V}) \in \{x\colon x \subseteq z\}.$$

So

$$z \not\subseteq w``\mathcal{V} .\supset. z \cap {}^-(w``\mathcal{V}) \in \{x\colon \Lambda \neq x \subseteq z\}$$

(by (3)) $$\supset. z \cap {}^-(w``\mathcal{V}) \in \arg \beta. \qquad (11)$$

From (1) and (4) we have, by 26.6 and the last hypothesis, that $w \notin \breve{\Psi}_{\beta z}``\mathcal{V}$. That is, by 32.2,

$$(y)(\langle y, z \cap {}^-(w``\mathcal{V})\rangle \notin \beta).$$

So $z \cap {}^-(w``\mathcal{V}) \notin \arg \beta$. So, by (11), $z \subseteq w``\mathcal{V}$. This and (10) and (9) and (6) are q.e.d.

To argue conversely from the numeration theorem to the axiom of choice, say in the form '$(z)(\exists w)(w \text{ Slr } z)$', take any class z and any numeration y of $\bigcup z$.This selector of z is then obtainable: the function w which, applied to any $x \in z \cap {}^-\{\Lambda\}$, gives as $w`x$ that member of x that gets the earliest number under the numeration y. I pass over the details.

A familiar phenomenon among infinite classes is that you can correlate such a class with a proper part of itself. Cases of this were noted in §28 and §30; and see also the next to last sentence in the proof of 24.8, which shows that

(iii) $$\omega \subseteq z \in \text{NO} .\supset. z \simeq z \cup \{z\}.$$

This trait was used by Dedekind (1888) to define infinitude: an infinite class is a class x such that $(\exists y)(x \simeq y \subset x)$, or, to isolate the essential point, $(\exists y)(x \lesssim y \subset x)$. Proof that this condition is implied by infinitude in a more usual sense of the term, say '$\text{N} \lesssim x$' or :

(iv) $$(z)(x \simeq z \in \text{NO} .\supset. \omega \subseteq z),$$

requires the axiom of choice and provides an example of the use of the numeration theorem. Suppose x is an infinite class in the sense (iv). By the numeration theorem, $x \simeq z$ for some $z \in \text{NO}$.

By (iv), $\omega \subseteq z$ and so, by (iii), $z \simeq z \cup \{z\}$. So $z \cup \{z\} \preceq z \preceq x$, by 11.2. So $z \cup \{z\} \preceq x$ (granted transitivity of '$\preceq$', which turns on '$(v)(w)(v \mid w \in \mathcal{V})$'). So $z \cup \{z\} \subseteq u``x$, by 11.1, for some function $u$. If we assume '$C_1$', something $y$ is $x \cap {}^{-}(\breve{u}``\{z\})$; cf. 29.3. Since Func u, we have $z \subseteq u``y$ and $y \subset x$. So $z \preceq y \subset x$. But $x \preceq z$, by 11.2. So $x \preceq y \subset x$.

The most celebrated equivalent of the axiom of choice is Zermelo's theorem (1904) that every class can be well-ordered. More precisely: every class, unless it has but one member, is the field of a well-ordering. That is,

(v) $$(z)((\exists x)(z = \{x\}) \vee (\exists x)(\text{Wellord } x \,.\, z = (x \cup \breve{x})``\mathcal{V})).$$

This is evident from the numeration theorem, since a numeration y of z furnishes for the members of z a well-ordering $y \mid \mathfrak{E} \mid \breve{y}$ parallel to that of the numerating ordinals. But the well-ordering theorem was a major result historically, for Zermelo proved it ahead of the numeration theorem. Indeed, the above proof of the numeration theorem derives in part from Zermelo's proof of the well-ordering theorem.

How to argue conversely from (v) to '$(z)(\exists w)(w \text{ Slr } z)$' is evident from the argument sketched three paragraphs back.

A simpler and in a way stronger variant of (v) says just that the universe can be well-ordered:

(vi) $$(\exists x)(\text{Wellord } x \,.\, (x \cup \breve{x})``\mathcal{V} = \mathcal{V}).$$

We get this from (v), of course, by taking z as $\mathcal{V}$ (if $\mathcal{V} \in \mathcal{V}$); and conversely we get (v) from this by means of 21.9 with α as x and β as z (if $x \cap (z \times z) \in \mathcal{V}$). The respect in which (vi) is stronger than (v) is that set theories provide that $\mathcal{V} \in \mathcal{V}$ less commonly than that $x \cap (z \times z) \in \mathcal{V}$ for all x and z. Still it would be an odd set theory that could count (vi) stronger than (v) and still entertain (vi) as possibly true. It would have to be a set theory that admitted neither '$\mathcal{V} \in \mathcal{V}$' nor '$(x)((x \cup \breve{x})``\mathcal{V} \in \mathcal{V})$'; for the latter with (vi) gives '$\mathcal{V} \in \mathcal{V}$'.

The odds against (vi) are indeed not to be wondered at; for a universal well-ordering as of (vi) would share essential properties of $\mathfrak{E} \upharpoonright$NO, and the incapacity of NO to exist was noted in 24.4.

Might the effect of universal well-ordering be gained without the extravagant existence claim of (vi) by adopting the drastic line noted at the end of §31? Thus take β as the universal selector $\lambda_x \sigma x$, with no presumption that $\beta \in \mathcal{V}$. Then 32.3 would seem to assure a numeration of $\mathcal{V}$, and therewith a well-ordering of $\mathcal{V}$. But the trouble with this reasoning is that such use of 32.3 requires as extravagant existence assumptions as ever.

The drastic line considered at the end of §31 for the universal selector could of course be simply copied now for universal well-ordering, instead of our trying to get the one from the other. This would mean adopting a primitive predicate 'F' subject to the axioms:

$$\text{Wellord } \{\langle x, y\rangle : \text{F}xy\}, \qquad (x)(\exists y)(\text{F}xy \vee \text{F}yx).$$

There are notable equivalents of the axiom of choice that I have not touched on. One is Hausdorff's law that every partial ordering harbors a maximal ordering. That is, if z is a partial ordering ($z \mid z \subseteq z \subseteq {}^{-}I$) there is an ordering $x \subseteq z$ which is maximal in the sense that $x \subset y \subseteq z$ for no ordering y. Another equivalent, known as Zorn's lemma, says that if v is a class such that $\text{U}w \in v$ for every nest $w \subseteq v$ then v has a member u which is maximal in the sense $(y){\sim}(u \subset y \in v)$. Zorn's lemma can be got from Hausdorff's law as follows. Taking z in Hausdorff's law as

$$\{\langle s, t\rangle : s \subset t \,.\, s, t \in v\}$$

(if it exists), we are assured of a maximal ordering $x \subseteq z$. Its field is a nest $w \subseteq v$. By the hypothesis of Zorn's lemma, then, $\text{U}w \in v$. But $\text{U}w$ is easily seen to be maximal in the sense $(y){\sim}(\text{U}w \subset y \in v)$.[1]

[1] On the axiom of choice and its equivalents see further Bernays and Fraenkel, chap. VI; Rosser, *Logic for Mathematicians*, chap. XIV; Suppes, chap. VIII; Rubin.

33. The place of the axiom

Near the end of §29 we were brought up against the axiom of choice by the law of comparability '$x \precsim y \,.\mathbf{v}.\, y \precsim x$'. Let us now prove this law, invoking requisite premisses of comprehension and choice.

33.1 $\quad C_1 \,.\, (u)(v)(u \mid v \in \mathcal{V}) \,.\, A\Psi_{zx}, A\Psi_{wy} \in \mathcal{V}.$
$z \text{ Slr } \{u: u \subseteq x\} \,.\, w \text{ Slr } \{u: u \subseteq y\} \,.\!\supset\!:\, x \precsim y \,.\mathbf{v}.\, y \precsim x.$

Proof. By hypotheses and 32.3, there are *s* and *t* such that

$$\text{Cor}\ s, \quad \text{Cor}\ t, \tag{1}$$

$$s``\mathcal{V} = x, \quad t``\mathcal{V} = y, \tag{2}$$

$$\breve{s}``\mathcal{V}, \quad \breve{t}``\mathcal{V} \in \text{NO}. \tag{3}$$

By virtue of (3) and 23.21, $\breve{s}``\mathcal{V} \subseteq \breve{t}``\mathcal{V}$ or vice versa; say $\breve{s}``\mathcal{V} \subseteq \breve{t}``\mathcal{V}$. Then, by (2), $x = (s \mid \breve{t})``y$. Moreover, by (1), Func $s \mid \breve{t}$. Moreover, by 'C_1', $\breve{t} \in \mathcal{V}$, so that, by second hypothesis, $s \mid \breve{t} \in \mathcal{V}$. These results add up, by definition, to saying that $x \precsim y$. In the other case $y \precsim x$.

In the last sentence of §29 another simple law of class comparison was mentioned as depending on the axiom of choice. It amounts to the following, when 'C_1' and a premiss of choice are prefixed and one Greek letter is subdued.

33.2 $\quad C_1 \,.\, u \text{ Sln } \{v: (\exists w)(v = z \cap \breve{y}``\{w\})\} \,.\, \text{Func}\ y \,.$
$\alpha \subseteq y``z \,.\!\supset (\exists x)(\text{Cor}\ x \,.\, \alpha \subseteq x``z).$

Proof. By 'C_1',

$$y \restriction z \in \mathcal{V}. \tag{1}$$

By second hypothesis, since $z \cap \breve{y}``\{w\}$ is $\breve{\ }(y \restriction z)``\{w\}$,

$$u \text{ Sln } \{v: (\exists w)(v = \breve{\ }(y \restriction z)``\{w\})\}. \tag{2}$$

Since Func y,

$$\text{Func } y \restriction z. \qquad (3)$$

Substituting for 'y' in 32.1 on the strength of (1), we have that (3), (2), and 'C_1' imply that

$$\text{Cor } (y \restriction z) \restriction u, \quad (4) \qquad ((y \restriction z) \restriction u)``\mho = (y \restriction z)``\mho$$
$$= y``z. \qquad (5)$$

By (1) and 'C_1', there is something x such that $x = (y \restriction z) \restriction u$. Then $x``\mho = x``z$ and so, by (5), $x``z = y``z$ and so, by last hypothesis, $\alpha \subseteq x``z$. Also, by (4), Cor x.

We know that '$x \precsim y$ .v. $y \precsim x$' and kindred laws may depend on the axiom of choice or on the Schröder–Bernstein theorem or be trivial, according as we make one or another choice among natural definitions of '$\precsim$'. Now the situation within the elementary arithmetic of cardinal numbers is bound to be much the same, inasmuch as the '$\leqq$' of cardinal arithmetic parallels '$\precsim$':

(i) $$\bar{\bar{x}} \leqq \bar{\bar{y}} \;.\!\equiv\!.\; x \precsim y.$$

On our definitions, '$x \precsim y$ .v. $y \precsim x$' depends on the axiom of choice; hence we may be sure that the '$z \leqq w$ .v. $w \leqq z$' of infinite cardinal arithmetic will likewise depend on the axiom of choice if we define the '$\leqq$' fairly directly by means of the correspondence (i). On the other hand we may rest the definition of '$\leqq$' on considerations quite apart from (i); so we do when we take the cardinal numbers as certain ordinals in the von Neumann sense, for then '$\leqq$' for ordinals in general and cardinals in particular comes simply to '$\subseteq$'. On this approach '$z \leqq w$ .v. $w \leqq z$' comes out of 23.21, which, though perhaps not trivial, does not depend on the axiom of choice. But the moment '$z \leqq w$ .v. $w \leqq z$' has been got clear of the axiom of choice, in this way or another, we may be sure that the crosslink (i) itself has been made to depend on the axiom of choice instead.

Or take the proposition that a class generally has a cardinal number. Under the Frege–Whitehead–Russell version of cardinals, a class x simply has $\{y: y \simeq x\}$ as its cardinal number. This will not be empty, since $x \simeq x$; and its existence could be assured by comprehension axioms. There is no question here of the axiom of choice. But how does the proposition fare under the von Neumann version of cardinals? Here the cardinal of a class x is the earliest ordinal $\simeq x$; so that we need to show in general that there is an ordinal $\simeq x$. And at this point the axiom of choice does come in. We appeal to the numeration theorem, 32.3, to show that there is an ordinal number (viz., $\breve{}\mathrm{A}\Psi_{yx}$ "$\mho$, where y Slr $\{z: z \subseteq x\}$) that is $\simeq x$; and thus we assume that

$$(\exists y)(y \text{ Slr } \{z: z \subseteq x\}).$$

True, $\bar{\bar{x}}$ on the von Neumann plan is the ordinal number $\{y: y \in \mathrm{NO} \,.\, y \prec x\}$, and whether this exists is a question of comprehension axioms rather than of the axiom of choice. But this is a quibble. Cardinal numbers so defined will do their intended job of measurement only if in general $x \simeq \bar{\bar{x}}$ as intended; and this is a question after all of there generally being an ordinal $\simeq x$.

We know that contradiction issues from too sweeping comprehension axioms. The restrictions observed in such axioms vary from system to system; in particular they can cut in on ordinals in such a way as to deprive us of ordinals $\simeq x$ for occasional x, despite the axiom of choice. In particular the numeration theorem 32.3, appealed to just now, bore its share of comprehension premisses. This is the reason for my evasive use of 'generally' above. But the axiom of choice is still needed, as described, for the general run of x.

It is no criticism of the von Neumann approach that the axiom of choice is needed there, and not under the Frege–Whitehead–Russell approach, to assure that classes generally have cardinal numbers in a relevant sense. For, characteristically, the shift that makes one bundle of theorems independent of the axiom of choice only causes other equally urgent theorems to depend on it instead. In particular the axiom of choice comes to be needed under the Frege–Whitehead–Russell approach to show that the relation of less to greater among cardinal numbers is a well-ordering; whereas under the von Neumann approach this follows from '$NC \subseteq NO$' and 24.3 and 21.9 without the axiom of choice.

These and other examples that we have noted, conspicuously '$x \leq y . \lor . y \leq x$', bespeak the urgency of the axiom of choice. We may therefore regret that we cannot prove it from prior assumptions, and hope that it can be added to them without contradiction. On this last point we have reassurance from Gödel (1940). He takes as his starting point the von Neumann–Bernays system of set theory (§43), which includes substantial but not evidently unreasonable assumptions of infinite classes, and he shows that if it is consistent it remains consistent when the axiom of choice is added.

His argument exploits a device of von Neumann (1929) that Shepherdson has since called an *inner model*: he stakes out a special part of the universe of the von Neumann–Bernays set theory and shows that all axioms still hold when their variables are allowed to take as values only the things in that special part of the universe.

To make this more precise let us turn to the idea of *relativization*. Think of 'α' now as some actual *term*, i.e., a specific variable or some abstract in the noncommittal sense of 2.1. Now the variable bound by any quantification, say '$(x)Fx$' or '$(\exists x)Fx$', can be *restricted* (as I shall say) to that term by rewriting '$(x)Fx$' as '$(x)(x \in \alpha . \supset Fx)$' and '$(\exists x)Fx$' as '$(\exists x)(x \in \alpha . Fx)$'; and a free variable '$y$' of a formula can be restricted to that term by prefixing the condition '$y \in \alpha . \supset$' to the formula. *Relativizing* a formula to a given term, finally, consists in simultaneously restricting all variables of the formula to the term by the above methods (first having expanded any defined notations to the point where all bound variables of the formula were variables of quantification).[1]

The von Neumann–Bernays system, as Gödel formulates it, has eight comprehension axioms that play a basic role in his construction.[2] Each has the form:

$$(x)(y)(\exists z)(w)(w \in z \mathrel{.}\equiv \ldots w \ldots x \ldots y \ldots)$$

at worst; some lack 'x' and some lack also 'y', but by inventing vacuous occurrences we can view all eight as of that form. Thus each comprehension axiom affirms the existence, for all x and y, of a certain class which for short we may call x ① y in the case

---

[1] This notion of relativization, simpler than Gödel's, departs from his in two superficial respects. For one thing, I use a single general sort of variable where Gödel uses one sort of variable for sets in particular and another sort for classes in general. This is why I am able to explain relativization without treating separately, as Gödel did, of the two sorts of variables. But it is a stylistic matter, since, where 'a' is a set variable, Gödel's '$(a)Fa$' and '$(\exists a)Fa$' are translatable thus:

$$(x)(y)(x \in y \mathrel{.}\supset Fx), \qquad (\exists x)(\exists y)(x \in y \mathrel{.} Fx).$$

And in addition there is another divergence. Its effect is that relativization, in his sense, say to 'L' (below) is relativization in my sense to '$\{x: x \subseteq \mathrm{L}\}$'. This departure suits the term to further useful applications in the last chapters and in other recent literature (e.g., Oberschelp).

[2] For readers who would collate my synopsis with Gödel's original, here are the connections. Gödel's axiom Bl, p. 5, should be pictured for purposes of my synopsis as the comprehension axiom:

$$(\exists z)(w)(w \in z \mathrel{.}\equiv (\exists u)(\exists v)(u \in v \mathrel{.} \langle u, v\rangle = w)),$$

where my variables, unlike Gödel's lower-case variables, are general. Axioms B5–8 carry over with similar contortions. B3–4 carry over more directly. B2 drops in view of Gödel's remark below the middle of p. 35. Such, then, are seven of the eight comprehension axioms in question. The eighth is:

$$(x)(y)(\exists z)(w)(w \in z \mathrel{.}\equiv: (\exists u)(w \in u) : w = x \mathrel{.\vee.} w = y).$$

which is just so much of the content of Gödel's axiom A4, p. 3, as comes under the head of pure comprehension axiom. The residual content of A4 is separable as an axiom of sethood:

$$(x)(y)((w)(w \in z \mathrel{.}\equiv: w = x \mathrel{.\vee.} w = y) \supset (\exists w)(z \in w)).$$

To appreciate this the reader must keep in mind the difference in our conventions about variables, and also Gödel's omission, through misprint, of '(u)' from A4.

of the first of the axioms, x ② y in the case of the second, and so on.

Now Gödel specifies a transfinite sequence which he calls F. Subject to a certain qualification which I postpone, F is as follows, where my numerals denote ordinals. F‘0 is Λ. F‘1 up to F‘8 are respectively (F‘0) ① (F‘0) up to (F‘0) ⑧ (F‘0), hence Λ ① Λ up to Λ ⑧ Λ. F‘9 is F“9, hence {F‘0, . . . , F‘8}. F‘10 up to F‘17 are respectively (F‘0) ① (F‘1) up to (F‘0) ⑧ (F‘1). F‘18 is again F“18. F‘19 is (F‘1) ① (F‘0), and so on. In general F‘9x is F“9x, and F‘(9x + 1) up to F‘(9x + 8) are respectively (F‘y) ① (F‘z) up to (F‘y) ⑧ (F‘z) where $\langle y, z\rangle$ is the pair of ordinals that comes in the xth (from 0th) place in a standardized ordering of all pairs of ordinals. In particular thus F‘ω is F“ω or {F‘0, F‘2, . . .}, containing as members Λ and (F‘y) ① (F‘z), . . . , (F‘y) ⑧ (F‘z) for all finite y and z. Then F‘(ω + 1) is (F‘0) ① (F‘ω), and so on. Actually Gödel shows how to define F formally within the von Neumann–Bernays system.

The von Neumann–Bernays system has other axioms, of course, besides these eight of comprehension. Some are sethood axioms; for it is a system with ultimate clases (cf. §6). Now to the qualification that I postponed: x ① y, . . . , x ⑧ y are not all taken quite directly from the eight comprehension axioms, but are in part modified so as to assure that all eight will be sets when x and y are sets.

Gödel calls F“Ʋ the class of *constructible* sets, briefly L. Thus F is a numeration of L, and we are assured that there is a well-ordering of L (viz. F | Ɛ | ˘F; cf. §32). This can be proved within the von Neumann–Bernays system, as he points out, without of course invoking the axiom of choice.

Next Gödel establishes his inner model of the von Neumann–Bernays system (minus the axiom of choice) by showing that the axioms go over into theorems still of the system when they are relativized to:

$$\{x\colon x \subseteq \mathrm{L} \,.\, (y)(y \in \mathrm{L} \,.\!\supset\!.\, x \cap y \in \mathrm{L})\}.$$

It follows that there can be nothing in the axioms (short of internal inconsistency) to demand classes other than subclasses of L, or, therefore, sets other than members of L. In short, ‘UƲ = L’ is consistent with the axioms if they are consistent.[3] But from '$\mathsf{U}\mathcal{V} = \mathrm{L}$' we could deduce according to the preceding paragraph that there is a well-ordering of $\mathsf{U}\mathcal{V}$. Thence in turn, since $(x)(x \subseteq \mathsf{U}\mathcal{V})$, we could deduce by 21.9 that there is a well-ordering of any class x. Thence in turn we could deduce the axiom of choice. So the axiom of choice is consistent with these axioms if they are consistent.

The argument is not as simple as this sketch suggests. Between saying that the axioms demand no sets other than members of L, and saying that '$\mathsf{U}\mathcal{V} = \mathrm{L}$' is consistent with the axioms, there is a gap. For might we not find that in taking $\mathsf{U}\mathcal{V}$ as L we so disturb the interpretation of 'ϵ' that the formula which the definitions abbreviate as '$\mathsf{U}\mathcal{V} = \mathrm{L}$' comes to say something else, inconsistent with the axioms after all? Gödel proves not, but it takes proving.

Gödel's result does not apply to every set theory, but it carries over to the Zermelo system and the Zermelo–Fraenkel system (§§38–39, below). Such indeed was the original setting of Gödel's proof, as sketched in 1939. It may be instructive here to note how the result carries over from the von Neumann–Bernays system to the Zermelo–Fraenkel system. I owe the following reasoning to Dreben.

The Zermelo–Fraenkel system knows only sets, and is embedded in the von Neumann–Bernays system, in the sense that all theorems of the Zermelo–Fraenkel system hold as theorems about the sets of the von Neumann–Bernays system. Thus if in particular we could prove in the Zermelo–Fraenkel system that $\sim(z)(\exists w)(w \text{ Slr } z)$, we could prove in the von Neumann–Bernays system that not every set z has a selector w that is a set. But in that event we could also prove in the von Neumann–Bernays system simply that $\sim(z)(\exists w)(w \text{ Slr } z)$; for in that system all selectors of sets are sets (cf. p. 223n). Therefore '$(z)(\exists w)(w \text{ Slr } z)$' is consistent with the Zermelo–Fraenkel system if it is consistent with the von Neumann–Bernays system. Moreover there is a

[3] In Gödel's monograph the equation appears as '$\mathrm{V} = \mathrm{L}$'. But his V, the class of all sets, is in our notation $\mathsf{U}\mathcal{V}$. See §6.

proof (cf. p. 319) that the Zermelo–Fraenkel system is inconsistent outright if the other is. So Godel's theorem, that the von Neumann–Bernays system is consistent with the axiom of choice if consistent without, carries over.

There is an early result of Fraenkel's (1922) which, as improved by Lindenbaum and Mostowski (1938) and further by Mendelson (1958) and Shoenfield (1955), is roughly dual to this one of Gödel's. It is that the axiom of choice is independent of the rest of set theory. What Gödel showed was that the axiom of choice could not be disproved unless the rest of the system he was using was inconsistent; what Mendelson and Shoenfield showed was that the axiom also cannot be proved unless the rest of the system is inconsistent. The symmetry was imperfect in that Mendelson and Shoenfield used a set theory that was weaker than that used by Gödel: weaker on the score, specifically, of the axiom of *Fundierung*. More recently Cohen, bringing new ideas to bear, has overcome this limitation.

Gödel's consistency proof goes beyond the axiom of choice and covers the continuum hypothesis as well—and the generalized one at that (cf. §30). For he shows that if $\mathsf{U}\mathcal{V} = \mathrm{L}$ then the generalized continuum hypothesis holds too. (Incidentally, the latter itself implies the axiom of choice.[4]) And the special importance of Cohen's recent work is that he also shows the independence of the generalized continuum hypothesis.

---

[4] Sierpiński, 1947; Tarski and Lindenbaum. See Sierpiński, 1958, pp. 534ff.

PART THREE

AXIOM SYSTEMS

XI | RUSSELL'S THEORY OF TYPES

34. The constructive part

We have encompassed a substantial bit of set theory, in the foregoing chapters, without settling on any considerable existence assumptions. There were 7.10, 13.1, and 23.12, which gave us finite classes. Beyond these, we have made do with *ad hoc* existence premisses expressed within the theorems that used them.

In the remaining chapters I shall describe and contrast various of the substantial systems of existence assumptions that have figured prominently in the literature of set theory. I shall temper the historical approach with the logical, stressing the connections of structure between the systems, and the efficacy of departures.

The divergences among the systems are profound. Some of the systems to be studied will be incompatible even with 7.10. In the end I shall argue for modifying such systems while preserving their good points.

In this chapter I shall describe one pioneer system, Russell's *theory of types* of 1908. It is a system that evolved from Russell's tentative suggestions of 1903 with the help of an idea of Poincaré's.[1]

Poincaré tried to account for Russell's paradox as the effect rather of a subtle fallacy than of a collapse of irreducible prin-

---

[1] Russell, 1903, Appendix B; Poincaré, 1906, p. 307. There was a suggestion of Poincaré's idea already in Richard, 1905, as Poincaré points out.

ciples. He attributed it to what he called a vicious circle. The defining characteristic of the paradoxical class y is '$(x)(x \in y \mathrel{.{\equiv}.} x \notin x)$', and the paradox comes, as we know, of letting the quantified variable 'x' here take y itself as a value. It is, he suggested, illegitimate to include a class y, or any classes whose specification might presuppose y, in the range of a quantification that is used in specifying y itself. He called the suspect procedure *impredicative.*[2] We must not presuppose y in defining y.

Definition, in the clearest sense, is what occurs when a new notation is introduced as short for an old one. No question of legitimacy can arise in connection with definition, so long as a mechanical procedure is provided for expanding the new notation in all cases uniquely into old notation. Now what Poincaré criticized is not the definition of some special symbol as short for '$\{x: x \notin x\}$', but rather the very assumption of the existence of such a class; the assumption of the existence of a class y fulfilling '$(x)(x \in y \mathrel{.{\equiv}.} x \notin x)$'. We shall do better to speak not of impredicative definition but of impredicative specification of classes, and, what is the crux of the matter, impredicative assumptions of class existence.

And what now of the vicious circle? A circular argument seduces its victim into granting a thesis, unawares, as a premiss to its own demonstration. A circular definition smuggles the definiendum into the definiens, in such wise as to prevent expansion into primitive notation. But impredicative specification of classes is neither of these things. It is hardly a procedure to look askance at, except as one is pressed by the paradoxes to look askance at something or other.

---

[2] The word fared oddly. In 1906 Russell spoke of a membership condition as predicative, for one or another set theory, simply to mean that for that set theory there was a class corresponding to that membership condition. Poincaré followed this use of Russell's; it just happened that the membership conditions that he wanted to declare predicative in this sense were the ones not involving the quasi-circularity that he objected to. Straightway the term acquired the latter sense, and became independent of the former. Next Russell gave the term a more technical but kindred sense, as we shall see midway in this section. In all these senses the term must be firmly dissociated from 'predicate', which I continue to use in the sense explained early in §1.

For we are not to view classes literally as created through being specified—hence as dated one by one, and as increasing in number with the passage of time. Poincaré proposed no temporal implementation of class theory. The doctrine of classes is rather that they are there from the start. This being so, there is no evident fallacy in impredicative specification. It is reasonable to single out a desired class by citing any trait of it, even though we chance thereby to quantify over it along with everything else in the universe. Impredicative specification is not visibly more vicious than singling out an individual as the most typical Yale man on the basis of averages of Yale scores including his own.

So the ban urged by Russell and by Poincaré is not to be hailed as the exposure of some hidden but (once exposed) palpable fallacy that underlay the paradoxes. Rather it is one of various proposals for so restricting the law of comprehension:

$$(\exists y)(x)(x \in y \mathrel{.}\equiv Fx)$$

as to thin the universe of classes down to the point of consistency.

Still the proposal is less arbitrary than some alternatives, in that it realizes a constructional metaphor: it limits classes to what *could* be generated over an infinite period from unspecified beginnings by using, for each class, a membership condition mentioning only preexistent classes. Metaphor aside, the distinctive feature of such a set theory is that its universe admits of a (transfinite) ordering such that every class that is specified by a membership condition at all is specified by one in which the values of all variables are limited to things earlier in the ordering.

Moving now to the details of Russell's 1908 system,[3] we put the very notion of class aside for a while; for Russell's theory starts out in other terms.

For Russell the universe consisted of individuals in some sense, and attributes and relations of them, and attributes and relations of such attributes and relations, and so on up. His own

---

[3] I mention the 1908 paper for its priority. But the more usual and convenient place to look for the material is in the early portions of *Principia Mathematica*.

term for the attributes and relations was '*propositional functions*'. He used 'ϕ', 'ψ', . . . as variables for them. To say that x has the attribute ϕ, that x bears the relation ψ to y, and so on, he used the notation 'ϕx', '$\psi(x, y)$', etc. For *abstraction* of propositional functions from sentences he simply put circumflexed variables in the argument positions. Thus the attribute of loving y and that of being loved by x would be rendered respectively by '$\hat{x}$ loves y' and 'x loves $\hat{y}$', the analogues of the class abstracts '$\{x$: x loves $y\}$' and '$\{y$: x loves $y\}$'. The relations of loving and its converse, corresponding to $\{\langle x, y\rangle$: x loves $y\}$ and $\{\langle y, x\rangle$: x loves $y\}$, come out as '$\hat{x}$ loves $\hat{y}$' and '$\hat{y}$ loves $\hat{x}$', direction being determined thus by alphabetical order.[4]

When such abstracts occur in broader contexts, there is sometimes no telling whether to construe a circumflexed variable as making its abstraction from a short clause or from a longer containing clause, especially when several abstracts occur in the passage. Russell was spared this difficulty in practice, mainly because of a modified and superior notation for classes and relations—similar in essential respects to what we have been using in earlier chapters—which he introduced by contextual definition and adhered to in all elaborate work. But in expounding his basic theory let me try to make do with his basic notation, skirting its pitfalls.

He classified his individuals and propositional functions into so-called *orders* in the following way. Individuals were of order 0. Certain unspecified propositional functions of individuals were of order 1; not all. For the rest, the order of a propositional function was determined by considering the abstractive expression that names it. That order was taken as the least integer exceeding the order of all bound variables therein—all circumflexed variables, that is, and all quantified ones as well. By the order of a variable was meant the order of the values it takes; and it was essential to Russell's plan that each variable be restricted, implicitly if not by a visible index, to values of a single order. Thus it was that Russell kept the propositional function from figuring

---

[4] Whitehead and Russell, vol. 1, p. 200.

as a value of the bound variables used in specifying it; the propositional function was always of too high an order to be a value of such variables.

In the above account there is a characteristic give and take between sign and object: the propositional function gets its order from the abstractive expression, and the order of a variable is the order of the values. Exposition is eased by allowing the word 'order' a double sense, attributing orders at once to the notations and, in parallel, to their objects. Ideally the order of each variable may, to begin with, be thought of as shown by a numerical superscript; the order of each abstractive expression is then computed as above; and it carries over to the propositional function thereby named. Russell's own exposition simply blurred the distinction between the abstractive expression (or even the open sentence) and the propositional function (or attribute or relation); but that is a feature which I shall not copy, and shall have occasion to deplore.

Extensionality being what separates classes from attributes, Russell's business here is clearly with attributes rather than classes. For two attributes can be of different orders and hence surely distinct, and yet the things that have them can be the same. For example, the attribute $(\phi)(\phi\hat{x} \equiv \phi y)$, with '$\phi$' of order 1, is an attribute of y and y only, and again the attribute $(\chi)(\chi\hat{x} \equiv \chi y)$, with '$\chi$' of order 2, is an attribute of y and y only; yet their orders are respectively 2 and 3.

Relations, in the sense in which Russell's propositional functions may be spoken of as attributes and relations, are so-called *relations-in-intension*; that is, they are like attributes, and unlike mere classes of ordered pairs, ordered triples, etc., in being capable of distinctness from one another even though relating exclusively the same things. They can be pictured as attributes of ordered pairs, triples, etc. (But Russell did not give them this further analysis.)

Besides propositional functions of one variable, or attributes, and propositional functions of many variables, or relations, Russell recognized also propositional functions of no variables, or propositions; his theory of orders applied to propositions as well as to propositional functions of one or more variables. But I see no value in tracing this strand of the history.

Many attributes were, for Russell, of higher order by two or more than the things having the attributes. An example was seen in $(\phi)(\phi\hat{x} \equiv \phi y)$. Another example is $(\exists\phi)(\psi\phi \,.\, \phi\hat{x})$, the attribute of having an attribute that has the attribute ψ. Some attributes, on the other hand, were of just next higher order than the things having them. An example could be $(x)(\hat{\phi}x \equiv \psi x)$, the attribute of coextensiveness with ψ. Such attributes Russell called *predicative.*[5] The connection envisaged between this technical use of the word and the use lately attributed to Poincaré is that a class abstract ('$\{x\colon Fx\}$') specifies its class predicatively rather than impredicatively, in Poincaré's sense, when and only when the corresponding attribute abstract ('$F\hat{x}$') names a predicative attribute. Thus Russell, in admitting attributes that are not predicative in his sense, was not yet evidently flouting Poincare's precept so long as only predicative ones were made to determine classes.

Russell of course extended the term 'predicative' to propositional functions other than attributes. He called a dyadic relation predicative if its order was just next higher than that of the things bearing the relation, or than that of the things to which the relation was borne—whichever was the higher. Similarly for *n*-adic.

Russell's criterion of the order of a propositional function obviously presupposes that each variable be recognizably restricted to a single order. Actually he went further: each variable for attributes was meant to range only over attributes that are themselves of some one fixed order and whose *arguments*—the things having the attributes—are of some one fixed order too. Similarly each variable for relations was meant to range only over relations that are of a single order, and that admit arguments of only some one fixed order in first argument place, and arguments of just some one fixed order in second argument place, and so on. A full formal presentation of the theory would call perhaps for numerical superscripts on the propositional-function variables to indicate the order of the propositional functions con-

[5] 1908. Whitehead and Russell apply the term more narrowly, pp. 164ff.

cerned, and numerical subscripts to indicate the order of admissible arguments to those propositional functions; and in the case of relations the subscripts would have to be compound, to indicate the respective orders of admissible first arguments, second arguments, and so on to the appropriate number.

Russell required that the order of a propositional function exceed that of each of its arguments. When a propositional function is given outright by the abstraction notation, this restriction is already present in what was said before, viz., that the order is to exceed that of the circumflexed variables. But it is needed still as an added restriction when the propositional function merely figures as value of a variable. In such cases the restriction amounts, in terms of indices (superscripts and subscripts), to requiring that a variable's superscript exceed its subscripts. Not that Russell was so explicit.

The forms of notation 'ϕx', '$\phi(x, y)$', etc., expressing attribution were to be accepted as meaningful only if the order or orders of the argument or arguments were those appropriate to the propositional function attributed. In terms of indices this means that the superscript of the argument, or the superscripts of the several arguments, must match the subscript of the propositional function, or the respective subscripts thereof.

But in practice Russell suppressed the indices altogether by a convention of so-called *systematic ambiguity*. The convention was, in effect, that indices are to be imagined supplied in any way conformable to the foregoing grammatical restriction.

Occasions arose when Russell did want to include in his formula some information about the orders of variables, beyond the minimal requirement of grammatical conformity. Though not caring about absolute order, he wanted sometimes to indicate that the order of one or another propositional function was to be just next above that of its arguments. Rather than restore full indices for this purpose, he introduced an exclamation point after some of the occurrences of the propositional-function variable concerned, to indicate that the variable was to range over predicative propositional functions of some order or other. The notation is illustrated early in the next section.

In general it is is convenient in presenting formal systems of set theory to be able to assume the standard logic of truth functions and quantifiers as a fixed substructure requiring only the addition of axioms appropriate to the special set theory in question. We cannot adhere quite fully to this line in the present instance, because of an implicit multiplicity of sorts of variables. The implicit distinctive indices are already a departure from the standard logic of quantification with its single sort of variables. However, this departure can mainly be localized in laws like '$(x)Fx \supset Fy$' and '$Fy \supset (\exists x)Fx$' which provide for change of variables. These we have to restrict to the extent of requiring that the variable in the role of 'y' be of the same sort as that in the role of 'x'; that is, that it bear the same indices.[5]

Indices, when supplied, fix the orders of such propositional functions as are referred to by the variables themselves. Indirectly they fix also the orders of propositional functions named by expressions of abstraction; for we have said that the order is next higher than that of the highest bound variable. But this account covers only the abstractive expressions in which all variables are bound, by quantifiers or circumflex accents. To be able to say in general what expressions can legitimately be substituted under the law '$(x)Fx \supset Fy$' for variables bearing given indices, we have to assign an order also to abstractive expressions with free variables. It is easily seen that the further stipulation needed in this case is that the order of the abstractive expression must be reckoned as not less than that of the free variables (while still exceeding that of the bound ones); this suffices to prevent us from defeating the other restrictions by subsequent substitutions on the free variables in question. Russell was silent on this detail, but his usage conformed.

Over and above the variables (with their indices or exclamation points) and the logical notations of quantification and truth func-

---

[5] Many-sorted logic is examined further in §37, below. —Under the head of deviations from standard logic, mention might be made also of *9 of *Principia* for its general oddity of approach to quantification theory. But *9 figures only as an option to the more classical treatment in *10; moreover it hinges on orders of propositions, which I said I would not pursue.

tions, the special notations of Russell's theory are the notations of attribution ('ϕx', '$\phi(x, y)$', etc.) and the use of circumflex accents for the abstraction of propositional functions. Over and above the general logical laws of truth functions and quantifiers (restricted as above), the special principle of Russell's theory is just that of *concretion* (cf. 2.1):

$$\text{(i)} \qquad (F\hat{x})y \equiv Fy, \quad (F\hat{x}\hat{y})(z, w) \equiv Fzw, \quad \text{etc.}$$

Again it must in justice to Russell be said that he was incommunicative over these matters.

Let us see how Russell's paradox is avoided in his theory. Where ψ is the propositional function $\sim\hat{\phi}\hat{\phi}$ (the attribute of not being an attribute of self) we have, by concretion, that $(\chi)(\psi\chi \equiv \sim\chi\chi)$ and hence in particular that $\psi\psi \equiv \sim\psi\psi$. But Russell's restrictions obstruct this reasoning twice over. The combination '$\phi\phi$' is ruled out as ungrammatical to begin with, since the order of a propositional function is required to exceed that of its argument. And even if it were not thus ruled out, definition of ψ as $\sim\hat{\phi}\hat{\phi}$ would give ψ a higher order than its bound variable 'ϕ' and hence disallow our taking χ as ψ in the step that led to '$\psi\psi \equiv \sim\psi\psi$'.

35. Classes and the axiom of reducibility

We are glad to have found the theory too weak for the paradoxes. However, it proves too weak also for some reasoning in classical mathematics that we are scarcely prepared to relinquish. An example is the proof that every bounded class of real numbers has a least bound.

Let us suppose the real numbers developed in Russell's theory in a fashion parallel to the development in Chapter VI, but with attributes in place of classes, and the attribution of attributes in place of class membership. According to §18 and §19 the least bound of a bounded class z of real numbers was the class $\mathsf{U}z$, or $\{x\colon (\exists y)(x \in y \in z)\}$. So, in parallel, we may expect the least bound of a bounded attribute ϕ of real numbers in Russell's system to be the attribute $(\exists\psi)(\phi\psi \,.\, \psi\hat{x})$. Now the difficulty is that under Russell's doctrine of orders the least bound $(\exists\psi)(\phi\psi \,.\, \psi\hat{x})$ is of higher order than the real numbers ψ falling under the attribute ϕ whose least bound is sought.

Least bounds are needed for all the classical techniques of mathematical analysis that continuity underlies. But least bounds are no good for these ends unless they are accessible as further values of the same variables that have already been ranging over the numbers whose limits are sought. A least bound of higher order does not qualify as value of such variables, and so fails of its purpose.

Russell dealt with this difficulty by propounding his *axiom of reducibility: Every propositional function* ϕ *is coextensive with a predicative one*. That is,

$$(\exists\psi)(x)(\psi!x \equiv \phi x), \quad (\exists\psi)(x)(y)(\psi!(x, y) \equiv \phi(x, y)),$$

and so on. It may or may not happen, given a propositional function, that there is an abstractive expression designating a co-extensive propositional function (one true of the same things) and meeting the demands of predicativity—viz., exhibiting no bound variables of higher order than all circumflexed ones. But even failing any such actual expression, there still exists, all un-expressed, such a predicative propositional function; that is the import of the axiom of reducibility.

Applied to $(\exists\psi)(\phi\psi \,.\, \psi\hat{x})$, the axiom assures us that we may without loss construe 'ϕ' and 'ψ' here as ranging over predicative attributes. In other words, we may construe 'ϕ' and 'ψ' as ranging over attributes respectively of order $n + 2$ and $n + 1$, where n is the order represented by the 'x'. For each bounded attribute ϕ of order $n + 2$, of real numbers ψ of order $n + 1$, we are thus assured a least bound $(\exists\psi)(\phi!\psi \,.\, \psi!\hat{x})$. Moreover, by the axiom of reducibility again, there is a predicative χ coextensive with this $(\exists\psi)(\phi!\psi \,.\, \psi!\hat{x})$. Being predicative, χ will be of order just higher than that represented by its circumflexed argument place —hence $n + 1$ again. So we now have the required law: any bounded attribute of real numbers of given order $n + 1$ has a least bound which is of that same order $n + 1$.

But the price is paid of abandoning the constructional metaphor noted early in §34, and acquiescing rather in the paradigm of the most typical Yale man. For the axiom of reducibility regales us after all with attributes unspecifiable except by quantifying over attributes whose order is as high as their own. Whatever sense of security from paradox we may have drawn from the constructional metaphor is now, therefore, forfeited. Still the old proofs of paradox continue, it seems, to be effectively obstructed. In particular the obstruction to Russell's paradox remains just as it was.

The foundational portion of Whitehead and Russell's *Principia Mathematica*, taking up barely the first two hundred pages, contrasts markedly with the main body of that work. Propositional functions are in evidence only in the foundational part; thereafter the work proceeds in terms rather of classes and relations-in-extension. Talk of classes and relations-in-extension is founded on talk of propositional functions, by means of contextual definitions, somewhat as follows. As a preliminary step, the notation of membership is explained as merely an alternative notation for the attribution of a predicative attribute:

(i) '$x \in \phi$' for '$\phi ! x$'.

Thus far, no classes. But then class abstraction is defined in context thus:[1]

(ii) '$G\{x: Fx\}$' for '$(\exists\phi)((x)(\phi ! x \equiv Fx) \,.\, G\phi)$'

and quantification over classes is defined thus:[2]

(iii) '$(\alpha)G\alpha$' for '$(\phi)G\{x: \phi ! x\}$', '$(\exists\alpha)G\alpha$' for '$(\exists\phi)G\{x: \phi ! x\}$'.

---

[1] A construction having substantially the effect of (i) and (ii) is to be found already in Frege, 1893, pp. 52f.

[2] This 'α' of Russell's is a quantifiable class variable, and so not to be confused with the schematic use of 'α' to which we have become accustomed in Chapters I–X. Readers of my *Mathematical Logic* have been used to yet a third use of 'α': as a syntactic variable for variables. Russell's use will be limited to the present paragraph.

The effect is this: classes are the same as predicative attributes except that when we talk of them as classes we waive distinctions between coextensive ones. The waiving of such distinctions is accomplished in (ii). For to say that anything ('G') is true of a class $\{x: Fx\}$ is, according to (ii), to say that it is true of *some* predicative attribute ϕ—no matter which—such that $(x)(\phi! x \equiv Fx)$. In this way Russell provides for proof of the law of extensionality:

(iv) $(x)(x \in \alpha \mathrel{.{\equiv}.} x \in \beta) \,.\, \alpha \in \kappa \mathrel{.{\supset}.} \beta \in \kappa$

for classes without having had to assume the corresponding law for attributes, or even for predicative attributes. As remarked, it is only on the score of this law that there is point in distinguishing classes from attributes.

Talk of dyadic relations-in-extension is provided for by definitions parallel to (i)–(iii). The special variables for such relations are 'Q', 'R', etc., and the notation for saying that x bears R to y is 'xRy'. So the definitions are these:

(v) '$x\phi y$' for '$\phi!(x, y)$',

(vi) '$G\{xy: Fxy\}$' for '$(\exists\phi)((x)(y)(\phi!(x, y) \equiv Fxy) \,.\, G\phi)$',

(vii) '$(R)GR$' for '$(\phi)G\{xy: \phi!(x, y)\}$',
'$(\exists R)GR$' for '$(\exists\phi)G\{xy: \phi!(x, y)\}$'.

As they stand, (ii) and (vi) are unsatisfactorily ambiguous on the score of how much text to reckon to 'G' in any particular application of these definitions. Russell added a convention covering this point.

The doctrine of orders becomes much simplified insofar as we confine our attention to individuals, predicative attributes of individuals, predicative attributes of such attributes, and so on; for the orders of these things are respectively 0, 1, 2, ... The corresponding thing happens for classes, since classes are just predicative attributes minus the distinctions between coextensive ones. In this connection Russell favors the word 'type' instead of 'order'; thus individuals are of *type* 0, and classes whose members are of type n are classes of type $n + 1$.

Dyadic relations-in-extension come through with two-dimensional types: the type of a relation is fixed only when we specify the type of the things bearing the relation and the type of the things to which the relation is borne. The bidimensionality of these types gives rise to a staggering proliferation. The type of a relation of things of type m to things of type n may be called (m, n); the type of a class of such relations may be called $((m, n))$; and the type of a relation of such classes to such classes is then $(((m, n)), ((m, n)))$.[3] Orders, of course, were far worse. Russell spared himself such indices by his device of systematic ambiguity, or, as he comes to call it, *typical* ambiguity; but it is a device that we must view as roughly expository only, while thinking of the real system as retaining the full luxuriance of complex indices. For when the indices are complex, as required for relations, the plan of leaving them tacit proves too flexible. Whitehead and Russell found that to avoid Burali-Forti's paradox they had to restore type indices at points in the argument.[4]

We saw that Russell's constructivistic approach foundered in the real numbers, and that by then resorting to his axiom of reducibility he gave up constructivism. Now we must note further, while not questioning the wisdom of giving up the constructivism, that this was a perverse way of giving it up. For the axiom of reducibility implies the superfluousness of the very distinctions that give it substance. The argument is as follows.

If Russell's system with its axiom of reducibility is free of contradiction, then we may be sure that no contradiction would ensue if we were simply to repudiate all but predicative orders. We can declare the order of every attribute to be the next above that of the things having the attribute; and correspondingly for relations-in-intension. Given any reference to an attribute of order $n + k$ that is an attribute of objects of order n, we have merely to take that notation as referring rather to a coextensive attribute of order $n + 1$ by a systematic reinterpretation of

[3] So Carnap, *Logical Syntax*, p. 85.
[4] Vol. 3, p. 75.

Russell's notation; and correspondingly for relations-in-intension. For Russell's axiom of reducibility tells us that a coextensive attribute or relation-in-intension of the desired order, a predicative one, exists every time. If the axiom is foreseen, the better course is to obviate all need of it by talking of simple *types* of attributes and relations-in-intension from the start rather than of orders in any distinctive sense; there is an excuse for orders only if a weak constructive theory is to be adhered to and the axiom of reducibility withheld.[5]

One senses from a reading of Russell how he was able to overlook this point: the trouble was his failure to focus upon the distinction between "propositional functions" as attributes, or relations-in-intension, and "proposition functions" as expressions, viz., predicates or open sentences. As expressions they differed visibly in order, if order is to be judged by indices on bound variables within the expression. Failing to distinguish sharply between formula and object, he did not think of the maneuver of letting a higher-order expression refer outright to a lower-order attribute or relation-in-intension.

Russell had also an independent motive for retaining the extra orders. He thought these distinctions were helpful against a class of paradoxes not considered in foregoing pages: the paradoxes known nowadays as *semantic*. One of these, due to Grelling,[6] arises from the reflection that a predicate may be true of itself (like 'short', which is a short word, or 'English', which is English, or 'word', or 'predicate', or 'pentasyllabic'), or it may not (like 'long', 'German', 'verb', 'monosyllabic', and indeed most predicates). We get the paradox by asking whether 'not true of self' is true of itself. Another such paradox has come down from antiquity as the Epimenides paradox or the paradox of the liar. Its traditional forms can be variously quibbled over; the essential logic of it can perhaps be put most forcefully thus:

[5] This argument was advanced at greater length in pp. 5–8 of my dissertation (Harvard, 1932) and in "On the axiom of reducibility." And there is something of it in Hilbert and Ackermann, 1928 edition, pp. 114f.

[6] In Grelling and Nelson. The paradox has been wrongly attributed to Weyl.

'yields a falsehood when appended to its own quotation'
yields a falsehood when appended to its own quotation.

This tells us how to form a certain sentence, and tells us further that it is false; but the sentence which it tells us how to form is itself; so it is true if and only if false. A third semantical paradox, attributed to G. G. Berry, turns on the reflection that there are only finitely many English syllables; hence only finitely many natural numbers each of which is specifiable in fewer than 24 syllables; and hence a least natural number not specifiable in fewer than 24 syllables. But I have just specified it in 23 syllables. The literature also contains further semantic paradoxes.[7]

The notion that Russell's orders were relevent to such paradoxes is not one that I know how to make plausible while maintaining a distinction between attributes and open sentences, which he confused under the head of propositional functions. It seems clear in any event that by rights the semantic paradoxes should be blamed on special concepts foreign to the theory of classes or propositional functions: on denotation (or "truth of") in the case of Grelling's paradox, on falsehood (and hence truth) in the case of the Epimenides, and on specifiability in the case of Berry's. These three culpable notions are important ones, and the semantic paradoxes create a crisis with respect to them analogous to the crisis that Russell's paradox creates with respect to the notion of class membership. The notions of denotation, truth, and specifiability must be subjected to some sort of intuitively unanticipated restriction, in the light of these paradoxes, just as class existence must in the light of Russell's paradox and others. But the semantic paradoxes are of no concern to the theory of classes. This point was made in a way by Peano even before Russell's theory appeared, and it was urged by Ramsey in his critique of Russell's theory.[8]

Russell's theory, with its discrimination of orders for propositional functions whose arguments are of a single order, came to

[7] See Whitehead and Russell, vol. 1, pp. 60–65.
[8] Peano, 1906, p. 157; Ramsey, pp. 20–29. Ramsey cites the Peano passage.

be known as the "ramified theory of types"; and Ramsey's position was that it should be reduced to the so-called "simple" (or, in Sheffer's quip, "ramsified") theory of types. He did not, indeed, make his case as strong as he might. Sharing Russell's failure to distinguish clearly between attribute and expression, he in turn evidently missed the really decisive point: that the axiom of reducibility guarantees outright the dispensability of the ramified theory.

It must be remembered moreover that the simple theory of types, whether urged on this latter ground or in Ramsey's less decisive way, had already been the explicit working theory of Whitehead and Russell's *Principia Mathematica* anyway. Once Russell's contextual definitions of classes and relations-in-extension were at hand, the ramified substructure dropped from sight; all thought thenceforward was of types, in the simple sense, of classes and relations-in-extension.[9] Thus what Ramsey was urging, and I a few pages back, was in effect just the disavowal of an ill-conceived foundation.

One may as well dispense not merely with the initial ramification of orders of attributes and relations-in-intension, but with the attributes and relations-in-intension themselves. One may as well simply take Russell's classes and relations-in-extension as starting point, subject to the so-called simple theory of types to which they are already subject in *Principia*. As long as the ramification of orders is retained, so that two coextensive attributes may differ in order, there is evident need to distinguish coextensive attributes and hence to call them attributes instead of classes; but this reason for starting with attributes instead of classes lapses when we drop the ramification.

Russell had also a philosophical preference for attributes, and felt that in contextually defining classes on the basis of a theory of attributes he was explaining the obscurer in terms of the clearer. But this feeling was due to his failure to distinguish between propositional functions as predicates, or expressions, and propositional functions as attributes. Failing this, he could easily think

[9] "If we assume the existence of classes, the axiom of reducibility becomes unnecessary" (Whitehead and Russell, vol. 1, p. 58).

that the notion of an attribute is clearer than that of a class; for that of a predicate is. But that of an attribute is less clear.[10]

In Hilbert and Ackermann (1938, 1949) and elsewhere we find a notation reminiscent still of Russell's old theory of propositional functions. For classes and relations we find 'F', 'G', etc. with suppressible indices, and then instead of '$x \in \alpha$' and 'xRy' we find '$F(x)$' and '$G(x, y)$', reminiscent of Russell's 'ϕx' and '$\psi(x, y)$'. But the reminiscence is misleading. The values of 'F', 'G', etc. are no longer propositional functions but rather classes and relations-in-extension, by the only criterion: coextensive ones are identified.

This notation has the fault also of diverting attention from major cleavages between logic and set theory. It encourages us to see the general theory of classes and relations as a mere prolongation of quantification theory in which the hitherto schematic predicate letters are newly admitted into quantifiers and into other positions that were hitherto reserved to 'x', 'y', etc. (thus '(F)', '$(\exists G)$', '$H(F, G)$'). The existence assumptions, vast though they are, can become strangely inconspicuous; they come to be implicit simply in the ordinary old rule of substitution for predicate letters in quantification theory, once we have promoted those letters to the status of genuine quantifiable variables. Any comprehension statement, say of the form:

$$(\exists F)(x)(Fx \equiv \ldots x \ldots),$$

simply follows by such substitution from:

$$(G)(\exists F)(x)(Fx \equiv Gx),$$

which in turn follows from '$(x)(Gx \equiv Gx)$'.[11]

[10] See above, Introduction. I have treated themes of this section more fully in "Whitehead and the rise of modern logic"; also in *Word and Object*, pp. 118–123, 209f. See also Church, *Introduction to Mathematical Logic*, pp. 346–356.

[11] This point, noted by von Neumann as early as 1927 (p. 43), escaped Hilbert and Ackermann; they adopted comprehension axioms too (1938, p. 125). They mentioned that they could instead have resorted to a primitive notation of abstraction (which was Russell's way), but not that they could have dispensed with both. In 1949 (pp. 133ff) the surviving author adopted rather a rule of so-called definition, tantamount still to a primitive notation of abstraction. See further my paper "On universals," p. 78.

Such assimilation of set theory to logic is seen also in the terminology used by Hilbert and Ackermann and their followers for the fragmentary theories in which the types leave off after finitely many. Such a theory came to be called the predicate calculus (Church: functional calculus) of *n*th order (not to be confused with order in Russell's sense), where *n* is how high the types go. Thus the theory of individuals and classes of individuals and relations of individuals was called the second-order predicate calculus, and seen simply as quantification theory with predicate letters admitted to quantifiers. Quantification theory proper came to be called the first-order predicate calculus.

It was a regrettable trend. Along with obscuring the important cleavage between logic and "the theory of types" (meaning set theory with types), it fostered an exaggerated if foggy notion of the difference between the theory of types and "set theory" (meaning set theory without types)—as if the one did not involve outright assumption of sets the way the other does. And along with somewhat muffling the existence assumptions of the theory of types, it fostered a notion that quantification theory itself, in its '*F*' and '*G*', was already a theory about classes or attributes and relations. It slighted the vital contrast between schematic letters and quantifiable variables.

The notational style that I am deploring was in essential respects Russell's, of course, before it was Hilbert and Ackermann's. It was associated with failures to discriminate propositional functions as open sentences from propositional functions as attributes. Of those failures various ill consequences were noted in recent pages; and the notions last deplored are just an attenuated continuation of the series.

Speaking of slighting the contrast between schematic letters and quantifiable variables recalls the virtual theory, where I let schematic letters 'α' and '*R*' simulate class and relation variables. That mimicry, however, was the contrary of a muffling of existence assumptions. It was a simulation of existence assumptions, and it was overt.

36. The modern theory of types

The major improvement that Russell's theory of types underwent in the dénouement of §35 was the dropping of attributes and relations-in-intension in favor of classes and relations-in-extension. Now a further conspicuous improvement lies ready to hand: we can reduce the relations-in-extension to classes by adopting the Wiener–Kuratowski definition 9.1 of ordered pair. This is an expedient that postdates *Principia Mathematica*. Taking also the further step of defining class abstraction contextually, we end up with 'ϵ' as sole primitive notation apart from the quantifiers, variables, and truth functions.

Now that we have to do in principle only with individuals and classes and not with relations, types are really simple: individuals are of type 0 and classes whose members are of type *n* are of type *n* + 1. As variables we may use 'x', 'y', etc. with indices to indicate type. The atomic formulas of the theory are built by 'ϵ' from variables of consecutive types, in the fashion '$x^n \epsilon y^{n+1}$'; and the rest of the formulas are built from these atomic ones by quantification and truth functions.

What I picture as the contextual definition of class abstraction for the purpose is this:

(i) '$y^n \epsilon \{x^n : Fx^n\}$' for
$$`(\exists z^{n+1})((x^n)(x^n \epsilon z^{n+1} .\equiv Fx^n) . y^n \epsilon z^{n+1})',$$

(ii) '$\{x^n : Fx^n\} \epsilon y^{n+2}$' for
$$`(\exists z^{n+1})((x^n)(x^n \epsilon z^{n+1} .\equiv Fx^n) . z^{n+1} \epsilon y^{n+2})'.$$

The '*n*' is schematic, on a par with '*F*'. The actual sentences of the system would always have specific consecutive arabic numerals in place of the dummy indices '*n*', '*n* + 1', '*n* + 2'.

In place of (i) we could carry over our old noncommittal 2.1 thus:

$$`y^n \epsilon \{x^n : Fx^n\}' \text{ for } `Fy^n'.$$

But this would add no freedom now, as it did back there. For in the theory of types the existence of classes is assured categorically (by (iv), below) as long as indices are in order; and when indices are not in order the question does not arise, grammar being violated. For the theory of types, in short, (i) and this adaptation of 2.1 are equivalent definitions. So I prefer the version (i) here as bearing no misleading reminder of virtual classes and failure of existence.

For defining identity, the pattern of 2.7 is not now suitable; it would leave '$x^0 = y^0$' unaccounted for. But the pattern of 7.14 will serve:

(iii) '$x^n = y^n$' for '$(z^{n+1})(x^n \in z^{n+1} .\supset. y^n \in z^{n+1})$'.

Note that '$x^m = y^n$' makes sense only where m is n. The constraint comes in the combinations '$x^n \in z^{n+1}$' and '$y^n \in z^{n+1}$' which appear in the right side of (iii); for '$x^m \in z^{n+1}$' is meaningless where $m \neq n$.

Definitions from (ii) onward should be understood as adopted also with abstracts in place of free variables; thus (ii) also with '$\{w^{n+1}: Gw^{n+1}\}$' in place of the 'y^{n+2}', and (iii) also with '$\{w^{n-1}: Gw^{n-1}\}$' in place of the 'x^n' or 'y^n'. Actually I shall not need to continue the list of definitions anyway, for the adaptation of relevant definitions from previous chapters is obvious.

The economies of basic notation now achieved call for adjustments in the apparatus of axioms and rules of proof. As long as abstraction was admitted as a basic notation, the existence of any class $\{x^n: Fx^n\}$ was implicit simply in the rule of proof that allowed substitution of the abstract for variables, and in the law of concretion that equated '$y^n \in \{x^n: Fx^n\}$' to 'Fy^n'. Now, however, our basic notation is such as to afford no substitutes for variables except more variables. The way now to postulate the existence of classes $\{x^n: Fx^n\}$ is by an axiom schema of comprehension couched explicitly in variables thus:

(iv) $$(\exists y^{n+1})(x^n)(x^n \in y^{n+1} .\equiv Fx^n).$$

A further axiom schema is now wanted for *extensionality*:

(v) $$(x^n)(x^n \in y^{n+1} .\equiv. x^n \in z^{n+1}) . y^{n+1} \in w^{n+2} .\supset. z^{n+1} \in w^{n+2},$$

or briefly:

$$(x^n)(x^n \in y^{n+1} \mathrel{.{\equiv}.} x^n \in z^{n+1}) \supset. \; y^{n+1} = z^{n+1}.$$

It is the law that Russell was able to prove for classes without assuming it for attributes, thanks to his contextual definition of class notation; but now that we are starting with classes we need it as an axiom schema.

The theorems of the system are the formulas that follow from those axioms by the logic of quantifiers and truth functions. But the logic of quantifiers is still not quite the standard one, for our variables are still many-sorted (cf. §34). The laws '$(x)Fx \supset Fy$' and '$Fy \supset (\exists x)Fx$' hold only where 'x' and 'y' bear the same index.

This systematization of set theory, more elegant than Russell's original, is what one tends to think of today as Russell's theory of types. It seems to have been presented in this form first by Tarski and Gödel.[1]

It must be noted that the use of the definition of ordered pairs affects Russell's system in a way that goes beyond mere economy. For $\langle x^m, y^n \rangle$ is $\{\{x^m\}, \{x^m, y^n\}\}$; the $\{x^m, y^n\}$ therein is in turn $\{u^k : u^k = x^m \mathrel{.\mathbf{v}.} u^k = y^n\}$ for appropriate k; and, according to what we observed just after (iii), the k of '$u^k = x^m \mathrel{.\mathbf{v}.} u^k = y^n$' must for meaningfulness be both m and n, making $m = n$. Construing relations as classes of pairs in this sense requires us therefore to abandon all *heterogeneous* relations: all relations between things of unlike type. This sacrifice is defended by pointing out that whenever we want e.g. to speak of a relation $\{\langle x^n, y^{n+1} \rangle : Fxy\}$ between things of type n and things of type $n + 1$, we can as well speak of the corresponding relation $\{\langle \{x^n\}, y^{n+1} \rangle : Fxy\}$ between things uniformly of type $n + 1$. By thus applying the unit-class operator to the objects of lower type, as often as necessary to produce equality of type, we can get a serviceable proxy for any relation between things of unlike type. But the fact remains that the system is drastically affected, even if not for the worse; for there ceases to be a contrast e.g.

---

[1] Tarski, pp. 110, 113f; Gödel, 1931.

between $\{\langle x^n, y^{n+1}\rangle: Fxy\}$ and $\{\langle\{x^n\}, y^{n+1}\rangle: Fxy\}$, which there had been before.

Cantor's theorem affords an example of the appeal to relations between things of unlike type. Thus consider its lemma 28.16. The thesis in 28.16 is:

$$\text{(vi)} \qquad \text{Func}\, w \supset. \{x: x \subseteq z\} \nsubseteq w``z,$$

with of course no comprehension premiss any more. But we must be able to supply indices. According to the theory of types before Wiener, heterogeneous relations would be allowed and the indices would be related as in this example:

$$\text{(vii)} \qquad \text{Func}\, w^{(1,0)} \supset. \{x^1: x^1 \subseteq z^1\} \nsubseteq w^{(1,0)}``z^1.$$

Let us see why. Begin arbitrarily by giving 'z' the index '1'; any but '0' would do. Like '$x^m = y^n$', and for the same reason, '$x^m \subseteq y^n$' makes sense only where $m = n$; so 'x' in (vi) must, like 'z', receive the index '1'. Then $w``z^1$ must match $\{x^1: x^1 \subseteq z^1\}$ in type, for coherence of (vi). So $w``z^1$ must be a class whose members are of type 1. But its members are what bear w to members of z^1, which are of type 0. So w must be a heterogeneous relation $w^{(1,0)}$.

With ordered pairs defined, on the other hand, we have to make w homogeneous by raising its defective side, thus: $w^{(1,1)}$. The things in its right field are now to be the unit classes of what had been there; so instead of $w^{(1,0)}``z^1$ we shall have

$$w^{(1,1)}``\{\{v^0\}: v^0 \in z^1\}.$$

Actually $w^{(1,1)}$ becomes simply w^4, since its member pairs are classes of classes of things of type 1. So (vi) now runs:

$$\text{(viii)} \qquad \text{Func}\, w^4 \supset. \{x^1: x^1 \subseteq z^1\} \nsubseteq w^4``\{\{v^0\}: v^0 \in z^1\}.$$

Cantor's theorem itself, viz. 28.17 minus the comprehension premiss, ceases now to be '$z^1 \prec \{x^1: x^1 \subseteq z^1\}$' and becomes, in conformity with (viii), this:

$$\text{(ix)} \qquad \{\{v^0\}: v^0 \in z^1\} \prec \{x^1: x^1 \subseteq z^1\}.$$

It says no longer that z^1 has fewer members than subclasses, but, literally, that z^1 has fewer unit subclasses than subclasses. Still we can and doubtless would adjust our definitions so as to retain the notational form '$z^1 \prec \{x^1: x^1 \subseteq z^1\}$' after all. Since it would otherwise lapse as meaningless, we can simply explain it as short for (ix). In general we can explain '$z^{n+1} \prec u^{n+2}$', '$z^{n+1} \prec u^{n+3}$', '$z^{n+2} \prec u^{n+1}$', etc. as short for:

$$\{\{v^n\}: v^n \in z^{n+1}\} \prec u^{n+2},$$
$$\{\{\{v^n\}\}: v^n \in z^{n+1}\} \prec u^{n+3},$$
$$z^{n+2} \prec \{\{v^n\}: v^n \in u^{n+1}\},$$

etc., first defining the basic form '$z^{m+1} \prec u^{m+1}$' in the familiar manner of 11.1 and 20.3.

Let us observe the fate of Cantor's paradox under the two approaches. As noted in and about 28.20, the way to get the paradox from our present (vi) is by taking w as I and z as $\mathcal{V}$ and concluding that $\{x: x \subseteq \mathcal{V}\} \nsubseteq I``\mathcal{V}$, hence $\mathcal{V} \nsubseteq \mathcal{V}$. But to do this in (vii) we have to settle the indices for 'I' and '$\mathcal{V}$'. There is a $\mathcal{V}$ for each type of classes; the one suited to the position of 'z^1' in (vii) is $\mathcal{V}^1$, the class $\{y^0: y^0 = y^0\}$ of all individuals. As for I, however, the best we can do is $I^{(1,1)}$ or $I^{(0,0)}$; and neither can go for '$w^{(1,0)}$' in (vii). Clearly '$I^{(1,0)}$' violates even the old version of the theory of types, despite tolerance of heterogeneous relations; for identity is homogeneous regardless.

The paradox is obstructed differently in (viii). Here we can indeed take w^4 as I^4, the class of all pairs $\langle y^1, y^1\rangle$. Taking also z^1 as $\mathcal{V}^1$, as before, we have from (viii) that

$$\{x^1: x^1 \subseteq \mathcal{V}^1\} \nsubseteq \{\{v^0\}: v^0 \in \mathcal{V}^1\}.$$

But this is no paradox. $\{x^1: x^1 \subseteq \mathcal{V}^1\}$ is $\mathcal{V}^2$, hence the class of all classes of individuals, while $\{\{v^0\}: v^0 \in \mathcal{V}^1\}$ is the class of all unit classes of individuals. Naturally the former is not a subclass of the latter.

We can easily assure ourselves once and for all that this version of set theory is free from contradiction. For suppose the types were reinterpreted as cumulative in the following fashion. Take Λ alone as of type 0; take Λ again, and $\{\Lambda\}$, and nothing else, as of type 1; and thus, in general, take type n as comprising all and only those sets whose members belong to type $n - 1$. Thus reinterpreted, each quantification (thanks to its indices) covers only finitely many cases. Each closed sentence can be checked mechanically for truth or falsity under the reinterpretation. Here is a miniature theory as unproblematical as truth-function logic. Yet it is easily observed that the axiom schemata (iv) and (v) come out true in all cases when thus trivially reinterpreted. Clearly then they harbor no logical contradiction.[2]

Suppression of indices under Russell's convention of typical ambiguity becomes less urgent now that the definition of the ordered pair has eliminated heterogeneous relations and reduced the types to a simple progression. But the suppression can still be convenient. And, ironically, it becomes foolproof as it was not when it was more urgent. The excess of flexibility that showed itself in connection with the Burali-Forti paradox (cf. §35) is gone.

In §34 we contemplated briefly with Russell a system of orders that prevented impredicative specifications. We had not yet, with Russell, shattered constructivity with an axiom of reducibility. There were reasons, preeminently the need of least bounds of bounded classes of ratios, for shattering the constructivity. But there is also reason to cultivate it, part of the time, despite its inadequacy to classical analysis. It is a part of set theory that carries extra conviction, because of the construction metaphor which we appreciated in those pages. One can be glad to know that certain results are within the reach of constructive set theory even if one is prepared to enlist a nonconstructive theory for further purposes. Therefore I now return briefly to constructive set theory to suggest what can be done for it in the more modern setting of the present section.

It is in the axiom shema (iv) of comprehension that the only difference needs to be made between a constructive theory of

---

[2] Reflections of more or less this sort have appeared in the literature since 1928 (Hilbert and Ackermann). No such easy assurance of consistency remains available when one adds, as one must, the axiom of infinity (§39).

types and the nonconstructive one that we have just been examining. For the constructive theory we merely stipulate that the 'Fx^n' of (iv) is to stand for a formula with no bound variables of type above *n* and no free variables of type above $n + 1$. Note the echo, in this, of the definition of the order of a propositional function. The restriction serves precisely to limit the comprehension schema to the predicative specification of classes.

This predicativity restriction obstructs Cantor's theorem. For consider how (viii) would be proved. If we combine the essential argument of 28.16 with the homogeneity adjustment in (viii), we see that the trick in proving (viii) is to take x^1 as

$$\{v^0: v^0 \in z^1 \,.\, v^0 \notin w^4\text{`}\{v^0\}\}.$$

But the instance of the comprehension schema (iv) that we would need for existence of this class is:

$$(\exists x^1)(v^0)(v^0 \in x^1 \,.\!\equiv\!.\, v^0 \in z^1 \,.\, v^0 \notin w^4\text{`}\{v^0\}),$$

and the 'w^4' in this violates the predicativity restriction.

This obstruction of Cantor's theorem might itself be seen as a virtue. The ins and outs of infinite arithmetic have claimed attention because they seemed forced on us by the same intuitively acceptable principles that underlay classical mathematics. If our constructive set theory were adequate to all reasonable demands of really classical mathematics, we might see its inadequacy to infinite arithmetic as a happy escape.

But in fact it is of course not adequate to classical demands. Like Russell's theory without the axiom of reducibility, it fails over least bounds of bounded classes of ratios or real numbers. For the comprehension axiom affirming existence of the least bound $\bigcup z^2$ of a class z^2 would run:

$$(\exists x^1)(v^0)(v^0 \in x^1 \,.\!\equiv (\exists y^1)(v^0 \in y^1 \in z^2)),$$

and the 'y^1' and 'z^2' in this violate the predicativity restriction.[3]

---

[3] Forms of "constructive" or "predicative" set theory were championed by Weyl in 1918 and Chwistek in 1924 and 1925. New light has of late been shed on it from the side of proof theory. See Kreisel; also Wang, *Survey*, last part; also Fraenkel and Bar-Hillel, pp. 150–160, 196–264.

XII | GENERAL VARIABLES AND ZERMELO

37. The theory of types with general variables

It is not to be supposed that the convention of typical ambiguity, in suppressing the indices that are the distinctive marks of the many sorts of variables, has the effect of adapting the theory of types to the one-sorted or simple logic of quantification. Such a formula as '$(\exists y)(x)(x \in y)$', treated as typically ambiguous, is simply on a par with the schema:

$$(\exists y^{n+1})(x^n)(x^n \in y^{n+1})$$

with its schematic '*n*' for an unspecified index. Its generality is the schematic generality of standing for any one of a lot of formulas:

$$(\exists y^1)(x^0)(x^0 \in y^1), \quad (\exists y^2)(x^1)(x^1 \in y^2), \ \ldots$$

and not the generality that consists in quantifying undividedly over an exhaustive universe of discourse. Taken in the latter vein, '$(\exists y)(x)(x \in y)$' would say that there is a class y whose members exhaust all objects x of all types. Taken as typically ambiguous it does not.

There is reason to consider what such a many-sorted theory might look like when translated into a genuinely one-sorted idiom. For the many-sorted departs from the standard simple logic of quantification. Moreover the indices are cumbersome; and if we dispense with them by typical ambiguity, the departures from simple logic are actually aggravated. For the method of typical ambiguity requires that a formula be counted meaningless that cannot be fitted with indices conformable to the theory of types; and this has the effect that even the conjunction of two meaningful formulas can be meaningless, as witness '$x \in y \,.\, y \in x$'. Also the departures can be more subtle, as in the following example. The quantificational schema:

$$\text{(i)} \qquad (x)Fxy \supset (\exists z)Fyz$$

is valid, for it follows from '$(x)Fxy \supset Fyy$' and '$Fyy \supset (\exists z)Fyz$'. Moreover the seeming instance:

$$\text{(ii)} \qquad (x)(x \in y) \supset (\exists z)(y \in z)$$

of that valid schema is a meaningful formula by standards of typical ambiguity. Yet it would be fallacious to justify (ii) by citing (i), for the 'Fyy' in the general proof of (i) makes it impossible for that proof to be meaningfully interpreted to give (ii). The fact is that (ii) under typical ambiguity is not really of the form (i) but only seems to be. Proof of (ii) must proceed independently of (i), e.g. by proof of the consequent '$(\exists z)(y \in z)$' outright from the instance:

$$(\exists z)(x)(x \in z \;.\!\equiv.\; x = y)$$

of the typically ambiguous axiom schema of comprehension.

Convenience of proof is not the only reason for preferring to hold to the simple logic of quantification. Even apart from convenience there is the sense of its just being poor strategy to disrupt general logic for the avoidance of paradoxes that are peculiar to the special subject matter of set theory. This is the maxim of minimum mutilation, already aired in §7. And finally there is the value of standardization for comparison. When we want to compare set theories with one another in respect of content, or in respect of form with theories of other subjects, it is well to have one underlying logic.

The many-sorted formulation is not essential to the theory of types, considered merely as a doctrine as to what classes there are. We can quite well hold that classes are disposed in types without forbidding general variables. As remarked in §4, we can always reduce multiple sorts of variables to one sort if we adopt appropriate predicates. Wherever we might have used a special sort of variable, we may use instead a general variable and *restrict* it (§33) to the appropriate predicate.

Thus instead of using indexed letters as variables specifically for things of type *n* we may adopt a notation '$\mathrm{T}_n x$' to mean that x is of type *n*. Purposes formerly served by the forms of quantification '$(x^n)Fx^n$' and '$(\exists x^n)Fx^n$' come now to be served no less well by the forms:

$$(x)(\mathrm{T}_n x \supset Fx), \qquad (\exists x)(\mathrm{T}_n x \,.\, Fx).$$

And free variables need not detain us, since sentences with free variables are normally of use only as clauses of longer texts in which those variables are bound. So, at the cost perhaps of adopting new and unreduced predicates 'T_0', 'T_1', 'T_2', . . . , additional to 'ϵ', we get rid of the special indexed variables in favor of the general variables 'x', 'y', ...

Actually '$\mathrm{T}_n x$' for each *n* can be expressed in terms purely of 'ϵ' and logic, as we shall now see. '$(\exists z)(x, y \in z)$' assures sameness of type on the part of x and y; and conversely, since $x^n, y^n \in \mathcal{V}^{n+1}$, sameness of type on the part of x and y assures that $(\exists z)(x, y \in z)$. So we can express sameness of type. Further, if w just precedes y in type, and only then, w will be a member of something of the same type as y; for, $w^n \in \mathcal{V}^{n+1}$. So, combining our devices, we can put 'w just precedes x in type' thus:

$$(\exists y)(w \in y \,.\, (\exists z)(x, y \in z)),$$

i.e., $(\exists z)(w \in^2 z \,.\, x \in z)$. So let us define:

(iii) '$w\mathrm{PT}x$' for '$(\exists z)(w \in^2 z \,.\, x \in z)$'.

Now it is obvious how to render '$\mathrm{T}_n x$' for each *n*.

(iv) '$\mathrm{T}_0 x$' for '$(w){\sim}w\mathrm{PT}x$',

(v) '$\mathrm{T}_{n+1} x$' for '$(w)(\mathrm{T}_n w \supset w\mathrm{PT}x)$'.

The indexed variables of special range can be restituted by definition:

(vi) $\quad$ '$(x^n)Fx^n$' for '$(x)(T_n x \supset Fx)$'

and '$(\exists x^n)$' for '$\sim(x^n)\sim$', whence, by elementary logic,

(vii) $\quad$ $(\exists x^n)Fx^n \equiv (\exists x)(T_n x \,.\, Fx)$.

But this plan does away with Russell's grammatical restriction, which declared '$x^m \in y^n$' meaningless where $m + 1 \neq n$. Sense is now made of '$x^m \in y^n$' for all m and n. If $m + 1 \neq n$, then '$x^m \in y^n$' merely becomes false. That we can suddenly be so cavalier with Russell's grammatical restriction makes one wonder whether he needed to make it. The answer is that he did not. One sees how he was led to make it. The idea of getting the paradoxes to turn out neither true nor false but meaningless was an inviting one, and the idea of failure of definition through vicious circularity was of a piece with it. But his system itself, by the time he had it working, was working independently of these ideas. There was a hint of this point already in our observation on Russell's paradox at the end of §34: that it was blocked *both* by Russell's imputation of meaninglessness *and* by the limitation of range of the variable. And the point is established conclusively, for the theory of types with the Wiener simplification, by the consistency argument in §36. For the model in finite classes which we there appealed to depends in no way on meaninglessness of the type violations; '$x^n \in x^n$' and the like can there simply be called false.

Russell's grammatical restriction did serve a purpose in his system: it implemented his device of typical ambiguity. But we are through with that device when we convert to general variables.

We have our method of translating the theory of types into terms of general variables. Let us now bring it to bear on the axiom schemata of the theory, viz. (iv) and (v) of §36. Translating them with tacit understanding of universal quantifiers, we get:

(viii) $\quad$ $(\exists y)(T_{n+1}y \,.\, (x)(T_n x \supset: x \in y \,.\!\equiv Fx))$,

(ix) $\quad$ $T_{n+2}z \,.\, T_{n+1}x \,.\, T_{n+1}y \,.$
$\qquad (w)(T_n w \supset: w \in x \,.\!\equiv\!.\, w \in y) \,.\, x \in z \,.\!\supset\!.\, y \in z$.

But can we be sure that all the theorems derivable by the many-sorted logic of quantification from (iv) and (v) of §36 are also derivable by one-sorted logic from (iii)–(ix)? The distinctive laws of the many-sorted logic (cf. §34) were:

$$(y^n)((x^n)Fx^n \supset Fy^n), \qquad (y^n)(Fy^n \supset (\exists x^n)Fx^n).$$

According to (vi) and (vii), these now mean:

$$(y)(\mathrm{T}_n y \supset . \ (x)(\mathrm{T}_n x \supset Fx) \supset Fy),$$
$$(y)(\mathrm{T}_n y \supset . \ Fy \supset (\exists x)(\mathrm{T}_n x \, . \, Fx))$$

and so are obviously valid for one-sorted logic. But there was also a further and subtler source of power in the many-sorted logic that we must not lose sight of. As every logic student learns, the logic of quantification implicitly assumes nonemptiness of the range of values of the variables by allowing such inferences as that of '$(\exists x)Fx$' from '$(x)Fx$'. In a many-sorted logic of quantification, where the standard logical laws are accepted anew for each sort of variable, the effect of this implicit assumption is that for each sort of variable the range of values is guaranteed nonempty by the inferences admitted. Consequently, if with our switch to one-sorted logic we are not to lose some theorems that were available before, we must be sure to provide explicitly for this as a theorem for each n:[1]

(x) $$(\exists x)\mathrm{T}_n x.$$

Proof. If $(x) \sim \mathrm{T}_n x$ then $(x)\mathrm{T}_{n+1}x$ by (v) and so, by (viii), there is y such that $(x)(x \in y \ . \equiv Fx)$, whence Russell's paradox.

Now all theorems of the theory of types with special variables are preserved, in translation, in the theory of types with general variables. Still the latter system is more glaringly incomplete than the former, because of all the newly meaningful formulas whose proof or disproof we have not provided for. Several such,

---

[1] This point was taken into account by Herbrand, 1930, p. 62. In the ensuing proof I am indebted to David Kaplan and Bruce Renshaw.

clearly valid for the theory of types as we are picturing it, are as follows:

(xi) $x \in y \,.\supset.\, \mathrm{T}_n x \equiv \mathrm{T}_{n+1} y$,

(xii) $(\exists y)(x)(x \in y \,.\equiv.\, x \in z \,.\, Fx)$,

(xiii) $(\exists y)(x)(x \in y \,.\equiv.\, x \in^2 z)$.

If we accept (xi) as a further axiom, we can simplify (viii) and (ix) to:

(xiv) $(\exists y)(\mathrm{T}_{n+1} y \,.\, (x)(x \in y \,.\equiv.\, \mathrm{T}_n x \,.\, Fx))$,

(xv) $\mathrm{T}_{n+1} x \,.\, \mathrm{T}_{n+1} y \,.\, (w)(w \in x \,.\equiv.\, w \in y) \,.\, x \in z \,.\supset.\, y \in z$.

For (viii) is equivalent to:

$$(\exists y)(\mathrm{T}_{n+1} y \,.\, (x)(\mathrm{T}_n x \,.\, x \in y \,.\equiv.\, \mathrm{T}_n x \,.\, Fx)),$$

and the '$\mathrm{T}_n x \,.\, x \in y$' reduces by (xi) to '$x \in y$' in the presence of '$\mathrm{T}_{n+1} y$'. Similar reasoning equates (ix) to (xv).

From (xiv) we can get only as near to (xii) and (xiii) as this:

(xvi) $(\exists y)(x)(x \in y \,.\equiv.\, \mathrm{T}_n x \,.\, x \in z \,.\, Fx)$,

(xvii) $(\exists y)(x)(x \in y \,.\equiv.\, \mathrm{T}_n x \,.\, x \in^2 z)$.

The reasoning that would eliminate '$\mathrm{T}_n x$' here, and so give (xii) and (xiii), is as follows: in (xvi) take n so that $\mathrm{T}_{n+1} z$, or, if $\mathrm{T}_0 z$, take n as 0; and in (xvii) take n so that $\mathrm{T}_{n+2} z$, or, if $\mathrm{T}_0 z$ or $\mathrm{T}_1 z$, take n as 0. But these lines are closed to us because we have no axiom to show that everything z is of some type or other. Kaplan has a proof that we cannot express such an axiom or axiom schema; '$(\exists n)\mathrm{T}_n z$' will not do, for the '$n$' is schematic and hence inadmissible in the quantifier. But we may, if we like, add (xii) and (xiii) themselves as axiom schema and axiom.

Such was their status in Zermelo's pioneer set theory, which dates from the same year as Russell's theory of types: 1908.[2]

[2] Both assumptions were anticipated by Cantor in a letter of 1899 which was not published until 1932 (p. 444).

The axiom schema (xii) may be remembered from §5 as that of *Aussonderung* or *separation*, so called because it has the effect, given a class z, of segregating a part y of it. The axiom (xiii) is known as the axiom of the *sum*. Zermelo's system does diverge from the theory of types in others of its axioms, as we shall see in §39.

The question arises of dropping '$T_{n+1}x$' and '$T_{n+1}y$' from (xv). They are needed on two counts. One need of them is to prevent x and y from being individuals. Any individuals x and y would, for lack of members, be identified with one another and with the null classes of all types if (xv) were adopted without '$T_{n+1}x$' and '$T_{n+1}y$'. The other need of these is to assure sameness of type, and so prevent identifying the null classes of different types with one another.

It is likewise so as to assure the existence of a null class in every class type that '$T_{n+1}y$' is needed in (xiv). The clause is indeed superfluous if y has members, since the type of y is then fixed by that of its members, as specified in the clause '$T_n x$'.[3]

38. Cumulative types and Zermelo

Once the theory of types has been couched thus in general variables, simplifications suggest themselves that are substantive in character. Thus, suppose we were willing to equate the null classes of all class types. One of the two purposes of the clauses '$T_{n+1}x \,.\, T_{n+1}y$' in (xv) above would then lapse. The remaining purpose of those clauses, that of stipulating that x and y be classes and not individuals, can as well be served thereafter by '$\sim T_0 x \,.\, \sim T_0 y$'. This is a simplification, since the complexity of '$T_{n+1}x \,.\, T_{n+1}y$' in terms of 'ϵ' mounts with n.

Equating the null classes enables us likewise to change '$T_{n+1}y$' in (xiv) to '$\sim T_0 y$'. So (xiv) and (xv) become:

(i) $(\exists y)(\sim T_0 y \,.\, (x)(x \in y \,.\!\equiv.\, T_n x \,.\, Fx))$,

(ii) $\sim T_0 x \,.\, \sim T_0 y \,.\, (w)(w \in x \,.\!\equiv.\, w \in y) \,.\, x \in z \,.\!\supset.\, y \in z$.

(ii) is no longer an axiom schema, but a single axiom.

---

[3] The last few pages of this section and the first few pages of the next have been adapted in part from pp. 272–275 of my 1956 paper, with the kind permission of the editors of the *Journal of Symbolic Logic*.

Our equating of the null classes constrains us to drop (xi) of p. 271. Otherwise Λ could not belong to classes x and y of consecutive types.[1] The reasoning is as follows. If Λ belonged to classes of consecutive types, then Λ would be of two consecutive types, by (xi). Then let n be the least number such that $T_n\Lambda$ and $T_{n+1}\Lambda$. So $T_{n+1}\{\Lambda\}$ and $T_{n+1}\Lambda$. So, by (i) of p. 272, $\{\{\Lambda\}, \Lambda\}$ exists. By (xi), since $T_n\Lambda$, $T_{n+1}\{\{\Lambda\}, \Lambda\}$. So, by (xi), $T_n\{\Lambda\}$. But, by definitions (iii)–(iv) of p. 268, Λ PT $\{\Lambda\}$ and so $\sim T_0\{\Lambda\}$. So $n > 0$. By (xi), then, since $T_n\{\Lambda\}$, $T_{n-1}\Lambda$—contrary to leastness.

The clause '$\sim T_0 y$' in (i) remains needed in order to assure the existence of Λ, which is provided by this case of (i):

(iii) $(\exists y)(\sim T_0 y \,.\, (x)(x \in y \,.\!\equiv.\, T_0 x \,.\, \sim T_0 x))$.

Without '$\sim T_0 y$', (iii) would still affirm the existence of memberless objects y; but these might be merely the individuals, rather than Λ, were it not for '$\sim T_0 y$'. The purpose of '$\sim T_0 y$' in (iii) is, in short, to keep the individuals distinct from Λ. Likewise, as seen, the purpose of '$\sim T_0 x \,.\, \sim T_0 y$' in (ii) is to avoid identifying the individuals with Λ and one another. But we know from §4 how to dispense with these needs. We cannot indeed now follow Fraenkel in simply dispensing with individuals, for, under the theory of types, this would close the door to infinite classes and also to classical number theory (see §39). But we can profitably adopt the other expedient of §4: identify individuals with their unit classes.

At the outset of converting the theory of types to general variables we were faced with the need of supplementary interpretations of '$x \in y$' covering objects x and y not of consecutive types. We chose blanket falsity. The expedient now envisaged of identifying individuals with their unit classes involves making rather this exception to the blanket falsity: where x is an individual, count '$x \in x$' as true. Now (i) and (ii) reduce to:

(iv) $(\exists y)(x)(x \in y \,.\!\equiv.\, T_n x \,.\, Fx)$,

(v) $(w)(w \in x \,.\!\equiv.\, w \in y) \,.\, x \in z \,.\!\supset.\, y \in z$.

[1] Or of two types at all. But this is bad enough, and quicker to prove. I am indebted to Kaplan.

Moreover, the definition of '$\mathrm{T}_n x$' must be revised to suit the new idea of individual. Skipping '$x\mathrm{PT}y$', we can define

(vi) '$\mathrm{T}_0 x$' for '$(y)(y \in x .\equiv. y = x)$',
'$\mathrm{T}_{n+1} x$' for '$(y)(y \in x .\supset \mathrm{T}_n y)$'.

Types become cumulative; $\mathrm{T}_m x \supset \mathrm{T}_n x$ for all $m < n$.

The proof of (x) of p. 270 is not available under these definitions. We must now take '$(\exists x)\mathrm{T}_0 x$' as an axiom, but we still can prove '$(\exists x)\mathrm{T}_{n+1} x$', thus: by (iv), with '$x \neq x$' for '$Fx$', we have $(\exists y)(x)(x \notin y)$ and so, by (vi), $(\exists y)\mathrm{T}_{n+1} y$.

Such, then, is the theory of cumulative types with general variables. It has (iv), (v), '$(\exists x)\mathrm{T}_0 x$', and the definitions (vi). The (xi) of §37 drops; half of it is in (vi) and the other half is false for cumulative types. But (xii) and (xiii) of §37, which were *Aussonderung* and sum, are as good as ever with cumulative types. We could take them as added axioms.

A further Zermelo axiom of which I have thus far omitted mention is called that of the *power set*. It posits for each class z the class $\{x: x \subseteq z\}$, and it has its name from the fact that $\{x: x \subseteq z\}$ has $2^{\bar{z}}$ members (cf. §30). Because individuals were for him memberless, he had to put the power-set axiom substantially thus:

$$(\exists y)(x)(x \in y .\equiv. x \text{ is a class} . x \subseteq z).$$

The classitude clause is there lest all individuals tag along into y.

In the theory of types as of §37, with general variables but no further liberalization, the most we could have admitted in that vein is:

$$(\exists y)(x)(x \in y .\equiv. \mathrm{T}_n x . x \subseteq z).$$

The homogeneity clause '$\mathrm{T}_n x$' is needed lest the null classes of all types and all individuals tag along into y. (When $n = 0$, all individuals do enter y; but then nothing else does.) I did not stop for this law in §37, for it is immediate from (xiv) of that section.

Now that individuals have ceased to be memberless, however, '$\mathrm{T}_n x$' is no longer needed to shield y from the flood of them; and now that the null classes of all types are identified, '$\mathrm{T}_n x$' is no longer wanted to stem the flood of those. We could adopt with equanimity for our cumulative theory of types the unhedged power-set axiom:

$$(\exists y)(x)(x \in y \,.\!\equiv.\, x \subseteq z),$$

out-liberalizing even Zermelo.

The axiom system, thus supplemented, can be made more elegant. Before doing so let us improve our notation. It will be convenient now to reactivate the noncommittal definition 2.1 of '$x \in \{y: Fy\}$', in preference to (i) of §36, and so regain the freedom of virtual classes. Indeed all the decimally numbered definitions of earlier chapters can be reactivated. Even the definition 2.7 of identity is all right now that individuals have themselves as members. Thereupon the axiom schemata and axioms that we have been accumulating, viz. (iv), (v), the power-set axiom, '$(\exists x)\mathrm{T}_0 x$', and (xii)–(xiii) of §37, take on these condensed forms:

$$\alpha \cap \{x: \mathrm{T}_n x\} \in \mathcal{V}, \qquad x = y \,.\, x \in z \,.\!\supset\!.\, y \in z,$$

$$\{x: x \subseteq z\} \in \mathcal{V}, \qquad (\exists x)\mathrm{T}_0 x, \qquad z \cap \alpha \in \mathcal{V}, \qquad \mathsf{U}z \in \mathcal{V}.$$

Now instead of the axiom schema '$\alpha \cap \{x: \mathrm{T}_n x\} \in \mathcal{V}$' here we could as well take '$\{x: \mathrm{T}_n x\} \in \mathcal{V}$'; for '$\{x: \mathrm{T}_n x\} \in \mathcal{V}$' follows from '$\alpha \cap \{x: \mathrm{T}_n x\} \in \mathcal{V}$' by setting $\alpha = \{x: \mathrm{T}_n x\}$, and conversely '$\alpha \cap \{x: \mathrm{T}_n x\} \in \mathcal{V}$' follows from '$\{x: \mathrm{T}_n x\} \in \mathcal{V}$' along with the axiom schema '$z \cap \alpha \in \mathcal{V}$' of *Aussonderung*. And instead of '$\{x: \mathrm{T}_n x\} \in \mathcal{V}$', in turn, it is sufficient to postulate '$\{x: \mathrm{T}_0 x\} \in \mathcal{V}$'; for from this and the power-set axiom '$\{x: x \subseteq z\} \in \mathcal{V}$' and the definition of '$\mathrm{T}_{n+1} y$' we get '$\{x: \mathrm{T}_1 x\} \in \mathcal{V}$', and continuing thus we rise to '$\{x: \mathrm{T}_n x\} \in \mathcal{V}$' for any *n*. Moreover, having thus got our axiom system down to where it makes no use of the form of notation '$\mathrm{T}_n x$' except for the one case '$\mathrm{T}_0 x$', we may skip that whole form of notation and its definition (vi) and revert to '$x = \{x\}$' for the one case. So our axiom system is down to this:

$$x = y \,.\, x \in z \,.\!\supset\!.\, y \in z, \qquad (\exists x)(x = \{x\}),$$

$$\{x: x = \{x\}\},\ \{x: x \subseteq z\},\ z \cap \alpha,\ \mathsf{U}z \in \mathcal{V}.$$

Yet another axiom of Zermelo is eligible to be added now that types are cumulative: $\{x, y\} \in \mathcal{V}$, the *axiom of pairing*. For the theory of ordinary exclusive types it was not in general true; but it fits the theory of cumulative types, since any two things are of a same cumulative type.

A consequence of the axioms '$\{x, y\}$, $\mathsf{U}z \in \mathfrak{V}$' is that $x \cup y \in \mathfrak{V}$; for take z as $\{x, y\}$. Here again is something that fails for ordinary types but holds for cumulative.

The axioms we have now accumulated for cumulative types may conveniently be reassembled in two lists. There are *Zermelo's axioms* of power set, pairing, *Aussonderung*, sum, extensionality:

(vii) $$\{x: x \subseteq z\},\ \{x, y\},\ z \cap \alpha,\ \mathsf{U}z \in \mathfrak{V},$$
$$x = y \,.\, x \in z \,.\!\supset\!.\, y \in z$$

and there are the *axioms of individuals*:

(viii) $$(\exists x)(x = \{x\}), \qquad \{x: x = \{x\}\} \in \mathfrak{V}.$$

Zermelo did not depict his system as disposed in types. Still, moving to his system through this channel helps to relate these two pioneer systems.

Zermelo owned to a few additional axioms. There was the axiom of choice, which he originated and counted in, and an axiom of infinity, which we shall take up in §39. Also there was '$\{x\} \in \mathfrak{V}$', but this was redundant, since '$\{x, y\} \in \mathfrak{V}$' gives '$\{x, x\} \in \mathfrak{V}$'. Also there was '$\Lambda \in \mathfrak{V}$', but it can be got from the case '$z \cap \Lambda \in \mathfrak{V}$' of the axiom schema of *Aussonderung* '$z \cap \alpha \in \mathfrak{V}$'.

As we noted when the power-set axiom first came up, Zermelo's actual system was complicated by the distinction between class and individual. Hence the classitude clause in our first formulation of the power-set axiom. Likewise in the extensionality axiom '$x = y \,.\, x \in z \,.\!\supset\!.\, y \in z$' Zermelo had to limit '$x$' and '$y$' to classes. And it should be said in Zermelo's behalf that his counterpart of '$\Lambda \in \mathfrak{V}$' was to the effect rather that

$$(\exists y)(y \text{ is a class} \,.\, (x)(x \notin y))$$

and therefore not redundant as long as individuals were memberless; *Aussonderung* assured a memberless object but not necessarily a memberless class. In simplifying this whole aspect by my concept of individuals as $x = \{x\}$, I have departed from Zermelo.

Readers previously acquainted with Zermelo's system will have had to make allowance also for the drastic difference in style of presentation that comes with my use of 2.1 and noncommittal abstraction. Zermelo's system admits no universe class $\mathcal{V}$, and Zermelo had no use for class symbols without classes; so my rendering of *Aussonderung* as '$z \cap \alpha \in \mathcal{V}$' would look odd indeed to him and his readers, both in its '$\mathcal{V}$' and in its 'α'. The version of *Aussonderung* characteristic of the literature is rather (xii) of §37. (Even it is due partly to Skolem (1922–23), who was clearer than Zermelo on the schematic status of the 'Fx'.) But it must be borne in mind that the whole matter of virtual classes and noncommittal abstraction, convenient though it is and large though it looms, is pure definition; Zermelo's system becomes no other system when thus set forth.

What are listed in (vii), then, are Zermelo's axioms, modified drastically in style of presentation, but modified substantively only by revision of the idea of an individual and by exclusion of redundancies and the high-powered axioms of infinity and choice. Listed in (viii) are extras, not in Zermelo: the axioms of individuals. These have entered as descendents of the theory of types, transformed by my special doctrine of individuals. Zermelo's own system merely permits and does not require individuals in any sense, mine or another.

Fraenkel's remark that Zermelo's system needs no individuals, but only "pure" classes (§4), can be strengthened so far as the axioms (vii) are concerned: there need be only finite pure classes. These are the classes belonging to the trivial model that in §36 assured us of the consistency of the theory of types. So we are assured of the consistency of the Zermelo axioms (vii). Nor is contradiction to be feared from adding the axioms (viii) of individuals; for a single individual will fill that bill.

Having come thus far from the theory of types ordinarily so called, let us get our bearings by seeing how Russell's paradox and Cantor's theorem now fare. The contradiction in Russell's paradox is, in a word, '$\{x: x \notin x\} \in \mathcal{V}$'; and the only hope of getting it would be through the *Aussonderung* schema '$z \cap \alpha \in \mathcal{V}$', which gives '$z \cap \{x: x \notin x\} \in \mathcal{V}$'. But to get from this to '$\{x: x \notin x\} \in \mathcal{V}$' we need a z big enough that $\{x: x \notin x\} \subseteq z$', and there is no visible way to such a z. Zermelo's protection against the paradoxes consists essentially in eschewing too big classes.

Cantor's theorem confronts no such obstacle. The *Aussonderung* schema '$z \cap \alpha \in \mathcal{V}$' gives that

$$\text{(ix)} \qquad (z)(w)(z \cap \{y: y \notin w`y\} \in \mathcal{V}),$$

and from this we can argue precisely as in 28.17 that

$$(z)(z \prec \{x: x \subseteq z\}).$$

But of Cantor's paradox, which would come of taking z here as $\mathcal{V}$, there is no danger; for we do not have that $\mathcal{V} \in \mathcal{V}$. We can prove for each n that $\mathcal{V}^{n+1} \in \mathcal{V}$, i.e., $\{x^n: x^n = x^n\} \in \mathcal{V}$, for this is to say simply that $\{x: \mathrm{T}_n x\} \in \mathcal{V}$, and we saw that this is forthcoming from Zermelo's axioms (vii) if supplemented by (viii); but '$\mathcal{V} \in \mathcal{V}$', or '$\{x: x = x\} \in \mathcal{V}$', there is no way to prove. Here again we see Zermelo's protection against the paradoxes as his avoidance of too big classes; there is no class of everything.

Cantor's theorem, in the form just now proved, depended on the ordinary definition of '$\prec$'; no special maneuvers were needed, as in §36, for heterogeneous relations. For an effect of switching to cumulative types is that the ban on heterogeneous relations lapses—or, as we might say, heterogeneity itself lapses, since one of any two types is now included within the other. The crucial point is '$\{x, y\} \in \mathcal{V}$', now at hand, which gives '$\langle z, w\rangle \in \mathcal{V}$' for all z and w.

It is in some ways confusing to talk of cumulative types. You cease to be able to speak uniquely of *the* type of a class. Moreover, whereas a type includes all *lower* types, a thing of any type belongs to all *higher* types. So it might be preferable to redefine *the* type of a class as what we have been calling its lowest type in the cumulative sense. Thus an individual would be said to be of type 0; the null class would be said to be of type 1; and any other class would be said to be of type next higher than its highest-type members. By this account '$T_n x$' as of (vi) would be read 'x is of type n at most'. What had been cumulativeness of types would come to be described instead as finite heterogeneity of classes: the members of a class are allowed to be of finitely many different types (viz., any below its own type). However, all this is just another way of describing one and the same theory of classes: the theory epitomized in (vii) and (viii).

Whichever the more convenient designation of the theory, certainly the theory itself represents a gain in convenience over the ordinary theory of types. We have seen an illustration of this in its unrestricted tolerance of ordered pairs and hence of heterogeneous relations. It may be noted also that the von Neumann and Zermelo versions of natural number fare a little better here than under Russell's theory of types. For von Neumann the successor of x was $x \cup \{x\}$, which clearly conflicts with the theory of types. And Zermelo's version conflicts with the theory of types as soon as one tries to put two numbers, say x and its successor $\{x\}$, into a class. The new plan, with its tolerance of finite heterogeneity in classes, is free of these conflicts with von Neumann's and Zermelo's numbers.

39. Axioms of infinity and others

The theory of types was in trouble even over the Frege version of number. To put this difficulty in perspective, let us recall a point from §12. It emerged there that all we need for a classical theory of natural number is an arbitrary function S that applies always to its own results to give something new. Take an arbitrary argument of S to play the role of 0, and you can define all further accessories of number theory by the general routine seen in §11. But the needs of number theory will not be met if S fails to give something new each time. And the fact is that precisely this failure threatens the Frege S under the theory of types.

For the Frege successor of a number x is

$$\{z: (\exists y)(y \in z \,.\, z \cap {}^{-}\{y\} \in x)\};$$

and what is to prevent that $S`x = x$? Say we are working in the lowest type for numbers, viz. type 2, so that a number, say 5, is the class of all five-individual classes. And suppose there are only five individuals in the universe. Thus 5, in type 2, is $\{\mho^1\}$. Then 6, or S'5, in type 2, is

$$\{z^1: (\exists y^0)(y^0 \in z^1 \,.\, z^1 \cap {}^-\{y^0\} = \mho^1)\},$$

which, '$y \in z \,.\, z \cap {}^-\{y\} = \mho$' being contradictory, is Λ^2. But then 7, or S'6, is $S`\Lambda^2$, which reduces to $\Lambda^2$ too. So $S`x = x$ where x is 6 of type 2, granted that there are no more than five individuals.

The argument is general. If a type has fewer than *k* members, the number *k* two types up will equal its own successor (both being Λ). Under these circumstances elementary number theory breaks down. In particular the Peano axiom of subtraction '$S`x = S`y \,.\!\supset\!.\, x = y$' fails. Thus take the preceding examples, where $5 \neq \Lambda$ but $S`6 = 6 = S`5 = \Lambda$; here $S`6 = S`5$ and yet $6 \neq 5$.

The worst of it is that if one type is finite in its membership, each is; and then proper arithmetic is forthcoming in no type. To sustain arithmetic, on this version anyway, it is necessary and sufficient to postulate infinitely many individuals. One way of phrasing this *axiom of infinity* is by saying that there is a nonempty class x^2 each of whose members is a subclass of a further member.[1]

$$\text{(i)} \quad (\exists x^2)((\exists y^1)(y^1 \in x^2) \,.\, (y^1)(y^1 \in x^2 \,.\!\supset (\exists z^1)(y^1 \subset z^1 \in x^2))).$$

The axiom has been decried on the ground that the question whether there are infinitely many individuals is a question rather of physics or metaphysics than of mathematics, and that it is incongruous to make arithmetic depend upon it. Whitehead and

[1] This version is from Tarski, p. 243. Whitehead and Russell phrased it rather as saying that for every $x^2 \in N^3$ there is a class y^1 with x^2 members; in short, $\Lambda^2 \notin N^3$.

Russell were apologetic about the axiom, as they were about the axiom of choice; they entered both of them as explicit hypotheses in the theorems that required them, just as I did with most comprehension assumptions in Chapters VII–X.

The need for this axiom of infinity continues to plague the Frege account of number even when we liberalize the theory of types as in §38 to allow cumulative types, or finitely heterogeneous classes. For within any type, even thus liberalized, there will be a finite limit to how big a class can be, unless there are infinitely many individuals.

If we then find it a comfort that the liberalized theory allows us to resort instead to Zermelo's notion of number, this comfort suddenly terminates in its turn in trouble over mathematical induction. Classically one defines

(ii) 'N' for '$\{x: (y)(0 \in y \,.\, \text{S}``y \subseteq y \;.\!\supset\!.\; x \in y)\}$'

and then takes y as $\{z: Fz\}$ to infer that

(iii) $F0 \,.\, (z)(Fz \supset F(\text{S}`z)) \,.\, x \in \text{N} \;.\!\supset Fx.$

The by now familiar difficulty is that there is in general no assurance that $\{z: Fz\} \in \mathcal{V}$.

We overcame this difficulty in Chapter IV by revising (ii) to read:

(iv) 'N' for '$\{x: (y)(x \in y \,.\, \breve{\text{S}}``y \subseteq y \;.\!\supset\!.\; 0 \in y)\}$'

and then proving (iii) by taking y not as $\{z: Fz\}$ but as the finite class $\{z: z \leqq x \,.\, {\sim}Fz\}$. In 7.10 and 13.1 we postulated finite classes, and all was well. Now one expects this expedient to work equally in the present system of liberalized types or of Zermelo, since here again all finite classes are assured of existence. We have seen how 'Λ, $\{z\}$, $x \cup y \in \mathcal{V}$' all come out of (vii) of §38; the latter two give '$x \cup \{z\} \in \mathcal{V}$', and from '$\Lambda \in \mathcal{V}$' by n applications of '$x \cup \{z\} \in \mathcal{V}$' we can show any class of n members to exist.

The specific plan encounters obstacles. Our derivation of (iii) from the definition (iv) turned on 13.1, which does not follow from (vii) of §38.[2] However, Zermelo numbers can be caught also in other and more devious definitions than (ii) and (iv), and Zermelo showed in 1909 how to derive (iii) from such a definition without using any comprehension axioms other than (vii) of §38. (See p. 76n above.) Zermelo's natural numbers and von Neumann's have the great advantage over Frege's of requiring no axiom of infinity.

For higher reaches, the theory of real numbers and beyond, infinite classes are of course still needed on any approach; and accordingly Zermelo added an axiom of infinity. It was in effect '$\mathrm{N} \in \mathcal{V}$', in fact this:

$$\text{(v)} \qquad (\exists x)(\Lambda \in x \,.\, (y)(y \in x \,.\!\supset\!.\, \{y\} \in x)).$$

This postulates a class to which at least all natural numbers in Zermelo's sense belong. It is equivalent to '$\mathrm{N} \in \mathcal{V}$'; for N is itself an x fulfilling (v), and conversely if x fulfills (v) then $\mathrm{N} \subseteq x$ and so $\mathrm{N} \in \mathcal{V}$ by *Aussonderung*.

Now of course the induction schema (iii) follows; just take the y of (ii) as $\mathrm{N} \cap \{z\colon Fz\}$, which exists by '$\mathrm{N} \in \mathcal{V}$' and *Aussonderung*. This is the easy way to induction in Zermelo's system, when one is not out to shield number theory from the infinitistic assumptions that are eventually wanted anyway in other quarters.

However extravagant as a basis for induction, '$\mathrm{N} \in \mathcal{V}$' is scarcely more than a minimum provision for the real numbers (cf. §19). And it is an axiom of infinity which, unlike Whitehead and Russell's, says nothing of individuals.

But it severs the last ties with the theory of types. An infinite class of natural numbers of the Zermelo kind, or of the von Neumann kind, is antithetical to the theory even of cumulative types; for such a class pierces all type ceilings.[3] Indeed it was

[2] Zermelo's system, even when extended to include the axiom schema of replacement (below) and the axiom of choice, but excluding the axioms of *Fundierung* and infinity (below), is fulfilled by a model which violates 13.1. The model is the last of those given by Bernays, 1954, p. 83. I owe this observation to Kenneth Brown.

[3] I speak of finitely high types. An idea of transfinite types, due to von Neumann, will emerge early in §45.

simply not true that the theory even of cumulative types accommodated natural numbers of the Zermelo or von Neumann kind, in an interesting sense; for certainly we should not want to close the way to infinite classes of numbers, even while postponing the assuming of them.

Whitehead and Russell's axiom of infinity was called forth, we saw, by the subtraction law '$\text{S}`x = \text{S}`y \,.\supset.\, x = y$'. To put the matter another way, it was needed lest the natural numbers stop short. Equally it was needed lest the real numbers stop short. And its significance does not stop there. Each succeeding type is the class of all subclasses of its predecessor, and so, by Cantor's theorem, bigger than its predecessor. Assume infinitely many individuals, therefore, and you assume higher infinities without end (granted (iv) of §38).

Zermelo's axiom of infinity has the same significance for higher infinities, in his system, that Whitehead and Russell's had in theirs. For, given $\text{N} \in \mathfrak{V}$, we have by the power-class axiom in (vii) of §38 that $\{x\colon x \subseteq \text{N}\} \in \mathfrak{V}$; and it, by Cantor's theorem, is bigger than N. And so on upward.

Zermelo's axiom of infinity shatters type ceilings. Shattering them is a good move, freeing us of a burden that was comparable to the type indices even though the indices themselves were already gone. For under the theory of types even with general variables we were driven to Frege's version of natural numbers. This meant recognizing a different 5 in every type (above classes of individuals), a different 6 in every type (above classes of individuals), a different N in every type (above classes of classes of individuals). And there supervenes a similar reduplication, upward through the type hierarchy, of every detail of the theory of real numbers: $\frac{3}{5}$ turns up as a different thing in each succeeding type, and π does, and Rat itself, and Real. Retention of type indices is practically needed for all these constants, despite our reduction of the basic notation to general variables. In Zermelo's system, on the other hand, with its axiom of infinity and consequent abandonment of type ceilings, all such reduplication ceases.

We saw Zermelo's protection against paradoxes in his avoidance of too big classes.[4] For the converse assurance, that classes fail to exist *only* if they would be bigger than all that exist, there was only very partial provision in Zermelo's schema of *Aussonderung*. Full provision was added rather by Fraenkel and Skolem in the axiom schema of replacement. Condensed by our technique of virtual classes and noncommittal abstraction, that schema becomes:

(vi) $$\text{Func}\,\alpha \supset .\ \alpha``x \in \mathcal{V},$$

as already noted in §13. Zermelo's system thus strengthened is called the *Zermelo–Fraenkel* system.

This is not a principle to which the theory of types adheres. In the theory of ordinary or exclusive types, a class of as few as two members can be banned because of difference of type while an infinite class can exist within a type. And even in the theory of cumulative types one infinite class can be banned because of infinite ascent of types while another, free of that trait, is admitted; so here again the axiom schema of replacement would be out of place.

We saw that the theory of types makes trouble over Zermelo's and von Neumann's numbers. We must also recognize a reciprocal incompatibility: Zermelo's set theory makes trouble over Frege's numbers. For if we construe Frege's numbers without thought of types, so that n is simply the class of all n-member classes of whatever objects, then any number but 0 will have as many members as $\mathcal{V}$ itself does; and a class that big is incapable of existing in Zermelo's system (with the axiom schema (vi) of replacement), since its existence would make, by (vi), for the existence of $\mathcal{V}$. Thus take even Frege's 1, which is the class $\iota``\mathcal{V}$ of all unit classes; we have $\breve{\iota}``1 = \mathcal{V}$ and so, by (vi), $\mathcal{V} \in \mathcal{V}$ if $1 \in \mathcal{V}$. So we may be thankful that Zermelo's numbers and von Neumann's become available instead, with no strings attached.

When the axiom schema (vi) of replacement is adopted, note

[4] §38. The idea of avoiding the paradoxes by avoiding too big classes is older still than Zermelo's system. It was mentioned by Russell in his 1906 paper and by Cantor in his long-unpublished letter of 1899 (Cantor, p. 444).

that the axiom schema '$x \cap \alpha \in \mathcal{V}$' of *Aussonderung* drops out as superfluous. For, taking the α of (vi) as the function $I \restriction \alpha$, we get that $(I \restriction \alpha)$"$x \in \mathcal{V}$, which is to say $x \cap \alpha \in \mathcal{V}$. In the way of further condensation of axioms it has been shown by Ono that if we complicate (vi) to read:

$$\text{Func}\ \alpha \supset \alpha``\{y: (\exists z)(y \subseteq z \in x)\} \in \mathcal{V}$$

then we can drop as redundant not only '$x \cap \alpha \in \mathcal{V}$' but also '$\bigcup z \in \mathcal{V}$' and '$\{x: x \subseteq z\} \in \mathcal{V}$'. Ono's schema is equivalent to these axioms and (vi), given pairing or '$\{x\} \in \mathcal{V}$'.

We saw that both the axiom schema (vi) of replacement and Zermelo's axiom (v) or '$N \in \mathcal{V}$' of infinity are laws that mark the divergence of the Zermelo system from the theory of types even in its liberalized, cumulative form. Conversely the axioms of individuals, (viii) of §38, are transformed traces of the theory of types that serve no purpose in the Zermelo system once the latter has taken these divergent ways of eking out its powers.

The axiom schema of replacement is one of two well-known additions made to the Zermelo system by followers. The other is von Neumann's axiom of *Fundierung* or *regularity*:

$$(x)(x \neq \Lambda \,.\!\supset (\exists y)(y \in x \,.\, x \cap y = \Lambda)),$$

or, to exploit some abbreviations of ours, 'Fnd $\mathfrak{E}$'. This implies that $(z)(z \notin z)$, as seen in 20.4. More, it forbids any endless descent, repetitive or not, with respect to membership.[5] Clearly, by its consequence '$(z)(z \notin z)$' alone, it is not for us with our theory of individuals as $x = \{x\}$. And even if we resolve to foreswear individuals in this or any sense, 'Fnd $\mathfrak{E}$' remains a

[5] This consequence is called the *Fundierungsaxiom* too, or the weaker form thereof. Mendelson calls the stronger form the axiom of restriction. They can be proved equivalent using the axiom of choice; but not otherwise unless the system is inconsistent. See Mendelson, pp. 201f. The idea of excluding endless descents dates from Mirimanoff (1917). He did not impose this restriction by a direct axiom, but he imposed it at one remove: his axioms that provided for the existence of $\bigcup x$, $\{y: y \subseteq x\}$, and the like were limited to classes x that do not subtend endless descents with respect to membership. Von Neumann gave the axiom its general formulation within his system in 1929, and showed that the adding of it leaves his system consistent if it was consistent before. (See also von Neumann, 1925, §VI.) Zermelo added it to his own system in 1930.

restraint on other counts. It implies e.g. that $\mathcal{V} \notin \mathcal{V}$, also that $^-\{x\} \notin \mathcal{V}$, also that $^-\text{N} \notin \mathcal{V}$, since each of these classes would be a member of itself if it existed.

Granted, these non-existences are implied anyway by others of Zermelo's axioms, and the *Fundierung* axiom saves steps; it would have shortened our definition 22.15 of 'NO' and some related proofs, and it would have freed '$\sim(x < x)$' from the premiss '$x \in \text{N}$' that it needed in 13.20. It is one way of doing things, one of the variant set-theoretic devices to know about. If the classes it precludes are not wanted, its sweep is gratifyingly clean. If on the other hand a comprehension principle with desirable features of its own conflicts with it, there is no *a priori* reason for it to stand.

One might even go beyond the axiom of *Fundierung* and adopt rather the corresponding axiom schema:

$$\alpha \neq \Lambda \,.\supset (\exists y)(y \in \alpha \,.\, \alpha \cap y = \Lambda).$$

Another schema that comes to the same thing is:

$$\{x\colon x \subseteq \beta\} \subseteq \beta \,.\supset.\, \beta = \mathcal{V},$$

as may be seen by thinking of β as $\bar{\alpha}$.

Twice lately we adduced consistency proofs of incipient set theories, by citing a simple model in finite sets. This particular model is precluded once we adopt an axiom of infinity, whether that of the theory of types or the '$\text{N} \in \mathcal{V}$' of the Zermelo system. Consistency becomes more questionable, and consistency proofs become more urgent. But they also become more difficult and less conclusive. The more elaborate the apparatus to which a consistency proof appeals, the more room there is for questioning the consistency of that apparatus itself and so for questioning the conclusion that the apparatus was used to establish. In the more speculative axiomatizations of set theory the most we can usually aspire to in the way of a consistency proof is a proof that one such system is consistent if another somewhat less mistrusted one is consistent. We shall see something in this vein in §44.

XIII | STRATIFICATION AND ULTIMATE CLASSES

40. "New foundations"

We saw that in the Zermelo system, particularly with the axiom schema of replacement added, class existence is a question of size. Thus $\mathcal{V} \notin \mathcal{V}$. Further $(x)(\bar{x} \notin \mathcal{V})$; for otherwise $x \cup \bar{x} \in \mathcal{V}$ and so $\mathcal{V} \in \mathcal{V}$. Thus the universe is not closed with respect to the functions of the Boolean algebra of classes. Boolean algebra survives only relativized (§33); a class x has as complement only $y \cap \bar{x}$, relative to an arbitrary class y in lieu of $\mathcal{V}$. The same situation indeed obtained under the theory of types, but there it was less conspicuous, since each type was closed under the Boolean operations and any thought of a class transcending types was closed off as a matter of course.

Zermelo's system in its main outlines came of the theory of types (in Chapter XII, not historically) by the switch to general variables and cumulative types. Now there is also a different way of departing from the theory of types. To prepare ourselves for this alternative departure, we shall reflect for two paragraphs on how it was that the theory of types excluded the paradoxes.

The law of comprehension:

$$\text{(i)} \qquad (\exists y)(x)(x \in y \mathrel{.{\equiv}} Fx)$$

is in general what we restrict to avoid the paradoxes. In the theory of types, however, logic itself was weakened to a many-sorted form; and what was then required of (i) was only, as of other formulas, that 'ϵ' be flanked always by variables with consecutive ascending indices. Or, under typical ambiguity, the requirement was that there be a way of so *supplying* indices that 'ϵ' comes to be thus flanked. Let us speak of a formula without indices as *stratified* if it is so constituted, i.e., if there is a way of so supplying indices that 'ϵ' comes to occur always between consecutive ascending indices.

So the overt restriction that the theory of types (with typical ambiguity) imposes on the law of comprehension is that every instance of it be stratified. Equivalently we can state the restriction more narrowly: it is that the formula put for 'Fx' in the law of comprehension be stratified. The reason this is equivalent is that whenever the formula represented by 'Fx' is stratified, so is '$x \epsilon y .\equiv Fx$', since 'y' can always be given the index next above that given to 'x'. The reason 'y' can always be given this index is that 'y' does not recur in the formula represented by 'Fx' (not free anyway, and if bound it can be relettered). And the reason 'y' is not a free variable of the formula represented by 'Fx' in (i), finally, is clear to all readers who weathered the remark on substitution toward the middle of §1.

The alternative departure from the theory of types that suggests itself, finally, is this: that we reconstrue unindexed variables as truly general variables (rather than as typically ambiguous), but yet keep the restriction on (i) that the particular formulas put for 'Fx' must be stratified. Such is the system called "NF," "New foundations," from the title of the paper in which I proposed it. It has just the axiom of extensionality and, for stratified 'Fx', the axiom schema (i). The version of individuals is again $x = \{x\}$, the definition of '$x = y$' is again '$(z)(z \epsilon x .\equiv. z \epsilon y)$', and indeed the definitions generally of Chapters I–III can be carried over. In particular the axiom condenses to:

(ii) $$x = y \,.\, x \epsilon z \,.\supset.\, y \epsilon z,$$

which is the same as 4.1 and as in (vii) of §38. The axiom schema condenses to:

(iii) $$\{x\colon Fx\} \epsilon \mathcal{V} \qquad (\text{'}Fx\text{' stratified}).$$[1]

[1] The reader will perceive that this parenthetical tag is itself a condensation. In full it means, "Substitute only stratified formulas for 'Fx' here."

Because of this stratification proviso, the definitions having to do with number in §12 and §22 are ill suited to NF. We succeed better in proving existence of requisite classes in NF when we construe numbers in the Frege–Whitehead–Russell way than by following von Neumann or Zermelo.[2] Happily the obstacle that Zermelo's set theory raised to Frege numbers as oversize classes is not raised by NF.

A couple of points about the stratification test should be mentioned. As described, the test involves assigning the same index to all recurrences of a variable; still, we can as well treat a bound variable as a different variable whenever requantified, and so account the formula:

$$(x)(x \in y) \supset (\exists x)(y \in x)$$

stratified. This ruling is a matter only of convenience, since relettering could otherwise be resorted to for the same end.

The other point is that the notion of stratification applies in theory only to primitive notation. If a formula contains defined notations, these must be imagined expanded far enough to expose all implicit primitive epsilons for the space of stratification tests.

In NF there are no types. Nor is it required that formulas be stratified to be meaningful. Stratification is simply an ultimate, irreducible stipulation to which a formula is to conform *if* it is to qualify as a case of 'Fx' in the particular axiom schema (i). The classes thus provided by (i) are not reduplicated from type to type; they are absolute. $\mathcal{V}$, for instance, whose existence is assured by (i) because '$x = x$' is stratified, is the whole universe. Again $\bar{z}$, whose existence is assured by (i) because '$x \notin z$' is stratified, is the true and unlimited complement of z. The universe of NF indeed affords the Boolean algebra of classes.

Stratification is not necessary to the existence of a class. It is necessary merely to direct proof of existence by (i) (or (iii)). Indirectly we can often prove the existence also of classes that are given by unstratified membership conditions. For example,

---

[2] The theory of cardinal and ordinal numbers in the sense of Whitehead and Russell is developed from NF in great detail by Rosser in *Logic for Mathematicians*.

we have by (i) that

$$(z)(w)(\exists y)(x)(x \in y \;.\equiv:\; x \in z \;.\mathrm{v}.\; x \in w),$$

or in short $(z)(w)(z \cup w \in \mathcal{V})$, since '$x \in z \;.\mathrm{v}.\; x \in w$' is stratified. But *then* we can proceed to take the w as $\{z\}$; for, by (iii), $\{z\} \in \mathcal{V}$, and furthermore our variables are general. We conclude in this indirect way that $z \cup \{z\} \in \mathcal{V}$. We could not have proved this by just one step of (i) (or (iii)), since '$x \in z \;.\mathrm{v}.\; x = z$' is unstratified. But by indirection of this sort we get part of the benefit of a cumulative theory of types.

We also miss part. Ordered pairs are indeed forthcoming unrestrictedly: (iii) gives that '$(z)(w)(\langle z, w\rangle \in \mathcal{V})$', and then substitution gives unstratified cases such as '$(z)(\langle z, \{z\}\rangle \in \mathcal{V})$'. Even so, NF retains something very like the ban on heterogeneous relations: we do not get any such theorem schema as '$\{\langle z, \{z\}\rangle: Fz\} \in \mathcal{V}$' from (iii) either directly or with help of subsequent substitution. On this score NF is less liberal than the cumulative theory of types.

In important ways, on the other hand, NF is more liberal than the cumulative theory of types. It is not subject to ceilings; $\mathcal{V} \in \mathcal{V}$, after all. Far from having specially to postulate an infinite class as Whitehead and Russell did and as Zermelo did, NF gets one outright in $\mathcal{V}$; and (iii) assures no end of members of it, e.g. Λ, $\{\Lambda\}$, $\{\{\Lambda\}\}$, and so on. By this last consideration, indeed, the $\mathcal{V}$ of NF literally meets the condition on 'x' in Zermelo's axiom of infinity ((v) of §39).

It is not a foregone conclusion that NF dodges the paradoxes just because the theory of types does.[3] Can we say really that NF adheres to the comprehension axiom schema of the theory of types, after all? Only if we hasten to add that, in transmuting the typically ambiguous variables into general variables, NF perilously strengthens the rules of inference. For we saw that the formula:

$$\text{(iv)} \qquad (x)(x \in y) \supset (\exists z)(y \in z)$$

---

[3] I mean always the theory of types without the axiom of infinity, except where otherwise indicated.

((ii) of §37) can be affirmed outright as a case of the valid schema '$(x)Fxy \supset (\exists z)Fyz$' of the logic of quantification when our variables are taken as general, and not when they are taken merely as typically ambiguous.

We noted that the example (iv) happened to hold true even with its variables typically ambiguous, but true by set theory and not by the logic of quantification alone. Take the variables as general, and (iv) is logically valid; take them as typically ambiguous and (iv) is not logically valid, but is still provable in the theory of types. Now we may wonder whether this is always the way, or whether on the contrary

(A) Some stratified formula, though logically valid when its variables are taken as general, is not provable in the theory of types when the variables are reconstrued as typically ambiguous.

An equivalent of (A) is this:

(B) Some stratified theorem of NF is not provable in the theory of types when the variables are reconstrued as typically ambiguous.

If (A) is true then obviously (B) is, since the logically valid formula is *ipso facto* a theorem of NF. Conversely, then, assume (B); to prove (A). Let T be the stratified theorem as of (B). So T is provable by logic from some axioms of NF: (ii) and some cases of (iii), call them $(\text{iii})_1, \ldots, (\text{iii})_n$. Hence the conditional C, whose antecedent consists of (ii), $(\text{iii})_1, \ldots, (\text{iii})_n$ and whose consequent is T, is logically valid. Further, C is stratified; for each of (ii), $(\text{iii})_1, \ldots, (\text{iii})_n$, and T is stratified, and we can insulate each from the others by universally quantifying its free variables. Now (ii) and the cases of (iii) hold also in the theory of types, when definitions are expanded and variables are reconstrued as typically ambiguous (cf. (v) and (iv) of §36). Yet T, with variables similarly reconstrued, is not there provable (cf. (B)). Nor, then, is C; and so (A) holds.

If (A) and (B) are false, as the example (iv) prepared us to imagine, then the consistency of NF follows from that of the theory of types. For, if any contradiction is provable in NF, then so are all, including stratified ones; and these, failing (B), would then be provable in the theory of types as well.

Nor let us be stampeded to the contrary conclusion by NF's show of strength in producing Zermelo's axiom of infinity. It, after all, is unstratified; NF could still remain as weak as the theory of types in stratified matters. In fact it does not; (B) proves true; but we shall have to await §41 for the evidence.

(B) closes off what would have been an easy proof of the consistency of NF, but it does not impute inconsistency. So let us press on hopefully. Specker (1958, 1962) shows that the question of the consistency of NF is equivalent to the question whether the theory of types, in the form (iv) and (v) of §36, remains consistent when we add to it a sheaf of *axioms of typical ambiguity* as follows. In any sentence, without free variables, raise all indices by 1; then the biconditional equating the original sentence and the resulting sentence qualifies as an axiom of typical ambiguity. Intuitively the import of these axioms is that one type is formally like another.

Specker's result is more interesting than reassuring; for Cantor's theorem, in making all types differ in size, lends only implausibility to the axioms of typical ambiguity. However, it is a question not of truth of those axioms, but only of their being consistent with (iv) and (v) of §36; and this, as Specker suggests (1962, pp. 117–119), is less implausible.

41. Non-Cantorian classes. Induction again

To prove along the lines of 28.16 and 28.17 that $z \prec \{x\colon x \subseteq z\}$ we need that

$$(w)(z \cap \{y\colon y \notin w`y\} \in \mathcal{V});$$

and whereas this was forthcoming in Zermelo's system and the theory of cumulative types (cf. (ix) of §38), it is not forthcoming from (iii) of §40, because '$y \notin w`y$' is unstratified. Here is another illustration of the respect in which NF is less liberal than the theory of cumulative types. On this point NF is in much the same situation as was the ordinary theory of types with pairs defined (cf. (viii) and (ix), §36). Thus what we succeed in proving in NF is not '$z \prec \{x: x \subseteq z\}$' but rather the counterpart of (ix) of §36, briefly '$\iota``z \prec \{x: x \subseteq z\}$'.

But there is a difference still, on this point, between NF and the theory of types with pairs defined. In the theory of types with pairs defined, '$z \prec \{x: x \subseteq z\}$' as of the ordinary definition came out not false but meaningless; consequently we were free to enlist (ix) of §36 (in effect '$\iota``z \prec \{x: x \subseteq z\}$') as redefinition of '$z \prec \{x: x \subseteq z\}$' and so sustain Cantor's theorem after all. In NF, on the other hand, '$z \prec \{x: x \subseteq z\}$' as of the ordinary definition (11.1, 20.3) is as meaningful as is '$\iota``z \prec \{x: x \subseteq z\}$', and the two are not to be confused. The latter is a theorem of NF. But the former—Cantor's theorem proper, '$z \prec \{x: x \subseteq z\}$' —is for NF true for some z and false for others. Clearly it is false where z is $\mathcal{V}$. NF is spared '$\mathcal{V} \prec \{x: x \subseteq \mathcal{V}\}$', or '$\mathcal{V} \prec \mathcal{V}$', by a breakdown in the very proof of '$z \prec \{x: x \subseteq z\}$'. Zermelo's system was spared it rather by not having $\mathcal{V}$.

Very well; in NF we escape '$\mathcal{V} \prec \mathcal{V}$' for lack of '$z \prec \{x: x \subseteq z\}$'. But we do not lack '$\iota``z \prec \{x: x \subseteq z\}$' as a theorem, nor therefore do we escape '$\iota``\mathcal{V} \prec \{x: x \subseteq \mathcal{V}\}$', i.e., '$\iota``\mathcal{V} \prec \mathcal{V}$'. Is this paradoxical? Surely '$\iota``z \prec z$' seems paradoxical for any z, since Func $\breve{\iota}$ and $z \subseteq \breve{\iota}``(\iota``z)$ and so presumably $z \preceq \iota``z$, contrary to '$\iota``z \prec z$'. But see the *non sequitur*: the step to '$z \preceq \iota``z$' presupposed that $\breve{\iota} \in \mathcal{V}$. From the counterinstance '$\iota``\mathcal{V} \prec \mathcal{V}$' of '$z \preceq \iota``z$' we must then conclude, to the contrary, that $\breve{\iota} \notin \mathcal{V}$. Then also $\iota \notin \mathcal{V}$ (for, by (iii) of §40, $(x)(\breve{x} \in \mathcal{V})$).

One does expect $z \simeq \iota``z$, so there is oddity here even if not contradiction. Yet the theory of types with pairs defined was no better on the point; just less outspoken. There '$\iota$' or '$\{\langle x, y\rangle: x = \{y\}\}$' was meaningless, and so was '$z \simeq \iota``z$' or '$z \simeq \{\{v\}: v \in z\}$' and so were '$z \preceq \{\{v\}: v \in z\}$' and '$\{\{v\}: v \in z\} \prec z$' until, saving the surface, we reconstrued these last two systematically as having the same senses respectively as:

$$\{\{v\}: v \in z\} \preceq \{\{v\}: v \in z\}, \qquad \{\{v\}: v \in z\} \prec \{\{v\}: v \in z\}.$$

NF is no odder over these matters than the theory of types with pairs defined, except in being able to say more.

Not, of course, that $(z)(\iota``z \prec z)$. It all depends on $z$. Yes, $\iota``\mathcal{V} \prec \mathcal{V}$; still, for many or most z, $z \simeq \iota``z$. Anything $z$ thus well behaved is in Rosser's terminology *Cantorian*. Thus a class $z$ is Cantorian if $z \simeq \iota``z$. For Cantorian z, Cantor's theorem '$z \prec \{x: x \subseteq z\}$' holds as usual. It is just that $\mathcal{V}$ along with sundry other outsize classes (among them NO) is not Cantorian.

Classes that are not Cantorian behave unconventionally in various connections. Specker has shown that they cause the relations of less to greater among cardinal numbers to fail of being a well-ordering.[1] I shall indicate something of the nature of his remarkable proof.

We noted toward the end of §30 that $^{=}\{z: z \subseteq x\} = 2^{\bar{\bar{x}}}$. Specker introduces a variant sense of '2^y' to make '$y < 2^y$' stratified; he identifies $^{=}\{z: z \subseteq x\}$ rather with $2^{^{=}(\iota``x)}$—which is the same as $2^{\bar{\bar{x}}}$ when x is Cantorian. More fully, he provides that

$$\text{(i)} \qquad y = {}^{=}(\iota``x) \;.\supset.\; 2^y = {}^{=}\{z: z \subseteq x\},$$

$$\text{(ii)} \qquad y > {}^{=}(\iota``\mathcal{V}) \;.\supset.\; 2^y = \Lambda.$$

If y is precisely $^{=}(\iota``\mathcal{V})$, then (i) gives $2^y = {}^{=}\mathcal{V}$ and (ii) gives $2^{2^y} = \Lambda$. If $y < {}^{=}(\iota``\mathcal{V})$, we have both $2^y \neq \Lambda$ and $2^{2^y} \neq \Lambda$. In general the class whose members are y, 2^y, 2^{2^y}, and so on, to and excluding Λ, Specker calls $\phi(y)$. Thus, for any cardinal number y,

$$\text{(iii)} \qquad y \leqq {}^{=}(\iota``\mathcal{V}) \;.\supset.\; y, 2^y \in \phi(y),$$

$$\text{(iv)} \qquad y > {}^{=}(\iota``\mathcal{V}) \;.\supset.\; \{y\} = \phi(y).$$

---

1 1953. Rosser and Wang had already shown that no model of NF—no interpretation of 'ϵ' compatible with the axioms—could make well-orderings of both the less-to-greater relation among ordinals and that among finite cardinals, unless at the cost of not interpreting the '=' of NF as identity. Note that the relevant versions of cardinals and ordinals are as in Whitehead and Russell.

Specker defines Ty as how many unit subclasses there are in a class of y members. Thus

(v) $$\mathrm{T}\bar{\bar{x}} = {}^{=}(\iota``x).$$

When x is Cantorian, of course $\mathrm{T}\bar{\bar{x}} = \bar{\bar{x}}$. For any cardinal numbers, as Specker proves,

(vi) $$y \leqq {}^{=}(\iota``\mathrm{V}) \;.\supset.\; \mathrm{T}2^{y} = 2^{\mathrm{T}y},$$

(vii) $$\phi(y) \text{ is finite } .\equiv.\; \phi(\mathrm{T}y) \text{ is finite},$$

(viii) $$x \leqq y \;.\equiv.\; \mathrm{T}x \leqq \mathrm{T}y,$$

(ix) $$y \leqq \mathrm{T}z \;.\supset (\exists x)(y = \mathrm{T}x).$$

Next suppose (a) that $\phi(y)$ has but one member. Still $\mathrm{T}y \leqq {}^{=}(\iota``\mathrm{V})$ by (v) and so, by (iii), we have $\mathrm{T}y$, $2^{\mathrm{T}y} \in \phi(\mathrm{T}y)$; so in this case $\phi(y) \prec \phi(\mathrm{T}y)$. Or suppose (b) that $\phi(y)$ has several members. They are y and those of $\phi(2^{y})$; so, if $\phi(2^{y}) \prec \phi(2^{\mathrm{T}y})$, it follows that $\phi(y) \prec \phi(\mathrm{T}y)$. But, by (vi), $2^{\mathrm{T}y} = \mathrm{T}2^{y}$. So

$$\phi(2^{y}) \prec \phi(\mathrm{T}2^{y}) \;.\supset.\; \phi(y) \prec \phi(\mathrm{T}y).$$

From this and the finding under (a) it follows by induction, for all cardinal numbers y such that $\phi(y)$ is finite, that $\phi(y) \prec \phi(\mathrm{T}y)$. Supposing now *per impossible* that the relation of less to greater among cardinals is a well-ordering, let z be the least cardinal which (like ${}^{=}\mathrm{V}$ or ${}^{=}(\iota``\mathrm{V})$) is such that $\phi(z)$ is finite. Then, as we just saw, $\phi(z) \prec \phi(\mathrm{T}z)$. So $z \neq \mathrm{T}z$. Still $\phi(\mathrm{T}z)$ is finite, by (vii); so, by the leastness of z, $z < \mathrm{T}z$. So, by (ix), $z = \mathrm{T}x$ for some x. So $\mathrm{T}x < \mathrm{T}z$. So, by (viii), $x \leqq z$. But also, since $z = \mathrm{T}x$, $\phi(\mathrm{T}x)$ is finite. So, by (vii), $\phi(x)$ is finite. So, by leastness of z $x = z$. So $\mathrm{T}x = \mathrm{T}z$. That is, $z = \mathrm{T}z$; a contradiction.

It was remarked in §40 that the Frege version of cardinals is the one for NF. And it was remarked in §33 that the proof that the relation of less to greater among these cardinals is a well-ordering depends, unlike the proof of the corresponding fact about von Neumann's cardinals, upon the axiom of choice. For this reason Specker's negative theorem is not a contradiction. But it is, as he points out, a disproof of the axiom of choice in NF.

The result can be accommodated, as Rosser remarks (1954), by conceding failure of the axiom of choice for non-Cantorian classes and reserving still the right to assume it for Cantorian classes. So what we have is just another case, and a beauty, of unconventional behavior on the part of non-Cantorian classes. There is a question whether it is to be more deplored than 'ι"$z \prec z$', which was unconventional already. Classical results can still be got in NF by inserting, where needed, a premiss that a class concerned is Cantorian. One could look upon NF as merely more general, in this respect, than set theories where everything is Cantorian.

Our next topic of concern in connection with NF is an abrupt comedown from infinite cardinals and the axiom of choice. It is the humdrum matter of mathematical induction over natural numbers. This story begins as in (ii) and (iii) of §39: classically we would define N in terms of 0 and S as in (ii) of §39 and then we would get the schema (iii) of induction by taking y as $\{z: Fz\}$. As usual the difficulty comes in showing that $\{z: Fz\} \in \mathcal{V}$. In NF, specifically, this difficulty comes when the formula in the role of 'Fz' is not stratified. The next phase of the story is still as in §39: we try inverting (ii) to (iv) so as to base induction on finite classes, since our comprehension schema gives '$\Lambda, x \cup \{y\} \in \mathcal{V}$' and so guarantees all finite classes. And again we come to the same *impasse* as in §39: we need, despite the finite classes, a proof that

$$\text{(x)} \qquad x \in \mathrm{N} \,.\supset.\, \{z: z \leqq x \,.\, {\sim}Fz\} \in \mathcal{V},$$

and there is no evident way of getting it without induction.

In Zermelo's system, which we were concerned with in those pages of §39, this obstacle was negotiated by postulating '$\mathrm{N} \in \mathcal{V}$' and then inferring (x) above, or even '$\mathrm{N} \cap \{z: Fz\} \in \mathcal{V}$', by *Aussonderung*. This course is not open to NF, for obviously

Aussonderung itself fails for NF; with '$\mathcal{V} \in \mathcal{V}$' it would give '$\mathcal{V} \cap \alpha \in \mathcal{V}$' and so '$\alpha \in \mathcal{V}$' unconditionally. We could simply add (x) above as a further axiom schema, or again we could add a form of 13.1; but not without a sense of defeat.

Here in NF we are to be understood as working with the Frege numbers, out of motives of stratification lately noted, rather than with the numbers of Zermelo or von Neumann. Now the Frege numbers were immune to the induction trouble of §39, at least in the theory of types. But that was because arithmetic was conducted in each type separately. A pride of NF, on the contrary, is that the type-to-type reduplication of numbers is done away with. This fusing of types invites some unstratified formulas, and so induction trouble can recur.

On the other hand it will be supposed that NF is free of the finitude trouble that touched the Frege arithmetic under the theory of types. An axiom of infinity was there needed, (i) of §39, to assure uniqueness of subtraction. Here, it will be supposed, NF is in the clear. It has, we saw, infinite classes—notably $\mathcal{V}$—without *ad hoc* postulation.

However, finitude and infinity are deceptive. We already saw to our surprise that although both Zermelo's system and NF provide all finite classes (Λ, $x \cup \{y\} \in \mathcal{V}$), and although mathematical induction requires no infinite classes (cf. Ch. IV), still there was induction trouble in both systems. And now can we be sure that the access that NF provides to infinite classes is of quite the sort needed to assure uniqueness of subtraction? It will be recalled that the subtraction trouble comes in Frege–Russell arithmetic when a natural number *n* turns out to be Λ because no class has enough members (viz. *n*) to qualify as a member of *n*. If we can show on the contrary that no natural number reduces thus to Λ—in short, that $\Lambda \notin \mathrm{N}$—then our troubles about the uniqueness of subtraction are over.[2] But can we prove in NF that $\Lambda \notin \mathrm{N}$? Granted, $\mathcal{V} \in \mathcal{V}$; granted, $\mathcal{V}$ has no end of members Λ, $\{\Lambda\}$, $\{\{\Lambda\}\}$, . . . , all distinct; still, just try to prove that $\Lambda \notin \mathrm{N}$.

---

[2] '$\Lambda \notin \mathrm{N}$' recalls a version of the axiom of infinity in §39, note 1.

A natural plan would be to prove it by induction. We easily prove that $0 \neq \Lambda$ (for the Frege 0, viz. $\{\Lambda\}$). If we can prove further that $(x)(x \neq \Lambda \,.\supset.\, S`x \neq \Lambda)$ for the Frege S, then we can conclude by mathematical induction that $(x)(x \in N \,.\supset.\, x \neq \Lambda)$, or briefly $\Lambda \notin N$. Induction is all right here, for there is no failure of stratification; $\{x\colon x \neq \Lambda\} \in \mathcal{V}$. The problem is how to prove that $(x)(x \neq \Lambda \,.\supset.\, S`x \neq \Lambda)$, i.e., that $\breve{S}``\{\Lambda\} \subseteq \{\Lambda\}$.

No way suggests itself of getting a foothold. So we try for a more substantial induction: we try proving of each $x \in N$ not just that $x \neq \Lambda$ but that some specific class, determined by x, is a member of x. And what class? By all means $\{y\colon y < x\}$; there are x numbers $< x$. So we proceed to prove that

$$\{y\colon y < 0\} \in 0,$$
$$(x)(x \in N \,.\, \{y\colon y < x\} \in x \,.\supset.\, \{y\colon y < S`x\} \in S`x).$$

The task is not formidable. But then the remaining step fails us, the inductive step to:

$$z \in N \,.\supset.\, \{y\colon y < z\} \in z.$$

For the trouble now is that '$\{y\colon y < x\} \in x$' turns out to be unstratified when expanded according to definitions appropriate to the Frege numbers, and so resists induction. Orey shows this induction to be unmanageable in NF if NF is consistent.

One may have been tempted to feel that the failure in NF of induction for unstratified conditions was unlikely to stand in the way of inferences we want to make. One is then disabused by the above example.

The question whether '$\Lambda \notin N$' could be proved in NF was recognized for a while, in various publications, as an open question. Indeed '$\Lambda \notin N$' was bound to be unproved as long as (B) of §40 above was an open question. For '$\Lambda \notin N$' is not provable in the theory of types; this can be shown by showing that it is not true ('$\Lambda \in N$' is) in the model universe of finite classes that was used in §36 to establish the consistency of the theory of types. Moreover, '$\Lambda \notin N$' is stratified. So, if it is a theorem of NF, (B) is true.

On the basis of his disproof for NF of the axiom of choice, Specker stated (*ibid.*) that '$\Lambda \notin N$' is indeed a theorem of NF. (So (B) is true.[3]) Something of the connection of ideas may be seen thus: the axiom of choice is true for finite classes (31.3), yet false in NF; so there are infinite classes in NF; so $\Lambda \notin N$. Of course this sketch is not of itself conclusive; we already knew there was an infinite class $\mathcal{V}$ in NF, and were not thereby enabled to prove that $\Lambda \notin N$. But our ground for calling $\mathcal{V}$ infinite had been only the egregiously unstratified consideration that Λ, $\{\Lambda\}$, $\{\{\Lambda\}\}$, $\ldots \in \mathcal{V}$. Specker's route works because essential formulas along the way are stratified.[4]

The demonstrability of '$\Lambda \notin N$' suggests that the non-Cantorian classes, with all their unconventional behavior, are not just a harmless annex to an otherwise well-behaved universe, but a valuable intermediary in proving desirable theorems about the well-behaved objects themselves. For it is the failure of the axiom of choice for non-Cantorian classes that has enabled Specker to prove '$\Lambda \notin N$', which itself says nothing of non-Cantorian classes.

But NF must still be said to leave something to be desired in respect of mathematical induction. Granted that the most notable failure of mathematical induction has been saved by Specker in '$\Lambda \notin N$', the fact remains that mathematical induction of unstratified conditions is not generally provided for in NF. This omission seems needless and arbitrary. It hints that the standards of class existence in NF approximate insufficiently, after all, to the considerations that are really central to the paradoxes and their avoidance.

42. Ultimate classes added

The primitive predicate '$\in$' divides the purposes of classes into (a) the purpose, after epsilon, of having members, and (b) the

---

[3] That (B) is true was first brought to my attention by Putnam; see my "Unification of universes," p. 270. His argument likewise uses Specker's results.

[4] Nicholas Goodman has supplied the details in a Harvard honors thesis, 1961.

purpose, before epsilon, of being members. Now our worries early and late over mathematical induction have been worries over the existence of classes that were needed solely for purpose (a). In order to derive the schema of mathematical induction from the definition of N, we need a class $\{x\colon Fx\}$ or N $\cap$ $\{x\colon Fx\}$ or $\{x\colon x \leqq z \,.\sim Fx\}$, on alternative approaches, as value of a variable of that definition; and it is a variable that stands only at the right of 'ϵ'. So the idea suggests itself of buttressing NF against the failure of induction, and any other failures of this pure post-epsilon type, by postulating the missing classes in a halfway status limited to purpose (a). Now virtual classes as of 2.1 serve only purpose (a), but the trouble with them is that they are not values of variables. For induction we do need $\{x\colon Fx\}$ or the like as a value of the variable in the definition of N. So what are wanted are precisely the *ultimate classes* (§§2, 6).

Without reactivating the paradoxes we can postulate unreservedly, for every membership condition, a class (perhaps ultimate) whose members are precisely the *sets* fulfilling that membership condition. That is, since to call x a set is merely to say that $(\exists z)(x \in z)$,

(i) $$(\exists y)(x)(x \in y \,.\!\equiv\!.\, (\exists z)(x \in z) \,.\, Fx).$$

Or, since

(ii) $$(\exists z)(x \in z) \equiv\!.\, x \in \cup\mathcal{V},$$

we may say more succinctly:

(iii) $$\alpha \cap \cup\mathcal{V} \in \mathcal{V}.$$

The underlying definitions may be understood still to be as in Chapters I–III, thus carrying no presumption that $\alpha \in \mathcal{V}$ or $\mathcal{V} \in \mathcal{V}$ or $\cup\mathcal{V} \in \mathcal{V}$. From (iii) we do get that $\cup\mathcal{V} \in \mathcal{V}$, of course, by taking α as $\cup\mathcal{V}$ or as $\mathcal{V}$. Whether $(\exists z)(\cup\mathcal{V} \in z)$, however, i.e., $\cup\mathcal{V} \in \cup\mathcal{V}$, or whether $\cup\mathcal{V}$ is an ultimate class, is another question, which we are free to settle by further postulation.

$\cup\mathcal{V}$, then, is the class of all sets. It is the most inclusive of all classes. Granted, $\mathcal{V}$ is yet more inclusive, if there are ultimate classes; for they belong to $\mathcal{V}$ (everything does) and not to $\mathsf{U}\mathcal{V}$. But the catch is that $\mathcal{V} \notin \mathcal{V}$ (if there are any ultimate classes); thus $\mathsf{U}\mathcal{V}$ is still the most inclusive class there *is*. If there are no ultimate classes, $\mathsf{U}\mathcal{V} = \mathcal{V}$; such was the way of the unsupplemented NF. Such, for that matter, was 8.8, which is to say 7.11; but remember that the '$\{x\} \in \mathcal{V}$' on which 7.11 depended is itself repudiated if we posit ultimate classes. After all, '$x \in \{x\}$' says only that $x = x$, since we are still using class abstraction noncommittally as in 2.1; so we have $(x)(x \in \{x\})$ still and therefore, if x is an ultimate class, $x \in \{x\}$ and yet $(y)(x \notin y)$ and so $\{x\} \notin \mathcal{V}$.

Reference to the class of all sets as $\mathsf{U}\mathcal{V}$ will not have been seen in other literature, since it rests on my noncommittal use of class abstraction, specifically of '$\mathcal{V}$'. Sometimes a special symbol '$\mathfrak{M}$' is defined for the class of all sets. And in *Mathematical Logic* I used 'V', which there stood not for our '$\{u : u = u\}$' but for '$\hat{u}(u = u)$', hence '$\mathsf{U}\mathcal{V}$'. In general

(iv) '$\hat{u}Fu$' for '$\{u : Fu\} \cap \mathsf{U}\mathcal{V}$',

as explained in §6.

This distinction between $\mathcal{V}$ and V, and the corresponding point about $\{x\}$ (cf. §6), would have required notice even if there had been no prior *Mathematical Logic* to placate and the idea of supplementing NF with ultimate classes were being propounded here for the first time. NF all of itself, after all, with $\mathcal{V}$ as $\{u : u = u\}$ or $\hat{u}(u = u)$ as you please (these being the same when there are no ultimate classes), gave that $\mathcal{V} \in \mathcal{V}$. Add ultimate classes and you get that $\mathcal{V} \in \mathcal{V}$ still or that $\mathcal{V} \notin \mathcal{V}$, according as you tie the symbol '$\mathcal{V}$' to the object—first and last the class $\hat{u}(u = u)$ of all sets—or to the noncommittal abstraction expression '$\{u : u = u\}$', as I do. Similarly for '$\{x\}$' and other examples.

We are getting our enlarged universe by adding ultimate classes to the universe of NF. The resulting system might be called an enlargement of the system of NF. But it is not an *extension* of that system, in the technical sense of the term; it is not obtainable by adding axioms to those of NF. We added (iii), or '$\hat{u}Fu \in \mathcal{V}$', true. But we cannot simply keep the old comprehension schema of NF, viz. '$\{x: Fx\} \in \mathcal{V}$' ('$Fx$' stratified). We saw just now that '$\{x: x = x\} \in \mathcal{V}$', e.g., now becomes false. So does '$\{y: y = x\} \in \mathcal{V}$' as we saw. In order to keep the ontological content of the old comprehension schema of NF uncorrupted we have to relativize it (cf. §33) to '$\cup\mathcal{V}$'; what was existence for NF becomes sethood. Thus where NF said '$\{x: Fx\} \in \mathcal{V}$' we must now switch to '$\hat{u}Fu \in \cup\mathcal{V}$' and also restrict to sets (i.e., to '$\cup\mathcal{V}$') any variables hidden under the 'F'. What we may call our *sethood axioms* comprise, in short, relativizations to '$\cup\mathcal{V}$' of '$\hat{u}Fu \in \cup\mathcal{V}$' with stratified formulas in place of 'Fu'.

So our new system consists of these sethood axioms and in addition the wholly unrestricted comprehension schema '$\hat{u}Fu \in \mathcal{V}$' and the axiom of extensionality. This last is still '$x = y \,.\, x \in z \,.\!\supset\!.\, y \in z$' ((ii) of §40), and supposes still the definition of '$x = y$' as '$(z)(z \in x \,.\!\equiv\!.\, z \in y)$', or 2.7. And note that there is a new urgency to this definition now that ultimate classes are with us; '$(z)(x \in z \,.\!\equiv\!.\, y \in z)$' is no longer a live alternative, for it would make all ultimate classes identical.

Such is the system of my *Mathematical Logic*, later editions. In the first edition I relativized the sethood condition insufficiently, failing to restrict the bound variables to sets; and the result was that the system led to the Burali-Forti paradox, as Rosser showed (1942). The saving restriction of the bound variables is due to Wang (1950). The idea of admitting ultimate classes at all goes back to von Neumann (1925) and, in a way, to König (1905) and Cantor (1899).[1]

---

[1] The Cantor source is the letter, unpublished until 1932 (pp. 443f). The pair of contrasting terms 'set' and 'class' appeared already there and also in König. Whether to see Cantor's classes (other than sets) as virtual or as real is, as noted in §2 above, indifferent to the context. Seeing them as real is perhaps less farfetched, and certainly it fits König's phrasing best. But neither Cantor nor König cited the succinct condition of sethood '$(\exists y)(x \in y)$'. To have done that would have clearly suggested that classes other than sets were intended among the real values of variables. Strictly speaking '$(\exists y)(x \in y)$' figures only indirectly in von Neumann, for that matter, but that is only because of his unconventional starting point in functions (cf. §43 below). It comes to the fore when the approach is standardized.

Let us refer to the system, not the book, as ML. What belongs to it is only what is said in terms of 'ϵ', quantification, and truth functions. The whole matter of virtual classes and noncommittal abstraction is, as stressed in §38, style. Whether 'x is a set' comes to be rendered '$x \epsilon \mathrm{V}$' as in *Mathematical Logic* or '$x \epsilon \cup\mathcal{V}$' as in these pages is a difference only in definitions, extrinsic to ML; indeed '$(\exists y)(x \epsilon y)$', without definitions, fits either medium.

What launched us on ML, early in this section, was the trouble in NF over mathematical induction. Clearly ML removes this difficulty. We can define N again as in (ii) of §39:

(v) 'N' for '$\{x\colon (y)(0 \epsilon y \,.\, \mathrm{S}``y \subseteq y \,.\!\supset\!.\, x \epsilon y\}$'

and then derive the induction schema, (iii) of §39, by taking y as $\hat{u}Fu$, assured as we are that $\hat{u}Fu \epsilon \mathcal{V}$ categorically. It must be observed, however, that N has suffered a subtle change in the process. The above definition of N means something different for ML from what it did for NF, because the range of 'y' comes to include ultimate classes.[2] If we had wanted to assure that N be the same thing for ML as for NF, we would have restricted the quantification to sets. Our not doing so was in line with our policy on '$\mathcal{V}$' and '$\{x\}$' lately mentioned: a case of tying a defined sign to the abstraction expression rather than to the object. That plan is especially attractive in the present instance because *if* there is really a difference—if

(vi) $$\{x\colon (y)(0 \epsilon y \,.\, \mathrm{S}``y \subseteq y \,.\!\supset\!.\, x \epsilon y)\} \neq \{x\colon (y)(y \epsilon \cup\mathcal{V} \,.\, 0 \epsilon y \,.\, \mathrm{S}``y \subseteq y \,.\!\supset\!.\, x \epsilon y)\}$$

—then the class on the left is clearly the tighter one, and the class on the right contains extras. Obviously 0, 1, 2, and their suite belong to both classes; an inequality is bound therefore to discredit the right-hand expression, not the left, as a version of 'N'.

The class on the right will of course not contain extras if there is a set y whose members are exactly 0, 1, 2, and their suite. On

[2] Remarked by Rosser, 1952.

the contrary, the class on the right will then be precisely that set y, as desired. Conversely, if there is no such set y, then the class on the right will contain extras. For the formula proves to be stratified (when 'S' has the Frege sense of successor); hence the class qualifies as a set under the sethood axioms; hence it would itself count as a set y of precisely 0, 1, 2, and their suite unless it contained extras. To sum up, then, the class on the right is in any event a set, and it is the set precisely of 0, 1, 2, and their suite if such a set there be. And the class on the left differs from that on the right only if, on the contrary, there is no set precisely of 0, 1, 2, and their suite.

Can we in any event depend on the class on the left, the tighter of the two, to comprise precisely 0, 1, 2, and their suite? No; Henkin has a neat proof that no definition whatever of N can enable us to prove that N contains just 0, 1, 2, and their suite, without extras. His argument shows that so long as '$0 \in N$', '$1 \in N$', '$2 \in N$', etc. all hold, there can be no contradiction in supposing an extra $x \in N$ too—an x such that

(vii) $$x \in N, \quad x \neq 0, \quad x \neq 1, \quad x \neq 2, \ldots$$

ad infinitum. His argument is in effect this: since a proof can use only finitely many premisses, any proof of contradiction from (vii) will use only finitely many of the premisses (vii); but any such *finite* lot is *true* for some x.

We noted already in Chapter II that quantification over classes enabled us to formulate notions that would otherwise have been beyond us. The prime example was in effect the idiom 'and their suite', whether in '0, 1, 2, and their suite' or in the notion of ancestor. We noted also, from that chapter onward, that the universe of classes over which we quantify is an unsettled matter, varying from theory to theory. Similar variation is to be apprehended, then, in the notions formulated with the help of such quantification. This is a relativity theme that was stressed by Skolem (1922–23). And in particular it applies to the deceptively familiar words 'and their suite'; such is the startling conclusion of Henkin's simple argument.

Where contradictions cannot be deduced, models exist: such is the force of Gödel's 1930 theorem of the completeness of logic. By Henkin's argument, then, any set of conditions fulfilled by the natural numbers must admit also of what he calls a *nonstandard model*: an interpretation that lets in extras. One can see that '$<$' will not even well-order the extras, if Peano's axioms are present.

Gödel (1931) called a system *ω-inconsistent* when there was a formula, say 'Fx', such that each of '$F0$', '$F1$', . . . *ad infinitum* could be proved in the system but '$(\exists x)(x \in \mathrm{N} \,.\, {\sim}Fx)$' could be proved too.[3] In these terms, Henkin's argument shows the consistency of an ω-inconsistent system.[4] For interpret 'F' as true of everything except for some one object x which fulfills (vii).

A theory that is ω-inconsistent in the above sense sounds intolerable even if consistent. But one quickly sees from Henkin's argument (as Henkin did) that the term and its definition are misleading. If a system is consistent and yet has '$(\exists x)(x \in \mathrm{N} \,.\, {\sim}Fx)$' and '$F0$', '$F1$', . . . all as theorems, and we grant the interpretation of '0', '1', . . . as names of the numbers, then clearly the trouble lies in interpreting 'N' as 'number' and not more broadly. Such is ω-inconsistency. Henkin's argument in connection with (vii) showed that even under the best circumstances 'N' *can* be interpreted as having extra members; but ω-inconsistency is the situation where 'N' *must* be so interpreted. In this situation it is sometimes possible to devise a narrowed redefinition of 'N' that puts an end to such enforcement of extras (though by Henkin's argument the narrowed N could still be consistently reinterpreted to include extras). And sometimes it is not possible; for we can imagine its happening, in a particular system, that for every formulable condition that is demonstrably fulfilled by each of 0, 1, 2, etc. *ad infinitum* there is another condition that we can prove to be fulfilled still by each of 0, 1, 2, etc. and yet not by all things fulfilling the first condition. This is the chronic form of ω-inconsistency, not to be cured by im-

---

[3] Gödel, 1931, p. 187. See also Tarski, pp. 279n, 287f.

[4] Tarski and Gödel also showed the consistency, each, of an ω-inconsistent system; and Henkin cites related observations by Skolem and Malcev. What is special about Henkin's argument is its directness and simplicity.

proving the version of 'N'; every improved version stands improvement in turn. Systems thus afflicted I have called *numerically insegregative.*[5] In these terms the matters talked of as ω-inconsistency become easier to picture.[6]

But to return to (vi). Henkin's argument shows that ML or any other system, if consistent, admits a perverse interpretation under which both of the expressions in (vi) will cover more than the numbers. But his argument does not show that ML does not also admit a benign interpretation under which one or both expressions cover just the numbers. We do not know that ML is numerically insegregative.

If either of the classes described in (vi) fails to comprise precisely 0, 1, 2, and their suite, it will of course be because of failure of existence of needed classes, or sets, as values of the 'y'. What then if we resort again to the inversion expedient of §11? This would mean defining N as

$$\{x\colon (y)(x \in y\,.\,\check{\mathrm{S}}``y \subseteq y\,.\supset.\, 0 \in y)\}$$

and resting our case on the existence of all finite classes. Yet Henkin's argument is general. How can this definition fail? The question is confused. If we think that only finite classes matter in this inverted definition, it is because we are already thinking of 0, 1, 2, and their suite without extras.

An element of this last discussion that needs further attention also apart from Henkin's theorem is the question of the sethood of N. It was remarked that the class on the right in (vi) is a set; but what of that on the left, which is N according to (v)? The quantification in (v) is not restricted to sets as would be required for a sethood axiom. We might of course still seek an indirect proof in ML that N is a set; for, just as existence can sometimes be proved indirectly in NF despite failure of stratification, so

---

5 "On ω-inconsistency."

6 Rosser remarked (1952) that an ω-consistent theory could have an ω-inconsistent part. This sounds paradoxical. But there is nothing odd about a numerically segregative system with a numerically insegregative part; the containing system has more machinery for numerical segregation.

sethood can sometimes be proved indirectly in ML despite failure of stratification or failure of restriction of quantifiers. But no; Rosser has proved, remarkably, that sethood of N as defined in (v) is not provable in ML directly or indirectly unless ML is inconsistent.[7]

This does not mean that we cannot consistently add '$\mathrm{N} \in \mathrm{U}\mho$' to ML as a further sethood axiom, *ad hoc*. One's aesthetic sensibilities are of course against such a move. But the theory of real numbers cannot come to much unless N, or anyway no end of its infinite subclasses, are sets. For the real numbers are, with one exception, infinite subclasses of N; and they have to be sets if we are to put them in classes or subject them to functions. Granted, real numbers could be differently construed; but I see no reason to suppose that they can be so construed as to lighten this sort of problem.

A place other than induction where ultimate classes prove of service can be seen by following the non-Cantorian classes of NF (§41) into ML. In the transition from NF to ML the definition of '$\leq$' undergoes an invisible but substantial change like that which the definition of 'N' was seen to undergo. By 'invisible' I mean that the letter of the definition is unchanged. By 'substantial' I mean that the content is nevertheless changed, by the broadening of the range of the bound variables. The definition:

$$\text{`}y \leq z\text{' for `}(\exists w)(\mathrm{Func}\, w \,.\, y \subseteq w``z)\text{'}$$

has the effect in ML that $y \leq z$ even if there is no set w, but only an ultimate class w, such that $\mathrm{Func}\, w \,.\, y \subseteq w``z$; and in such a case NF would deny that $y \leq z$, though the definition stays literally the same. Now a non-Cantorian class was a class $z$ such that $\iota``z \prec z$. There is no such thing in ML (under the invisibly but substantially changed sense of '$\prec$'); on the contrary, $(z)(z \leq \iota``z)$—indeed $(z)(z \simeq \iota``z)$—since $z = \breve{\iota}``(\iota``z)$ and $\mathrm{Func}\, \breve{\iota}$ and, for ML, $\breve{\iota} \in \mho$ (even though $\breve{\iota} \notin \mathrm{U}\mho$). The ultimate class $\breve{\iota}$,

[7] 1952, p. 241.

added (with ι) to the universe of discourse in expanding NF to ML, has made the difference.

Everything of NF survives in the sets of ML; it is just that what the non-Cantorian goes over into ceases to seem anomalous. If x is non-Cantorian in NF, then x is a set in ML such that '$x \subseteq w``(\iota``x)$' fails for every function $w \in \mathsf{U}\mathcal{V}$ (though holding where $w = \breve{\iota}$). Still $x \lesssim \iota``x$ in the ML sense of '$\lesssim$', so there is no anomaly.

Another boon of ultimate classes is that with the passing of the non-Cantorian there passes also that remarkable failure of the axiom of choice, a failure that turned on non-Cantorian classes. Intuitively the relation is as follows. The axiom of choice failed for NF in that there was a non-Cantorian set x of exclusive sets that was without a selection set. In ML this same x is still a set of exclusive sets that is without a selection set, but it need no longer lack a selection class. The axiom of choice fails still in the strong form 'Every set of exclusive sets has a selection set', but there is no indication that it cannot still consistently be assumed for ML in the form 'Every set (even: Every class) of exclusive sets has a selection class'.

And what now of Cantor's theorem itself? To prove along the lines of 28.16 and 28.17 that $z \prec \{x\colon x \subseteq z\}$ we need that

$$(w)(z \cap \{u\colon u \notin w`u\} \in \mathcal{V}).$$

But ML gives this. For any member of z (or of anything real) is a set; so

$$z \cap \{u\colon u \notin w`u\} = \hat{u}(u \in z \,.\, u \notin w`u);$$

and we have categorically that $\hat{u}Fu \in \mathcal{V}$. Thus Cantor's theorem is proved in ML without special premiss or other restriction.

What then of Cantor's paradox? It is a matter of taking the z of Cantor's theorem '$z \prec \{x\colon x \subseteq z\}$' as $\mathcal{V}$ and so getting '$\mathcal{V} \prec \{x\colon x \subseteq \mathcal{V}\}$', i.e., '$\mathcal{V} \prec \mathcal{V}$'. But we cannot, since $\mathcal{V} \notin \mathcal{V}$ in ML. ML escapes Cantor's paradox not as NF did, by a breakdown in the proof of '$z \prec \{x\colon x \subseteq z\}$', but as Zermelo's system did: by not having $\mathcal{V}$.

This account of ML will startle readers of *Mathematical Logic*, until they reflect on what was said about confusing $\{u\colon Fu\}$ with $\hat{u}Fu$. ML does not give '$z \prec \hat{u}(u \subseteq z)$' in general; an exception comes where $z = \mathrm{U}\mathcal{V}$, since $\hat{u}(u \subseteq \mathrm{U}\mathcal{V})$ is $\mathrm{U}\mathcal{V}$ and of course '$\mathrm{U}\mathcal{V} \prec \mathrm{U}\mathcal{V}$' is false.

Let us see how one would try in vain to prove in ML the variant version '$z \prec \hat{u}(u \subseteq z)$' of Cantor's theorem. What one would try to produce, for every function w, is a member of $\hat{u}(u \subseteq z)$ not belonging to $w\text{``}z$. Under the plan of 28.16 and 28.17 the candidate would be, again, $z \cap \{u\colon u \notin w\text{`}u\}$, in other words $\hat{u}(u \in z \,.\, u \notin w\text{`}u)$. But the trouble is that this subclass of z might not be a set and so not be a member of $\hat{u}(u \subseteq z)$. The argument that it is always a set is obstructed by the unstratified character of '$u \notin w\text{`}u$'.

So we may say that Cantor's paradox is averted either by a nonexistence or by a nonsethood, depending on whether the paradox is sought along the lines of '$\{u\colon Fu\}$' or '$\hat{u}Fu$'.

A similar double story holds for Russell's paradox itself. On the one hand

$$\{u\colon u \notin u\} \in \{u\colon u \notin u\} \;.\!\equiv.\; \{u\colon u \notin u\} \in \mathcal{V} \,.\, \{u\colon u \notin u\} \notin \{u\colon u \notin u\}$$

(cf. 6.13), from which as usual we conclude on pain of contradiction that $\{u\colon u \notin u\} \notin \mathcal{V}$. And on the other hand

$$\hat{u}(u \notin u) \in \hat{u}(u \notin u) \;.\!\equiv.\; \hat{u}(u \notin u) \in \mathrm{U}\mathcal{V} \,.\, \hat{u}(u \notin u) \notin \hat{u}(u \notin u),$$

from which we conclude that $\hat{u}(u \notin u) \notin \mathrm{U}\mathcal{V}$; nor does a sethood axiom say otherwise, thanks to the unstratified character of '$u \notin u$'. Thus the class $\{u\colon u \notin u\}$ of all classes that are not members of themselves does not exist, whereas the class $\hat{u}(u \notin u)$ of all sets that are not members of themselves does exist but is an ultimate class.

XIV VON NEUMANN'S SYSTEM AND OTHERS

43. The von Neumann–Bernays system

I used the device of ultimate classes to enlarge NF. Von Neumann used it in 1925 to enlarge Zermelo's system. But von Neumann's enlargement of Zermelo's system stopped short of the full force of the axiom schema '$\hat{u}Fu \in \mathcal{V}$' (or (iii) of §42). His system gives '$\hat{u}Fu \in \mathcal{V}$' where the formula in the role of '*Fu*' has all its bound variables restricted to sets, and not in general otherwise. I shall follow Wang in calling this restricted sort of enlargement *predicative*, as against the unrestricted sort that led from NF to ML. Poincaré's use of 'predicative' (§34) thus becomes somewhat extended, since in restricting the bound variables of the class abstract to sets von Neumann does not necessarily keep $\hat{u}Fu$ out of the range of values of its bound variables. But the term is pat nevertheless, as will emerge in §44.

Von Neumann's enlargement of Zermelo's system with ultimate classes is, we see, restrained. A liberalization will soon be noted on the side of sets. If the sets were to be precisely Zermelo's classes, they might be specified by relativizing Zermelo's comprehension axioms to '$\bigcup\mathcal{V}$'. In particular the Zermelo schema '$x \cap \alpha \in \mathcal{V}$' of *Aussonderung* would become:

$$x \in \bigcup\mathcal{V} \;.\supset.\; x \cap \alpha \in \bigcup\mathcal{V}$$

but with further relativization, to '$\bigcup\mathcal{V}$', of whatever abstract we put for 'α'. Or equivalently, since such relativization assures according to the preceding paragraph that $\alpha = z$ for some z, we could adopt just the single axiom of *Aussonderung*:

(i) $$x \in \mathrm{U}\mathcal{V} \mathrel{.\supset.} x \cap z \in \mathrm{U}\mathcal{V}.$$

Zermelo's further comprehension axioms:

$$\{x, y\}, \ \{u \colon u \subseteq x\}, \ \mathrm{U}x \in \mathcal{V}$$

(cf. (vii) of §38) go over into von Neumann's system by straight relativization to 'U$\mathcal{V}$', in effect, thus:

(ii) $$x, y \in \mathrm{U}\mathcal{V} \mathrel{.\supset.} \{x, y\}, \hat{u}(u \subseteq x), \ \mathrm{U}x \in \mathrm{U}\mathcal{V}.$$

Corresponding to Zermelo's axiom of infinity '$\mathrm{N} \in \mathcal{V}$', von Neumann has in effect a sethood axiom:[1]

(iii) $$\mathrm{N} \in \mathrm{U}\mathcal{V}.$$

He has the usual extensionality axiom. Also he has the axiom of *Fundierung* (§39), but let us think of it as an optional accessory.

By considerations precisely parallel to those that carried us from the Zermelo schema '$x \cap \alpha \in \mathcal{V}$' of *Aussonderung* to the single axiom (i), we are carried from the axiom schema of replacement ((vi) of §39) to this single axiom:

$$x \in \mathrm{U}\mathcal{V} \,.\, \mathrm{Func}\ y \mathrel{.\supset.} y``x \in \mathrm{U}\mathcal{V}.$$

Reactivating our definition 11.1, we can put the axiom also thus:

(iv) $$z \preceq x \in \mathrm{U}\mathcal{V} \mathrel{.\supset.} z \in \mathrm{U}\mathcal{V}.$$

A class is a set, that is, if no bigger than some set; so von Neumann. But in the end he settles on a stronger axiom of replacement, whereby a class is a set if and only if it is not as big as the class of all sets. I.e.,

(v) $$x \in \mathrm{U}\mathcal{V} \mathrel{.\equiv.} x \prec \mathrm{U}\mathcal{V}.$$

---

[1] As remarked in connection with (v) of §39, Zermelo's actual axiom diverged trivially from '$\mathrm{N} \in \mathcal{V}$'. Von Neumann's diverged more from '$\mathrm{N} \in \mathrm{U}\mathcal{V}$'; see second page below.

This implies (i) and so eliminates it as axiom. For, by (v) and the hypothesis of (i), $x \prec \mathsf{U}\mathcal{V}$. But $\mathsf{U}\mathcal{V} \precsim x \cap z \,.\!\supset\!.\, \mathsf{U}\mathcal{V} \precsim x$, by 28.2. So $x \cap z \prec \mathsf{U}\mathcal{V}$. Further $x \cap z \in \mathcal{V}$, even by von Neumann's predicative form of '$\hat{u}Fu \in \mathcal{V}$'; so we can substitute '$x \cap z$' in (v) and conclude from '$x \cap z \prec \mathsf{U}\mathcal{V}$' that $x \cap z \in \mathsf{U}\mathcal{V}$, q.e.d.

From (v) we can even get the axiom of choice, as von Neumann showed. The essential idea is as follows. We have by von Neumann's predicative '$\hat{u}Fu \in \mathcal{V}$', if somewhat indirectly, that NO $\in \mathcal{V}$. The argument from the Burali-Forti paradox which led us to 'NO $\notin \mathcal{V}$' in 24.4 leads here only to 'NO $\notin \mathsf{U}\mathcal{V}$'. Now this in turn, by (v), gives that $\mathsf{U}\mathcal{V} \precsim$ NO. So, by definition, there is a function that assigns every set to a distinct ordinal. But this, in view of the well-ordering of NO, assures the well-ordering of the whole universe $\mathsf{U}\mathcal{V}$ of sets. Thence we get the axiom of choice.

We can give the axiom (v) a more elementary form. Since $(y)(y \subseteq \mathsf{U}\mathcal{V})$, we get easily that

$$\mathsf{U}\mathcal{V} \precsim x \,.\!\supset (y)(y \precsim x)$$

(cf. 28.1). Conversely, we easily get from von Neumann's predicative '$\hat{u}Fu \in \mathcal{V}$' that $\mathsf{U}\mathcal{V} \in \mathcal{V}$, so that, by 6.11,

$$(y)(y \precsim x) \supset\!.\, \mathsf{U}\mathcal{V} \precsim x.$$

Combining, we see that we can put '$(y)(y \precsim x)$' for '$\mathsf{U}\mathcal{V} \precsim x$', hence '$(\exists y)(x \prec y)$' for '$x \prec \mathsf{U}\mathcal{V}$'. Also '$x \in \mathsf{U}\mathcal{V}$' reduces to '$(\exists y)(x \in y)$'. So (v) becomes:

(vi) $$(\exists y)(x \in y) \equiv (\exists y)(x \prec y).$$

The idea that a class be a set unless it is too big is, by the way, curiously pat from a German point of view. 'Menge' is the technical German for 'set', and 'Unmenge' the vernacular for an excessive multitude.

Von Neumann's actual system differed greatly in appearance from what I have described. He treated primarily not of classes but of functions, and derived his classes from them. It was Bernays (1937, 1941) who reworked the system into the more familiar form of a set theory focused upon membership. The system as I have been describing it is therefore best referred to as the von Neumann–Bernays set theory, particularly if with Bernays we shun the axiom (v), which implies the axiom of choice, and limit ourselves to the schema (iv). Summed up, then, with *Fundierung* also left aside, the von Neumann–Bernays system comprises (ii)–(iv), the extensionality axiom '$x = y \,.\, x \in z \,.\supset.\, y \in z$', and the schema '$\hat{u}Fu \in \mathcal{V}$' taken predicatively.

But only in effect. In fact von Neumann got by with a finite list of axioms, to the exclusion of schemata; and Bernays followed suit. Specifically, the comprehension schema '$\hat{u}Fu \in \mathcal{V}$', taken predicatively, can be proved as a theorem schema if in its stead we adopt just the seven comprehension axioms:

$$\text{(vii)} \qquad \mathfrak{E} \upharpoonright \cup\mathcal{V},\ \breve{x},\ \text{cnv}_2 x,\ \text{cnv}_3 x,\ x``\mathcal{V},\ x \times \cup\mathcal{V},\ x \cap \overline{y} \in \mathcal{V}$$

where $\text{cnv}_2 x$ and $\text{cnv}_3 x$ are

$$\{\langle u, \langle v, w\rangle\rangle : \langle v, \langle w, u\rangle\rangle \in x\}, \qquad \{\langle u, \langle v, w\rangle\rangle : \langle u, \langle w, v\rangle\rangle \in x\}.$$

I am still not following Bernays to the letter. Bernays adopts distinctive variables for sets and for classes, and treats sets not as special classes but only as corresponding to classes. On this point I stay rather with von Neumann, identifying sets with the corresponding classes.[2] On the axiom of infinity all three of us diverge: I gave '$N \in \cup\mathcal{V}$', Bernays postulated an infinite set in Dedekind's sense (§32), and von Neumann postulated a nested set with no most inclusive member. But no matter; we easily derive each of these from each, given the rest of the system (except that we need the axiom of choice, or (v), for Bernays's case). Again my assortment of comprehension axioms in (vii) departs from Bernays's and is nearer to Gödel's version (1940); but the effect is the same.

---

[2] So did Gödel, in his 1940 adaptation of the von Neumann-Bernays system. Gödel had special variables for sets, but the sets were classes. See above, §33, note 1.

Finally, my recourse to '$\hat{u}Fu$', '$\mathcal{V}$', and '$\mathsf{U}\mathcal{V}$' gives the system a cast not to be found in other renderings. However, as twice remarked, these are expository devices only. So the system as I have formulated it is what I shall be calling the von Neumann–Bernays system.

This system does not make directly for mathematical induction in all cases, as ML did; for this system does not assure, like ML, the impredicative cases of '$\hat{u}Fu \in \mathcal{V}$'. But no matter, since in Zermelo's system the induction problem has already been met head on by Zermelo's axiom of infinity, which became (iii) in the von Neumann–Bernays system. This is not an axiom that could be dispensed with even given the impredicative '$\hat{u}Fu \in \mathcal{V}$' that does assure induction. For without the axiom of infinity there would be no proof in Zermelo's system of the existence of infinite classes; and without its analogue there would be no proof in the von Neumann–Bernays system of the existence of infinite sets.

The proof of Cantor's theorem '$z \prec \{x\colon x \subseteq z\}$' fails in the von Neumann–Bernays system if we define '$y \preceq z$' again as in 11.1 and §42. For the proof requires existence of $z \cap \{u\colon u \notin w`u\}$ for functions w, whereas the predicative form of the comprehension schema '$\hat{u}Fu \in \mathcal{V}$' does not assure that existence unless $w \in \mathsf{U}\mathcal{V}$. If on the other hand we modify the definition of '$y \preceq z$' to read:

(viii) '$y \preceq z$' for '$(\exists w)(\text{Func}\, w \,.\, w \in \mathsf{U}\mathcal{V} \,.\, y \subseteq w``z)$',

then the proof of '$z \prec \{x\colon x \subseteq z\}$' for ML that we noted in §42 can be paralleled in the von Neumann–Bernays system. Moreover the derivation of Cantor's paradox '$\mathcal{V} \prec \mathcal{V}$' from '$z \prec \{x\colon x \subseteq z\}$' is averted, here as there, by the fact that $\mathcal{V} \notin \mathcal{V}$.

The proof of Cantor's theorem in the form '$z \prec \hat{x}(x \subseteq z)$' breaks down here, again as in ML, because of non-sethood of $\hat{u}(u \in z \,.\, u \notin w`u)$ for some functions $w$. The only difference between this system and ML, on this point, is in how the assurance of sethood of $\hat{u}(u \in z \,.\, u \notin w`u)$ fails. In ML it failed because '$u \notin w`u$' is not stratified. Now it fails because in general no set is forthcoming that we can show $\hat{u}(u \in z \,.\, u \notin w`u)$ to be a subclass of, or not larger than. If in particular z is a set, then we do have sethood of $\hat{u}(u \in z \,.\, u \notin w`u)$, by substitution of '$z$' and '$\hat{u}(u \notin w`u)$' for '$x$' and '$z$' in (i); so Cantor's theorem is indeed forthcoming in the form:

(ix) $$z \in \mathsf{U}\mathcal{V} \;.\supset.\; z \prec \hat{x}(x \subseteq z),$$

in addition to '$z \prec \{x\colon x \subseteq z\}$'. Here Cantor's paradox threatens again, in the new form '$\mathsf{U}\mathcal{V} \prec \mathsf{U}\mathcal{V}$'; for $\hat{x}(x \subseteq \mathsf{U}\mathcal{V})$ is indeed $\mathsf{U}\mathcal{V}$. But this threat of paradox simply affords, through (ix), a *reductio ad absurdum* proof that $\mathsf{U}\mathcal{V} \notin \mathsf{U}\mathcal{V}$: the class of sets is not, for this system, a set. (It was for ML.) Of course we knew this already from (v), when (v) was still with us.

Again Russell's paradox invites inspection in two forms. The form using '$\{u\colon u \notin u\}$' fares as noted for ML in §42. The form using '$\hat{u}(u \notin u)$' requires us to conclude, as in §42, that $\hat{u}(u \notin u) \notin \mathsf{U}\mathcal{V}$; nor is there any evident way of proving the contrary, for want of a set that we can show $\hat{u}(u \notin u)$ to be a subclass of, or no larger than.

44. Departures and comparisons

Aussonderung, '$\alpha \cap z \in \mathcal{V}$', is the most distinctive mark of Zermelo's system. '$\mathsf{U}\mathcal{V} \in \mathcal{V}$' is inconsistent with the axioms of Zermelo's system. Still '$\mathsf{U}\mathcal{V} \in \mathcal{V}$' is not inconsistent with '$\alpha \cap z \in \mathcal{V}$' itself. '$\mathsf{U}\mathcal{V} \in \mathcal{V}$' and '$\alpha \cap z \in \mathcal{V}$' simply add up to '$\alpha \cap \mathsf{U}\mathcal{V} \in \mathcal{V}$'. For obviously they imply it, and conversely we can get both from it as follows. To get '$\mathsf{U}\mathcal{V} \in \mathcal{V}$' from '$\alpha \cap \mathsf{U}\mathcal{V} \in \mathcal{V}$', substitute '$\mathsf{U}\mathcal{V}$' for '$\alpha$'. To get '$\alpha \cap z \in \mathcal{V}$' from '$\alpha \cap \mathsf{U}\mathcal{V} \in \mathcal{V}$', substitute '$\alpha \cap z$' for '$\alpha$' and reflect that $z \cap \mathsf{U}\mathcal{V} = z$.

But '$\alpha \cap \mathsf{U}\mathcal{V} \in \mathcal{V}$' amounts in turn to the impredicative comprehension schema '$\hat{u}Fu \in \mathcal{V}$'; cf. (iii) of §42. So we see that what may be called the skeletal impredicative theory of sets and ultimate classes, viz., '$\hat{u}Fu \in \mathcal{V}$' together with extensionality ('$x = y \,.\, x \in z \;.\supset.\; y \in z$'), stands in a very simple relation to what may be called the skeletal Zermelo system, viz., '$\alpha \cap z \in \mathcal{V}$' together with extensionality. The relation is just that the one is the other plus '$\mathsf{U}\mathcal{V} \in \mathcal{V}$'. The skeletal impredicative theory of sets and classes is what we get from the skeletal Zermelo system if, instead of adding Zermelo's further axioms, we take another turning and add the deviant axiom '$\cup\mathcal{V} \in \mathcal{V}$'.

I momentarily present the skeletal impredicative theory of sets and classes in this light only because we usually do not. Usually we think of it not as coordinate with Zermelo's system or NF or the like, but as something to superimpose on such a system. The skeletal impredicative theory of sets and classes leaves open the question what to take as $\cup\mathcal{V}$, the class of sets; and so, superimposing, we take as $\cup\mathcal{V}$ the universe of NF or of Zermelo or whatever. If we take it as that of NF, we have ML. If we take it as that of Zermelo, we have a system somewhat similar to von Neumann's.

Such superimposition is not, of course, mere addition of axioms. Enlargement is not extension (see §42). Simply to pool the skeletal impredicative theory with Zermelo's full system would be to add '$\cup\mathcal{V} \in \mathcal{V}$' to Zermelo's full system and engender contradiction. To *enlarge* the Zermelo system, by *superimposing* the skeletal impredicative theory, we would relativize the Zermelo comprehension axioms to '$\cup\mathcal{V}$' and then add the result to the skeletal impredicative theory. When we enlarged NF to ML we relativized the comprehension schema of NF to '$\cup\mathcal{V}$' and added the result to the skeletal impredicative theory. Such, in brief, is *impredicative enlargement*.

An argument due to Wang (1950) shows that such enlargement never engenders contradiction. If, given a consistent set theory without ultimate classes, you relativize its axioms to '$\cup\mathcal{V}$' and superimpose the '$\hat{u}Fu \in \mathcal{V}$' and '$x = y \,.\, x \in z \,.\!\supset.\, y \in z$' of the skeletal impredicative theory of sets and ultimate classes, the result will be consistent. This means in particular that, if NF is consistent, so is ML. For concreteness I shall sketch Wang's argument for the case of NF and ML; but it is the same for other cases.

He appeals to the Skolem–Löwenheim theorem, which says that any consistent set of quantificational schemata comes out true under an interpretation in the universe of natural numbers. Suppose then that NF is consistent. It follows that there is a numerical relation R such that all theorems of NF come out true when the variables are reconstrued as ranging over the natural numbers and 'ϵ' is reconstrued as expressing R. In particular then this corollary:

$$(z)(z \epsilon x .\equiv. z \epsilon y) \supset: x \epsilon w .\equiv. y \epsilon w$$

of the extensionality axiom comes out true when thus reconstrued. So we see that if numbers x and y are such that entirely the same numbers bear R to x as to y, then x and y are wholly indistinguishable in terms of R. Therefore the reinterpretation of 'ϵ' as R and of the universe as numbers will continue to fulfill NF even though we *cull* the numbers thus:[1] whenever entirely the same numbers bear R to each of various numbers $x_1, x_2, \ldots$, abolish all but the least of $x_1, x_2, \ldots$. For the abolished numbers are indistinguishable in terms of R from the retained ones. Now Wang proceeds to formulate a two-sorted version of ML, with small variables for sets and capital variables for classes. Sets cease to count as classes and come, as with Bernays (1937), merely to correspond to classes. Only set variables are allowed on the left of 'ϵ'. The comprehension schema, the sethood axioms, and the extensionality axiom (see §42) become respectively:

(i) $(\exists Y)(x)(x \epsilon Y .\equiv Fx)$,

(ii) $(\exists y)(x)(x \epsilon y .\equiv Fx)$
('Fx' stratified and without capitals),

(iii) $(z)(z \epsilon x .\equiv. z \epsilon y) . Fx .\supset Fy$.

Consider next a variant interpretation of this two-sorted ML, as follows. Take the range of the small variables as comprising the natural numbers, culled as above. Take the range of the capital variables as comprising all the subclasses of the range of the small variables. Take 'ϵ' before small letters as R, and before capitals as membership. This reinterpretation fulfills (iii); for, thanks to the culling, x *is* y when $(z)(z \epsilon x .\equiv. z \epsilon y)$. Further,

---

[1] In this phase of the argument I lean rather on Wang, 1951, p. 289, where he fills a gap of his 1950 proof.

the reinterpretation fulfills (ii), since NF comes out true with 'ϵ' as R and the universe as the culled numbers. And finally the reinterpretation fulfills (i), for we shall assume the consistency of the naïve theory of classes of numbers. Thus the two-sorted ML proves consistent. The remainder of the argument is a humdrum matter of showing that since the two-sorted ML is consistent so is ML proper.

This result—that ML is consistent if NF is—embodies the main reason for continued interest in NF. For ML is more satisfactory than NF. It is free of the limitations on induction, it is free of the anomaly of non-Cantorian sets, it knows no limitation of Cantor's theorem, and it overcomes the failure of the axiom of choice. And these advantages are mere illustrations of the sort of convenience conferred on every hand by the adding of the ultimate classes. So much more convenient is ML than NF that it is surely preferable unless perhaps for the increased risk of inconsistency that all this added strength would seem to entail. How welcome, then, the proof that ML is consistent if NF is. And if proofs are to be sought that ML is consistent provided that certain theories more plausible still than NF are consistent, the best strategy in seeking such proof is to try to prove that NF is consistent if those other theories are.

If a system without ultimate classes is consistent, so is its impredicative enlargement—such is Wang's theorem, argued just now for NF and ML. An argument advanced in another connection by Mostowski (p. 112n) can be used to show further that *any formula is already a theorem of the original system if, when relativized to* '$\mathrm{U}\mathfrak{V}$', *it becomes a theorem of the enlarged system.* Restated in application to NF and the two-sorted ML of (i)–(iii), the point is that every theorem of the latter system is a theorem also of NF if lacking in capitals. Mostowski's proof, when thus applied, runs as follows. Let $\mathfrak{F}$ be any formula without capitals that is not provable in NF. Then NF with the negation of $\mathfrak{F}$ added as a new axiom is consistent. Then, by Wang's theorem, the impredicative enlargement of this system is consistent too. But it is the two-sorted ML with the negation of $\mathfrak{F}$ added. So $\mathfrak{F}$ is not a theorem of the two-sorted ML.

The von Neumann–Bernays system is not related to the Zermelo–Fraenkel system as ML is to NF. The von Neumann–Bernays system foregoes strength that Wang's theorem would allow: the impredicative '$\hat{u}Fu \in \mathcal{V}$'. That the von Neumann–Bernays system is consistent, if the Zermelo–Fraenkel system is, has been known independently of Wang's theorem. One argument to that effect was given by Miss Novak, and another by Rosser and Wang (pp. 124ff), who credited Mostowski with independently discovering it. The crux of Rosser and Wang's proof is that predicativity on the part of '$\hat{u}Fu \in \mathcal{V}$' achieves, for the classes so added to a set theory, Poincaré's objective (§34) of ordered generation. As remarked in (vii) of §43, each class so added is either $\mathfrak{E} \restriction \cup \mathcal{V}$, or else $\breve{x}$ or $\mathrm{cnv}_2 x$ or $\mathrm{cnv}_3 x$ or $x``\mathcal{V}$ or $x \times \cup \mathcal{V}$ for some preassigned x, or $x \cap \overline{y}$ for some preassigned x and y. If we begin with a theory of sets admitting of a model in natural numbers, then its enlargement by ordered generation of classes in the above fashion can by a simple rearrangement be given a model in natural numbers too. But any consistent theory has a model in natural numbers. So, if the underlying theory of sets is consistent, the enlargement is too.

All classes of the Zermelo–Fraenkel system are obviously sets of the von Neumann–Bernays system. The converse, that only those classes are sets of the von Neumann–Bernays system, is not obvious; but it follows easily from the constructions of Rosser, Wang, and Mostowski, as those authors showed. More precisely, what they showed is that any formula can be proved in the Zermelo–Fraenkel system if the relativization of the formula to '$\cup \mathcal{V}$' can be proved in the von Neumann–Bernays system. In 1954, Shoenfield went farther and gave a direct rule (a "primitive recursive" one, in the jargon of proof theory) whereby to find a proof in the Zermelo–Fraenkel system of any formula, given a proof of its relativization in the von Neumann–Bernays system.

It is brought home by the nature of these arguments how little burden was put on ultimate classes in the von Neumann–Bernays system. Wang's theorem about the other situation, the impredicative, becomes the more surprising. No wonder its proof required so substantial an assumption as that the naive theory of classes of natural numbers is consistent. Even that assumption was slight, of course, compared to the question of the consistency of NF or ML or the like.

That the predicative '$\hat{u}Fu \in \mathcal{V}$' is resoluble into seven single axioms as in (vii) of §43 seems a reflection of the weakness of the predicative assumption. Presumably the impredicative '$\hat{u}Fu \in \mathcal{V}$', as of ML, cannot be reduced thus to a finite selection of cases.

Yet NF is finitely axiomatizable. Hailperin has shown how to get its comprehension schema, in effect '$\{u\colon Fu\} \in \mathcal{V}$' with '$Fu$' stratified, from ten of its instances. Putnam even goes on then to show how to get it from a single one of its instances; he shows that any finite lot of comprehension axioms can be got down to one. His argument is that any two can be reduced to one, as follows. The two may, to begin with, be pictured thus:

$$\{x\colon Fxy_1 \ldots y_m\},\ \{x\colon Gxz_1 \ldots z_n\} \in \mathcal{V}$$

where '$Fxy_1 \ldots y_m$' and '$Gxz_1 \ldots z_n$' stand for particular sentences with free variables as shown. Then, where 'p' is short for:

$$(y_1) \ldots (y_m)(\{x\colon Fxy_1 \ldots y_m\} \in \mathcal{V}),$$

the two can be combined into this equivalent single one:

$$\{v\colon Fvw_1 \ldots w_m \,.\, {\sim}p \,.\mathsf{v}.\, Gvz_1 \ldots z_n \,.\, p\} \in \mathcal{V}.$$

On the other hand a bit of set theory can be surprisingly modest and yet fail of finite axiomatizability. A discovery of Kreisel and Wang's, extended by Montague,[2] is that a consistent set theory based on the single primitive predicate '$\in$' cannot be finitely axiomatized if it provides that

$$x \cap \alpha,\ x \cup \{y\} \in \mathcal{V}, \qquad x = y \,.\, x \in z \,.\supset.\, y \in z.$$

[2] 1957, 1961. The appearance of discrepancy in my formulation is due, again, to my use of noncommittal abstraction. —The stipulation that there are no extra predicates is essential in view of a theorem of Kleene's ("Two papers"): any consistent system can be extended to a consistent finitely axiomatized system if we add predicates.

Since these provisions are part of Zermelo's system, it follows in particular that Zermelo's system itself, if consistent, is not finitely axiomatizable.[3] This is surprising, considering that von Neumann's finitely axiomatized system is an enlargement of Zermelo's system. But remember that it is only an enlargement, not an extension; that would indeed make both systems inconsistent by Montague's result.

Waiving the benefits of finite axiomatization, such as they may be, I find the von Neumann–Bernays system as of §43 not without its attractions when '$\hat{u}Fu \in \mathcal{V}$' is freed for impredicative cases. For further beauty we may supplant (iv) of §43 again by (v). This impredicative *extension*, as we can now correctly call it, of the von Neumann–Bernays system has the sethood axioms:

$$\mathrm{N} \in \mathrm{U}\mathcal{V}, \qquad x \in \mathrm{U}\mathcal{V} \;.\!\equiv\!.\; x \prec \mathrm{U}\mathcal{V},$$

$$x, y \in \mathrm{U}\mathcal{V} \;.\!\supset\!.\; \{x, y\},\ \hat{u}(u \subseteq x),\ \mathrm{U}x \in \mathrm{U}\mathcal{V}$$

and the impredicative comprehension schema '$\hat{u}Fu \in \mathcal{V}$' and the axiom of extensionality.[4] One point of latitude to look to if contradiction threatens is the '$\prec$' in one of the above axioms: whether to base its definition on 11.1 or on (viii) of §43.

But the system shares a serious drawback with ML, and with von Neumann's unextended system, and any other system that invokes ultimate classes: the drawback, deplored in §7, of violating 7.10, to say nothing of 13.1. Two values conflict. We want to be able to form finite classes, in all ways, of all things that there are assumed to be—even of any infinite classes that there are assumed to be; and the trouble is that ultimate classes will not belong.

Perhaps a kind of reconciliation can be managed by softening the note of ultimacy: letting ultimate classes belong to some classes after all, but only to smaller ones. To call x a set would be to say no longer that $(\exists y)(x \in y)$, but that $(\exists y)(x \in y \,.\, x \preceq y)$.

---

[3] This result goes back, as Montague points out, to 1954 (McNaughton) or, with inadequate proofs, to 1952 and 1953 (Wang, Mostowski)

[4] Such, approximately, is the system NQ (von Neumann–Quine) of Wang (1949), or BQ (Bernays–Quine) of Stegmüller (1962).

At last we have been contemplating a variant of the set concept $\mathfrak{M}$, departing from $\cup\mathcal{V}$. Such deviation is not quite unprecedented. Ackermann has propounded a system in which $\mathfrak{M}$ is taken neither as $\cup\mathcal{V}$ nor in the alternative manner last contemplated, but left undefined along with 'ϵ'.

For Ackermann's system we may define $\hat{u}Fu$ as $\mathfrak{M} \cap \{u: Fu\}$. One of the axiom schemata amounts then to '$\hat{u}Fu \in \mathcal{V}$'. Another of the axiom schemata is in effect the sethood schema:

$$\text{(iv)} \qquad y_1, \ldots, y_n \in \mathfrak{M} \;.\supset.\; \hat{u}Fuy_1 \ldots y_n \in \mathfrak{M}$$

('$Fuy_1 \ldots y_n$' devoid of further free variables and '$\mathfrak{M}$').

It does not require restriction of the hidden bound variables to sets, nor of course is there talk of stratification; instead there is the exclusion of '$\mathfrak{M}$'. In addition Ackermann has in effect the two sethood axioms:

$$\cup\mathfrak{M} \subseteq \mathfrak{M}, \qquad x \subseteq y \in \mathfrak{M} \;.\supset.\; x \in \mathfrak{M},$$

and the usual axiom of extensionality. Appreciation of this system mounts as Ackermann shows how to derive Zermelo's axioms from it—not only all the axioms (vii) of §38 but even the axiom of infinity.[5] These come through weakened to the extent of carrying hypotheses limiting various of the variables to sets; still, we get a model of Zermelo's system by identifying Zermelo's universe with Ackermann's $\mathfrak{M}$.

Ackermann's system, unlike Zermelo's, shares with ML and von Neumann's the drawback of not granting existence unreservedly to finite classes. But what is hardest to accept in Ackermann's system is the inelegance of the added primitive term '$\mathfrak{M}$' (or the corresponding predicate). Moreover, this looks irremediable. Seeing how (iv) hinges on presence or absence of '$\mathfrak{M}$' in a formula, there is little hope of making '$\mathfrak{M}$' eliminable by definition.

---

[5] Ostensibly also the axiom schema of replacement; but Lévy, "On Ackermann's set theory," found a fault in the proof. Lévy showed further that Ackermann's system is consistent if the Zermelo-Fraenkel system is consistent.

45. Strength of systems

If one deductive system is an extension of another, in that its theorems comprise all those of the other system and more, then in a way the one is stronger than the other. But this basis of comparison is poor on two counts. First, it fails where each of two systems has theorems not in the other. Second, it hinges on accidents of interpretation and not just on structure. Thus, to take a trivial illustration, suppose we have a system with just '=' and '*R*' as primitive two-place predicates, subject to the usual axioms of identity and an axiom of transitivity of '*R*'; and suppose we extend the system by adding reflexivity, '$(x)(xRx)$'. The extended system is stronger only insofar as we equate its '*R*' with the original '*R*'. If we reinterpret its 'xRy' rather in terms of the original '*R*' as '$x = y$ .v. xRy', then all its theorems are provable in the unextended system.

A less trivial illustration is suggested by Russell's method, noted in (i)–(iv) of §35, of assuring extensionality for classes without having had to assume it for attributes. Given a set theory without the axiom of extensionality, we could extend the system by adding that axiom; and yet we might show that all the theorems of the extended system were reinterpretable by Russell's method into theorems already provable in the unextended system.

So a more significant standard of strength comparison is what may be called the *reinterpretational* one. If we can so reinterpret the primitive nonlogical signs of the one system—just 'ϵ', typically, for set theory—as to cause all the theorems of that system to become translations of theorems of the other, then the latter system is at least as strong as the former. If a similar trick cannot be done the other way around, then the one system is stronger than the other. In general, of course, there is trouble in showing that a similar trick cannot be done the other way around.

Strength in a further significant sense—*ordinal* strength, we might say—admits of this strikingly numerical measure: the least transfinite ordinal number that the system cannot prove to exist. Any not conspicuously deficient set theory can of course prove the existence of transfinite numbers without end, but this does not mean getting them all. What is so characteristic of the transfinite is that we then go on iterating the iteration, and iterating the iterating of iterations, and so on, until somehow our apparatus buckles; and the least transfinite number after the buckling of the apparatus is how strong the apparatus was.

An axiom that can be added to a system to the visible end of increasing ordinal strength is the axiom that there is an inaccessible number beyond ω (see end of §30). An endless series of further axioms of this sort is possible, postulating ever further inaccessible numbers and raising always the ordinal strength.

There is also another way of using ordinal numbers as a measure of the strength of systems. To begin with we extend the theory of cumulative types (§38) into transfinite types, following von Neumann,[1] by accrediting to the xth type, for each ordinal x, all classes whose members are all of types below x. Thus the universe of the theory of cumulative types in §38, lacking transfinite types, is itself the ωth type. When the axioms of a set theory are fulfilled by taking the universe as such a type, Montague and Vaught call the type a *natural model* of the set theory. Thus Zermelo's set theory, short of the axiom of infinity, has the ωth type as a natural model; such, in present terms, is what transpired in §38.[2] Finally the ordinal strength (in a second sense) of a given set theory is the least ordinal x such that the xth type is a natural model of the theory. Thus the ordinal strength of Zermelo's set theory without the axiom of infinity is at most ω; but also obviously not less than ω; so ω. That of Zermelo's set theory with the axiom of infinity is $\omega + \omega$, as Tarski remarks (1956). That of the von Neumann–Bernays system is, according to Shepherdson, one more than the first inaccessible number after ω.

I turn next to the *proof-theoretic* criterion of relative strength. In his proof of the impossibility of a complete number theory

---

[1] 1929. See also Bernays, 1948; Mendelson, p. 202.

[2] Also in my "Unification of universes."

(1931) Gödel introduced a method of numbering, now well known, that enabled him to talk in effect about formulas and deductive procedure while talking literally in a purely arithmetical vein about numbers. Since number theory can be developed in set theory, this means that the class of theorems (really Gödel numbers of theorems) of a given set theory can be defined in that same set theory, and various things can there be proved about it. But Gödel showed, as a consequence of his incompletability theorem, that one thing the set theory cannot (if it is consistent) prove about the class of its own theorems is that it is consistent; i.e., say, that '0 = 1' is not in it. When the consistency of one set theory can be proved in another, the latter is the stronger (unless of course both are inconsistent). Kemeny showed in this way that Zermelo's system is stronger than the theory of types.[3]

A method then comes ready to hand for generating, from any given set theory, an endless series of further ones, each stronger in the proof-theoretic sense than its predecessors, and each consistent if its predecessors were consistent. All you have to do is add a new arithmetical axiom, via Gödel numbering, to the effect that the previous axioms were consistent. You can even make a single strong system of this whole progression of axioms; but then you can continue as before with a new axiom affirming the consistency of all that. We see the familiar pattern of transfinite recursion setting in. The strength of a system of accumulated axioms specified along these lines is limited only by the potentialities of transfinite recursion—the ordinal strength, in turn—of the medium of communication in which we are specifying that infinite fund of axioms.[4]

In thinking of the strength of a system of set theory we think first of richness of universe. Such is ordinal strength. Such is the

---

[3] Here Zermelo's system is without the axiom schema of replacement; the theory of types is of course without transfinite types; and both have their axioms of infinity. See Kemeny; also Wang and McNaughton, p. 35.

[4] On the strengthening of systems by adding consistency axioms or the like see Gödel, 1931, note 48a; Rosser and Wang, pp. 122ff; Wang, "Truth definitions"; Feferman.

strength added by an axiom of infinity or the axiom schema of replacement. Such is the strength gained for von Neumann's theory of sets and ultimate classes by his strengthening of the schema of replacement (§43), or again by impredicative extension (§44).

But extending a system need not enrich its universe. The added axiom can as well settle an open question of existence in the opposite way, by ruling for poverty. *Fundierung* did that. So did the continuum hypothesis.

Such also was the tendency of a *Beschränktheitsaxiom* that Fraenkel advocated for the Zermelo system: an axiom to the effect that there is nothing in the universe beyond what has to be there according to the other axioms. Fraenkel did not reduce this to a sharp formulation, and von Neumann remarked upon difficulties in the way of doing so.[5] With the help of the notion of relativization seen late in §33 we can formulate a rigorous axiom *schema* of *Beschränktheit* as '$\mathfrak{A}\alpha \supset. \alpha = \mathcal{V}$' where '$\mathfrak{A}\alpha$' stands for the relativization, to '$\{x: x \subseteq \alpha\}$', of the conjunction of the rest of the axioms; but this version requires that the rest of the axioms be finite in number, so it does not work as an adjunct to Zermelo's system. It does work as an adjunct to von Neumann's, though, and to NF, these being finitely axiomatizable (§44).

Gödel's '$\mathsf{U}\mathcal{V} = \mathrm{L}$', discussed late in §33, is near kin of that *Beschränktheitsschema*. Like that schema, it rules for poverty. Of course Gödel merely entertained '$\mathsf{U}\mathcal{V} = \mathrm{L}$' in the course of proving the consistency of the axiom of choice and the consistency of the continuum hypothesis; he did not *favor* it as one does the axiom of choice and more basic axioms. Still, lovers of conceptual and ontological economy could so favor it; and indeed it is sometimes referred to as the axiom of constructibility. As remarked in §33, it implies the axiom of choice and the continuum hypothesis.

It is hard to say whether the axiom of choice is for poverty or for richness. It repudiates all the selectionless classes of exclusive

[5] Fraenkel, *Einleitung*, pp. 355f; von Neumann, 1925, p. 230f.

classes. But it guarantees selections. It is implied by Gödel's poverty-directed '$\mathsf{U}\mathcal{V} = \mathrm{L}$'.

Axioms exploiting the inner-model idea (cf. §33) are not always, like *Beschränktheit* and '$\mathsf{U}\mathcal{V} = \mathrm{L}$', poverty-directed. Some make for ordinal strength. By identifying the universe with a specified inner model you hold things down. But by postulating inner models, or declaring them to be sets, you can step things up. Thus, given a system of set theory with a finite set of axioms, let '$\mathfrak{A}x$' again stand for the conjunction of them relativized to '$\{y: y \subseteq x\}$'. *Beschränktheit* would give '$\mathfrak{A}x \supset. x = \mathcal{V}$', hence also '$(x){\sim}\mathfrak{A}x$' if $\mathcal{V} \notin \mathcal{V}$. But instead we might in the opposite spirit postulate that $(\exists x)\mathfrak{A}x$ or even that $(\exists x)(x \in \mathsf{U}\mathcal{V} \,.\, \mathfrak{A}x)$, thereby implying the existence of a class x and perhaps even a set x not otherwise discoverable in the universe of the system and perhaps bigger than any otherwise available.

For theories that, like Zermelo's, cannot be got down to finitely many axioms, of course this plan will not work. But the following modification will. We can no longer consider a conjunction of all the axioms, but we can still consider separately each finite conjunction of axioms without limit, or, more simply, we can consider separately each theorem that follows from the axioms; and we can take '$\mathfrak{A}_1 x$', '$\mathfrak{A}_2 x$', ... as standing severally for the relativizations of these. Then we can adopt '$(\exists x)\mathfrak{A}_n x$' (or '$(\exists x)(x \in \mathsf{U}\mathcal{V} \,.\, \mathfrak{A}_n x)$') as added axiom for each n, taking an axiom schema to cover the lot. Lévy ("Axiom schemata"), building upon work of Mahlo and Shepherdson, has shown that axiom schemata of this sort can be equivalent to ones that postulate steep flights of inaccessible numbers.

Bernays's system of 1961, an improvement of Lévy's system, will well illustrate this interesting trend.[6] Unlike Bernays's 1958 system, where the so-called classes were only virtual, this is a theory of sets and real, quantifiable classes. Its distinctive axiom

---

[6] My account of it will depart from his in conspicuous ways. Partly this is because I keep the expository convenience of noncommittal abstraction. And do not stop reading his paper short of the turning points that come at p. 21 and p. 47.

schema is stronger still than '$(\exists x)(x \in \mathsf{U}\mathfrak{V} \,.\, \mathfrak{A}_n x)$', in three respects: it provides further that $\mathsf{U}x \subseteq x$ and

$$(y)(z)(y \subseteq z \in x \;.\supset.\; y \in x),$$

and it lets '$\mathfrak{A}_n x$' stand for the relativization not just of a theorem but of any truth. We may put it thus, using still our language of noncommittal abstraction:

$$\text{(i)} \qquad p \supset (\exists x)(\mathsf{U}x \subseteq x \in \mathsf{U}\mathfrak{V} \,.\, Px \,.\, (y)(z)(y \subseteq z \in x \;.\supset.\; y \in x))$$

where any sentence goes for 'p' and, for 'Px', its relativization to '$\{y: y \subseteq x\}$'. In addition Bernays adopts the axiom of extensionality and in effect the sethood axiom '$\{y, z\} \in \mathsf{U}\mathfrak{V}$'. He shows in effect that the full impredicative comprehension schema as of ML follows: '$\alpha \cap \mathsf{U}\mathfrak{V} \in \mathfrak{V}$', or '$\hat{u}Fu \in \mathfrak{V}$' (cf. §42). Similarly for the sethood axioms corresponding to Zermelo's comprehension axioms of the sum, the power class, *Aussonderung*, and infinity (here '$\mathrm{N} \in \mathsf{U}\mathfrak{V}$') and to the axiom schema of replacement. And he shows that the system is the equal of Lévy's in its yield of inaccessible numbers.

For a constructivistic set theory, with its economy of means, there is both philosophical and aesthetic motivation. And there is a methodological motive as well, knowing as we do the threat of paradox. There are all these counsels for keeping things down as best we can without quite stifling classical mathematics. And on the other hand there are motives for stepping things up. That there is again an aesthetic one can scarcely be doubted. Also a practical motive for generosity in the ontology of set theory is coming to be felt from the side of abstract algebra and topology, as MacLane has stressed (p. 25), because of "the big totalities involved (all groups, all spaces, all . . .)." In these connections even a generous set theory can prove inadequate if it is one of those that renounce the biggest classes. So there may be a premium on something like ML and NF, which do not make existence or sethood depend on limits of size. One might try combining such a system with the devices of Lévy and Bernays last alluded to; for these devices are formidable promoters of ordinal strength, though at present they operate within the framework of set theories that renounce the biggest classes. Also MacLane sketches an idea for salvaging some biggest classes as needed. Let me seize this opportunity to leave the reader with a sense of how open the problem of a best foundation for set theory remains.

SYNOPSIS OF FIVE AXIOM SYSTEMS

Modern theory of types:

Comprehension (§36(iv)): $(\exists y^{n+1})(x^n)(x^n \in y^{n+1} .\equiv Fx^n)$.

Extensionality (§36(v)):

$$(x^n)(x^n \in y^{n+1} .\equiv. x^n \in z^{n+1}) . y^{n+1} \in w^{n+2} .\supset. z^{n+1} \in w^{n+2}.$$

Annex (besides axiom of choice): Infinity (§39(i)):

$$(\exists x^2)((\exists y^1)(y^1 \in x^2) . (y^1)(y^1 \in x^2 .\supset (\exists z^1)(y^1 \subset z^1 \in x^2))).$$

Zermelo:

Power set, pairing, *Aussonderung*, sum (§38(vii)):

$$\{z: z \subseteq x\}, \{x, y\}, x \cap \alpha, \mathrm{U}x \in \mathcal{V}.$$

Extensionality (§38(vii)): $x = y . x \in z .\supset. y \in z$.

Infinity (§39(v)):

$$(\exists x)(\Lambda \in x . (y)(y \in x .\supset. \{y\} \in x)), \qquad \text{or} \qquad \mathrm{N} \in \mathcal{V}.$$

Annexes (besides axiom of choice):

Replacement (§39(vi), supplanting *Aussonderung*):

$$\mathrm{Func}\ \alpha \supset. \alpha``x \in \mathcal{V}.$$

Fundierung (§39): Fnd $\mathfrak{E}$.

New Foundations (NF):

Comprehension (§40(iii)): $\{x: Fx\} \in \mathcal{V}$. ('*Fx*' stratified)

Extensionality: $x = y . x \in z .\supset. y \in z$.

Mathematical Logic (ML):

Comprehension (§42(iii)): $\hat{u}Fu \in \mathfrak{V}$.

Sethood (§42): '$\hat{u}Fu \in \mathsf{U}\mathfrak{V}$' relativized to '$\mathsf{U}\mathfrak{V}$', with '$Fu$' stratified.

Extensionality: $x = y \,.\, x \in z \,.\!\supset\!.\, y \in z$.

Von Neumann–Bernays:

Comprehension (§43): $\hat{u}Fu \in \mathfrak{V}$ ('Fu' relativized to '$\mathsf{U}\mathfrak{V}$') or finitely (§43(vii)): $\mathfrak{E} \restriction \mathsf{U}\mathfrak{V}$, $\breve{x}$, $\mathrm{cnv}_2 x$, $\mathrm{cnv}_3 x$, $x``\mathfrak{V}$, $x \times \mathsf{U}\mathfrak{V}$, $x \cap \overline{y} \in \mathfrak{V}$.

Power set, pairing, sum (§43(ii)):

$$x, y \in \mathsf{U}\mathfrak{V} \,.\!\supset\!.\, \hat{u}(u \subseteq x), \{x, y\}, \mathsf{U}x \in \mathsf{U}\mathfrak{V}.$$

Extensionality: $x = y \,.\, x \in z \,.\!\supset\!.\, y \in z$.

Infinity (§43(iii)): $\mathrm{N} \in \mathsf{U}\mathfrak{V}$.

Replacement (§43(iv)): $z \preceq x \in \mathsf{U}\mathfrak{V} \,.\!\supset\!.\, z \in \mathsf{U}\mathfrak{V}$.

Annex: *Fundierung* Fnd $\mathfrak{E}$.

Ways of strengthening:

Comprehension: $\hat{u}Fu \in \mathfrak{V}$ (outright).

Replacement (§43(v)): $x \in \mathsf{U}\mathfrak{V} \,.\!\equiv\!.\, x \prec \mathsf{U}\mathfrak{V}$

LIST OF NUMBERED FORMULAS

A bookmark among these pages will save effort in checking references to decimally numbered formulas. Those theorems and theorem schemata will be omitted here, however, which were not cited by number outside their own sections; so this list should not be used to check cross references within a section.

2.1	'$y \in \{x: Fx\}$' for 'Fy'.
2.2	'$\alpha \subseteq \beta$' for '$(x)(x \in \alpha .\supset. x \in \beta)$'.
2.3	'$\alpha \subset \beta$' for '$\alpha \subseteq \beta \not\supseteq \alpha$'.
2.4	'$\alpha \cup \beta$' for '$\{x: x \in \alpha .\vee. x \in \beta\}$'.
2.5	'$\alpha \cap \beta$' for '$\{x: x \in \alpha . x \in \beta\}$'.
2.6	'$\bar{\alpha}$' or '$^{-}\alpha$' for '$\{x: x \notin \alpha\}$'.
2.7	'$\alpha = \beta$' for '$(x)(x \in \alpha .\equiv. x \in \beta)$', or '$\alpha \subseteq \beta \subseteq \alpha$'.
2.8	'Λ' or '$\{\ \}$' for '$\{z: z \neq z\}$'.
2.9	'$\mathcal{V}$' for '$\{z: z = z\}$', or '$^{-}\Lambda$'.
4.1	*Axiom.* $y = z . y \in w .\supset. z \in w$.
5.1	$\alpha = \{x: Fx\} .\equiv (x)(x \in \alpha .\equiv Fx)$.
5.3	$\sim(x)(x \in y .\equiv. x \notin x)$.
5.4	$\sim(x)(x \in y .\equiv \sim(x \in^2 x))$.
5.5	'$\{x: Fx\} \in \beta$' for '$(\exists y)(y = \{x: Fx\} . y \in \beta)$'.
6.1	$Fy \equiv (\exists x)(x = y . Fx)$.
6.2	$Fy \equiv (x)(x = y .\supset Fx)$.
6.4	$\alpha = \alpha$.

6.6 $\alpha = \beta \,.\, F\alpha \,.\!\supset F\beta.$

6.7 $\alpha = \beta \,.\!\supset\!.\, F\alpha \equiv F\beta.$

6.8 $x \in \mathcal{V}.$

6.9 $\alpha \in \mathcal{V} \,.\!\equiv (\exists x)(x = \alpha).$

6.11 $\alpha \in \mathcal{V} \,.\, (x)Fx \,.\!\supset F\alpha, \qquad \alpha \in \mathcal{V} \,.\, F\alpha \,.\!\supset (\exists x)Fx.$

6.12 $\alpha \in \beta \,.\!\supset\!.\, \alpha \in \mathcal{V}.$

6.13 $\alpha \in \{x\colon Fx\} \,.\!\equiv\!.\, \alpha \in \mathcal{V} \,.\, F\alpha.$

6.14 $\alpha \notin \Lambda.$

6.15 $(x)(x \in \alpha) \equiv\!.\, \alpha = \mathcal{V}, \qquad (x)(x \notin \alpha) \equiv\!.\, \alpha = \Lambda.$

6.16 $(x)Fx \equiv\!.\, \{x\colon Fx\} = \mathcal{V} \,.\!\equiv\!.\, \{x\colon \sim Fx\} = \Lambda.$

7.1 '$\{\alpha\}$' for '$\{z\colon z = \alpha\}$', '$\{\alpha, \beta\}$' for '$\{\alpha\} \cup \{\beta\}$'.

7.4 $\{x\} \subseteq \alpha \,.\!\equiv\!.\, x \in \alpha.$

7.6 $x \in \{x\}, \qquad x, y \in \{x, y\}.$

7.7 $\{x\} = \{y\} \,.\!\equiv\!.\, x = y.$

7.8 $\{x, y\} = \{z\} \,.\!\equiv\!.\, x = y = z.$

7.9 $\{x, y\} = \{x, w\} \,.\!\equiv\!.\, y = w.$

7.10 *Axiom.* $\Lambda, \{x, y\} \in \mathcal{V}.$

7.11 $(\exists y)(x \in y).$

7.12 $\{\alpha\} \in \mathcal{V}.$

7.13 $\{\alpha, \beta\} \in \mathcal{V}.$

7.14 $\alpha = z \,.\!\equiv (x)(z \in x \,.\!\supset\!.\, \alpha \in x).$

8.1 '$\mathsf{U}\alpha$' for '$\{x\colon x \in^2 \alpha\}$'.

8.2 $\mathsf{U}\{x\} = x.$

8.3 $\mathsf{U}(\alpha \cup \beta) = \mathsf{U}\alpha \cup \mathsf{U}\beta.$

8.5 $\mathsf{U}\alpha \subseteq \beta \,.\!\equiv (x)(x \in \alpha \,.\!\supset\!.\, x \subseteq \beta).$

8.6 $x \in \alpha \,.\!\supset\!.\, x \subseteq \mathsf{U}\alpha.$

8.8 $\mathsf{U}\mathcal{V} = \mathcal{V}.$

8.9 '$\bigcap\alpha$' for '$\{x\colon (y)(y \in \alpha \,.\!\supset\!.\, x \in y)\}$'

8.13 $\beta \subseteq \bigcap\alpha \,.\!\equiv (x)(x \in \alpha \,.\!\supset\!.\, \beta \subseteq x).$

8.14 $x \in \alpha \,.\!\supset\!.\, \bigcap\alpha \subseteq x.$

8.15 $\bigcap\Lambda = \mathcal{V}.$

8.18 '$(\iota x)Fx$' for '$\mathsf{U}\{y\colon (x)(Fx \equiv\!.\, x = y)\}$'.

8.20 $(x)(Fx \equiv\!.\, x = y) \supset\colon Fz \equiv\!.\, z = (\iota x)Fx.$

8.21 $y = (\iota x)(x = y).$

8.22 $\sim(\exists y)(x)(Fx \equiv.\ x = y) \supset.\ (\iota x)Fx = \Lambda.$

9.1 ‘$\langle\alpha, \beta\rangle$’ for ‘$\{\{\alpha\}, \{\alpha, \beta\}\}$’.

9.2 $\langle x, y\rangle = \langle z, w\rangle .\supset.\ x = z \,.\, y = w.$

9.3 $\langle x, y\rangle = \langle z, w\rangle .\equiv.\ x = z \,.\, y = w.$

9.4 ‘$\{\ldots x_1 \ldots x_2 \ldots x_n \ldots : Fx_1x_2 \ldots x_n\}$’ for
‘$\{z: (\exists x_1)(\exists x_2) \ldots (\exists x_n)(Fx_1x_2 \ldots x_n \,.$
$z = \ldots x_1 \ldots x_2 \ldots x_n \ldots)\}$’.

9.5 $\langle z, w\rangle \in \{\langle x, y\rangle : Fxy\} .\equiv Fzw.$

9.6 ‘${}^{\cdot}\alpha$’ for ‘$\{\langle x, y\rangle : \langle x, y\rangle \in \alpha\}$’.

9.7 ${}^{\cdot}\alpha = \alpha \cap {}^{\cdot}\mathcal{V}.$

9.8 ${}^{\cdot}\alpha \subseteq \beta .\equiv (x)(y)(\langle x, y\rangle \in \alpha .\supset.\ \langle x, y\rangle \in \beta).$

9.9 ${}^{\cdot}\alpha = {}^{\cdot}\beta .\equiv (x)(y)(\langle x, y\rangle \in \alpha .\equiv.\ \langle x, y\rangle \in \beta).$

9.11 ‘$\alpha \times \beta$’ for ‘$\{\langle x, y\rangle : x \in \alpha \,.\, y \in \beta\}$’.

9.12 ‘$\breve{\alpha}$’ or ‘${}^{\smile}\alpha$’ for ‘$\{\langle x, y\rangle : \langle y, x\rangle \in \alpha\}$’.

9.13 ‘$\alpha \mid \beta$’ for ‘$\{\langle x, z\rangle : (\exists y)(\langle x, y\rangle \in \alpha \,.\, \langle y, z\rangle \in \beta)\}$’.

9.14 ‘$\alpha``\beta$’ for ‘$\{x: (\exists y)(\langle x, y\rangle \in \alpha \,.\, y \in \beta)\}$’.

9.15 ‘I’ for ‘$\{\langle x, y\rangle : x = y\}$’.

9.16 ‘$\alpha \upharpoonright \beta$’ for ‘$\alpha \cap (\mathcal{V} \times \beta)$’.

9.17 ‘$\beta \upharpoonleft \alpha$’ for ‘$\alpha \cap (\beta \times \mathcal{V})$’.

10.1 ‘Func α’ for ‘$\alpha \mid \breve{\alpha} \subseteq I \,.\, \alpha = {}^{\cdot}\alpha$’, or
‘$(x)(y)(z)(\langle x, z\rangle, \langle y, z\rangle \in \alpha .\supset.\ x = y) \,.\, \alpha = {}^{\cdot}\alpha$’.

10.2 ‘arg α’ for ‘$\{x: (\exists y)(\alpha``\{x\} = \{y\})\}$’, or
‘$\{x: (\exists y)(z)(\langle z, x\rangle \in \alpha .\equiv.\ z = y)\}$’.

10.3 Func Λ.

10.4 Func I, arg $I = \mathcal{V}$.

10.5 Func $\{\langle x, y\rangle\}$.

10.6 Func α . Func β $.\supset$ Func $\alpha \mid \beta$.

10.7 Func $\alpha \,.\, y \notin \breve{\alpha}``\mathcal{V}$ $.\supset$ Func $\alpha \cup \{\langle x, y\rangle\}$.

10.8 Func $\alpha \supset$ Func $\alpha \cap \beta$.

10.10 Func ${}^{\cdot}\alpha \equiv.\ \breve{\alpha}``\mathcal{V} \subseteq \text{arg}\,\alpha$
$\equiv.\ \breve{\alpha}``\mathcal{V} = \text{arg}\,\alpha.$

10.10a Func $\alpha \,.\, \breve{\alpha}``\mathcal{V} \subseteq \breve{\beta}``\mathcal{V} \,.\, \beta \subseteq \alpha .\supset.\ \alpha = \beta.$

10.11 ‘$\alpha`\beta$’ for ‘$(\iota y)(\langle y, \beta\rangle \in \alpha)$’.

10.15 $w \notin \text{arg}\,\alpha .\supset.\ \alpha`w = \Lambda.$

10.17 Func ${}^{\cdot}\alpha \equiv (x)(\alpha``\{x\} \subseteq \{\alpha`x\}).$

10.18 $x \in \text{arg}\,\beta .\supset. (\alpha \mid \beta)`x = \alpha`(\beta`x).$

10.20 $\Lambda`\alpha = \Lambda$.

10.21 '$\lambda_x(\ldots x \ldots)$' for '$\{\langle y, x\rangle : y = \ldots x \ldots\}$'.

10.22 Func $\lambda_x(\ldots x \ldots)$.

10.23 $\ldots y \ldots \epsilon\ \mathcal{V} .\equiv.\ y \epsilon \arg \lambda_x(\ldots x \ldots)$.

10.24 $\ldots y \ldots \epsilon\ \mathcal{V} .\supset.\ \lambda_x(\ldots x \ldots)`y = \ldots y \ldots$.

10.25 'ι' for '$\lambda_x\{x\}$'.

10.26 $\iota`x = \{x\} \neq \Lambda$.

10.27 $x \epsilon \arg \iota$.

10.28 $\langle\{x\}, y\rangle \epsilon\ \iota .\equiv.\ x = y$.

10.29 $\breve{\iota}`\{x\} = x$.

11.1 '$\alpha \lesssim \beta$' for '$(\exists x)(\text{Func}\ x \,.\, \alpha \subseteq x``\beta)$'.

11.2 '$\alpha \simeq \beta$' for '$\alpha \lesssim \beta \lesssim \alpha$'.

12.1 '$\beta \leqq \alpha$' or '$\alpha \geqq \beta$' for '$(z)(\alpha \epsilon z \,.\, \breve{\iota}``z \subseteq z .\supset.\ \beta \epsilon z)$'.

12.2 '$\beta < \alpha$' or '$\alpha > \beta$' for '$\{\beta\} \leqq \alpha$'.

12.3 'N' for '$\{x: \Lambda \leqq x\}$'.

12.4 $x \leqq x$.

12.5 $x \leqq y \leqq z .\supset.\ x \leqq z$.

12.6 $x \leqq \{x\}$.

12.7 $x < \{x\}$.

12.8 $x < y \leqq z .\supset.\ x < z$.

12.9 $x < y .\supset.\ x \leqq y$.

12.10 $x < y < z .\supset.\ x < z$.

12.11 $x \leqq y .\supset:\ x = y .\vee\ (\exists z)(y = \{z\})$.

12.12 $w \leqq x .\equiv (z)(x \epsilon z \,.\, (y)(\{y\} \epsilon z .\supset.\ y \epsilon z) .\supset.\ w \epsilon z)$.

12.14 $\Lambda \epsilon \text{N}$.

12.15 $x \epsilon \text{N} .\supset.\ \{x\} \epsilon \text{N}$ (i.e., $\iota``\text{N} \subseteq \text{N}$).

12.16 $x \epsilon \text{N} .\supset:\ x = \Lambda .\vee\ (\exists y)(x = \{y\})$.

12.17 $x \leqq \Lambda .\equiv.\ x = \Lambda$.

12.18 $\sim(x < \Lambda)$.

12.19 '$\{,,,\alpha\}$' for '$\{x: x \leqq \alpha\}$'.

12.20 $x \epsilon \{,,,x\}$.

12.21 $\{,,,\Lambda\} = \{\Lambda\}$.

13.1 *Axiom schema.* Func $\alpha \supset.\ \alpha``\{,,,x\} \epsilon\ \mathcal{V}$.

13.2 Func $\alpha \,.\, \beta \subseteq \alpha``\{,,,x\} .\supset.\ \beta \epsilon\ \mathcal{V}$.

13.3 $\{,\,,x\} \cap \alpha \in \mathcal{V}.$

13.4 $\mathrm{Func}\,\alpha \,.\, \breve{\alpha}``\mathcal{V} \subseteq \{,\,,x\} \;.\supset.\; \alpha \in \mathcal{V}.$

13.5 $x \in \alpha \,.\, (y)(\{y\} \in \alpha \;.\supset.\; y \in \alpha) \;.\supset.\; \{,\,,x\} \subseteq \alpha.$

13.7 $Fw \,.\, (y)(Fy \supset F\{y\}) \,.\, w \leqq x \;.\supset Fx.$

13.9 $F\Lambda \,.\, (y)(Fy \supset F\{y\}) \,.\, x \in \mathrm{N} \;.\supset Fx.$

13.10 $F\Lambda \,.\, (y)(y \in \mathrm{N} \,.\, Fy \;.\supset F\{y\}) \,.\, x \in \mathrm{N} \;.\supset Fx.$

13.11 $x \leqq y \;.\equiv:\; x = y \;.\mathrm{v}.\; x < y.$

13.12 $x < \{y\} \;.\equiv.\; x \leqq y.$

13.13 $x \leqq \{y\} \;.\equiv:\; x = \{y\} \;.\mathrm{v}.\; x \leqq y$

(i.e., $\{,\,,\{y\}\} = \{,\,,y\} \cup \{\{y\}\}$).

13.16 $x \in \mathrm{N} \;.\equiv:\; x = \Lambda \;.\mathrm{v}.\; \Lambda < x.$

13.17 $x \in \mathrm{N} \;.\supset:\; \Lambda < x \;.\equiv.\; x \neq \Lambda.$

13.18 $x \leqq y \in \mathrm{N} \;.\supset.\; x \in \mathrm{N}.$

13.19 $x \in \mathrm{N} \;.\equiv.\; \{x\} \in \mathrm{N}.$

13.20 $x \in \mathrm{N} \;.\supset \sim(x < x).$

13.21 $x \in \mathrm{N} \;.\supset:\; x \leqq y \leqq x \;.\equiv.\; x = y.$

13.22 $x, y \in \mathrm{N} \;.\supset:\; x \leqq y \;.\equiv \sim(y < x).$

14.1 'Seq' for '$\{x\text{: Func } x \,.\, (\exists y)(\breve{x}``\mathcal{V} = \{,\,,y\})\}$'.

14.2 '$\alpha^{|\beta}$' for '$\{\langle x, y\rangle\text{: } (\exists z)(z \in \mathrm{Seq} \,.\, \langle x, \beta\rangle, \langle y, \Lambda\rangle \in z \,.$

$z \mid \iota \mid \breve{z} \subseteq \alpha)\}$'.

14.3 $\alpha^{|\Lambda} = I.$

14.6 $\alpha^{|\{x\}} = \alpha \mid \alpha^{|x}.$

14.7 $\alpha^{|\{\Lambda\}} = {}^{\cdot}\alpha.$

14.9 $x \notin \mathrm{N} \;.\supset.\; \alpha^{|x} = \Lambda.$

14.10 $\alpha^{|\{x\}} = \alpha^{|x} \mid \alpha.$

14.11 $x \in \mathrm{N} \,.\, \arg \alpha = \mathcal{V} \;.\supset.\; \arg \alpha^{|x} = \mathcal{V}.$

14.12 $\mathrm{Func}\,\alpha \supset \mathrm{Func}\,\alpha^{|x}.$

14.13 $I^{|x}`\Lambda = \Lambda.$

15.1 '$*\alpha$' for '$\{w\text{: } (\exists z)(w \in \alpha^{|z})\}$'.

15.2 $\langle x, x\rangle \in {}^*\alpha$ (i.e., $I \subseteq {}^*\alpha$).

15.5 $\langle x, y\rangle \in \alpha \,.\, \langle y, z\rangle \in {}^*\alpha \;.\supset.\; \langle x, z\rangle \in {}^*\alpha$

(i.e., $\alpha \mid {}^*\alpha \subseteq {}^*\alpha$).

15.7 $\alpha``\beta \subseteq \beta \;.\equiv.\; {}^*\alpha``\beta = \beta.$

15.10 $Fz \,.\, (x)(y)(\langle y, x\rangle \in \alpha \,.\, Fx \;.\supset Fy) \,.\, \langle w, z\rangle \in {}^*\alpha \;.\supset Fw.$

15.11 $*\alpha = I \cup (\alpha \mid *\alpha)$.

15.13 $x \geqq y \,.{\equiv}.\, \langle x, y\rangle \in *\iota$.

15.14 $\mathrm{N} = *\iota``\{\Lambda\}$.

16.1 '$\alpha + \beta$' for '$\iota^{|\beta`}\alpha$'.

16.2 '$\alpha\cdot\beta$' for $(\lambda_x(\alpha + x))^{|\beta`}\Lambda$'.

16.3 'α^β' for '$(\lambda_x(\alpha\cdot x))^{|\beta`}\{\Lambda\}$'.

16.4 $x \notin \mathrm{N} \,.{\supset}.\, \alpha + x = \alpha\cdot x = \alpha^x = \Lambda$.

16.7 $x\cdot\Lambda = \Lambda$.

16.8 $y \in \mathrm{N} \,.{\supset}.\, x\cdot\{y\} = x + x\cdot y$.

16.12 $x \in \mathrm{N} \,.{\supset}.\, x\cdot y \in \mathrm{N}$.

16.14 $y \in \mathrm{N} \,.{\supset}.\, x \leqq x + y$.

16.18 $x, y \in \mathrm{N} \,.{\supset}.\, x + y = y + x$.

16.19 $x, y, z \in \mathrm{N} \,.{\supset}.\, (x + y) + z = x + (y + z)$.

16.20 $x, y, z \in \mathrm{N} \,.\, x + z = y + z \,.{\supset}.\, x = y$.

16.25 $x \in \mathrm{N} \,.{\supset}.\, \{\Lambda\}\cdot x = x$.

16.26 $x, y \in \mathrm{N} \,.{\supset}.\, x\cdot y = y\cdot x$.

16.28 $x, y, z \in \mathrm{N} \,.{\supset}.\, (x\cdot y)\cdot z = x\cdot(y\cdot z)$.

16.29 $x, y \in \mathrm{N} \,.{\supset}:.\, x\cdot y = \Lambda \,.{\equiv}:\, x = \Lambda \,.\mathbf{v}.\, y = \Lambda$.

16.30 $x, y \in \mathrm{N} \,.\, y \neq \Lambda \,.{\supset}.\, x < x + y$.

16.31 $x, y, z \in \mathrm{N} \,.\, x \leqq y \,.{\supset}.\, x\cdot z \leqq y\cdot z$.

16.32 $x, y, z \in \mathrm{N} \,.\, x\cdot z < y\cdot z \,.{\supset}.\, x < y$.

16.33 $x, y, z \in \mathrm{N} \,.\, z \neq \Lambda \,.\, x < y \,.{\supset}.\, x\cdot z < y\cdot z$.

16.34 $x, y \in \mathrm{N} \,.\, x\cdot x < y\cdot y \,.{\supset}.\, x < y$.

17.1 '$\alpha;\beta$' for '$\alpha + (\alpha + \beta)\cdot(\alpha + \beta)$'.

17.4 $z, w \in \mathrm{N} \,.{\supset}:\, z;w \in \{x;y\colon x, y \in \mathrm{N} \,.\, Fxy\} \,.{\equiv}\, Fzw$.

18.1 'α/β' for '$\{z;w\colon z, w \in \mathrm{N} \,.\, z\cdot\beta < \alpha\cdot w\}$'.

18.8 $x, y, z, w \in \mathrm{N} \,.\, {\sim}(z = w = \Lambda) \,.{\supset}:$

$x/y \subseteq z/w \,.{\equiv}.\, z;w \notin x/y$.

18.10 'Rat' for '$\{x/y\colon x, y \in \mathrm{N} \,.\, y \neq \Lambda\}$'.

18.12 'Real' for '$\{\bigcup z\colon z \subseteq \mathrm{Rat}\} \cap {}^{-}\{\{\Lambda\}/\Lambda\}$'.

18.13 $\mathrm{Rat} \subseteq \mathrm{Real}$.

20.2 'Fnd α' for '$(x)(x \subseteq \breve{\alpha}``x \,.{\supset}.\, x = \Lambda)$'.

20.3 '$\alpha \prec \beta$' or '$\beta \succ \alpha$' for '${\sim}(\beta \preceq \alpha)$'.

20.4 Fnd $\alpha \supset .\ \langle x, x\rangle \notin \alpha.$

20.5 $\{x\colon {\sim}Fx\} \in \mathcal{V}\ .\ \mathrm{Fnd}\ \alpha\ .\ (y)((x)(\langle x, y\rangle \in \alpha\ .\!\supset Fx) \supset Fy)$
$.\!\supset Fz.$

20.6 $\{x\colon x \in (\alpha \cup \breve{\alpha})\text{“}\mathcal{V}\ .\ {\sim}Fx\} \in \mathcal{V}\ .\ \mathrm{Fnd}\ \alpha\ .$
$(y)((x)(\langle x, y\rangle \in \alpha\ .\!\supset Fx)\ .\ y \in (\alpha \cup \breve{\alpha})\text{“}\mathcal{V}\ .\!\supset Fy)\ .$
$z \in (\alpha \cup \breve{\alpha})\text{“}\mathcal{V}\ .\!\supset Fz.$

20.7 $\alpha \subseteq \beta\ .\ \mathrm{Fnd}\ \beta\ .\!\supset \mathrm{Fnd}\ \alpha.$

21.1 ‘Connex α’ for
‘$(x)(y)(x, y \in (\alpha \cup \breve{\alpha})\text{“}\mathcal{V}\ .\!\supset .\ \langle x, y\rangle \in \alpha \cup \breve{\alpha} \cup I)$’.

21.2 ‘Ordg α’ for ‘$\alpha \mid \alpha \subseteq \alpha \subseteq \overline{\ }I$. Connex α’.

21.4 ‘Wellord α’ for ‘Fnd α . Ordg α’.

21.5 Ordg $\alpha\ .\ x, y \in (\alpha \cup \breve{\alpha})\text{“}\mathcal{V}\ .\ \alpha\text{“}\{x\} = \alpha\text{“}\{y\}\ .\!\supset .\ x = y.$

21.7 ‘$\beta 1 \alpha$’ for ‘$\beta \in \alpha\text{“}\mathcal{V}\ .\ \beta \notin \breve{\alpha}\text{“}\mathcal{V}$’.

21.8 Ordg $\alpha\ .\ x1\alpha\ .\ y1\alpha\ .\!\supset .\ x = y.$

21.9 Wellord $\alpha \supset$ Wellord $\alpha \cap (\beta \times \beta).$

22.1 ‘$\acute{S}$’ for ‘$\lambda_x(x \cup \{x\})$’.

22.2 ‘C’ for ‘$\lambda_x(\acute{S}^{|x\text{‘}}\Lambda)$’.

22.8 ‘ω’ for ‘$_*\acute{S}\text{“}\{\Lambda\}$’.

22.9 $\Lambda \in \omega.$

22.10 $\acute{S}\text{“}\omega \subseteq \omega.$

22.11 $x \in \omega\ .\!\supset .\ x \cup \{x\} \in \mathcal{V}.$

22.12 $x \in \omega\ .\!\supset .\ x \cup \{x\} \in \omega.$

22.13 ‘$\mathfrak{E}$’ for ‘$\{\langle y, z\rangle\colon y \in z\}$’.

22.14 $\mathsf{U}\beta \subseteq \beta\ .\!\supset .\ \mathfrak{E}\restriction\beta = \mathfrak{E} \cap (\beta \times \beta).$

22.15 ‘NO’ for ‘$\{x\colon \mathsf{U}x \subseteq x\ .\ \mathrm{Wellord}\ \mathfrak{E}\restriction x\}$’.

23.1 $\Lambda, \{\Lambda\} \in \mathrm{NO}.$

23.2 $\Lambda \neq x \in \mathrm{NO}\ .\!\supset .\ \Lambda \in x.$

23.3 $x \in \mathrm{NO}\ .\!\supset .\ x = \mathsf{U}(x \cup \{x\}).$

23.4 $x \in \mathrm{NO}\ .\!\supset .\ x \notin x.$

23.5 $x \in \mathrm{NO}\ .\!\supset {\sim}(x \in^2 x).$

23.6 $x \in y \in \mathrm{NO}\ .\!\supset .\ x \subset y.$

23.8 $x \in \mathrm{NO}\ .\!\supset .\ x \subset \mathrm{NO}.$

23.9 $\text{UNO} \subseteq \text{NO}.$

23.10 $x, y \in z \in \text{NO} .\supset: x \in y .\text{v}. y \in x .\text{v}. x = y.$

23.11 $\alpha \subseteq \text{NO} .\supset. \alpha \cap \bigcap\alpha = \Lambda.$

23.12 *Axiom schema.* $\text{Func}\,\alpha . x \in \text{NO} .\supset. \alpha``x \in \mathcal{V}.$

23.13 $\text{Func}\,\alpha . x \in \text{NO} . \beta \subseteq \alpha``x .\supset. \beta \in \mathcal{V}.$

23.15 $\text{Func}\,\alpha . \breve{\alpha}``\mathcal{V} \subseteq x \in \text{NO} .\supset. \alpha \in \mathcal{V}.$

23.16 $(y)((x)(x \in y .\supset Fx) . y \in \text{NO} .\supset Fy) . z \in \text{NO} .\supset Fz.$

23.18 $\alpha \subseteq \breve{\mathfrak{E}}``\alpha .\supset. \alpha \cap \text{NO} = \Lambda.$

23.19 $\bigcup\alpha \subseteq \alpha \subset z \in \text{NO} .\supset. \alpha \in z.$

23.21 $x, y \in \text{NO} .\supset: x \subseteq y .\text{v}. y \subseteq x.$

23.22 $x, y \in \text{NO} .\supset: x \subseteq y .\text{v}. y \in x.$

23.23 $x, y \in \text{NO} .\supset: x \in y .\text{v}. y \in x .\text{v}. x = y.$

23.24 $\bigcup\alpha \subseteq \alpha \subset \text{NO} .\equiv. \alpha \in \text{NO}.$

23.25 $\alpha \subseteq \text{NO} .\supset: \bigcup\alpha \in \text{NO} .\text{v}. \bigcup\alpha = \text{NO}.$

23.26 $x \in y \in \text{NO} .\supset: x \cup \{x\} \in y .\text{v}. x \cup \{x\} = y.$

23.27 $\Lambda \neq \alpha \subseteq \text{NO} .\supset. \bigcap\alpha \in \alpha.$

24.3 Wellord $\mathfrak{E}\restriction\text{NO}.$

24.4 $\text{NO} \notin \mathcal{V}.$

24.9 $x \in \text{NO} .\supset. x \cup \{x\} \in \text{NO}.$

25.1 ‘SEQ α’ for ‘Func $\alpha : \breve{\alpha}``\mathcal{V} \in \text{NO} .\text{v}. \breve{\alpha}``\mathcal{V} = \text{NO}$’.

25.2 ‘Aγ’ for ‘$\bigcup\{w$: SEQ w .

$(y)(y \in \breve{w}``\mathcal{V} .\supset. \langle w`y, w\restriction y\rangle \in \gamma)\}$’.

26.1 $\text{Func}\,\text{A}\gamma\restriction y . \langle x, y\rangle \in \text{A}\gamma .\supset. \langle x, \text{A}\gamma\restriction y\rangle \in \gamma . \text{A}\gamma\restriction y \in \mathcal{V}.$

26.3 $\breve{\text{A}\gamma}``\mathcal{V} \in \text{NO} .\text{v}. \breve{\text{A}\gamma}``\mathcal{V} = \text{NO}.$

26.4 $\text{Func}\,\gamma \supset \text{SEQ}\,\text{A}\gamma.$

26.5 $\text{Func}\,\gamma . y \in \breve{\text{A}\gamma}``\mathcal{V} .\supset. \langle \text{A}\gamma`y, \text{A}\gamma\restriction y\rangle \in \gamma.$

26.6 $\text{Func}\,\gamma . \breve{\text{A}\gamma}``\mathcal{V} \in \mathcal{V} .\supset. \text{A}\gamma \notin \breve{\gamma}``\mathcal{V}.$

27.1 ‘Φ_α’ for ‘$\{\langle x, z\rangle: \alpha``\{x\} = z``\mathcal{V} :\cdot z = \Lambda .\supset x1\alpha\}$’.

27.2 ‘eα’ for ‘AΦ_α’.

27.3 ‘Cor β’ for ‘Func β . Func $\breve{\beta}$’.

28.1 $\alpha \subseteq \beta \lesssim \gamma .\supset. \alpha \lesssim \gamma.$

28.2 $\alpha \lesssim \beta \subseteq \gamma .\supset. \alpha \lesssim \gamma.$

28.7	$\alpha \precsim \{,,,x\} \,.\, \text{Func}\, \beta \,.\!\supset\!.\, \beta\text{“}\alpha \precsim \alpha.$
28.10	$\alpha \precsim \{,,,x\} \,.\!\supset\!.\, \alpha \in \mathcal{V}.$
28.12	$\alpha \precsim \beta \precsim \{,,,x\} \,.\!\supset\!.\, \alpha \precsim \{,,,x\}.$
28.16	$\alpha \cap \{y\colon y \notin \beta\text{‘}y\} \in \mathcal{V} \,.\, \text{Func}\, \beta \,.\!\supset\!.\, \{x\colon x \subseteq \alpha\} \nsubseteq \beta\text{“}\alpha.$
28.17	$(w)(\alpha \cap \{y\colon y \notin w\text{‘}y\} \in \mathcal{V}) \supset.\, \alpha \prec \{x\colon x \subseteq \alpha\}.$
29.1	‘C_1’ for ‘$(x)(y)(x \cap \bar{y}, \breve{x}, x\text{“}\mathcal{V}, x \restriction y \in \mathcal{V})$’.
29.3	$\text{C}_1 \supset (x)(y)(x \cap y, x\text{“}y \in \mathcal{V}).$
30.1	‘$\bar{\bar{\alpha}}$’ or ‘$^{=}\alpha$’ for ‘$\{x\colon x \in \text{NO} \,.\, x \prec \alpha\}$’.
30.2	‘NC’ for ‘$\{x\colon x = \bar{\bar{x}}\}$’.
30.3	‘ω_α’ for ‘$\text{e}(\mathfrak{E} \cap ((\text{NC} \cap \bar{\omega}) \times \text{NC}))\text{‘}\alpha$’.
31.1	‘$\beta\ \text{Sln}\ \alpha$’ for ‘$(y)(y \in \alpha \,.\, y \neq \Lambda \,.\!\supset (\exists x)(\beta \cap y = \{x\}))$’.
31.2	‘$\text{Ch}\ \alpha$’ for ‘$\text{Func}\ \breve{}(\mathfrak{E} \restriction \alpha) \supset (\exists w)(w\ \text{Sln}\ \alpha)$’.
32.1	$\text{C}_1 \,.\, \text{Func}\, y \,.\, \beta\ \text{Sln}\ \{z\colon (\exists w)(z = \breve{y}\text{“}\{w\})\}$ $.\!\supset\!.\, \text{Cor}\ y \restriction \beta \,.\, (y \restriction \beta)\text{“}\mathcal{V} = y\text{“}\mathcal{V}.$
32.3	$\text{C}_1 \,.\, \beta\ \text{Slr}\ \{x\colon x \subseteq z\} \,.\, w = \text{A}\Psi_{\beta z}$ $.\!\supset\!.\, \text{Cor}\ w \,.\, w\text{“}\mathcal{V} = z \,.\, \breve{w}\text{“}\mathcal{V} \in \text{NO}.$

Note also these from §6:

‘$\hat{u}Fu$’ for ‘$\{u\colon (\exists z)(u \in z) \,.\, Fu\}$’ or ‘$\text{U}\mathcal{V} \cap \{u\colon Fu\}$’,

‘V’ for ‘$\hat{u}(u = u)$’ or ‘$\text{U}\mathcal{V}$’,

‘$\iota\alpha$’ for ‘$\hat{u}(u = \alpha)$’.

BIBLIOGRAPHICAL REFERENCES

This list includes only such works as happen to have been alluded to, by title or otherwise, in the course of the book.

Ackermann, Wilhelm, "Zur Axiomatik der Mengenlehre," *Mathematische Annalen 131* (1956), 336–345.

——*See also* Hilbert.

Bachmann, Heinz, *Transfinite Zahlen* (Berlin: Springer, 1955).

Bar-Hillel, *see* Fraenkel.

Behmann, Heinrich, *Mathematik und Logik* (Leipzig, 1927).

Bernays, Paul, "A system of axiomatic set theory," *Journal of Symbolic Logic 2* (1937), 65–77; *6* (1941), 1–17; *7* (1942), 65–89, 133–145; *8* (1943), 89–106; *13* (1948), 65–79; *19* (1954), 81–96.

——"Zur Frage der Unendlichkeitsschemata in der axiomatischen Mengenlehre," in A. Robinson, ed., *Essays on the Foundation of Mathematics* dedicated to Fraenkel (Jerusalem: Hebrew University, 1961).

——and A. A. Fraenkel, *Axiomatic Set Theory* (Amsterdam: North-Holland, 1958).

——*See also* Hilbert.

Brown, K. R., and Hao Wang, "Finite set theory, number theory and axioms of limitation," *Mathematische Annalen 164* (1966), 26–29.

——"Short definitions of the ordinals," *Journal of Symbolic Logic 31* (1966), 409–414.

Burali-Forti, Cesare, "Una questione sui numeri transfiniti," *Rendiconti di Palermo 11* (1897), 154–164. Translation in van Heijenoort.

Cantor, Georg, *Gesammelte Abhandlungen mathematischen und philosophischen Inhalts*, E. Zermelo, ed. (Berlin, 1932). The most relevant papers date from the years 1878–1899.

Carnap, Rudolf, *The Logical Syntax of Language* (London and New York, 1937; paperback, Paterson, N.J.: Littlefield and Adams, 1960).

Church, Alonzo, *The Calculi of Lambda Conversion* (Princeton, 1941).
——*Introduction to Mathematical Logic* (Princeton: Princeton University Press, 1956).
Chwistek, Leon, "The theory of constructive types," *Annales de la Société Polonaise de Mathématique 2* (1924), 9–48; *3* (1925), 92–141.
Cohen, P. J., *Set Theory and the Continuum Hypothesis* (New York: Benjamin, 1966).
Dedekind, Richard, *Stetigkeit und irrationale Zahlen* (Brunswick, 1872).
——*Was sind und was sollen die Zahlen?* (Brunswick, 1888).
Feferman, Solomon, "Transfinite recursive progressions of axiomatic theories," *Journal of Symbolic Logic 27* (1963 for 1962), 259–316.
Fraenkel, A. A., *Einleitung in die Mengenlehre* (3d ed., Berlin, 1928).
——*Abstract Set Theory* (Amsterdam: North-Holland, 1953; 2d ed., 1961).
——"Der Begriff 'definit' und die Unabhängigkeit des Auswahlaxioms," *Sitzungsberichte der Preussischen Akademie der Wissenschaften.* phys.-math. Kl., 1922, 253–257
——"Zu den Grundlagen der Cantor-Zermeloschen Mengenlehre," *Mathematische Annalen 86* (1922), 230–237.
——and Y. Bar-Hillel, *Foundations of Set Theory* (Amsterdam: North-Holland, 1959).
——*See also* Bernays.
Frege, Gottlob, *Begriffsschrift* (Jena, 1879). Translation in van Heijenoort.
——*Die Grundlagen der Arithmetik* (Breslau, 1884); trans. by J. L. Austin, *The Foundations of Arithmetic* (2d ed., Oxford: Blackwell, 1953; paperback, New York: Harper, 1960).
——*Grundgesetze der Arithmetik* (Jena: vol. 1, 1893; vol. 2, 1903).
Gal, *see* Novak.
Gödel, Kurt, *The Consistency of the Continuum Hypothesis* (Princeton, 1940).
——"Die Vollständigkeit der Axiome des logischen Funktionenkalküls," *Monatshefte für Mathematik und Physik 37* (1930), 349–360. Translation in van Heijenoort.
——"Ueber formal unentscheidbare Sätze der Principia Mathematica und verwandter Systeme," *Monatshefte für Mathematik und Physik 38* (1931), 173–198. Translation in van Heijenoort.
——"Consistency-proof for the generalized continuum hypothesis," *Proceedings of the National Academy of Sciences 25* (1939), 220–224.
Grelling, Kurt, *Mengenlehre* (Leipzig, 1924).
——and L. Nelson, "Bemerkungen zu den Paradoxien von Russell und Burali-Forti," *Abhandlungen der Fries'schen Schule 2* (1907–8), 300–334
Hailperin, Theodore, "A set of axioms for logic," *Journal of Symbolic*

Logic 9 (1944), 1–19.
Halmos, Paul, *Naive Set Theory* (Princeton: van Nostrand, 1960).
Hausdorff, F., *Grundzüge der Mengenlehre* (Leipzig, 1914).
Henkin, Leon, "Completeness in the theory of types," *Journal of Symbolic Logic 15* (1950), 81–91.
Henson, C. W., III, "Cantorian Well-Orderings in Quine's New Foundations," dissertation, M. I. T., 1967.
Herbrand, Jacques, *Recherches sur la Théorie de la Démonstration* (Warsaw, 1930).
Hessenberg, Gerhard, *Grundbegriffe der Mengenlehre* (Göttingen, 1906).
Hilbert, D., and W. Ackermann, *Grundzüge der theoretischen Logik* (Berlin, 1928; 2d ed., Berlin: Springer, 1938; 3d ed., 1949); translation of 2d ed., *Principles of Mathematical Logic* (New York: Chelsea, 1950).
——and P. Bernays, *Grundlagen der Mathematik* (Berlin, vol. 1, 1934; vol. 2, 1939).
Kemeny, J. G., "Type Theory versus Set Theory," dissertation, Princeton, 1949; abstract in *Journal of Symbolic Logic 15* (1950), 78.
Kleene, S. C., *Introduction to Metamathematics* (New York: van Nostrand, 1952).
——"Two papers on the predicate calculus," *Memoirs of the American Mathematical Society* (1952), No. 10.
König, Julius, "Ueber die Grundlagen der Mengenlehre und das Kontinuumproblem," *Mathematische Annalen 61* (1905), 156–160. Translation in van Heijenoort.
Kreider, D. L., and H. Rogers, Jr., "Constructive versions of ordinal number classes." *Transactions of the American Mathematical Society 100* (1961), 325–369.
Kreisel, G., "La prédicativité," *Bulletin de la Société Mathématique de France 88* (1960), 371–391.
——and H. Wang, "Some applications of formalized consistency proofs," *Fundamenta Mathematicae 42* (1955), 101–110.
Kuratowski, Casimir, "Sur la notion de l'ordre dans la théorie des ensembles," *Fundamenta Mathematicae 2* (1920), 161–171.
Lévy, Azriel, "On Ackermann's set theory," *Journal of Symbolic Logic 24* (1960, for 1959), 154–166.
——"Axiom schemata of strong infinity in axiomatic set theory," *Pacific Journal of Mathematics 10* (1960), 223–238.
Lindenbaum, A., and A. Mostowski, "Ueber die Unabhangigkeit des Auswahlaxioms und einiger seiner Folgerungen," *Comptes rendus des séances de la Société des Sciences et des Lettres de Varsovie*, Classe III, *31* (1938), 27–32.
——*See also* Tarski.

MacLane, Saunders, "Locally small categories and the foundations of set theory," in *Infinitistic Methods*, proceedings of a 1959 symposium (Warsaw, 1961), pp. 25–43.

McNaughton, Robert, "A non-standard truth definition," *Proceedings of the American Mathematical Society 5* (1954), 505–509.

——*See also* Wang.

Mahlo, P., "Zur Theorie und Anwendung der ρ_0-Zahlen," *Berichte über die Verhandlungen der Sächsischen Akademie der Wissenschaft zu Leipzig* (*math.-ph. Kl.*) *64* (1912), 108–112; *65* (1912–3), 268–282.

Martin, R. M., "A homogeneous system for formal logic," *Journal of Symbolic Logic 8* (1943), 1–23.

Mendelson, Elliott, *Introduction to Mathematical Logic* (Princeton: van Nostrand, 1964).

——"The axiom of Fundierung and the axiom of choice, "*Archiv für mathematische Logik und Grundlagenforschung 4* (1958), 65–70.

Mirimanoff, D., "Les antinomies de Russell et de Burali-Forti et le problème fondamental de la théorie des ensembles," *L'Enseignement Mathématique 19* (1917), 37–52.

Montague, Richard, "Non-finite axiomatizability," in *Summaries of Talks at Summer Institute for Symbolic Logic* (Ithaca: mimeographed, 1957), pp. 256–259.

——"Semantical closure and non-finite axiomatizability," in *Infinitistic Methods*, proceedings of a 1959 symposium (Warsaw, 1961), pp. 45–69.

——and R. L. Vaught, "Natural models of set theories," *Fundamenta Mathematicae 47* (1959), 219–242.

Mostowski, Andrzej, "Some impredicative definitions in the axiomatic set theory," *Fundamenta Mathematicae 37* (1950–51), 111–124.

——"On models of axiomatic systems," *Fundamenta Mathematicae 39* (1953 for 1952), 133–158.

——*See also* Lindenbaum.

Myhill, John, "A derivation of number theory from ancestral theory," *Journal of Symbolic Logic 17* (1952), 192–197.

Nelson, *see* Grelling.

Neumann, J. von, "Zur Einführung der transfiniten Zahlen," *Acta Litterarum ac Scientiarum Regiae Universitatis Hungaricae Francisco-Josephinae* (*sect. scient. math.*) *1* (1923), 199–208. Translation in van Heijenoort.

——"Eine Axiomatisierung der Mengenlehre," *Journal für reine und angewandte Mathematik 154* (1925), 219–240; *155* (1926), 128. Translation in van Heijenoort.

——"Zur Hilbertschen Beweistheorie," *Mathematische Zeitschrift 26* (1927), 1–46.

——"Die Axiomatisierung der Mengenlehre," *Mathematische Zeitschrift 27* (1928), 669–752.

——"Ueber die Definition durch transfinite Induktion und verwandte Fragen der allgemeinen Mengenlehre," *Mathematische Annalen 99* (1928), 373–391.

——"Ueber eine Widerspruchsfreiheitsfrage in der axiomatischen Mengenlehre," *Journal für reine und angewandte Mathematik 160* (1929), 227–241.

Novak, I. L. (Mrs. Steven Gal), "A construction for models of consistent systems," *Fundamenta Mathematicae 37* (1950–51), 87–110.

Oberschelp, Arnold, "Untersuchungen zur mehrsortigen Quantorenlogik," *Mathematische Annalen 145* (1962), 297–333.

Ono, Katuzi, "A set theory founded on unique generating principle," *Nagoya Mathematical Journal 12* (1957), 151–159.

Orey, Steven, "New foundations and the axiom of counting," *Duke Mathematical Journal 31* (1964), 655–660.

Parsons, Charles, "A note on Quine's treatment of transfinite recursion," *Journal of Symbolic Logic 29* (1964), 179–182.

Peano, Giuseppe, *Arithmetices Principia* (Turin, 1889). Translation in van Heijenoort.

——*Formulaire de Mathématiques* (Paris, 1901).

——"Super theorema de Cantor–Bernstein," *Rendiconti di Palermo 21* (1906), 360–366; reprinted with "Additione" in *Revista de Mathematica 8* (1902–6), 136–157.

——"Sulla definizione di funzione," *Atti della Reale Accademia dei Lincei* (*Rendiconti, classe di scienza*) *20* (1911), 3–5.

Poincaré, Henri, "Les mathématiques et la logique," *Revue de Métaphysique et de Morale 13* (1905), 815–835; *14* (1906), 17–34, 294–317.

Putnam, Hilary, "Axioms of class existence," in *Summaries of Talks at Summer Institute for Symbolic Logic* (Ithaca: mimeographed, 1957), pp. 271–274.

Quine, W. V., *A System of Logistic* (Cambridge, Mass., 1934).

——*Mathematical Logic* (New York, 1940; rev. ed., Cambridge, Mass.: Harvard University Press, 1951; paperback, New York: Harper, 1962).

——*O Sentido da Nova Lógica*, 1942 Brazilian lectures (São Paulo: Martins, 1944); Spanish translation by Mario Bunge, *El Sentido de la Nueva Lógica* (Buenos Aires: Nueva Visión, 1958).

——*Methods of Logic* (New York: Holt, 1950; rev. ed., Holt, Rinehart, and Winston, 1959).

——*Word and Object* (Cambridge, Mass.: M.I.T. Press, 1960).

——*Selected Logic Papers* (New York: Random House, 1966).

——"A theory of classes presupposing no canons of type," *Proceedings of the National Academy of Sciences 22* (1936), 320–326.

——"On the axiom of reducibility," *Mind 45* (1936), 498–500.

——"New foundations for mathematical logic," *American Mathematical Monthly 44* (1937), 70–80; reprinted with additions in Quine, *From a Logical Point of View* (Cambridge, Mass.: Harvard University Press, 2d ed., 1961).

——"Whitehead and the rise of modern logic," in P. A. Schilpp, ed., *The Philosophy of A. N. Whitehead* (Evanston, Ill., 1941), pp. 125–163. Reprinted in *Selected Logic Papers.*

——"Element and number," *Journal of Symbolic Logic 6* (1941), 135–149. Reprinted in *Selected Logic Papers.*

——"On universals," *Journal of Symbolic Logic 12* (1947), 74–84.

——"On ω-inconsistency and a so-called axiom of infinity," *Journal of Symbolic Logic 18* (1953), 119–124. Reprinted in *Selected Logic Papers.*

——"Unification of universes in set theory," *Journal of Symbolic Logic 21* (1956), 267–279.

——"A basis for number theory in finite classes," *Bulletin of the American Mathematical Society 67* (1961), 391f.

——and Hao Wang, "On ordinals," *Bulletin of the American Mathematical Society 70* (1964), 297f.

Ramsey, F. P., "The foundations of mathematics," *Proceedings of the London Mathematical Society 25* (1925), 338–384; reprinted in Ramsey, *The Foundations of Mathematics and other Logical Essays* (London, 1931; paperback, Paterson, N. J.: Littlefield and Adams, 1960).

Richard, Jules, "Les principes des mathematiques et le problème des ensembles," *Revue générale des sciences pures et appliquées 16* (1905), 541. Translation in van Heijenoort.

Robinson, R. M., "The theory of classes. A modification of von Neumann's system," *Journal of Symbolic Logic 2* (1937), 29–36.

Rogers, *see* Kreider.

Rosser, J. B., *Logic for Mathematicians* (New York: McGraw-Hill, 1953).

——"The Burali-Forti paradox," *Journal of Symbolic Logic 7* (1942), 1–17.

——"The axiom of infinity in Quine's New Foundations," *Journal of Symbolic Logic 17* (1952), 238–242.

——Review of Specker, *Journal of Symbolic Logic 19* (1954), 127f.

——and Hao Wang, "Non-standard models for formal logic," *Journal of Symbolic Logic 15* (1950), 113–129.

Rubin, Herman and J. E., *Equivalents of the Axiom of Choice* (Amsterdam: North Holland, 1963).

Russell, Bertrand, *The Principles of Mathematics* (Cambridge, England, 1903; 2d ed., New York, 1938).

——*Introduction to Mathematical Philosophy* (London, 1919).

——"On denoting," *Mind 14* (1905), 479–493; reprinted in Russell, *Logic and Knowledge* (London: Allen and Unwin, 1956), and in Feigl and Sellars, eds., *Readings in Philosophical Analysis* (New York: Appleton-Century-Crofts, 1949).

——"On some difficulties in the theory of transfinite numbers and order types," *Proceedings of the London Mathematical Society 4* (1906), 29–53.

——"Mathematical logic as based on the theory of types," *American Journal of Mathematics 30* (1908), 222–262; reprinted in Russell, *Logic and Knowledge* (London: Allen and Unwin, 1956).

——*See also* Whitehead.

Scott, Dana, "Quine's individuals," in E. Nagel *et al.*, eds., *Logic, Methodology, and Philosophy of Science* (Stanford: Stanford University Press, 1962), pp. 111–115.

Shepherdson, J. C., "Inner models for set theory," *Journal of Symbolic Logic 16* (1951), 161–190; *17* (1952), 225–237; *18* (1953), 145–167.

Shoenfield, J. R., "A relative consistency proof," *Journal of Symbolic Logic 19* (1954), 21–28.

——"The independence of the axiom of choice" (abstract), *Journal of Symbolic Logic 20* (1955), 202.

Sierpiński, Waclaw, *Cardinal and Ordinal Numbers* (Warsaw, 1958).

——"Une remarque sur la notion d'ordre," *Fundamenta Mathematicae 2* (1921), 199f.

——"L'hypothèse généralisée du continu et l'axiome du choix," *Fundamenta Mathematicae 34* (1947), 1–5.

Skolem, Thoralf, "Einige Bemerkungen zur axiomatischen Begründung der Mengenlehre," *Conférences au 5e. Congrès [1922] des Mathématiciens Scandinaves* (Helsingfors, 1923), pp. 218–232. Translation in van Heijenoort.

——"Ueber einige Grundlagenfragen der Mathematik," *Skrifter Utgitt av Det Norske Videnskaps-Akademi i Oslo, Kl. I* (1929), No. 4.

Specker, Ernst, "The axiom of choice in Quine's New foundations for mathematical logic," *Proceedings of the National Academy of Sciences 39* (1953), 972–975.

——"Dualität," *Dialectica 12* (1958), 451–465.

——"Typical ambiguity," in E. Nagel *et al.*, eds., *Logic, Methodology, and Philosophy of Science* (Stanford: Stanford University Press, 1962), pp. 116–124.

Stegmüller, Wolfgang, "Eine Axiomatisierung der Mengenlehre, beruhend auf den Systemen von Bernays und Quine," in M. Käsbauer *et al.*, eds., *Logik und Logikkalkül* dedicated to Britzelmayr (Freiburg: Verlag Alber, 1962), pp. 57–103.

Suppes, Patrick, *Axiomatic Set Theory* (Princeton: van Nostrand, 1960).

Tarski, Alfred, *Logic, Semantics, Metamathematics: Papers from 1923 to 1938*, trans, by J. H. Woodger (Oxford: Clarendon Press, 1956).

——"Ueber unerreichbare Kardinalzahlen," *Fundamenta Mathematicae 30* (1938), 68–89.

——"Notions of proper models for set theories," *Bulletin of the American Mathematical Society 62* (1956), 601.

——and A. Lindenbaum, "Communication sur les recherches de la théorie des ensembles," *Comptes Rendus de la Société des Sciences et des Lettres de Varsovie (classe III), 19* (1926), 299–330.

van Heijenoort, J., ed., *From Frege to Gödel: A Source Book in Mathematical Logic, 1879–1931* (Cambridge, Mass.: Harvard University Press, 1967).

Vaught, *see* Montague.

von Neumann, *see* Neumann.

Wang, Hao, *A Survey of Mathematical Logic* (Peking, 1962; Amsterdam: North-Holland, 1963).

——"On Zermelo's and von Neumann's axioms for set theory," *Proceedings of the National Academy of Sciences 35* (1949), 150–155.

——"A formal system of logic," *Journal of Symbolic Logic 15* (1950), 25–32.

——"Arithmetic translations of axiom systems," *Transactions of the American Mathematical Society 71* (1951), 283–293.

——"The irreducibility of impredicative principles," *Mathematische Annalen 125* (1952), 56–66.

——"Truth definitions and consistency proofs," *Transactions of the American Mathematical Society 73* (1952), 243–275; reprinted in Wang, *Survey*.

——"The axiomatization of arithmetic," *Journal of Symbolic Logic 22* (1957), 145–158; reprinted in Wang, *Survey*.

——"Eighty years of foundational studies," *Dialectica 12* (1958), 466–497; reprinted in Wang, *Survey*.

——and R. McNaughton, *Les Systèmes Axiomatiques de la Théorie des Ensembles* (Paris: Gauthier-Villars, 1953).

——*See also* Brown; Kreisel; Quine; Rosser.

Weyl, Hermann, *Das Kontinuum* (Leipzig, 1918).

Whitehead, A. N., "The logic of relations, logical substitution groups, and cardinal numbers," *American Journal of Mathematics 25* (1903), 157–178.

——and B. Russell, *Principia Mathematica* (Cambridge, England: vol. 1, 1910; vol. 2, 1912; vol. 3, 1913; 2d ed., 1925–1927; paperback, to *56: New York: Cambridge University Press, 1961).

Wiener, Norbert, "A simplification of the logic of relations," *Proceedings of the Cambridge Philosophical Society 17* (1912–14),

387–390. Reprinted in van Heijenoort.

Zermelo, Ernst. "Beweis, dass jede Menge wohlgeordnet werden kann," *Mathematische Annalen 59* (1904), 514–516. Translation in van Heijenoort.

——"Untersuchungen über die Grundlagen der Mengenlehre," *Mathematische Annalen 65* (1908), 261–281. Translation in van Heijenoort.

——"Sur les ensembles finis et le principe de l'induction complète," *Acta Mathematica 32* (1909), 185–193.

——"Ueber Grenzzahlen und Mengenbereiche," *Fundamenta Mathematicae 16* (1930), 29–47.

Zorn, Max, "A remark on method in transfinite algebra," *Bulletin of the American Mathematical Society 41* (1935), 667–670.

INDEX

Lester V. Hoffman's help with this index is gratefully acknowledged, and likewise his help and Barnet Weinstock's in proofreading the book.

Abstract: set theory 5; objects 10; algebra 329
Abstraction 16–18, 28, 34, 39, 251, 259f; Greek letters for 18, 33, 47; of relations 21, 28, 59, 61, 249, 252; as noncommittal 35, 275, 277, 284, 320n, 327n; two forms 45f, 301–303; of functions 70–73; of attributes 244, 249; as primitive 257n; law of, *see* Comprehension axiom *and* Comprehension premiss
Accumulate 177–184
Ackermann, Wilhelm 254n, 257f, 264n, 322
Adaptor 177n
Addition, *see* Sum
Aggregate 1. *See also* Class; Union
Aleph 210–215
Algebra 328f; Boolean 17f, 26, 50, 64, 287, 289; of relations 26, 64
Analysis 4f, 23, 250, 264f
Ancestor 28f, 53, 74f, 101, 105, 304
Ancestral 76n, 101–106; induction 104, 140f, 144f
Antinomy, *see* Paradox
Antisymmetry 23, 147
Anzahl (having *x* members) 78, 81f. *See also* Cardinal; Size
Application: of functions 68, 70; of number 81, 135
Argument 24f, 65, 68f, 246f
Asymmetry 23, 146
Atomic 9f, 14, 259
Attribute 26, 243–247, 249–251; vs. class 2f, 245, 252, 256–259; vs. expression 9, 19, 245, 254–258
Attribution 2, 21, 28, 59f, 62, 249
Aussonderung 37, 88n, 165, 328, 331; in Zermelo 37f, 271f, 276–278, 284, 315; fails for NF 38, 297; in cumulative types 274–276; in von Neumann 310–312
Axiom 11, 30, 87f, 164f, 331f; of individuals 32n, 270, 275–277, 285; of null class 50, 88f, 276; of pairing 50, 88f, 275f, 311, 331f; Peano's 91, 110, 280, 305; of constructivity 237, 326f; of sethood 236, 302, 311f, 323, 328; finitely many 313, 320f, 326; of reducibility 250–254, 256, 264f; of sum 272, 274, 276, 328, 331f; of power set 274–276, 311, 328, 331f; of typical ambiguity 292; in BQ 321n; in Ackermann 322; strength of 323–329; and inaccessible numbers 324, 328; of consistency 325; of *Beschränktheit* 326f; in Lévy 328. *See also Aussonderung;* Bernays; Choice; Comprehension axiom;

Extensionality; *Fundierung;* Infinity; Neumann; Replacement; Types; Zermelo

Bachmann, Heinz 210n, 214n
Bar-Hillel, Yehoshua 265n
Bauer-Mengelberg, S. 4n
Behmann, Heinrich 19f
Bernays, Paul 12n, 15n, 224n, 328; and Fraenkel (1958) 20f, 35, 45f, 174, 224n, 230n, 327; 1937–54 series 20f, 152n, 155n, 282n, 313, 317, 324n; von Neumann- 234–238, 313f, 319, 321, 324, 332
Bernstein, F. 204, 207f, 232
Berry, G. G. 255
Beschränktheit 326f.
Bestimmtheit, *see* Extensionality
Biconditional 12f
Boolean algebra 17f, 26, 50, 64, 287, 289
Bound 54f, 120, 128; law of least 120, 130–132, 200, 249f, 264f
BQ 321n
Brown, K. R. 88, 154, 157n, 282n
Burali-Forti, Cesare 171, 253, 264, 302, 312

Cantor, Georg 2, 5, 130, 212; 1899 letter 3, 20f, 37n, 88n, 271n, 284n, 302; size comparison of classes 78, 87, 199f; ordering 142n, 151, 153; paradox 171n, 202, 263, 278, 308f, 314f; law or theorem 201f, 210, 213, 262f, 265, 277f, 283, 292–294, 308f, 314f, 318; cardinals 209f, 212f
Cantorian 294–296, 299, 307f, 318
Cardinal number 135, 208–216; and axiom of choice 233f; in NF 289, 294–296. *See also* Size
Carnap, Rudolf 253n
Cartesian product 22, 64
Cauchy, A. L. 136n
Chain 101n
Choice, axiom of 88n, 199, 208, 217–220, 231; equivalents of 220, 222–226, 228–230; consistency of 234–238, 327; fails for NF 296, 299, 308, 318; in Zermelo 276f; in von Neumann 312f
Church, Alonzo 70f, 257f
Chwistek, Leon 265n
Circumflex 45f, 51, 244, 247, 250, 301f, 314
Class 1–3, 20, 243; missing 5, 36, 171; of classes 29, 47f; everything a class 32f, 47; expressing existence of 39, 43–46. *See also* Attribute; Comprehension; Set; Too big; Ultimate; Virtual
Classitude 31–33, 274, 276
Closure condition 28, 74
Cohen, P. J. 238
Committal, *see* Noncommittal
Commutativity, failure of 158
Comparability 150, 171, 190f, 208, 231f
Complement 18, 22, 62, 72, 287, 289
Complex number 137f
Comprehension axiom 35–38, 50f, 86–88, 164, 218, 241, 331f; in Cantor 20; in von Neumann 235–237, 310, 313, 320; finitely many 313, 320f; covert 257, 260; in theory of types 260, 267, 269, 287, 290; predicative and otherwise 264f, 310, 313, 320–322, 329; in Zermelo 271f, 274–277; in NF 288, 299; in ML 300, 302; in Ackermann 322. *See also* Sethood
Comprehension premiss 143, 183, 193f, 201f, 222; for real numbers 131–133; abbreviated 204
Concretion 16, 44, 260; for relations 21, 61f, 64, 124; for functions 73; for attributes etc. 249
Confinement 64, 148f, 155, 165. *See also* Relativization
Connexity 22, 64, 94, 146f. *See also* Comparability
Consistency 37, 286, 325; of axiom of individuals 32n; of axiom of choice 234–238, 326; of theory of types 263f, 269, 277, 286, 291f, 298; of Zermelo 277; of NF 291f; of ML 302, 307, 316–320; of von Neumann 319; of Ackermann 322n; axioms of 325
Constructible 236–238, 326

Constructive 243, 251, 253f, 264f, 328
Contextual definition 16, 19, 39, 244, 251, 256, 259-261; of description 70
Continuity 23, 133, 250
Continuum 134, 213f, 238, 326
Contraction 18n, 36n
Contradiction, *see* Consistency; Paradox
Convention of free substitution 52, 58f, 68, 88, 108
Converse 22, 25, 64, 72, 204
Correlation, Correspondence 78, 145, 149f, 184–186, 203f
Counting 78, 82, 199, 211. *See also* Enumeration; Numeration
Course of values 139–141, 143f, 175–177
Culling 317f
Cumulative types 274–279, 281f, 284, 287; finite 263, 269; and NF 290, 292f; transfinite 282n, 324
Cut 129
Cycle 36, 86, 95, 195. *See also Fundierung*

Dedekind, Richard 78n, 80n, 92n, 101n, 129, 228, 313
Definiteness, *see* Extensionality
Definition 13, 208, 242, 277, 303. *See also* Contextual; Recursion
Denotation 255
Density 134
Denumerable 211
Description 56–58, 68, 70f, 88, 108
Directification 80, 174f
Domain 25, 65
Dot 62–64, 72
Dreben, Burton 237
Dummett, Michael 76n
Dummy 9f, 18, 259

Elementary number theory 92, 110f, 325. *See also* Natural number
Empty universe 10, 38, 270. *See also* Null class
Enlargement 301, 310, 316–319, 321
Enumeration 185f, 211f; theorem 150, 152, 161, 186–190

Epimenides 254f
Epsilon: number 212f; operator 224n. *See also* Membership
Ersetzung, *see* Replacement
Exclamation point 247f
Excluded middle 51
Existence 28, 243. *See also* Comprehension; Noncommittal; Virtual
Exponents, law of 116. *See also* Indices; Power
Extension 301, 316, 320f, 323, 325
Extensionality 2, 30–34, 331f; in Russell 245 252, 260f, 264, 269, 323; in Zermelo 276, 315, 317; in further systems 288, 302, 313, 321f, 328

Feferman, Solomon 325n
Field 22, 25, 145f; confined 64, 148f, 157, 170
Finite classes 140f, 195–199, 218; existence of 38, 50f, 86f, 195, 198, 218, 281, 297; for arithmetic 75–77, 82, 86, 102, 281f, 297; model in 263f, 269, 277, 286, 298. *See also* Infinite
First exception 140–142
Follow logically 11
Founded 141–143, 145f, 285
Fraenkel, A. A. 5, 171n, 205n, 265n, 326; on pure classes 32, 273, 277; axiom of replacement 88n, 284; Bernays- 174n, 224n, 231n; Zermelo- 237f, 284, 319
Frege, Gottlob 3n, 16n, 70f, 78, 82, 251n, 304; ancestral 29n, 74, 101, 103n; natural number as size class 82, 152, 214, 279, 281, 284, 289, 297f, 304; cardinal 214, 233f, 289, 295
Friedman, Joyce 85n
Function 23–25, 65–73; existence of 89; specified by recursion 174; von Neumann on 302n, 313. *See also* Propositional
Functional calculus 258
Fundierung 157n, 238, 285f, 311, 313, 326, 331f

Generality, two sorts 266

Generating sequence function 175–177, 185, 226
Generation 175–179; of universe 236, 243, 319
Getchell, Charles 72n
Godfrey, Colin 185n
Gödel, Kurt 12n, 111, 157n, 261, 305, 325; 1940 set theory 20f, 24f, 76n, 156n, 223n, 234–238, 313, 326f
Goodman, Nicholas 299n
Grammatical restriction 247, 249, 260, 263, 267; abrogation of 269f, 273, 287–289, 293
Greater, *see* Less
Greek letter 18, 21, 33f, 41, 47f, 62, 251n
Grelling, Kurt 76n, 254f
Grenzzahl 214
Grid 121, 125, 127, 200
Grounded 37
Grouping 72f

Hailperin, Theodore 320
Halmos, Paul 177
Hausdorff, F. 230
Hemmendinger, David 94n
Henkin, Leon 304–306
Herbrand, Jacques 270n
Hessenberg, Gerhard 147n
Heterogeneous, Homogeneous 261–265, 274, 278f, 281, 290
Hilbert, David 12n, 15n, 171n, 224, 254n, 257f, 264n

Identity 12–15, 30, 40–43, 52; of indiscernibles 14f; with Greek letters 18, 33–35, 47f; of relations 22, 63; as relation 22, 64f, 70f, 193, 263; in theory of types 260; in Zermelo 275; in NF 288, 294n; in ML 302. *See also* Extensionality
Image 22, 25f, 64
Imaginary number 137f
Impredicative, *see* Predicative
Inaccessible number 214, 324, 327f
Inclusion 18, 22, 54, 62f; between real numbers 125–128, 135; as relation 140f, 146f; between ordinals 153, 162, 166f, 232
Incompleteness of number theory 111, 325
Inconsistency, ω- 305f. *See also* Consistency; Paradox
Indices 244–248; for mere types 253f, 257, 259–265; translated 266–268; survivals 283, 288f; in Specker 292
Individual 29–33, 38; axioms of 32n, 270, 275–277, 285; benefits of assimilation 35, 47, 58, 277; conflict with *Fundierung* 86, 95, 286; in theory of types 243f, 252, 258f, 268, 272, 280; in cumulative types 273f, 278f; in Zermelo 274, 276f, 282; in NF 288
Induction: ancestral 105, 140f, 144f; transfinite 144f, 147, 165, 176. *See also* Mathematical
Infinite classes 51, 87f, 199f, 228f, 273, 321; inversion obviates 75f, 86, 92, 102, 197, 281, 306; and real numbers 120, 131. *See also* Finite
Infinity, axiom of 280–283, 285, 290, 292, 297, 324, 327f, 331f; and consistency proofs 264n, 286; in von Neumann 311, 314; in Ackermann 322
Initial ordinal 213, 215f
Inner model 234, 236, 327f
Insegregative 306
Integer 102, 121, 127, 130, 136. *See also* Natural number
Interpretation 10f, 14f, 316–318, 323. *See also* Model
Intersection 18f, 22, 55f, 62, 164, 169
Intransitivity 23
Inversion 75f, 86, 102, 197, 281, 296, 306
Irrational number 119–121, 131
Irreflexivity 22, 146
Isomorphism 145, 149, 152f, 159, 184, 186f
Iteration 79–82, 96–101, 160, 174f, 324

Kaplan, David 270f, 273n
Kemeny, J. G. 325
Kleene, S. C. 139n, 320n

König, Julius 205n, 212n, 302
Kreider, D. L. 214n
Kreisel, Georg 265n, 320
Kuratowski, Casimir 58, 147n, 259

Lambda 70–73
Larger, *see* Smaller
Left field 22, 25, 64
Length 5, 149–152, 158f, 184f
Less ($<$, $\leqq$): in natural numbers 77, 79, 81–85, 92–95, 106, 109–111, 116; in real numbers 125–128, 135–137; as ordering 141–143, 145–147; in ordinals 153, 159, 162–164, 166–168, 170f; in cardinals 209f, 232–234, 294–296
Letter, *see* Greek; Predicate; Schematic
Leuer, Constance 102n
Lévy, Azriel 322n, 327f
Lexicographic ordering 212n
Limit 132, 250; -ordinal 151, 156, 179, 215; -cardinal 214. *See also* Bound
Lindenbaum, Adolf 238
Löwenheim, Leopold 316
Logic 5, 9–12, 18, 26, 29, 34, 51; principles tacit 6, 50, 64; existential minimum 10, 38, 270; conditions on substitution 11, 43, 224, 248, 261, 266, 287f; vs. set theory 257f; completeness of 305

MacLane, Saunders 328f
Maclaurin, Colin 136n
McNaughton, Robert 321n, 325n
Mahlo, P. 327
Malcev, A. 305n
Many-sorted 31, 270; Gödel 235n; theory of types 248, 261, 266–269; Bernays 313; ML 317f
Martin, R. M. 19n, 76n
Mathematical induction 76f, 86, 90–94, 105; course-of-values 139–141, 143f; for classes 196–198; in Zermelo 218f; in NF 296–300; in ML303, 318; in von Neumann 314
Maximal 230
Meaningful, *see* Grammatical
Membership 16f, 28–31, 33, 35, 38–40, 48; fore and aft 16, 39, 299f; for theory of types 19, 259, 268; as predicate 29–31, 33, 39, 81f, 289, 303, 323; condition 35, 44, 170, 218, 242f, 300; as relation 157, 163, 168, 184, 216, 313; for Hilbert and Ackermann 257f; reinterpreted 317, 323; in individuals, *see* Individual. *See also Fundierung;* Set; Ultimate
Mendelson, Elliott 214n, 238, 285n, 324n
Menge 20, 312, 322. *See also* Set
Minimal 141f
Mirimanoff, D. 37, 88n, 285n
ML 302–309, 320f, 328, 332; consistency of 316–318
Model 135, 305; inner 234, 236, 327f; in finite classes 263f, 269, 277, 286, 298; nonstandard 303–307; numerical 316–319; natural 324
Montague, Richard 320f, 324
Mostowski, Andrzej 238, 318f, 321n
Multiplication, *see* Product
Multiplicity, *see* Size
Mutilation, minimum 51, 267
Myhill, John 76n

Natural model 324
Natural number: defined from 0 and S 74–77, 86, 102, 106f; existence of N or its subclasses 75, 133; use 77–79, 81, 135, 208f; sum, product, power 79f, 107–116, 174f; variously defined from scratch 81–83, 135, 152–154; elementary theory of 92, 110f, 325; pairs of 122–124; how many 200, 211; in theory of types 279–281; in Zermelo's set theory 281–284; in NF 289, 297–299; in ML 303f, 306f; extra 303–306; sethood of N 303–307. *See also* Finite; Mathematical
Negation: of number 102, 135–137; of class, *see* Complement
Nelson, Leonard 254n
Nest 125, 147, 167, 230, 313

Neumann, J. von 177n, 282n, 285, 302n, 311f, 326; ultimate classes 3, 46n, 310; concept of number 81f, 152–155, 161, 165, 209, 211, 215f, 233, 281f, 289, 296f; -Bernays 234–238, 313f, 319, 321f, 332
NF 32n, 38, 46, 288–293, 331; Specker on 292, 294–296, 299; induction in 296–300; compared to ML 302f, 308, 316–319; finite axioms 320
Nominalism 9, 26f, 256f
Noncommittal 32, 38, 87, 218, 241, 277, 281; abstraction 35, 39, 45f, 301, 303
Nonstandard model 303–307
Notion 21
Novak, I. L. 319
NQ 321n
Null class 19, 30, 44f, 52, 65; axiom of 50, 88f, 276; in theory of types 272–274
Null relation 22
Number: irrational 119–121, 131; ratio 119–121, 124–134; complex 137f; imaginary 137f; relation 153. *See also* Cardinal; Natural; Ordinal; Real
Numeration 226–229, 233, 236

Oberschelp, Arnold 235n
Ohe, Akira 166n
Omega 151, 211–213, 215f; -consistency 305f
Ono, Katuzi 285
Orey, Steven 298
Opacity 2n
Open class 129
Open sentence: as determining a class 1–3, 5, 35, 60, 218, 242f, 300; vs. attribute 19, 245, 254–258
Order: preserving 149, 187f; -type (Cantor) 153, 158; of a propositional function 244–250, 253–256, 265; of a predicate calculus 258
Ordered: pair 58f, 122f, 259, 261f, 278, 290; set 148; generation of universe 236, 243, 319
Ordering 141f, 145–151, 159, 185; partial 146f, 230; lexicographic 210n; of universe 229f, 236, 243, 319
Ordinal number 150f, 184f; versions of 152–154, 156f, 286; arithmetic of 158–160, 178–180, 186, 198f, 215; laws of 161–173; and cardinal 209, 211–213, 216, 233; in NF 289, 294; in von Neumann-Bernays 312; as measuring strength 323–325, 327–329
Oversize 278, 284, 287, 289, 311f, 328f

Pair: unordered 19, 47–51; ordered 58f, 122f, 259, 261f, 278, 290
Pairing, axiom of 50, 88f, 275f, 311, 331f
Paradox 36f, 50f, 233, 267, 328; Russell's 3f, 36, 39, 60, 202, 241f, 249, 251, 255, 269, 277f, 309, 315; Burali-Forti's 171, 253, 264, 302, 312; Cantor's 202, 263, 278, 308f, 314f; and theory of types 241–243, 249, 251, 255, 263, 269, 287; semantic 254f; and Zermelo 277f, 284; and NF 290, 293, 299; and ML 300, 308f; and von Neumann 315
Parsons, Charles 180n
Partial ordering 146f, 230
Peano, Guiseppe 121, 130, 136, 205n, 255; on functions 24f, 68; axioms 92, 111, 280, 305
Poincaré, Henri 241–243, 246, 310, 319
Point set 5
Power: of natural number 79f, 107–109, 116, 175; of ratio 119; of real number 134, 136; of ordinal 151, 160, 179f, 212; of cardinal 209f, 213; of continuum 213n; -set 213n, 274–276, 311, 328, 331f; of relation, *see* Iteration. *See also* Cardinal; Size; Strength
Predicate 10, 12; -letter 9–11, 16f, 19; vs. attribute 9, 19, 245, 254–258; primitive 13–16, 18, 38, 223, 230, 322; epsilon as 29–31, 33, 39, 81f, 289, 303, 323; to resolve many-sorted logic 31, 268f; -calculus 258

Predication, *see* Attribution
Predicative, Impredicative 242; in theory of types 246f, 250–254, 264f; in von Neumann and beyond 310, 312–316, 318–321, 328
Primitive 223f. *See also* Predicate
Product: Cartesian 22, 64; of natural numbers 79f, 107–109, 111, 113–116, 175; of ratios 119; of real numbers 134, 136; of complex numbers 137; of ordinals 151, 158, 160, 178–180, 216; of cardinals 209, 216; logical, *see* Intersection; of relations, *see* Resultant
Productation 180
Progression 37, 151
Proof theory 265n, 319, 324f
Proper: class, *see* Ultimate; inclusion 18, 22; ancestral 101n, 103f
Property, *see* Attribute
Proposition 245
Propositional function 19, 71n, 244–251, 254–258, 265
Pure class 32, 273, 277
Putnam, Hilary 299n, 320

Quantification: over attributes 19, 244–246, 251; over classes 20, 28f, 39f, 48, 79, 251n; over relations 59f, 252; over numbers 74, 81, 111. *See also* Logic; Many-sorted; Variable

Ramified 256
Ramsey, F. P. 255f
Range 25
Ratio 119–121, 124–134
Ray 121, 127, 200
Real number 119f, 125, 128–134; not indiscernible 14f; arithmetic of 134f; negative 135–137; how many 200, 213n; in theory of types 249f, 265
Recursion 79f, 96, 108–110, 174–176; transfinite 160, 177–183, 185f, 226, 325; course-of-values 175f
Reducibility, axiom of 250–254, 256 264f
Reduction 82f, 135
Reduplication 263, 272, 283, 289, 297
Reflexivity 22
Regularity, *see Fundierung*
Reinterpretation 323
Relation: virtual 21–26, 88f; abstraction and attribution of 21, 28-59–62 249, 252; algebra of 26, 64; as class of pairs 59–64; -number 153; -in-intension 243–245, 247, 253f, 256; -in-extension (Russell) 251–254, 256f, 259; heterogeneous, homogeneous 261–265, 274, 278f, 281, 290
Relational part 62–64, 72
Relativization 234–236, 302, 310f, 316, 318f, 326–328
Relettering 17, 289
Renshaw, Bruce 270n
Replacement, axiom schema of 88, 284f, 311–313, 322n, 325f, 328, 331f
Restriction 234, 268, 302f, 310
Resultant 22, 64, 100
Richard, Jules 212n, 241n
Right field 22, 24f, 64f, 96
Robinson, R. M. 157n, 166n
Rogers, Hartley, Jr. 214n
Rosser, J. B. 61, 230n, 306, 319, 325n; on NF 289n, 294, 296; on ML 302f, 307
Roupas, Graham 92n
Rubin, H. and J. E. 230n
Russell, Bertrand 46, 70, 103n, 197n, 284n; paradox 3f, 36, 39, 60, 202, 241f, 249, 251, 255, 269f, 277f, 309, 315; concretion 16n, 19; notation 18n, 45n, 68; terminology 25, 142n; versions of number 82n, 129f, 153, 214, 233f, 289, 294; propositional functions and their orders 241–258, 264f, 271; classes and their types 252f, 256, 259, 261, 269, 279, 323; axiom of infinity 280f, 283, 290

Schematic letter: for predicates 9–11, 90, 257f, 277; vs. variable 10, 19, 39f, 79, 82, 251n, 257f; for abstracts 18f, 21, 41, 47f, 59f, 62, 251n; for numerals 79, 259, 266, 271

Schröder, Ernst 204, 207f, 232
Scope 72, 252
Scott, Dana 32n
Script 46
Second number class 212
Segment 149, 158f
Selection 217f, 221, 308
Selector 220–224, 226, 230
Semantic paradox 254f
Separation, *see Aussonderung*
Sequence 185; finite 80, 96, 174–176; infinite 174–177; -function 177–179, 185, 226; transfinite 177–180, 226, 236
Series number 80
Series 142n, 185
Set 1, 3f, 20, 45f, 50f, 55f; -theory 1, 3–6, 32, 51, 71n, 74, 135, 258, 267, 329; distinct from class 35, 313, 317; modified version 51, 321f; selector as 223; -hood axioms 236, 302, 311f, 322, 327f; in enlarged systems 300f, 315f; N as 303–307
Sheffer, H. M. 256
Shepherdson, J. C. 234, 324, 327
Shoenfield, J. R. 238, 319
Sierpiński, Waclaw 147n, 213n, 238n
Sign and object 9, 19, 26f, 245, 254–258, 303
Size of class: numbers to measure 77–79, 81, 135, 150f, 208f; same ($\simeq$) 78f, 145, 203f, 208f. *See also* Cardinal; Smaller; Too big
Skeletal 315f
Skolem, Thoralf 88n, 224, 277, 284, 304f, 316
Smaller ($\prec$, $\preceq$) 142, 145, 193–195, 200, 204, 210f; defined 78f, 87, 141, 199, 203, 307, 321. *See also* Cantor's theorem and paradox; Comparability
Solid 129
Specifiable 2, 15, 255. *See also* Predicative
Specker, Ernst 292, 294–296, 299
Stegmlüler, Wolfgang 321n
Stratification 288–292, 296–298, 302, 304, 306f, 309
Strength of systems 323–329
Subclass, *see* Cantor's theorem; Inclusion; Power set
Subscript 247f
Substitution: of sentences 11, 257, 288; of abstracts and Greek letters 39–44, 260; conventions of free 52, 58f, 68, 108; of primitive term 224; many-sorted restraint 248, 261, 266, 287f
Substitutivity: of biconditional 12f; of identity 12f, 34, 40, 42f. *See also* Extensionality
Subtraction, Peano axiom of 92, 280, 283, 297
Successor 81–84, 86; in von Neumann 81, 152, 154–156, 165, 169, 171–173; unconstructed 74, 77, 92, 101f, 105, 149, 209, 213, 279; one-to-one 92, 280, 283, 297; -ordinal 151, 173, 179
Sum: of natural numbers 79f, 107–115, 175; of ratios 119; of real numbers 134, 136; of complex numbers 137; of ordinals 151, 158–160, 178, 186; of cardinals 209f, 216; axiom of 272, 274, 276, 328, 331f; logical, *see* Union
Summation 179f, 214
Superscript, *see* Indices
Suppes, Patrick 157n, 209n, 230n
Symmetry 22
Systematic ambiguity 247, 253. *See also* Typical

Tarski, Alfred 214, 238n, 261, 280n, 305n, 324
Term 9, 71, 234
Theorem 11, 261
Theory 9–16, 18, 28, 38, 267, 304; strength of 323–329
Too big 278, 284, 287, 289, 311f, 328f
Torrey, J. C. 59n
Transfinite: induction 144f, 147, 165f, 176; recursion 160, 178–183, 185f, 211, 226, 325
Transitivity 23, 146
Trichotomy 208. *See also* Comparability
True of 1, 254f
Tymoczko, A. T. 216

Types, theory of: early or ramified 243–256; Hilbert and Ackermann 257f; classical modern 259–264, 331; consistency 263f, 269, 277, 286, 291f, 298; constructive modern 264f; with general variables 268–272; cumulative 273–276, 278f; with axiom of infinity 280f, 283; transfinite 282n, 324; compared with other systems, 284, 287–293, 298
Typical ambiguity 253, 264, 266f, 269, 288, 290f; axioms of 292; systematic ambiguity 247

Ullian, J. S. 189n
Ultimate class 3f, 20, 45f, 50f, 55f; modified version 51, 321; imposed in enlarging 300–302, 315–319; consequences for ML 303, 307–309
Union 18f, 22, 53–56, 62, 70. *See* also Sum, axiom of
Unit class 18f, 31f, 48–52, 81, 147; function 73, 83, 105f, 293–295; endless descent 86f, 95, 195; to adjust types 261–263, 278, 293–295
Universal class 19, 45, 263; vs. V of ML 45f, 55n, 237n, 301–303; existence of 45, 222f, 229, 277, 287, 289f, 297
Universal selector 223f, 230
Universe 15, 28; not empty 10, 38, 270; relativity to 304; richness of 326–329

Validity 10–13, 26, 37, 267, 291
Value of a function 23–25, 68–70
van Heijenoort, John 3n, 4n
Variable 224, 242f, 250, 304; vs. schematic letter 10, 19, 39f, 79, 82, 251n, 257f; bound 11, 17, 61, 70; of abstraction 17 *and see* Circumflex; relettered 17, 289; existential import of 20, 28f; general 31, 235n, 248, 266–270, 274, 288; restricted 234, 268, 302f, 310, 322; order of 244–247; syntactic 251n. *See also* Indices; Many-sorted; Quantification; Substitution; Virtual and real
Vaught, R. L. 324
Vicious circle 242f, 269
Virtual and real 4, 16, 19–21, 26f, 35, 70, 258; classes 16–19, 38f, 45–48, 259f, 275–277, 284, 300, 302, 327n; relations 21–25, 59–62, 88f; benefits from the real 28f, 48, 53, 58, 65, 70, 74f, 78f, 82; ratios 119
von Neumann, *see* Neumann

Wang, Hao 13n, 76n, 88, 320f, 325n; on Dedekind 92n, 101n; on predicativity 265n, 310; on NF and ML 294, 302, 316–319
Waterhouse, William 69n, 105n
Well-ordering 142, 145f, 149, 157, 173, 189; length of 149–153, 157–159, 161, 184–186; of ordinals 170f, 212, 234, 294n; theorem of 229f
Weyl, Hermann 254n, 265n
Whitehead, A. N. 80n, 103n, 142n, 197n, 244n, 246n, 251, 253, 255f; concretion 16n, 19n; notation 18n, 45n, 68; versions of number 129f, 153, 214, 233f, 289, 294; axiom of infinity 280, 283, 290
Wiener, Norbert 58, 259, 262, 269

Yosida, Natuhiko 165n

Zermelo, Ernst 4, 76n, 152n, 157n, 205n, 214; axiom system in general 32, 46, 271f, 274–278, 284f, 287, 289, 296f, 310, 321f, 324–328, 331; *Aussonderung* 37f, 271f, 276–278, 284, 315; version of number 81–83, 138, 151, 153f, 209, 279, 281f, 297; choice and well-ordering 217, 229; axiom of infinity 282, 285, 287, 290, 292, 311; -Fraenkel 237f, 284, 319
Zero 81–84, 86, 298; unconstrued 74, 77, 92, 209, 279
Zorn, Max 230